Super Continent

THE LOGIC OF EURASIAN INTEGRATION

Kent E. Calder

STANFORD UNIVERSITY PRESS
Stanford, California

Published under the auspices of the Johns Hopkins University
SAIS Reischauer Center for East Asian Studies

Stanford University Press
Stanford, California

Printed in the United States of America on acid-free, archival-quality paper

Library of Congress Cataloging-in-Publication Data

Names: Calder, Kent E., author.
Title: Super continent : the logic of Eurasian integration / Kent E. Calder.
Description: Stanford, California : Stanford University Press, 2019. |
  Includes bibliographical references and index.
Identifiers: LCCN 2018038995 | ISBN 9781503608153 (cloth ; alk. paper) |
  ISBN 9781503609617 (pbk. ; alk. paper) | ISBN 9781503609624 (epub)
Subjects: LCSH: Eurasia—Foreign economic relations. | Eurasia—Economic
  integration. | Eurasia—Economic conditions. | Eurasia—Foreign relations. |
  Geopolitics—Eurasia. | China—Foreign economic relations—Eurasia. |
  Eurasia—Foreign economic relations—China.
Classification: LCC HF1583 .C36 2019 | DDC 337.5—dc23
LC record available at https://lccn.loc.gov/2018038995

Cover design: George Kirkpatrick

Typeset by Newgen in 10.5/13.5

Contents

Figures, Maps, and Tables

TABLES

Preface

THE EXPANSES OF EURASIA have fascinated me ever since I was a boy. As I was growing up, it was terra incognita—exotic, foreign territory, and much of it off-limits to American citizens. As I began my academic career, the continent was in volatile transition, a world of fragile regimes whose demise opened up intriguing new worlds, epitomized by the fall of the Berlin Wall and the collapse of the shah's regime in Teheran. Today, Eurasia is being reconfigured once again. Its western and eastern poles are moving into an ever-deeper embrace, with global political-economic implications.

Those fateful developments, unfolding before our eyes, configure the story presented in the pages to follow. A century ago and more ago, a Super Continent began to rise on American shores, its connectivity assured by infrastructure—a transcontinental railway, consolidated by the Golden Spike at Promontory Point (1869), and a canal from the Atlantic to the Pacific, completed across Panama (1914). Only a few years ago, a second Super Continent began to rise across Eurasia as well.

What to make of this new Super Continent as it begins to rise has been one of the central intellectual concerns of my career. It animated my first post-doctoral academic endeavor—a course on comparative Asian political economy, cotaught at Harvard in the fall of 1979 with Roy Hofheinz, only months after the advent of China's Four Modernizations. That course in turn inspired a book, *The Eastasia Edge*, coauthored with Hofheinz, that was among the first to view East Asian political-economic development comparatively and to consider how Asian growth might broaden beyond Japan to wide areas of the surrounding continent.

After writing a book at Princeton on Japanese domestic political economy, I came back to the transformation of Eurasia in *Pacific Defense*, published in 1996. That volume considered the rising energy interdependence between Northeast Asia and the Persian Gulf, and the corollary importance of the energy sea lanes. The ensuing *East Asian Multilateralism* (2008), *Pacific Alliance* (2009), coedited with Francis Fukuyama; and *The Making of Northeast Asia* (2010), coauthored with Min Ye, have all dealt with regionalist themes.

The clearest intellectual precursor of this volume, however, is *The New Continentalism* (2012). In that book, published eighteen months before Xi Jinping announced his Belt and Road Initiative, I outlined the critical junctures that both opened Eurasia as a whole to the prospect of deeper political-economic embrace following the collapse of the Soviet Union, and also provided the incentives for that interaction. I am gratified that *The New Continentalism* has now been translated into Japanese, Korean, Mongolian, and Chinese, and provides some basis, elaborated before the BRI emerged as policy, for understanding the considerations that led Xi Jinping to propose it.

I began thinking of a sequel to *The New Continentalism* within months of its original publication in May 2012—an inclination that grew ever stronger as Chinese leadership began stressing transcontinental political-economic relationships as core dimensions of national grand strategy. Beijing's announcement of the Asian Infrastructure Investment Bank, and the decision of major European powers to join it, convinced me still further that my earlier instincts about deepening trans-Eurasian interaction were correct. By mid-2014 I was hard at work on the current volume.

Many people and many events over the past several years have deepened my understanding of the historic transformation of Eurasia occurring before our eyes. The Boao Forum for Asia, in which I have participated six times since 2011, has been a key element of that. Through Boao, I have gained a much more fine-grained sense of Chinese aspirations on regional and global matters, as well as the quality and biases of Chinese leadership. The 2017 Belt and Road Forum in Beijing, in which I participated as an active observer, as well as seminars at SAIS Europe, the National University of Mongolia, and Nanyang University RSIS in Singapore helped deepen those perceptions still further.

For my understanding of this transcontinental equation, I am indebted to a range of scholars and policy makers in Europe, Asia, and the United States. Among them have been Zbigniew Brzezinski, Fukuda Yasuo, Dominique de Villepin, Bilahari Kausikan, Volker Stanzel, Vali Nasr, Eliot Cohen, Erik Jones, Kishore Mahbubani, Michael Plummer, David Shambaugh, David Shear, Bekhbat Khasbazar, Batbayar Tsedendamba, Enksaikan Jargalsaikhar, Lynn White, William Frucht, Alicia Campi, and Jacopo Pepe. I owe a special debt of gratitude to Dr. Pepe, a brilliant young researcher with the German Council on Foreign Relations (DGAP), who spent the better part of two years at the Reischauer Center for East Asian Studies that I head, first as a dissertation fellow, and later as an adjunct professor at SAIS. We co-taught two courses, and Jacopo contributed significantly, together with Alicia Campi, to a series of conferences and panels on Eurasia's transformation that we organized in locations ranging from Poznań, Berlin, and Toronto to Hong Kong, Tokyo, and Ulaanbaatar, Mongolia. We all share a mutual fascination with geography and its centrality in political-economic analysis that suffuses this work.

The SAIS Reischauer Center for East Asian Studies has been my intellectual home for the past fifteen years, and the collegial atmosphere, as well as warm support, that I have enjoyed there has been invaluable to the genesis and evolution of this book. Zongyuan Liu, Rachel Xian, Sophie Yang, Tom Ramage, Jonathan Hall-Eastman, Evan Sankey, Jaehan Park, Olivia Schieber, and Toshiko Calder, among others, have all contributed in different ways at the Reischauer Center to the development of this volume. Apart from all this, at the vital interface of research, graphics, and technical integration, I owe Yun Han my deepest thanks. She has contributed tirelessly and selflessly to tasks large and small, ranging from detailed fact checking to penetrating conceptual analysis, at all hours of the day and night, in ways that words cannot easily express. I also appreciate the expert contributions of Stanford University Press and its affiliates.

Many hands, in short, have helped build the sturdy foundations for this work. For the edifice erected thereon, and all the associated imperfections, however, I must take responsibility. Hopefully the reader will feel, in reading these lines, some share of the fascination I have always felt for the emergence, before our eyes, of a new continental incarnation of global import, comparable only to what emerged on American soil a century and more ago.

Reischauer Center for East Asian Studies
Johns Hopkins SAIS
Washington, DC
December 2018

Introduction

GEOGRAPHY SEEMS AN IMMUTABLE VERITY OF NATURE, not to mention of human existence. Yet changes in the practical meaning of geography often occur, and can truly transform the world. Indeed, it was creative reconfigurations of North America, achieved by visionary infrastructure building, that transformed the United States into first a Super Continent and then a global power during the five momentous decades between the Civil War and World War I.

The first fateful step toward America's conversion into a Super Continent was the driving of the Golden Spike in the desert of Utah, at Promontory Point, just before 1 p.m. on May 10, 1869. That ceremonial act completed construction of the Transcontinental Railway, linking America's east and west coasts overland. It reduced the overland travel time between New York and California from six months to two weeks, and obviated the need for dangerous alternatives: either a six-week sea voyage around Cape Horn, or an equally treacherous combination of sailing to Central America, and crossing the Isthmus of Panama by rail, exposed to yellow fever in the crossing.[1]

American entrepreneurs, publicists, and statesmen, driven by dreams of Manifest Destiny, had begun dreaming of extending America to the Pacific more than six decades before. Thomas Jefferson, in an 1812 letter to John Jacob Astor, foresaw the day when American settlers would cover the length of the Pacific coast with "free and independent Americans, unconnected with us but by the ties of blood and interest."[2] Thomas Hart Benton in 1820 was even more ambitious, stressing not only the value of America's march to the Pacific but also the mutual worth, to both America and East Asian peoples also, of trans-Pacific ties.[3]

Concrete proposals for a transcontinental railroad began emerging in the 1830s, with Asa Whitney, a New York merchant who had recently visited China, making a proposal in 1845 for a railroad from Lake Michigan to the mouth of the Columbia River in Oregon.[4] Over the following decade, proposals proliferated, with Secretary of War Jefferson Davis's 1856 report narrowing the discussion to five routes.[5]

Behind the proliferation of proposals was a steady transformation across the first half of the nineteenth century in both American territorial scale and in related political-economic interests. By 1803 the Louisiana Purchase had created an American heartland in the Mississippi Valley. The Oregon Treaty and the Mexican War extended American territory to the west coast. And the Gold Rush of 1849, followed by California's accession to statehood status in 1850, established a sturdy American anchor on the Pacific.

In 1860 Theodore Judah's eminently realistic proposal for a route through Iowa, Nebraska, and across the Sierra Nevada to Sacramento ended the routing debate.[6] President Buchanan was persuaded, and Republicans included Judah's proposed route in their national platform for the 1860 presidential campaign.[7] The election of Abraham Lincoln sealed the matter, with Lincoln enthusiastically signing the Pacific Railroad Act, providing financing and land grants for the railroad, in 1862.[8]

Together with mundane economic considerations, especially prominent among the builders themselves, geopolitics also figured in the building of the transcontinental railway. As William Gilpin, arguably America's first geopolitician, wrote presciently in 1860, America's "intermediate geographical position between Asia and Europe and their populations, invests her with the powers and duties of arbiter between them."[9] In narrower political-military terms, the Lincoln White House was concerned, amidst the Civil War, with a mix of threats from rivals. Confederate incursions had reached as far as New Mexico, while England was financing railroads across Canada. Meanwhile France was also building a transcontinental railway across Mexico, creating the danger that both Britain and France could potentially have closer contact with California than the Union's east coast, distracted by bitter conflict, actually did.[10]

Although geopolitical concerns, rendered urgent by the exigencies of civil war, may have figured prominently in creating the continentalist policy framework, it was private enterprise that brought the transcontinental railway to actual fruition. Leland Stanford, who became governor of California in 1861, played a key role, both in government and later as president of the Central Pacific Railway, which built the tortuous railway segment across the Sierra Nevada, employing 15,000 Chinese workers.[11] Thomas Durant, general manager of the Union Pacific, who became fabulously rich by early acquiring nearly half of his firm's outstanding shares, also played a key role.[12] The Golden Spike thus critically furthered America's transformation from a regional nation hugging the Atlantic seaboard into a bicoastal power with a functioning window on the Pacific as well.

The second key geographical transformation in America's ascent to global power—also accomplished through new infrastructural connections—was the building of the Panama Canal. As in the case of the transcontinental railroad, the actual construction was preceded by a lengthy period of conceptualization, change in national political-economic incentives, and consensus building. The result was a clear conversion of America's international standing from regional into full-fledged global power.

Conceptualization began even before completion of the transcontinental railway itself, although not by Americans. In 1869 Count Ferdinand de Lesseps, an entrepreneurial French aristocrat, completed construction of the Suez Canal, with an eye to revolutionizing world shipping through constructed waterways. In May 1879 he convened the International Congress for the Study of an Interoceanic Canal, to build support for an analogous sea-level waterway in Panama, for which he began construction in 1881. In 1889 his company was liquidated, however, after losing 20,000 men and spending $287 million in his futile quest.[13]

Just as de Lessep's abortive venture was ending, Alfred Thayer Mahan, America's preeminent grand strategist, in 1890 published his most important work, *The Influence of Sea Power upon History, 1660–1783*.[14] Mahan did not directly press for the building of a Panama Canal and was mildly skeptical that one could be completed, due to the lack of plausible commercial incentives. Mahan did, however, note presciently that if a canal *were* built, it would enhance the economic and strategic importance of the Caribbean, stimulate American commerce, and necessitate the building of a much more powerful US Navy. His work was widely read and became a catalyst for the expansionism in the Caribbean and the Pacific that finally did lend geo-economic momentum in Washington to the effort to build a Panama Canal.

The geo-economic argument for a Panama Canal was simple. A waterway across the narrow 50-mile-wide isthmus would connect the Atlantic and the Pacific, cutting almost 7,900 miles off the distance between New York and San Francisco, or 5,700 miles off the distance between New York and Yokohama, Japan. The sailing time for ships of the day, travelling at 15 knots/hour, would be cut to a third of previous levels.[15]

The imperative for a US Navy capable of operating in both the Atlantic and the Pacific was strengthened by the American acquisition of Hawaii in 1898 and the Philippines in 1899.[16] The military implications were graphically demonstrated in the Spanish-American War, when it took the USS *Oregon* 67 days to arrive in Cuba from San Francisco. Nearly two months had passed since the outbreak of the war, as the battleship pursued its circuitous 14,700-mile voyage around South America to enter the fray.[17]

Shortly after war's end, following the assassination of President McKinley, Theodore Roosevelt, a hero of the recent conflict, ascended to America's highest office. In short order he inspired Panamanian independence, with the USS *Nashville* anchored offshore the Panamanian capital to lend highly visible support. Three months later, in February 1904, the Hay-Bunau-Varilla Treaty was ratified, providing Panama with a $10 million payment and a $250,000 annual annuity, in return for US sovereignty in perpetuity over a ten-mile-wide Canal Zone.[18] In June 1906 the US Congress approved a proposal for a lock canal, strongly supported by President Roosevelt.[19] Construction began almost immediately, and the first ship sailed through the newly opened Panama Canal in mid-August 1914, just three weeks after World War I began.

With the canal finally open, Americans celebrated a new era of American global influence that geography, transformed through infrastructure, had made possible. Mahan naturally pointed to the strategic implications as a force multiplier: "The relation of the Canal to the Navy is that it opens a much shorter line of communication between the Atlantic and Pacific coasts, and thereby does enable a given number of ships—a given strength of fleet—to do a much greater amount of work."[20] He noted that "The Canal, in short, is a central position, from which action may be taken in either direction, and it is also a decisive link in a most important line of communications."[21] Others pointed, over the decades, to the economic benefits. One analyst in 1929, for example, calculated that during the first twelve years of its regular operation (fiscal 1915–1927), the canal saved the American people at least $1 billion— approximately 2.5 times the entire original cost of construction.[22]

US history shows clearly how imaginatively conceived infrastructure can literally reconfigure geography and, in the course of redrawing the map, that new connectivity can also transform the face of world affairs. The Transcontinental Railroad and the Panama Canal in combination consolidated North America as a Super Continent, integrated economically and strategically, with a powerful, flexible presence in both the Atlantic and Pacific. Is a similar process of connection, or possibly reconnection, in progress across Eurasia today?

Super Continent

1

Eurasian Reconnection and Renaissance

EURASIA, AS WE SHALL SEE, is in the throes of historic transition. Despite its geographic coherence, epitomized by the lack of major physical barriers separating Europe and Asia, together with important cultural contiguities,[1] the sprawling continent was long Balkanized into a maze of conflicting jurisdictions. It is now regaining coherence in the post–Cold War world, as China rises and grows closer to Europe in the wake of Soviet collapse, American disengagement, and a quiet logistics technology revolution. Connectivity through massive infrastructure construction is collapsing distance while reconfiguring both Eurasia and world affairs, just as it did a century ago on the American continent.

For more than seven decades the United States has clearly dominated the global political economy, secure in its standing, detached from Old World turbulence, on its own invulnerable Super Continent. Those seven decades, however, are but a tiny fraction of the millennia over which another Super Continent—Eurasia—has dominated world history. Most recently it was the Europeans who held sway, both within that space and globally—from the voyages of discovery and the Industrial Revolution into the twentieth century. Across the bulk of previous recorded history, however, the global fulcrum lay far to the eastern side of that Super Continent—preponderantly within China, and secondarily in India, Persia, and the Levant. Collectively, at the dawn of the sixteenth century, as the voyages of exploration to the New World were beginning, Eurasia generated 89 percent of global gross domestic product (GDP).[2] China alone contributed 25 percent of that total, and India 24 percent, due not only to teeming population but also equally to technical prowess.[3]

It was, after all, Asian nations that invented paper, movable type, and gunpowder, pioneering in mathematics, biology, and geometry amidst their European brethren's slumber during less enlightened times in the West. North America—in no sense a Super Continent for centuries to come—remained terra incognita to the rest of the world. On the eve of the Industrial Revolution in 1750, Asia's share of global output remained around 60 percent.[4] It was not until after 1870, following the Franco-Prussian War, that Europe and the United States actually generated a larger share of the world's product than did Asia.

A Historic Transition

Powered by sweeping social changes and a revolution in manufacturing, Europe and North America surged ahead of Asia during the nineteenth and early twentieth centuries.[5] By 1950, the United States had passed Western Europe as the largest generator of global product. Meanwhile, Asia's portion had fallen to only two-thirds of US output,[6] despite a population nine times as large.[7]

In the long eye of history, the American surge was not to last. The US global share peaked in 1950, as indicated in Figure 1.1. Then Europe, Japan, and finally continental Asia began to revive. By the beginning of the twenty-first century, a resurging and increasingly interactive Eurasia had begun to claim, in terms of raw global GDP proportion, the traditional preeminence that it had sustained across the years before Columbus reached the New World, and Vasco da Gama arrived in India, more than five centuries ago.

Eurasia Reconnected

Europe spearheaded the initial Old World revival, aided in its post–World War II restructuring by the Marshall Plan. The parallel catalyst for postwar East Asian economic recovery was Japan, supplemented in the wake of the Vietnam War by Korea itself. In both the Japanese and continental Asian cases (especially South Korea, but China as well), revival was enhanced by the formidable strength of America's post–World War II economy, and the related expansion of transpacific trade. Eurasian reconnection was not a factor in all this transpacific prosperity.

Following the oil shocks of the 1970s, however, the Persian Gulf surged forward, sustained by its massive oil and gas reserves and growing demand

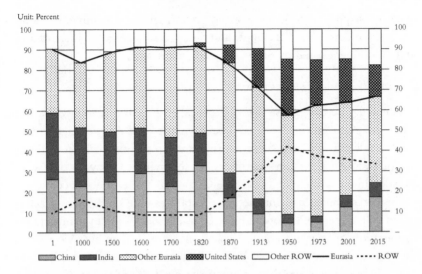

Unit: Percent

FIGURE 1.1 The fall (and rise) of Eurasia (1–2015 AD)

SOURCES: For GDP figures between 1 and 2001 AD, see Angus Maddison, *The World Economy: Historical Statistics* (Paris: OECD, 2003), Table 8b. World GDP, 20 Countries and Regional Totals, 1–2001 AD, https://doi .org/10.1787/9789264104143-en; For 2015 GDP, see World Bank, "GDP, PPP (Constant 2011 International $)," *World Development Indicators*, accessed July 2, 2018.

NOTES: GDP figures between 1 and 2001 AD are in 1990 international dollars, while 2015 GDP is in 2011 international dollars. ROW indicates "Rest of world."

for them from Eurasian continental neighbors to the east. Driving the recent transformation from an Atlantic to a Eurasian-centered global political economy has been an even broader transcontinental dynamic, spearheaded by Chinese growth, Soviet collapse, logistical advances, and European transformation. The People's Republic of China (PRC) in 1973 accounted for less than 5 percent of global GDP in purchasing power parity (PPP) terms. That share more than tripled to 17 percent in 2015, by which time China had already passed the US as the world's largest economy. Together with the twenty-eight independent, mostly advanced members of the European Union, as well as China's Asian neighbors, the collective GDP of the Eurasian continent in 2015 had climbed to almost 70 percent of the global total, as Figure 1.1 suggests.

Initially Chinese growth, like Japanese and Korean expansion before it, was driven by export dependence on the US market. America continues, of course, to be an important economic partner for Asia today, and a vital security ally for many of its key nations. Yet since the end of the Cold War a new dynamic has quietly arisen—as yet largely unnoticed, but with increasing political-economic momentum. That fateful new development on the global

scene, now quietly accelerating world growth and transforming its geopolitics, is the reconnection of Eurasia and the gradual emergence there of a new
Super Continent based on Sino-European interaction.

Connectivity and Its Consequences

Connectivity across Eurasia has a provenance of more than two thousand
years. Imperial Rome and China's Han Dynasty, after all, exchanged artifacts
before the birth of Christ, with intermittent transcontinental trade continuing for over a millennium thereafter. Yet following the voyage of Vasco da
Gama to India, and Columbus to the Caribbean as the fifteenth century was
waning, transcontinental interaction abruptly assumed a more abstract and
distant cast. An era of European imperialism, Soviet socialism in one country,
a generation of war and political chaos, and a variety of autarkic national-
isms, not to mention the Cold War—all complicated transnational relations
across Eurasia, rendering the nations at the heart of the continent economically constrained and marginal in the calculus of world affairs.

Following the collapse of the Soviet Union, the reconnection of Eurasia
has intensified, and accelerated rapidly since the global financial crisis of 2008.
China's Belt and Road Initiative (BRI) is a belated if substantial part of this.
Yet China's rise itself is but a subplot in a larger and more substantial drama.
Logistics and information revolutions as well as the political-economic transformation of Europe, Russia, and Southeast Asia, together with the geo-
economic frustrations of India and Iran, are all part of the chronicle. The sum
story of reconnection, in short, is much more than the country-specific parts
of the whole to which we have so often myopically directed our gaze.

What seems incontestable is that an increasingly reconnected Eurasia
is now emerging—aided, but not created, by Xi Jinping's ambitious BRI.
Cargo trains between China and Europe, which only began running in 2011,
increased to more than 3,000 during 2017 alone, surpassing the previous six
years combined.[8] Those trains carried products such as PCs, clothing, and
auto parts westward, with whiskey, pharmaceuticals, baby formula, and machinery flowing eastward on the return.[9] The volume of maritime cargo,
technical contracts, and air flights across the continent are all expanding,
together with political-economic coordination mechanisms like the Asia-
Europe Meeting (ASEM), the Shanghai Cooperation Organization (SCO),
and the 16+1 summit-conference series between Eastern Europe and China.
Reconnection, in short, has become the order of the day.

The reconnection of Eurasia is by no means only a matter of cargo freight
or even diplomacy. It extends to communications and technology as well,

with deepening implications for the global economic and strategic futures. Huawei, now the world's largest producer of telecommunications equipment, as well as global mobile infrastructure,[10] is working closely with TUV SUD, the European Union's certification authority, on verification technologies for communications products. In April 2018 Huawei became the first company to achieve a CE type examination certificate (TEC) for its 5G products from these European authorities, and is working closely with them on common 5G standards.[11] Although deeply interdependent with Europe, Huawei has largely withdrawn from the United States, amid US Department of Justice investigations of its possible role in violating US Iran sanctions.[12]

How Globalization and Eurasian Reconnection Relate

Many ask how this deepening Eurasian transcontinental interplay differs from a more cosmopolitan globalization, broadly conceded to be sweeping the world since the mid-1970s.[13] The answer is threefold:

(1) *The historical point of departure is distinctive.* Eurasia, despite its venerable Silk Road history of connectivity, has for centuries been much more divided internally politically—not to mention Balkanized into unconnected, overregulated jurisdictions—than core economies elsewhere in the world. Connectivity thus has distinctively momentous geopolitical and geo-economic implications for Eurasia, as opposed to North America or other continents.

(2) *The geography is distinctive.* China and Europe are more than 30 percent closer overland than via sea routes[14]—a discrepancy intensified the further one plunges into the interior of these two central constituent parts of Eurasia, as indicated in Map 1.1. Such a pattern prevails on only the largest of continents, with Eurasia naturally representing the most extreme case on earth.

(3) *The techno-political context is distinctive.* Technological change, and regulatory adjustment with it, is uncommonly rapid today, in sectors of special relevance to Eurasia's reintegration such as land transport and telecommunications. The Logistics Revolution, accelerated by digitalization and the Internet of Things, is proceeding at warp speed early in the twenty-first century, with greater implications for Eurasia than for other regions due to that Super Continent's geography and to the pace of its economic advance. Public policy and private effort, especially China's Belt and Road Initiative (BRI), together with the efforts of firms like COSCO, Huawei, Ericsson, Alibaba, and Deutsche

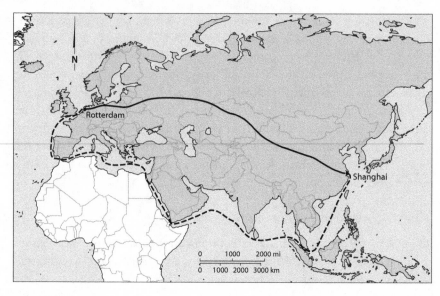

MAP 1.1 Land vs. sea routes

Bahn, are capitalizing on these long-term trends, with BRI and private efforts complementing one another in synergistic fashion.

Eurasia's Enduring Yet Dynamic Geo-Economic Centrality

On the Eurasian continent, at least, geography thus remains crucial to an understanding of regional political-economic interactions and their broader global significance. The simple size, population profile, and resource configuration of that huge land mass raise the possibility that geography *could* matter. In the emerging world of the twenty-first century, we argue, long neglected geographical traits—particularly the propinquity of population and natural resources within Eurasia—can assume fateful global geo-economic and geo-political importance as well.

Lending special future promise to the reconnection of Eurasia are the scale and complementarities innate to the continent itself, as suggested above. Eurasia is by far the world's largest and most central continent, with well over a third of the Earth's entire land area.[15] Beneath its soil lies nearly two-thirds of the world's oil and over 80 percent of conventional gas reserves, as shown in Table 1.1. Eurasia's constituent nations hold almost 85 percent of world foreign exchange reserves, while generating close to 70 percent of global GDP in PPP terms, not to mention nearly half of the world's manufactured

TABLE I.I
Eurasia's formidable scale in global context

	Land Area	GDP, Nominal	GDP, PPP	Total Reserves (incl. gold)	Proved Oil Reserves	Proved Gas Reserves
World	100.00	100.00	100.00	100.00	100.00	100.00
Eurasia (Asia + Europe)	40.96	61.93	69.41	83.72	59.33	80.81
Central Asia	3.03	0.33	0.68	0.30	1.84	11.29
Eastern Asia	8.88	24.04	24.97	42.89	1.51	2.83
South-Eastern Asia	3.35	3.50	6.33	7.66	0.74	4.10
South Asia	4.93	4.71	10.61	4.23	9.53	18.10
Western Asia	3.70	3.84	5.60	4.40	38.75	24.41
Eastern Europe	13.91	3.78	5.73	7.23	6.29	18.71
Northern Europe	1.31	5.80	3.89	3.38	0.62	0.99
Southern Europe	1.00	4.89	4.09	2.64	0.04	0.02
Western Europe	0.84	11.03	7.52	11.00	0.00	0.35
Rest of the World	59.04	38.07	30.59	16.28	40.67	19.19

SOURCES: World Bank, "Land Area (sq. km)," "GDP (Current US$)," "GDP, PPP (Constant 2011 International $)," and "Total Reserves (Includes Gold, Current US$)," *World Development Indicators*, accessed October 22, 2018; and BP, "Oil: Proved Reserves" and "Gas: Proved Reserves," *Statistical Review of World Energy*, June 2018.
NOTE: All regions and subregions are geographical, as defined and used by the United Nations Statistical Division.

goods.[16] They also generate innovative new technology, in sectors ranging from 5G telecommunications to high-speed rail.

Demography as a Catalyst

By most political-economic measures, of course—nominal GDP, service trade, and agricultural production, not to mention technology and military spending—the United States still remains preeminent. Both China and the other major nations of Eurasia have multiple problems of their own. Yet the nations of eastern Eurasia, in particular, have at least one powerful advantage in their resurgence toward global political-economic prominence— populations that are both generally industrious and also larger, by orders of magnitude, than anywhere else on earth.[17] As indicated in Table 1.2, three of the five most populous nations in the world lie in Eurasia, and six of the top ten. China, to repeat, is both the most populous and the most centrally located state within the populous economic core of the continent. The European Union, were it a nation, would rank third. The Eurasian nations, if considered collectively, would have over ten times the population of the United States.

The countries of eastern Eurasia are, generally speaking, not only populous, but also still on average relatively poor, with the exception of Japan, South Korea, Malaysia, and Singapore. Many, such as China and India,

TABLE I.2

Top ten most populous countries (2017)

Ranking	Country	Population (millions)	Growth Rate (annual %)	Eurasia
1	China	1,386.40	0.56	Yes
2	India	1,339.18	1.13	Yes
*	EU-28	512.46	0.24	Yes
3	United States	325.72	0.71	No
4	Indonesia	263.99	1.10	Yes
5	Brazil	209.29	0.78	No
6	Pakistan	197.02	1.95	Yes
7	Nigeria	190.89	2.60	No
8	Bangladesh	164.67	1.05	Yes
9	Russia	144.50	0.11	Yes
10	Mexico	129.16	1.26	No

SOURCE: World Bank, "Population, Total" and "Population Growth (Annual %)," *World Development Indicators*, accessed October 22, 2018.

TABLE I.3

The looming challenge of rising energy consumption in developing Eurasia

	China	India	Japan	EU-28	United States
GDP Per Capita, Constant 2010 US$ (2017)*	13.8	3.7	91.4	68.9	100.0
Food Supply Per Capita, kcal per day (2013)*	84.4	66.8	74.0	92.6	100.0
CO_2 Emissions Per Capita, metric tons (2014)*	45.7	10.5	57.8	38.7	100.0
Energy Use Per Capita, kg of oil equivalent (2014)*	32.2	9.2	49.9	44.3	100.0
Energy Use Per Capita (change between 2005-2014)	+60.5%	+41.3%	-14.6%	-14.8%	-11.3%

SOURCES: World Bank, "GDP Per Capita (Constant 2010 US$)" "$CO_2$ Emissions (Metric Tons Per Capita)" and "Energy Use (kg of Oil Equivalent Per Capita," *World Development Indicators*, accessed October 22, 2018; Food and Agricultural Organization of the United Nations, "Food Supply—Crops Primary Equivalent (kcal/capita/day)," *FAOSTAT*, updated February 5, 2018.
NOTE: * Country figures expressed as percentage of US levels.

include some fabulously wealthy people, but many more of painfully modest means. As a consequence, the per capita incomes and consumption levels of most East and Central Asian nations remain low by global standards, with far to go before reaching levels of the advanced industrial world. As indicated in Table 1.3, for example, India's per capita energy consumption remains no more than one-tenth that of the United States, and only a fifth that of the European Union, while its per capita caloric food intake is still only two-thirds that of the United States and three-quarters of the European average.

The large populations and low levels of per capita consumption in eastern Eurasia drive a fundamental emerging reality of this emerging Super Continent: *Eurasia, as it grows, is fated to loom large, in the aggregate, on the global economic stage, and in the global quest for food and resources.* The mathematics of its formidable population size, multiplied by its modest but rising per capita consumption, especially in the east of the continent, clearly drive this simple equation. With energy consumption and GDP levels that are both much lower in nominal terms than those of the United States, it is only a matter of time before China and possibly India will surpass America along both dimensions—in the calculus of nominal GDP as it already has in the scales of purchasing-power parity.

What do these historic economic changes concretely signify for the world in broader terms? If a more interactive Eurasian playing field is emerging, what does that mean for the profile of world affairs? These are the central questions that we confront.

It is important to remember that the question is *not* developments in any one country alone. *Connectivity* among nations is increasingly pervasive, synergistic with intranational change, and imparts increased momentum to developments in any one nation. Growth and technological progress in Asia or Europe alone is leveraged by their interaction.

Transformational change, through which technology radically reconfigures geography, is a hallmark of our extraordinary times. Nations are changing within, as middle classes emerge, even as inequalities intensify. Buffeted by deepening economic challenges from both within and without, transnational regions are also assuming new shapes. And these epic transformations at both national and regional levels have fateful implications for the world as a whole.

The Whole Is More than the Sum of the Parts

Few of the epic changes underway in our world today can be understood through one-country analysis—not even the rise of China. It is the *interaction* among parts of the broader system that often gives concrete developments in any one location their broader importance. Nowhere is this synergistic pattern more pronounced than in Eurasia, which is both massive and unique, as noted above.

To make analytical sense of the political-economic transitions now unfolding in Eurasia, and to grasp their broader implications, this research employs four interrelated concepts, chosen for their heuristic value: (1) geographic location, (2) critical junctures, (3) Crossover Points, and (4) distributive globalism. Together, these tools clarify the incentives and leverage of actors at various decision points; the prospects for system stability or transformation; and the resultant systemic profiles of particular processes of change. Collectively, they give us deeper insights into why Eurasia's reconnection is steadily progressing, despite challenging implications for the classical liberal order, and what the global implications thereof will ultimately be.

We conceive the utility of the foregoing concepts for our analysis in this volume as follows:

(1) *Geographic Location.* Determines resource endowments and latent connectivity potential. Contrary to the frequent assertions of globalist commentators, the world is *not* flat, either in reality or for many geo-economic purposes.

(2) *Critical Junctures.*[18] Describe the character of critical change periods, such as the 2008 global financial crisis, and provide microlevel insights into the timing, sequence, and causality through which political-economic systems and their constituent institutions change in the way that they do.

(3) *Crossover Points.*[19] Describe broad periods of transition, such as the December 1991 collapse of the Soviet Union, in structural terms. Provide macrolevel insights into the nature of systemic transitions.[20]

(4) *Distributive Globalism.*[21] Describes systems of governance characterized by distributive as opposed to regulatory allocation. Readily generates "win-win" arrangements between benefactors and recipients due to payoff structures involving concentrated benefits and diffuse, widely distributed costs. This concept generates insights into the nature of international order at the macro level, based on incentive structures at the micro level. It also generates predictions for system stability and prospects for transformation.

To succinctly conceptualize the process of systemic transformation, and to help assess its functional significance, we focus first on the notion of Crossover Points. Crossover Points can exist at various levels of social activity, and we identify three of particular significance relative to the ongoing transformation of Eurasia's role in global affairs today.

China's Crossover Point

Change in China matters to the continent—not only due to China's scale and momentum but also due to its geographical positioning. The PRC, at the economic heart of Eurasia, has been growing steadily for more than a generation, and became the second largest economy globally, in nominal terms, during 2010.[22] Three years later, in 2013, China became the largest nation globally in PPP terms.[23]

In no nation of global consequence is the pace of change more rapid or the implications more globally consequential than in China. The PRC, after all, has the largest population on earth and has sustained for over three decades one of the highest long-term economic growth rates in history for a major nation. As a consequence, China's own domestic consumption patterns—of food, energy, and raw materials—have assumed major significance beyond its borders.

Location, a basic and enduring variable, makes a much greater difference in shaping political-economic outcomes than often appreciated. China would not make nearly so much difference to global affairs if it were in the South Pacific, like Australia or New Zealand. The PRC is instead situated in the heart of populated Eurasia, surrounded by fourteen neighboring countries.[24] Across most of recorded history, connectivity among these nearby nations has been poor, despite resource complementarities and industrious labor, with their economies remaining remarkably static as a consequence.

China of course is surrounded by the Himalayas, Gobi Desert, Tibetan plateau, Taklamakan Desert, Tian Shan mountains, Southeast Asian jungles, and the Pacific Ocean. It has historically been isolated from the rest of Eurasia, rather than interconnected. That is why its rising recent connectivity with neighbors, as catalyst for an explosively growing continent, is so important today. The transformation of a huge nation like China, so centrally located, thus naturally has historic continental implications.

For many years, China's rising economic strength was hidden, until dramatically revealed in the 2008 global financial crisis, when it steadily grew, amid broader recession elsewhere. This underlying Chinese strength did not at first translate into strongly proactive diplomacy or political-military strategy. The Hu Jintao administration largely followed Deng Xiaoping's dictum of "hiding strength and biding time."[25] This pattern has shifted decisively, however, under President Xi Jinping, especially since the enunciation of the One Belt One Road (OBOR) program in October 2013.[26] At last China has moved to consolidate a fractious Eurasia, exercising leadership capacities implicit in its new economic strength and geopolitical centrality.

China's Crossover Point under President Xi has had three main dimensions: domestic, political-military, and diplomatic. In domestic terms, there has been increasing emphasis on the centrality of the Communist Party in national affairs, and a related allocative preference toward less-developed outlying regions in the West, the Northeast, and the Southwest as well.[27] In the political-military sphere, China has continued to expand military spending commensurate with its rapid economic growth. Diplomatically, China has reached out more systematically and strategically under the Belt and Road Initiative to Russia, Europe, Central Asia, Southeast Asia, and the Middle East.

As its economy, global dependence, and defense budget have grown, China has significantly expanded military power-projection capacities, in such areas as cruise missiles, reconnaissance satellites, stealth weaponry, artificial intelligence, and aircraft carriers.[28] The PRC has simultaneously restructured the People's Liberation Army, consolidating seven military regions into five theater commands.[29] China has also more assertively reinforced its territorial claims in the South and East China Seas, both by building artificial islands and by strengthening its naval presence.[30] Most recently, it has begun reconciliation, based on its rising geo-economic strength, with a variety of Eurasian neighbors, including longstanding US allies such as the Philippines, Korea, Japan, and several NATO nations. The PRC has thus begun to neutralize asymmetrical US influence far from Chinese shores, emerging as a major global rather than simply a regional power. Promoting connectivity has become a major tool for Beijing, complementing its rising hard power with a congenial distributive soft power that also furthers geopolitical objectives.

Eurasia's Crossover Point

Eurasia in the aggregate is a potential Super Continent, with resources, population, and geographic scale second to none. Yet until the late 1970s, that potential powerhouse was just a static, Balkanized corner of the world, divided among myriad conflicting jurisdictions, with little commerce or even reliable infrastructure connecting the disparate parts. China's Four Modernizations (1978), the collapse of the Soviet Union (1991), and the 2008 global financial crisis enhanced the *potential* for a more interactive and interdependent Eurasia across three fateful decades. That prospect, emerging slowly but surely over the past ten years, has been catalyzed since 2013 by the Ukraine crisis between Russia and the West as well as China's Belt and Road Initiative. Overall, the geo-economic changes within China since 1978 have triggered a broader Eurasian consolidation that can be seen most productively within the context of that Eurasian transformation as a whole.

On the far side of Russia and Central Asia, from the perspective of the Sino-Indian giants, lies the European Union (EU). The EU lies remarkably close in geographic terms, across the expanses of Eurasia, to the major centers of Asia. And a process of "continental drift," set in motion by post–Cold War Europe's integration and China's western development, is bringing industrial centers of the two regions ever closer together, as suggested in Map 1.2. Technological and domestic political-economic changes are imparting this drift with enhanced momentum.

Sino-European economic relations, in particular, have deepened sharply since the 2008 global financial crisis. China's growth, a common—and complementary—Sino-European focus on manufacturing, a revolution in intermodal logistics that is synergistic with that manufacturing emphasis, improved transcontinental infrastructure, and streamlined border-clearance procedures have all played important roles in deepening this historic linking between the antipodes of Eurasia. Ties between China and the former socialist nations of Eastern Europe (institutionalized through the 16+1 framework established in 2012), as well as those linking China and Southeast Asia, have deepened especially rapidly. Since the Iranian nuclear agreement of 2015 (the Joint Comprehensive Plan of Action, JCPOA), Indian economic ties with Europe have also grown, using as a transit point the Iranian port of Chabahar, only 550 nautical miles across the Arabian Sea from Prime Minister Modi's own home state of Gujarat. US withdrawal from JCPOA in mid-2018 complicates this Indian initiative and India's efforts to compete with China in developing ties to Europe.

Changes over the past three decades have also hastened the emergence of a more interactive Eurasia. A "New Europe" has emerged in the east from the former Warsaw Pact, growing rapidly and holding longstanding ties to China, Vietnam, Mongolia, and even North Korea, dating from socialist days. Meanwhile, a powerful central European manufacturing complex has emerged, considerably to the east of its predecessors, with synergistic complementarities to Asian continental economies, especially China. Logistical innovations, such as expedited freight forwarding and border clearance, accelerated by BRI infrastructure support, are also making transcontinental trade and transport ever easier and faster, helping integrated transcontinental production and distribution chains to develop. E-commerce, which actively employs new modes of communication such as business-to-business (B2B) and customer-to-customer (C2C) liaison, is accelerating this integration still further. On the political front, European fragmentation and social problems, including migration, are absorbing local attention and allowing Chinese influence to quietly increase, especially in Eastern Europe.

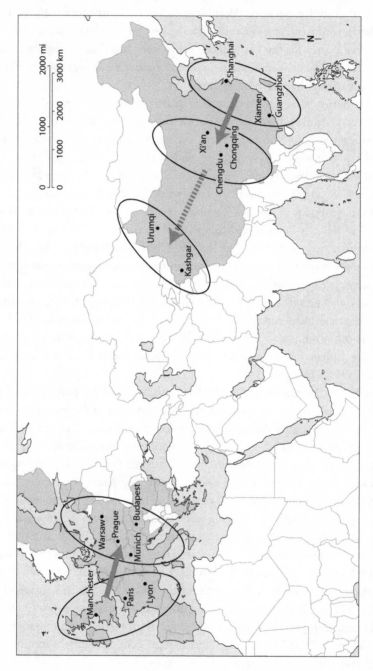

MAP 1.2 "Continental Drift" brings Europe and Asia closer in the post–Cold War world

Today the Asian Infrastructure Investment Bank, ASEM, the Conference on Interaction and Confidence-Building Measures in Asia (CICA), and the 16+1 cooperation framework, among major international organizations, link Europe and Northeast Asia at the west and east antipodes of the Eurasian continent. Meanwhile, the Shanghai Cooperation Organization (SCO) and the Eurasian Economic Union help integrate transit states into the broader chessboard as well. Over the past decade, transnational road, rail, pipeline, telecommunications, and electric power infrastructure across Eurasia have all expanded to a remarkable degree. The first scheduled Europe-bound freight train from China left Chongqing for Duisburg only in March 2011. Yet by September 2018, over 10,000 trips between Europe and China had been completed. More than one-third of this total occurred during 2017 alone, with over thirty trains per week moving transcontinentally in each direction.[31]

This deepening and well-used infrastructure, capitalizing on the revolution in intermodal logistics provoked by the digital revolution, is turning Eurasia into an increasingly interactive political-economic playing field. Integrated rail, road, air, and maritime transport, enabled by the digital revolution, is becoming increasingly competitive with maritime variants. This logistical revolution is provoking a rapid proliferation of transcontinental supply chains, with China at their core.

As the pages to come will demonstrate, dual Crossover Points—across Eurasia as a whole and within China more specifically—have latent synergistic potential. A historic consolidation within Eurasia is occurring, driven by developments in both China and its Eurasian partners to the west, from Central Asia all the way to Central Europe. And those dual consolidations create the deepening if distant prospect of a Eurasian Super Continent, potentially provoking a much broader and more consequential global reconfiguration, especially if the United States is oblivious or insensitive in its response.

A Global Crossover Point Impending?

Eurasia is by far the largest continent on earth in geo-economic terms, generating over 60 percent of nominal global GDP, and nearly 70 percent when calculated in PPP. It is home to around 70 percent of the world's people, and holds the bulk of global foreign-exchange reserves.[32] It has Super Continent potential. Yet it still lacks internal connectivity.

The largest nations of Eurasia—China, India, and Russia among them—are neighbors geographically and complementary in economic terms. This triad remains largely unbound, as yet, by infrastructural ties or well-institutionalized multilateral networks.[33] This propinquity of the largest continentalist powers has broad geo-economic implications, however, that could well mean greater interdependence and arguably more intense institutional ties, with deepening geopolitical implications, in coming years.

Complementarity begins in the economic realm. Russia, for example, is a major exporter of both energy and arms, and India a sophisticated producer of services, while China is a highly competitive manufacturer. Russia, its competitive problems elsewhere in the world notwithstanding, is a major exporter of energy and arms to both the Asian giants. Despite geopolitical differences, there is powerful logic to the interdependence of this Eurasian triad, and collective geopolitical benefits to cooperation among its members, especially due to their shared centrality on the world's largest continent.

European experience suggests the frequent importance of smaller powers as catalysts for stable relations among their larger neighbors. Following World War II, for example, the Benelux nations (Belgium, Netherlands, and Luxembourg) played a key role in bringing France and Germany together as the core founding members of the European Economic Community. Belgian statesman Paul-Henri Spaak was chosen as the chairman of the European Coal and Steel Community; the head of the Spaak Committee, which played an influential role in establishment of the European Economic Community; and as the second secretary-general of NATO. He also served as Belgian prime minister and foreign minister, playing a central regional role in those national capacities as well.

Much depends, in short, on the ability of the largest Eurasian powers to collaborate with one another—yet also on the converse intensity of their mutual rivalry and competition. Should those massive nations cohere, their collaboration would accelerate the coming of a global Crossover Point where Asia takes central prominence in world affairs; should they quarrel, that Crossover Point could be delayed or fail entirely to materialize.

Intra-Eurasian geopolitical rivalries, including border conflicts between China and India across the Himalayas, doubtless remain.[34] Yet the key nations of Eurasia—preeminently China and the European states—are forging new ties with alternate centers of global affairs, apart from the United States. Most significantly, as we shall see, they are developing fresh relationships with their Eurasian neighbors, renewing historic Silk Road ties that had largely languished since Vasco da Gama's historic sea voyage from Europe to India over five centuries before.

Particularly important in propelling deepening connectivity and interaction across Eurasia are several middle-power *regionalist integrators*, with special incentives to pursue continental integration, even in opposition to broader globalization. They are playing similar regional roles to those of the Benelux nations in Europe six decades ago. Small and middle powers such as Erdoğan's

Turkey, Mirziyoyev's Uzbekistan, Nazarbayev's Kazakhstan, and Lukashenko's Belarus—maneuvering among larger nations like Xi Jinping's China and Vladimir Putin's Russia—have all for a variety of reasons actively sought to bring Eurasian neighbors together in subglobal Eurasian continentalist associations, with the smaller powers playing surprisingly important catalytic roles.

Also prominent among these would-be continentalists is Iran, with the eleventh largest population and the second largest energy reserves on the continent. Due to its estrangement from the United States, Iran emphatically rejects US-centric globalism but finds Eurasian continentalism quite congenial, and has actively been seeking membership in the regionalist SCO. Iran manifests the most extreme case of continentalist bias. Yet it is far from the only nation striving to construct a continentalist order that minimizes the influence of the United States. Eurasian continentalism is a convenient vehicle for doing so, as the United States is—quite distinctively among major nations of the world—not a Eurasian nation.

Multilateral regional organizations with potential significance in orienting Eurasian states toward broader collective global roles are beginning to evolve, as they did in Europe half a century ago. ASEM, CICA, and the SCO, for example, founded in 1996, 1999, and 2001 respectively, include a broader selection of Eurasian nations, but none include the United States. The SCO, in particular, has begun to play a substantive role in deepening personal ties among Eurasian leaders and providing a forum for policy coordination, especially since 2017 when India as well as Pakistan joined and Iran became an active observer. A decade ago the SCO was active mainly in the counterterrorism area, but its functions have expanded recently into energy and infrastructure, with BRI as a major catalyst to its effectiveness.[35]

The large nations of Eurasia, as many have argued, do have "big power" consciousness and divergent geopolitical aims. They exist, however, in a changing continental context, in which their relative influence is shifting, smaller powers are growing more active, and connectivity is sharply rising. The distributive policies of China's BRI, in particular, accelerate that connectivity process and are especially seductive in doing so, due to an allocative character that concentrates benefits and diffuses costs.

Connectivity and Political Economy: A Theoretical Perspective

To understand how connectivity relates to real-world political economy, both domestic and international, it is crucial first to grasp the grassroots-level incentive structures at work. Our point of departure is the important analytical distinction made by Theodore Lowi among three functional categories of policy decisions—distributive, regulatory, and redistributive.[36] The costs and benefits generated in the three types of cases are, as Lowi points out, crucially different. Table 1.4 suggests implications for concrete systems of international order.

TABLE I.4

Systems of international order

		Rules Based	
		Yes	No
Leadership Structure	Unitary	REGULATORY (Bretton Woods System)	TRIBUTARY (Traditional Chinese World Order)
	Plural	CONCERT OF POWERS (Congress of Vienna)	DISTRIBUTIVE REGIONALISM/ GLOBALISM (Belt and Road Initiative)

Regulatory and redistributive policies diffuse benefits to broad categories of individuals but concentrate costs. While equitable in many ways due to their broad application to general classes of people and situations, policies in these categories tend to provoke conflict and implementation resistance precisely because costs are so clearly concentrated and benefits are diffuse. Distributive policies, by contrast, have politically congenial traits: they concentrate benefits and diffuse costs. Not surprisingly, distributive policies, often derided as "pork-barrel politics," have been a mainstay of durable democratic regimes across history, ranging from the New Deal of Franklin D. Roosevelt to the conservative Liberal Democratic Party government of Japan.[37]

Lowi's distinctions, centering on the contrasting incentive structures that different policy types create, is relevant to international as well as domestic politics. In the international sphere, "regulatory" systems are rule based, with the universality, fragility, and propensity toward conflict that flows from the incentive structures they generate. By contrast, "distributive" systems tend to be low conflict and politically seductive, precisely because they concentrate benefits and diffuse costs.

Conceptually, these distinctions generate a typology of international system types, based on the structure of costs and benefits generated and the degree of pluralism in the leadership of the international system in question.[38] A configuration with distributive characteristics that embodies aspirations to order international affairs in general can be described as "distributive globalism." China's Belt and Road Initiative of recent years falls into this category, and the US Marshall Plan of the late 1940s shared some of the same general characteristics.

The foregoing categories are simply abstract types, and do not correspond precisely to any specific systems in the real world. They are, however, evocative. The classic Bretton Woods system of the early post–World War II years was clearly regulatory; China's BRI of recent years is clearly distributive. This distinction, we suggest, has important consequences for both the normative acceptability and the political acceptability of both types of systems in the broader world.

Distributive Globalism as a Resolution?

In the preceding section we introduced the concept of *distributive globalism*, or a cosmopolitan orientation toward providing incentives that concentrate divisible benefits and diffuse prospective costs. This pragmatic type of international behavior, epitomized by China's BRI, promotes connectivity through support for infrastructure enhancements in multiple dimensions. Both in concept and in China's practice, distributive globalism operates on an ad hoc basis, without general rules and subject solely to mutual national consent, often just ruling-elite consent, in contrast to regulatory systems like the Bretton Woods framework, which have clear and transparent rules.

Patterns of connectivity, such as the presence or absence of roads, railroads, trading regimes, or communication systems, evolve through discrete human decisions. Those decisions necessarily involve the interaction of multiple participants, but come in three contrasting variants with sharply different implications for conflict and cooperation. Distributive policies, as Lowi noted, involve divisible goods, that can be allocated without regard to limited resources and hence can, through almost infinite disaggregation, minimize social conflict. Benefits are concentrated, while costs are widely distributed, and often largely invisible to participants. Distributive policies include the land-grant programs authorized by the 1862 Morrill Act, which generated funds for building of the US transcontinental railway. China's Belt and Road Initiative arguably often has this distributive, "win-win" character for those directly involved, which could well aid its global reception and consequent prospects for success, unless allocative patterns prove controversial. Since distributive benefits are typically allocated through established authorities, however, their attractiveness to such incumbents is much greater than to the opposition, creating potential complications when there is a change of power, as recently in Malaysia, Sri Lanka, and elsewhere.

One might ask how such a system relates to established theories of international relations, and also how practical it may be as a form of governance—both for Eurasia and possibly the world more generally in future years. Since both distributive regionalism and distributive globalism lack any set of clearly specified rules, other than the consent of the contracting parties, distributive globalism cannot be easily classed as idealistic. In the hands of China, centrally located as it is in the geo-economic heart of a continent like Eurasia that is sorely lacking in connectivity, such policies have clear realist implications. They do have an aspect of "checkbook diplomacy" and can potentially create "debt traps" for recipients, with perverse developmental consequences, as appears to have happened recently in Sri Lanka, Malaysia, Pakistan, and the Maldives.[39] The Chinese variant, however, like the US Marshall Plan in earlier years, is far from a unilateral "tributary system," as we shall see, and is but part of a much broader and more pluralistic process of Eurasian reconnection that builds on history yet far transcends it. If it proves to be fiscally responsible and can cope with potential domestic backlash, especially from disadvantaged opposition groups, distributive globalism, partially in the form of China's BRI, could ultimately be an effective way to change the modus operandi of international affairs, particularly given the scale of China's financial reserves. It could also potentially secure a global leadership role for both China and possibly other illiberal powers, while insulating domestic interests in such countries from the turbulence of full domestic liberalization.

In Conclusion

The two and a half centuries since the Industrial Revolution were, in the long eye of world history, an anomalous interlude. They represented a fleeting era of American political-economic dominance, combined with Eastern fragmentation, that could now be entering its twilight years. A clear erosion of economic liberalism, manifest in Brexit and the trade policies of Donald Trump, is one central development. Also important are the dramatic growth and transformation of the Chinese political economy, the rise of a new Eurasian continentalism, and explosively growing "South–South" trade.

These historic changes take place against a backdrop of enduring, embedded geo-economic realities that are all too often ignored. China lies at the geographic heart of the largest and most populous continent on earth, surrounded by dynamic neighbors in East and Southeast Asia. And the PRC has the largest population and the third largest geographical expanse in the world. China borders on fourteen countries and is strategically positioned in relation to many more. It has the largest foreign-exchange reserves on earth. Yet China's connectivity with the rest of Eurasia—indeed, with the broader world—is historically poor.

Connectivity initiatives at the heart of the BRI could thus, if realized, have a synergistic effect on China's power and influence. Yet by supplying infrastructure and promoting political-economic stability through distributive policies, they could energize its neighbors and transcontinental partners as well. Infrastructure, ranging from railroads to electric power grids and telecommunications systems, enables mutually beneficial transactions including trade, investment, and cultural exchange. It also opens prospects for deepened Eurasian synergies across the continent, such as the China-inspired 16+1 Forum, even as it intensifies tensions in neglected parts of the continent as well.

Deepening Eurasian interdependence, especially the increased connectivity between major economic centers such as China and Europe, magnifies the systemic impact of classical globalism's erosion. It also accelerates a fateful transformation of world affairs as a whole that benefits China but involves far more than the rise of China alone. Through distributive globalism Eurasia is thus being reconnected and a Super Continent is arising, normative implications notwithstanding. The dimensions of this development and the global implications, are subjects of the pages to come.

The Silk Road Syndrome

WE HAVE JUST SEEN HOW THREE MOMENTOUS, largely post—Cold War developments—the rise of China, the collapse of the Soviet Union, and the transformation of Europe—have given birth to an ever-more-interactive Eurasia, assuming the potential dimensions of a Super Continent. This is by no means the first time, however, that Europeans, Chinese, and others across the Eurasian landmass have dealt intensively with one another. To the contrary, East-West intellectual and economic interaction across Eurasia has a venerable heritage.

For the past two centuries and more, since the Industrial Revolution, world affairs have revolved preeminently around the Atlantic basin. First Britain and then the United States have been the preeminent international powers. Today, with the rise of multiple Asian nations, and deepening transcontinental ties between Asia and Europe, the era of undiluted Atlantic supremacy is unquestionably ending. Patterns of an earlier age are returning, and it behooves us to understand those atavistic historical paradigms.

Given its geo-economic scale and internal complementarities, a transcontinental Eurasia has always had immense latent potential for influence in world affairs. At times—the days of Genghis Khan and Kublai Khan, for example—a consolidated Eurasia has arguably played the role of Super Continent. The critical uncertainty has always been internal cohesion and identity—not just at the continental but even at the national level. In reality, any sort of transcendent social consciousness beyond the civic has often been lacking in Eurasia, across the centuries. This chapter chronicles the checkered, tortured course of continental interdependence and shared consciousness over the years, while also considering the deepening potential consequences of such cohesion for the global system as a whole.

Tracing the once and future prospects of Eurasian continentalism has special relevance in today's world, because of how Eurasia is configured geographically and what it excludes. As Chapter 1 suggested, China lies amidst the most fertile, habitable, and populous portion of eastern Eurasia, with Germany in a comparable, if less dominant, position within the West.[1] The largest political economy in the world apart from China—the United States—is conspicuously detached and distant from the Eurasian land mass. Its closest allies—Britain and Japan—are detached as well. The United States has never had aspirations to be a Eurasian land power itself, and would no doubt find it geopolitically difficult to become one, despite its pervasive global influence. The geographical barriers to China's west, across the great Eurasian plain to Europe, are limited. Any deepening consolidation of Eurasian continentalism thus tends to enhance the geopolitical influence of China, Russia, Germany, and France on the global stage, at the possible expense of the United States and other maritime powers.

In conceptualizing this complex transcontinental linkage—neither national nor civic—and its various socioeconomic incarnations over the centuries, we employ the concept of "syndrome," first developed by the renowned physician Ibn Sina (Avicenna, 980–1037), and frequently employed even today in the realm of medicine.[2] We use the term *syndrome* more broadly to suggest the persistent recurrence over history of particular response elements. Ibn Sina defined a syndrome as a set of "composite" interactions, consistently occurring together.

In the Eurasian context, diverse peoples of Europe and Asia, across the centuries, have had to address a common underlying set of recurring transcultural, social, and geo-economic realities, closely correlated with one another, and reflecting the particulars of Eurasian geography. The continent, after all, is vast, containing multiple and sometimes overlapping jurisdictions, many lightly governed spaces, and a diversity of peoples with limited transcultural understanding. Eurasia's world has historically *not* often been Westphalian—more typical have been complex national entities like the Holy Roman and Ottoman Empires, together with a variety of city-states. In such a world of limited, overlapping sovereignties, brokers naturally attain prominence, while leadership needs to be assertive and dictatorial to unify large parts of the continent. Socioeconomic transactions have generally involved nonhierarchical, transcultural bargaining and mediation, often lacking in both transparency and effective sanctions. This pattern of personalistic and nontransparent bartering has prevailed both within what nominally passed as nations and between them.

It was nearly 2,150 years ago that a Chinese imperial envoy, Zhang Qian, first voyaged to the west, into the Fergana Valley of Central Asia, on a diplomatic mission with fateful longer-term consequences for regional trade.[3] Fourteen hundred years later, Marco Polo popularized the notion of East-West cultural exchange, with his epic two-decade overland voyage from Venice to China (1271–1292). And a bit more than 140 years ago, an aristocratic German adventurer, Baron Ferdinand von Richthofen, in 1877 coined the term *Silk Road*, traversing the territory that Zhang and Polo had trodden centuries before.

Both the abstract concept and the physical reality of the Silk Road have thus been around for some time. Broadly speaking, in both concept and reality, the "Silk Road" has generally denoted a cross-cultural interaction of the East and the West, devoid of American dominance. There has been tremendous variation across history in the intensity of human interaction along the different "Silk Roads," not to mention in the very popularity of the Silk Road concept itself.[4] Yet many features have been recurrent, as we shall see.

In this chapter we review the varied yet structurally parallel usages of "Silk Road" over history, in diverse corners of the world, relating them to the actual history of East-West transcontinental interaction among East and South Asia, Europe, the former Soviet Union, the Middle East, and to some extent Africa. This context will allow us to grasp with the greatest possible clarity commonalities particular to the "Silk Road Syndrome." It will therefore show us the historic nature of the transformations toward Eurasian interdependence and centrality now unfolding in the "post-post-" Cold War world, together with their unprecedented global systemic implications.

The Classic Silk Roads of History

From the early Stone Age, as human beings began to use polished stone tools to grow crops and tend domesticated animals, Eurasians began dividing into two distinct societies, one sedentary and the other nomadic, and separated geographically by the Caucasus mountains in the west and the Altai/Tian Shan ranges to the east. Along the fertile rim of the continent, hunters became farmers. Across the vast Eurasian steppe, however, they herded livestock, including horses, cattle, and sheep. From time to time, the movements of nomads and their livestock threatened the settled lives of farmers, whose crops could be easily destroyed by marauding nomadic herds.

At times displaced nomads migrated westward in search of more fertile grasslands in western Asia and ultimately Eastern Europe. The Huns, followed by the Turks, were prominent among them.[5] Thus emerged the genetic ties linking the peoples of Northeast Asia and Eastern Europe, flowing from common ancestry in the grasslands of Mongolia. Those ties continue to link the peoples of Eurasia to this day, east and west, at an elementary, existential level.[6]

Around 600 BC, horseback riding began spreading across the Eurasian steppe. Within two hundred years nomads adjoining the agricultural zones of Eurasia started combining horsemanship with archery to "become masters of the horse as a military machine."[7] With these cavalries emerging, organized trade and communication across the vast steppe linking Europe and Asia began. It was, after all, the nomads who began bringing the diverse peoples of East and West together, across the vast distances of Central Eurasia.

The production of silk was already an ancient art in China, appearing first in the third millennium BC. Silk weaving and textiles were common there—referred to even in folk songs three millennia ago, during the Zhou Dynasty (1046–256 BC).[8] Yet silk remained rare and an object of great attraction among nomads to the west and north of China itself.

Meanwhile, in ancient China, a revolution of military affairs was brewing. Seven agricultural states, including the Qin, Zhao, and Yan, were emerging in the fifth century BC and jousting with both each other and the agile nomads to the north for supremacy and survival. Grasping the tactical advantages of the nomads' sophisticated use of horses, the state of Zhao, under King Wuling, reconfigured its military in the fourth century BC, stressing mobile horseback combat. Zhao's approach grew general across the Middle Kingdom, increasing the need for hardy, speedy horses with great endurance that could only be bred on the vast grasslands of the steppe.

Thus emerged the early basis for trade across Eurasia—speedy horses of the steppe, in return for the elegant silk of the plains. There were other important commodities—jade from the mines of Xinjiang were an early and persistent candidate. But silk for horses was the stable equation. That was the basis on which the Silk Road began to thrive.

The first documented traveler along what later became the Silk Road was Zhang Qian, an emissary of the Han court. Zhang was dispatched westward to negotiate with the Yuezhi, a nomadic group traditionally friendly to the Han, in the hopes that they would conclude an alliance against the Xiongnu, a more hostile group of nomads from whom today's Mongolians are arguably descended.[9] Zhang was captured by the Xiongnu and spent a decade among them, marrying and fathering children. Ultimately, however, he escaped, wending his way westward to the Fergana Valley in today's Uzbekistan. In 129 BC, Zhang finally reached the court of the Yuezhi on the banks of the Oxus River, returning to report the details of his remarkable thirteen-year journey across the "Western Regions" to Emperor Wu. Zhang's original report has unfortunately been lost, but his travel was recounted meticulously by several distinguished historians of the day.[10]

As indicated in Map 2.1, there were four basic permutations of the classic Silk Road. These included two variants in the east (to the north and the south of the Taklamakan Desert) and two more in the west (to the north and the south of the Caspian Sea). The eastern terminus of these multiple Silk Roads was typically the Chinese capital—variously Chang'an (today's Xian), Luoyang, Khanbaliq,[11] and Beijing over the centuries. The established western termini included prominent centers of continental Europe in their day, such as Rome and Venice during the periods of their preeminence.

Along the way the classic Silk Road twisted west from China across the Gobi Desert and either north or south of the still more desolate Taklamakan, toward Kashgar, and from there across Central Asia. From Samarkand, one route, opened by the Turks in the sixth century,[12] wound north of the Caspian and across the Volga into the heartland of Russia. Another more travelled thoroughfare crossed Persia south of the Caspian and ventured into Turkey toward Constantinople (Istanbul). From there it proceeded across the Bosporus into Europe.

Although the Silk Road is popularly conceived as a single, continuous unit, there have thus in reality been multiple routes traversing Eurasia. And there have actually been remarkably few periods, prior to the recent past, when individuals have been physically or politically able to travel the Silk Road as a whole. Zhang Qian, the first recorded traveler, only journeyed roughly a third of the way, from Chang'an to the Fergana Valley. And his trip took thirteen years. Marco Polo did reportedly travel the entire length of the road in the thirteenth century, but his voyage took over twenty years. Silk and other traded goods did, to be sure, pass from one end to the other in many periods, beginning with commerce between the Han Dynasty and the Roman Empire. Yet commerce and the broader flow of information were generally conducted through middlemen, who themselves had no direct personal experience with the Silk Road as a whole.

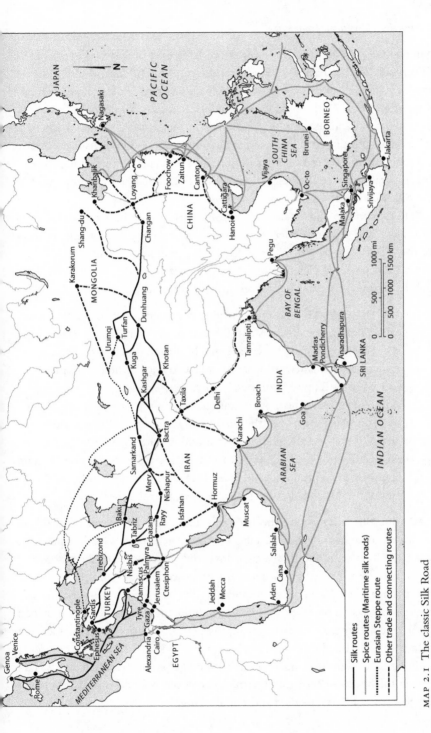

MAP 2.1 The classic Silk Road

SOURCE: United Nations Educational, Scientific and Cultural Organization, "About the Silk Road," *Silk Roads: Dialogue, Diversity & Development*, accessed June 24, 2018, https://en .unesco.org/silkroad/about-silk-road.

Distinctive Silk Road Traits

Middlemen—of all varieties—thus loom large over the classic history of the Silk Road. At the individual level, traders, innkeepers, and priests, who ran the way stations and places of refuge where travelers took shelter, were always important. At the broader sociopolitical level, city-states and empires, which naturally acquired powerful stakes in Silk Road commerce where it flourished, also played key roles in facilitating trade and information flows— covarying with political stability in the city-states and empires along its way. Nation-states in the Westphalian sense have been remarkably unimportant in the Silk Road's history over the centuries.

The coherence and vitality of the Silk Road oscillated sharply across its history. When powerful rulers and dynasties arose along a substantial portion of the Silk Road's length, commerce and communication also flourished; as centralized power declined, commerce conversely grew more difficult. The Silk Road thus held particular coherence in three rough periods:

(1) **150 BC–AD 250**. This was roughly the interval between Zhang Qian's diplomatic missions and the end of the Han dynasty. This period of Chinese outreach overlaps much of the history of the Roman Empire, which lasted from 27 BC until AD 395, when the Eastern and Western Empires definitively split.

(2) **AD 600–1000**. This was roughly the era of the Tang dynasty (618–907), and Persia between the final Islamic conquest of that nation (around 651) and the end of the Saffarid empire there (1003).

(3) **AD 1200–1400**. This approximated the interval between the Mongol conquest of Central Asia and Iran (1221), on the one hand, and the end of the Yuan dynasty (1368) in China, on the other.

During this latter period the Mongols held sway over virtually all of the Eurasian landmass and greatly facilitated commerce across its vast expanse. It was the Mongols, interestingly, who invented the concept of the passport, a document committing the protection of a powerful ruler and thus assuring safe passage. The Mongolian passport, known as a *gerege*, assured both safe passage and access to relay stations throughout the empire. It also provided fresh food and remounts, epitomizing the political-economic guarantees that helped the Silk Road in its heyday to flourish.[13]

Political-economic guarantees were always helpful in facilitating trade. Except at the height of Mongol supremacy, however, political jurisdiction along the Silk Road was fragmented and middle-range governance was crucial to its prosperity. The Silk Road thus gave birth to a series of once-important yet long-forgotten Central Asian kingdoms that prospered from trade, only to later fade into oblivion, as economic intercourse waxed and waned across the continent. Even in their heyday, these fragile regimes totally lacked the mass legitimacy and institutional strength typical of modern-day Western nation-states.

The first of the important "middleman" kingdoms, bridging east and west along the Silk Road, was the Parthian Empire. It dominated Persia for over four centuries, from 247 BC until AD 224. Then came the Kushan Empire, which helped to transmit Buddhism from India to China, built the famous Bamiyan Buddha later destroyed by the Taliban, and ruled Afghanistan, as well as parts of India and Central Asia, from 130 BC to AD 300. Caravan and trading cities such as Petra, Palmyra, and Sogdiana were also important, both in this early period, and for close to a thousand years thereafter, as was the Byzantine Empire until its collapse in AD 1453 with the fall of Constantinople to the Turks.

The importance of the classic Silk Road to the evolution of Chinese, Western, and Islamic civilizations is little known but difficult to overstate. The role of spices in Chinese cuisine, introduced from Persia during the Tang dynasty, was one concrete and enduring result of such confluence, as was the role of paper and gunpowder introduced from China into the West. Chinese pottery also graced both the Islamic world and the West. Religious concepts likewise flowed along the trade routes—Buddhism, Manichaeism, and Nestorian Christianity all traveled together with the silk. All this was largely achieved, however, through the power of markets, random military action, and interpersonal trading networks. There was only a limited role for political authority—and none at all for strategic decisions by the nation-state.[14]

For well over a thousand years the classic Silk Road was the principal conduit between East and West, linking the central poles of world civilization across Eurasia, the largest landmass on earth and a potential Super Continent. Conspicuously, the Western Hemisphere was a mere sideshow, totally isolated from the main flow of world affairs. Yet the global political economy as a whole was in no sense integrated the way it was later to become.

With two epic voyages of discovery within a single decade—Christopher Columbus's voyage to the Americas in 1492 and Vasco da Gama's to India in 1498—the world's horizons suddenly opened beyond Eurasian continentalism. The Americas, Africa, Northwestern Europe's seafaring centers, and the Atlantic Ocean that linked them all became increasingly important from a global perspective, with the Industrial Revolution enhancing the preeminence of Europe still further. The Silk Road, including its Central Asian way stations and East Asian terminus, faded into relative insignificance for centuries to come. Meanwhile, the seaways prospered and the maritime powers that controlled them rose to global dominance.

What the Classic Silk Road Was Not: A Vehicle for Chinese Dominance

Stereotypical popular views have emerged suggesting that a cosmopolitan China was a primary initiator and supporter of the historic Silk Roads. It does appear that Zheng He, the often-mentioned Ming-era Muslim Chinese (Hui) sea captain, was a historic figure. He sailed ships three times the size of the Santa Maria on seven long voyages as far as Zanzibar, spanning a twenty-eight-year period that began almost a century before Columbus. Zheng He, however, was an anomaly.

In actuality, very few of the voyagers who traveled on the Silk Roads, either overland or maritime, traversed even close to its entirety. And of those, very few of the traders on the overland Silk Roads outside China were ethnic Han Chinese. It was not just that Chinese travelers did not venture far along the Silk Road. They actually did not travel much overland beyond China at all. That makes China's ambitious goals today for the Belt portion of the Belt and Road Initiative (BRI), including the personal involvement of Chinese in Russia, Central Asia, and the Middle East, all the more remarkable. To be sure, Chinese have long been seafarers. Chinese merchants traveled to Southeast Asia and beyond even before the days of Zheng He. Yet they rarely ventured overland. That China has returned to its former economic preeminence is significant, but what is truly striking is that it is now striving itself to bind together the Eurasian continent, both on the sea and on the land, with potentially fateful implications.

Silk Road Visions in the Industrial Age and Beyond

In the late seventeenth century, visions of a transcontinental Eurasia began arising once again, in forms displaying some family resemblance to what had gone before. The first of the conscious modern continentalists was Russia—not surprising, since Russia was the first European power to extend physically to the Pacific. Korea, Japan, Turkey, and China have also developed continentalist visions, as will be clear in the coming pages. Mongolia,[15] Kazakhstan,[16] and Iran[17] have also seriously considered the issue. In all these cases, leaders had to strive mightily to bring coherence to continental ventures; not surprisingly, entropy—complicated by multiple overlapping jurisdictions—was the more common pattern.

The classic Silk Road and its more modern incarnations traversed in many cases geographically divergent routes. Yet they have faced a common geo-economic challenge—how to communicate and conduct economic transactions across cultures and formidable distance. By comparing these formulations we gain deeper insights into how geographic and cultural realities at the heart of the Silk Road syndrome continue to reassert themselves across the ages, even in the face of revolutionary changes in technology.

Russia's Road of Steel

Czarist Russia in the nineteenth century quite naturally became the first nation of the industrial era to try bridging the Eurasian continent, as it had earlier become the first nation since the Mongols of the thirteenth and fourteenth centuries to extend politically across that vast expanse. The legions of the czar reached the Sea of Okhotsk in 1639, but it was only much later that Russia began to take serious interest in Pacific affairs.

In February 1891, the decision to begin construction of the Trans-Siberian Railway was finally approved. To stress the importance that Czar Alexander III attached to this visionary new transcontinental infrastructure project, he ordered his heir-apparent, Czarevich Nicholas, to lay the cornerstone of the railway. The young, twenty-three-year-old Nicholas, soon to become Czar Nicholas II, gladly took this fateful step in late May 1891 at Vladivostok, launching the massive, geopolitically transformational project on its way.[18]

As the rails to the east were being laid over two long decades, the geo-economics and geopolitics of Northeast Asia were steadily changing in fateful ways. Japan was rising; in 1895 it defeated an ailing Qing China decisively—in return receiving Taiwan, major concessions in Manchuria, and a crushing indemnity settlement of 231.5 million taels of pure silver, amounting to nearly three times Japan's annual military budget.[19] Russia, increasingly proactive in Asia with the Trans-Siberian underway, conspired with France and Germany in the Triple Intervention to force Tokyo to disgorge its Manchurian concessions. Less than a decade later, in 1904, Japan sought revenge with a surprise attack on the czar's fleet at Port Arthur, preempting the prospective geopolitical leverage of the nearly complete Trans-Siberian Railway with a decisive victory in the Russo-Japanese War of 1904–5.

Finance, construction materials, and weather were major complications. To economize, the original railway was only single-track, with extensive provision for sidings where conflicting traffic was compelled to wait, often for interminable periods. The rails were typically light, and the bridges built of timber rather than metal or stone. Heavy frosts limited construction to only four months a year.

In the face of multiple constraints, construction was naturally slow, as noted above. The railway took twenty-five years to complete (1891–1916). And even after it was completed at last, during the Great War, transport along the new Trans-Siberian Railway remained tortuous, involving extended delays on sidings along the single-tracked line. Before long, derailings and all manner of accidents likewise proliferated, due to the economical and often shoddy construction methods employed. And the Russian Revolution of 1917, coupled with Japan's rising ascendancy in Asia, delayed for half a century the projection of decisive Russian power into Asia's heart, of which Alexander III, his son Nicholas II, and influential czarist finance minister Sergius Witte had all dreamed so long before.

Despite its defects, amid the undertow for Russia of Eurasian history, the Trans-Siberian has, over the past century, become a basic pillar of Eurasian continentalism—the underlying ribbon of steel that links Europe with Pacific Russia and by extension with much of Northeast Asia as well. As we shall see, Russia's trans-Siberian infrastructure was the focal point of Kim Dae-jung's Iron Silk Road concept in Korea two decades ago and Japanese corporate calculations during the 1990s and 2000s. Using the Trans-Siberian also figured recently in Vladimir Putin's Far East overtures, and in Korean president Moon Jae-in's calculations. Xi Jinping's BRI, however, seeks to transcend and to a substantial degree replace Russian infrastructure, as does Turkey's Middle Corridor Initiative.

Putin's Pacific Russia Concept

Russian explorers reached the coast of the Pacific and claimed it for the czar in 1639. Yet since the reign of Peter the Great—less than half a century later—Russia has emphatically seen itself as a Eurocentric nation, vast positions in Asia notwithstanding.[20] A few of Peter's successors, such as Nicholas II, appreciated the Pacific, as we have seen. Yet such visionaries were few and far between.

In recent history, Mikhail Gorbachev did sense the rising importance of the Pacific, expressed in his insightful July 1986 Vladivostok speech, as well as his historic August 1988 Krasnoyarsk address two years later. Broad and dynamic relations with India, China, and finally South Korea, culminating in Gorbachev's dramatic June 1990 summit dialogue with Korean president Roh Tae-woo in San Francisco, were among the creative hallmarks of his career, building on his historic acquiescence in the transformation of Eastern Europe. Yet Gorbachev disappeared from the global scene with the collapse of the Soviet Union, unable to achieve the realignment of international relations, including transcontinental ties with Asia, that he had so fervently sought.

Vladimir Putin, who assumed power in 1999, was decidedly Eurocentric, in the venerable Russian tradition. He was, after all, a native of St. Petersburg, founded by Peter the Great as Russia's "window on the West." Putin had served for five years with the KGB in East Germany during the fateful period of communism's collapse there (1985–1990), and spoke fluent German.[21] In his first term as president, Putin not surprisingly focused predominantly on European affairs.[22] He did, however, make the first Russian state visit to North Korea, participate in the 2000 G-8 summit in Okinawa, and travel to Seoul for a historic meeting with Kim Dae-jung in February 2001.

Putin's strong Pacific orientation of recent years began with his third inauguration in May 2012 as Russian president, followed four months later by hosting the Vladivostok APEC summit. The rise of Asia itself, in a global context, was clearly one major influence driving Putin's Asian pivot. Another was domestic economic complexities within Russia, especially rising investment needs against the painful backdrop of limited domestic savings. These dislocations made Asia increasingly important as a potential source of investment capital for fueling Russian economic development east of the Urals.

Asia's rise, through rapid economic growth, has led to sharp increases in energy demand—particularly for oil and gas. Russia's rich hydrocarbon endowments have been a natural bridge for deepened relations with Asia, just as they have become, in the post–Cold War world, one of Russia's most valued power resources in the world more generally. This new geo-economic reality has not been lost on Vladimir Putin, who had placed great priority in his third term on both energy-sector development and the use of energy as a tool of Russian foreign policy.[23] Energy has also been crucial to the post–Cold War well-being of the entire Russian political economy—the energy sector, after all, makes up 70 percent of total exports and generates over half of federal budget revenues.[24]

Influenced in part, no doubt, by China's BRI, Russia has added Siberian infrastructure development as a policy priority. Putin's first vice premier Igor Shuvalov, for example, proposed in September 2017 that the Japanese and

Russian governments should cooperate to connect Hokkaido and southern Sakhalin. He also proposed a connection between Tokyo and London via the Trans-Siberian Railway.[25]

Putin's Pacific Russia concept is provoking a globally important Russian pivot toward the Pacific, with six central dimensions.

(1) *Promotion of local, Siberian, and Russian Far East development.* The Russian Far East shares long borders with China. Only 4.3 million people live on the Russian side, however, facing over 26 million people on the other side.[26] The Russian Far East's development is thus important to Moscow for both economic and national-security reasons.

(2) *Acceptance of some limited interdependence with Asian neighbors.* Putin seems to find China particularly congenial, due to parallel soft-authoritarian values and national-security priorities; South Korea is also attractive for its midrange, cost-effective technology, and construction skills; and Japan also in technological dimensions.

(3) *Centrality of energy.* Energy is Russia's comparative advantage, and also an almost universal need of Russia's Asian neighbors.

(4) *Project finance from Russia's foreign economic partners.* Russia's massive resource development projects are highly capital intensive; the Power of Siberia gas pipeline now under construction between Yakutia and the Chinese border, for example, is projected to cost at least $70 billion.[27]

(5) *Substantial value-added within Russia.* Putin's administration has been clearly emphasizing downstream energy development projects in sectors such as petrochemicals, where value-added is higher than in pure resource-extraction areas.

(6) *Political-military dimension.* The Putin administration has attempted to draw in defense-relevant technology from Asian partners in sectors such as aerospace; it has also been willing and indeed eager to export arms to Asian nations, becoming the largest military supplier to both China and India, for example.

Some elements of Putin's approach to Asia, such as use of energy and transit infrastructure as tools for national leverage, are natural approaches for any Russian leader, rooted in national resource endowments and geographic positioning between Northeast Asia and Europe. Other aspects, including a willingness to seek financing from foreign partners and an emphasis on downstream energy value added, are more Putin specific, although they could be influenced as well by Russia's isolation from the global community following the Crimean annexation in March 2014. What is clear is that there is a strong and deepening Russian priority now—particularly since the Ukrainian crisis exploded at the end of 2013—on deepening ties with Asia. The nuances of that priority vary across the country, partly due to transport logistics, with the Russian Far East prioritizing Korea and Japan while western Siberia advantages China. That Russian enthusiasm, in turn, is strengthening Eurasian continentalism as a whole, with potentially significant long-term global implications.

Korean Continentalism: Nordpolitik, the Iron Silk Road, and Beyond

Korea lies at the very rim of the rapidly growing Eurasian continent—a "shrimp among whales" sandwiched between Russia and China, with Japan looming close by as well across contested seas. This delicate yet pivotal location, a source of strategic danger mixed with economic opportunity, has decisively shaped Korea's ambivalent response across the years to its continental positioning. More than almost any other nation, Korea oscillates sharply between security and economic priorities in its approach to the continent, while according the continent—particularly Russia—continuous attention and analytical priority.

Since post–World War II South Korea by itself has been a geopolitical island, separated from the Eurasian continent by an isolated and historically intransigent North Korea. The Republic of Korea's economic relations with Eurasia are thus linked to the evolution of North-South relations within the Korean peninsula itself. Only four months after Richard Nixon's historic visit to China, a North-South Joint Statement of July 4, 1972, established principles of Korean reunification.[28] The following year Park Chung-hee offered economic reciprocity to all the communist countries.[29]

Deteriorating inter-Korean relations, however, soon converted Park's *Nordpolitik* into little more than political rhetoric. This pattern of cyclical improvement and deterioration was to repeat itself frequently across the years. It was not until the late 1980s, under Roh Tae-woo, that South Korea began to develop a truly dynamic continental diplomacy.

Roh's so-called Northern Diplomacy was intended to encircle North Korea through deepened relations with Korea's giant communist neighbors to the north and west, which would in turn build opportunities for South Korea's powerful construction, steel, and other heavy industries. Roh's initiatives established the foundations on which Korean continentalism has proceeded for the past quarter century and more. These northern initiatives creatively linked both economic and security objectives, exploiting manifest synergies between them. Roh reached out first to the Soviet Union, beginning with sports diplomacy connected to the 1988 Seoul Olympics. Sports diplomacy was followed by trade diplomacy, including the establishment of a Soviet trade office in Seoul (April 1989) and a parallel South Korean trade office in Moscow (July 1989). These incremental steps ultimately led to the dramatic Gorbachev-Roh summit meeting in San Francisco (June 1990), mutual diplomatic recognition (September 1990), and Gorbachev's visit to South Korea (April 1991) just months before the collapse of the Soviet Union.

The Roh administration well recognized that its continentalist diplomacy with the Asian communist superpowers needed to be accompanied by at least gestures of conciliation toward North Korea, the erstwhile ally of Russia and China, and by appreciating the geographical link between these countries and the South. Seoul first agreed to the simultaneous UN admission of both North and South Korea in September 1991. It also signed a Basic Agreement with Pyongyang three months later, as the Soviet Union was collapsing, that aimed at mutual reconciliation through economic exchange and cooperation.[30] The focus, however, was increasingly on broader relationships across Eurasia, transcending Korean peninsular issues alone.

The collapse of the Soviet Union was a fateful catalyst for broader Korean diplomacy and economic ties across Eurasia. In August 1992, Korea established diplomatic relations with China, a development that had been at least four years in the making.[31] China, like the USSR, sent a large delegation to the 1988 Seoul Olympics, following up with further economic exchanges, a gradual upgrading of trade missions during 1991, and a bilateral trade pact in February 1992. After the Soviet collapse at the end of 1991, Korea also rapidly established ties with the new nations of Central Asia, where the bulk of the 500,000 Koryo-saram (ethnic Korean residents of the former USSR) were living.[32] In future years both Uzbekistan, the most populous nation of Central Asia, and Kazakhstan, Central Asia's largest constituent nation and most endowed with natural resources, were to become priority targets of Korean continentalist initiatives.

Each Korean president since the collapse of the USSR, except arguably Kim Young-sam, has had a clearly articulated Eurasia policy, which has been a major pillar of their global foreign policy as a whole.[33] Kim Dae-jung's vision (1998–2003) was of an "Iron Silk Road," centering on the development of railway lines across the Eurasian continent, with a focus on Russia. This prioritized, under the so-called Sunshine Policy of developing North-South linkages, two inter-Korean railway spurs: between Dorasan Station (South

Korea) and Kaesong (North Korea) on the west side of the peninsula; as well as the Donghae Line between Jeojin (South Korea) and Onjong-ri (North Korea) on Korea's east coast. Both lines were completed under Kim's successor Roh Moo-hyun, in 2003 and 2004 respectively, opening the serious prospect of transshipments across North Korea to Russia and beyond.

In addition to the Iron Silk Road vision, Kim Dae-jung also initiated a far-sighted dialogue on the concept of a Silk Road linking Asia and Europe via information technology as well as railway infrastructure. In his address to the European Parliament in 2001, Kim repeated his vision of a "Cyber Silk Road," or high-speed optical fiber information network across Eurasia, previously articulated at the 2000 ASEM summit in Seoul.[34] Of Korea's recent leaders, Kim Dae-jung was, together with Roh Tae-woo, arguably the most proactive architect of Korea's continentalist ties across Eurasia, in part due to his optimistic view of prospects for North-South relations within Korea itself.

If Roh and Kim were the architects and visionaries, Lee Myung-bak (2008–2013) was the pragmatic builder who brought Korean continentalist dreams to earth. Lee's New Asia Initiative called for a strategic partnership with Kazakhstan, which Lee visited seven times during his five-year presidency.[35] Relations with Eurasia were also deepened early in Lee's term with the launch in April 2008 of Korea's first astronaut on board a Soyuz flight to the International Space Station; Korea also undertook its first domestic launch of a satellite, with Russian assistance, in January 2013, a month before Lee left office.[36]

President Park Geun-hye, in the tradition of her forebearers since the late 1980s, announced her own Eurasia Initiative in October 2013.[37] Like Kim Dae-jung, her administration also gave attention to railway development and to building support for it through gestures such as backing for the month-long citizen railway journey across Eurasia, undertaken with Ministry of Foreign Affairs and Korean Railway Corporation support in 2015.[38] It also accorded priority to a new dimension of Korean continentalism: promotion of relationships with Russia and Europe across the Arctic. President Moon Jae-in followed this activist line regarding Korean Arctic development following his inauguration in mid-2017 as well.

In 2018 Moon pursued the classic line of continentalist diplomacy based on North-South rapprochement that was pioneered by his progressive forebearer, Kim Dae-jung, in the Sunshine Policy of two decades previously. His "New Northern Policy," involving a primary focus on Russia, contemplates cooperation on railway, ports, electric power, natural gas, shipbuilding, jobs, and fisheries, in addition to Arctic routes. It could potentially involve promoting the "Asian Super Grid," to establish an ultra-high-voltage power transmission network, including several of Northeast Asia's major economies.[39] Moon also propounded a "New Southern Policy" for intensive cooperation with ASEAN, beginning with Indonesia. This also would have an infrastructure focus, including a light-rail transit system for Jakarta.

The geographical constraint on Seoul's continental policies has always been North Korea, which stands between the DMZ and the Eurasian continent, and converts South Korea geo-strategically into an island. In April 2018 Moon held on South Korean territory the first of multiple bilateral summits with North Korean leader Kim Jong-un, at Peace House in Panmunjom.[40] He thus became the first South Korean head of state to actually host a North Korean leader. Beyond that first summit, following another DMZ meeting and Moon's return visit to Pyongyang in September 2018, lay the prospect of a future transit role for North Korea in Korea's deepening political-economic ties with the Eurasian continent. Due to Korea's geographical positioning and its lack of hydrocarbons, its national geostrategic interests, with respect to both energy and optimal transcontinental logistics, parallel those of Russia more than those of China, despite deep economic dependence on China.

Japan's Oscillating Silk Road Diplomacy

Unlike the major powers of Eurasia discussed above, Japan is an island nation, only intermittently engaged with the continent. "Before the modern period," as Prime Minister Abe Shinzō's advisor Kanehara Nobukatsu has pointed out, "the geopolitically favorable condition of being an island nation made both diplomatic strategy and alliance policies unnecessary."[41] Japan did serve in the Nara period as one terminus for the classic Silk Road—a fleeting reality that has persisted in Japanese imagination—but there was very little actual continental interaction. Like Britain on Eurasia's western flank, Japan long enjoyed a "splendid isolation" as it industrialized, and as economic interdependence with the broader world began to require at least a rudimentary strategy, Japan has allied with and devoted predominant strategic attention to other maritime powers—particularly Britain and the United States.

Japan's intermittent modern encounter with the Eurasian continent began in the mid-1890s with the Sino-Japanese War and its aftermath. Japan defeated China in the conflict, but was forced to disgorge many of its spoils by the Triple Intervention of three Eurasian continental powers—Russia, Germany, and France. The ensuing Russo-Japanese War of revenge had a significant continental dimension. That conflict was only a prelude to four decades of continuing warfare on the continent, centrally involving Japan, that cost arguably more than thirty million Asian lives.

Although the persistent thrust of Japanese grand strategy since Meiji has been maritime, several thinkers before World War II did suggest a Eurasian continental dimension.[42] Kawanishi Seikan invoked Karl Haushofer's argument that have-not empires were justified in expanding their territories to achieve critical mass to legitimate Tokyo's Greater East Asia Co-Prosperity Sphere.[43] Asano Risaburō advocated continentalist cooperation with the USSR and Germany, so as to compete effectively in world affairs with the Anglo-American maritime bloc.[44] Some important policy makers, such as Ishiwara Kanji, vice chief of staff of the Kwantung Army based in Manchuria, saw the continent during the late 1930s as a crucial redoubt for Japan in preparing for total war with the globally dominant Anglo-American powers.[45] Until the covert Battle of Nomonhan with Soviet forces in 1939, in which Japan was defeated and suffered heavy casualties, continental expansion was the main line of Japanese military advance in the lead-up to World War II.[46]

Following the war it took a quarter century and more for Japanese continental aspirations to revive. Neither China nor either of the Koreas nor the Soviet Union or any of its successor states signed the San Francisco Peace Treaty with Japan, and Japan did not establish diplomatic relations with the People's Republic of China until 1972. It was really the collapse of the USSR and the emergence of five fledgling independent Central Asian states at the end of 1991 that began to revive active Japanese ties with continental Eurasia and serious Japanese strategizing about the New Silk Road.

The Japanese corporate sector began analyzing future prospects for relations with Eurasia before the government became actively involved. In 1992 the Mitsubishi Corporation, in cooperation with Exxon Mobil and China's CNPC, began planning for a feasibility study on a 7,000-kilometer gas pipeline connecting Turkmenistan to Japan, via Kazakhstan and China.[47] In 1993, the Japan National Oil Corporation also began conducting feasibility studies for oil and gas development.[48]

Following an intensification of Japanese bilateral official development assistance, and multilateral support to Central Asia through the Asian Development Bank, Prime Minister Hashimoto Ryūtarō announced the birth of Japanese "Silk Road Diplomacy" in a 1997 speech to the Japan Association of Corporate Executives (Keizai Dōyūkai).[49] In 2004 the Central Asia Plus Japan Dialogue among foreign ministers was initiated, which met six times during 2004–2017;[50] in 2006 Koizumi Junichirō became the first Japanese prime minister to visit Central Asia,[51] followed by Abe Shinzō in 2015.[52]

Building on Hashimoto's 1997 "Silk Road Diplomacy" speech, Japan has periodically presented updated conceptualizations of its transcontinental commitments. In November 2006 Foreign Minister Asō Tarō included Central Asia and the Caucasus explicitly in his "Arc of Freedom and Prosperity."[53] A decade later Abe proposed a "Freedom Corridor" linking democratic Eurasian nations, at a 2016 Tokyo summit with Indian Prime Minister Modi, and in May 2017 elaborated on this with the "Asia-Africa Growth Corridor" (AAGC) concept.[54] While Aso's Arc had a clear continental aspect, Abe pivoted with his AAGC approach to a clear maritime strategy. In response to China's BRI, Japan's Silk Road diplomacy has been growing more active, and more collaborative with Indian and US efforts, although Abe also proved conciliatory to BRI in his late 2018 dialogue with China, demonstrating once again the oscillating character of Japan's Silk Road diplomacy.

Turkey's Middle Corridor Initiative

Central geographical positioning, including control over important trade routes, has long been a concern of the Turks and their ancestors, although specific priorities and strategies have changed over the years. The Ottomans, for example, placed high priority during their early days on achieving exclusive control over land trade routes from Europe across Asia. The current Turkish president Recep Tayyip Erdoğan has regarded transcontinental trade routes as a geo-economic tool also.

Domestic politics have also driven Turkish continental policies over the centuries. The Ottomans, by the late nineteenth century, had developed a geopolitical obsession with control of the Islamic holy cities of Mecca and Medina.[55] Such control was essential to legitimate the Ottoman sultan's politically important claims as caliph, or Defender of the Faithful, as the empire itself was declining. Erdoğan also uses continental policies to validate his Islamic credentials with his religious base in Anatolia.

Following establishment of the secular Turkish republic in 1923, Ataturk and other top Turkish leaders continued to be highly conscious of Turkey's pivotal location between East and West, but primarily as a bulwark of Western civilization against more parochial Eurasianist concerns. During the 1930s and 1940s, however, Eurasianist sentiments did begin to revive, on both the left and the right of Turkey's political spectrum, in opposition to Ataturk's military government and Western modernist shift. *Kadro*, an influential leftist magazine published between 1932 and 1934, expressed such Eurasianist sentiments. So did *Yön*, another left-wing magazine launched in the wake of a military coup in 1960, which enjoyed particular popularity following another Kemalist military takeover in 1980.[56] The Patriotic Party (Vatan Partisi), headed by Doğu Perincek, also provided support for Eurasianism from a nationalist, populist perspective, transcending left-right distinctions.

Eurasianism became mainstream in Turkey with the advent of the Justice and Development Party's Islamist administration, inaugurated in 2002. It was inspired intellectually by the works of Ahmet Davutoğlu,[57] an influential political science professor at Marmara and Beykent universities who became Turkish foreign minister in May 2009. Davutoğlu argued that a nation's value is based on its geopolitical location and historical depth—dimensions along which, he maintained, Turkey is uniquely endowed.[58] Geopolitically, Turkey lies on the Bosporus, and it is the historical successor to the Ottoman Empire. Through control of the Middle East, Central Asia, and the Balkans, the Ottomans unified the Islamic world, as Defender of the Faith. Davutoğlu contended that Turkey should also build on its Ottoman and Islamic heritage to forge a regional economic bloc that included both the Middle East and Central Asia, creating a Muslim security mechanism based on the Organization of the Islamic Conference, thus consolidating the global community of Muslim believers (*ummah*).[59]

Davutoğlu also argued that Turkey should, in the interest of "strategic depth," also normalize relations not only with Islamic neighbors like Syria, Iran, Iraq, or Indonesia, but equally with other major Eurasian powers, including China and Russia. Although Davutoğlu was ultimately dismissed in 2014 as foreign minister, President Erdoğan has continued to pursue the grand strategy that he enunciated, very much in the Eurasianist tradition. The Turkish president has been encouraged in this approach by increasingly strained relations with the West over a variety of issues, including the introduction of a presidential system granting him sweeping powers, Western refusal to crack down on his opponents overseas, his incarceration of Western citizens, and differences regarding Syria and the Kurds.

Diplomatically Erdoğan has cultivated close personal relations with Russian president Vladimir Putin and forged intimate energy ties with Russia through the Blue Stream pipeline project under the Black Sea, and more recently the TurkStream pipeline, which will supply Russian gas to southeastern Europe via Turkey.[60] He has also developed close personal ties with Chinese president Xi Jinping, appearing as one of the featured speakers, together with Putin, at

Xi's inaugural May 2017 Belt and Road Forum. Erdogan has also joined China's BRI, held joint military exercises with the People's Liberation Army, supported large Chinese investment in Turkish e-commerce, and visited Xinjiang on a state visit to China, thus helping to assuage separatist sentiment there.[61]

Turkey's Eurasia initiatives also have concrete policy and infrastructural dimensions, animated by a desire to establish Turkey's own direct political-economic ties across the continent to China, routed through the Turkic Central Asian republics of the former Soviet Union and thus avoiding Russian transit. This approach is known as the Middle Corridor Initiative, or Turkey's Silk Road.[62] The multimodal connectivity corridor runs from Turkey to Georgia and Azerbaijan (railway), through the Caspian Sea (by ferry), to Turkmenistan and Kazakhstan, and thence into China. For the Caspian Sea passage, the ports of Aktau and Turkmenbashi are used.

Considerable progress on the Middle Corridor Initiative, which benefits greatly from the rising technical efficiency of intermodal transport, has already been made. One of its crucial components, the Baku-Tbilisi-Kars (BTK) Railway, was inaugurated in October 2017. The Lapis Lazuli Transit, Trade, and Transport Route Agreement, to enhance economic cooperation and connectivity along the Middle Corridor, was signed by Afghanistan, Turkmenistan, Azerbaijan, Georgia, and Turkey in November 2017. The Caravanserai Project, initiated by Turkey, is working to coordinate customs clearance among the nations of this Middle Corridor, and numerous related infrastructure projects are also underway.[63] Erdoğan summarizes Turkey's intentions this way: "This initiative, realized in a vast geography, means establishing a brand-new system interconnected in economic, political, social, and cultural areas."[64] In its efforts to reconnect Eurasia, Turkey's approach is analogous, albeit in a smaller way, to China's BRI—and also in tension with Russian aspirations to dominate transit routes across the Eurasian continent.

China's Belt and Road Initiative

Few Chinese traversed the classic overland Silk Road beyond China's frontiers, as we have noted. And China never—except under the Mongols—exerted powerful geopolitical sway over the transcontinental trade routes. China's BRI, however, could be the vehicle for a variety of forms of influence over Eurasia—through "distributive globalism"—that China has never exerted before.

No country is more centrally located within the populated core of Eurasia than China, encircled as it is by fourteen neighbors and the major economic centers of the region. Location gives it diverse options for transcontinental commerce, including Central Asia, the Caucasus, and Turkey, as well as Russia. Beyond these neighbors, yet at a manageable distance, is another magnetic polar attraction: the European Union. Across four millennia and more of recorded history, the Chinese have often considered their geographic centrality a misfortune, inspiring of necessity construction of the Great Wall and other defensive measures. In an era of Chinese ascendancy like the early twenty-first century, however, centrality is increasingly seen as a distinct geopolitical and geo-economic advantage for the People's Republic. And scale gives China leverage as well.

China's geo-economic centrality is a potential advantage in an era of Chinese strength, because it allows Beijing to exert asymmetric influence over its neighbors through connectivity. Linking China to neighbors via high-speed railroads, highways, communications networks, and power grids not only generates economic efficiencies. Such connectivity also creates asymmetrical power relations at the national level, together with win-win connections to local politicians through impact on economic growth and real-estate prices.

China's economic centrality in Asia—and indeed globally—became clear following the global financial crisis of 2008. Beijing's massive stimulus package in response, and the symbolically important Beijing Olympics, both took place in the same year. Yet Chinese policy making curiously failed to exploit China's centrality within Eurasia until advent of Xi Jinping's administration in 2013. Jiang Zemin had, of course, begun actively promoting Western development within China itself during the late 1990s. And Hu Jintao included major southern and western China infrastructure projects in his mammoth stimulus plan of 2008. Yet Chinese policy makers did not clearly exploit the enormous latent potential of Eurasian continentalism to leverage China's regional and global roles until Xi Jinping.

When China finally did unveil its continentalist policies, as will be seen, they proved to be the most detailed and substantive of any Eurasian nation. Backed by Chinese economic firepower and the creation of new multilateral institutions at Chinese initiative such as the Asian Infrastructure Investment Bank, those policies showed prospect of having a major impact on the economic development of the continent. They provided a general vision of new roads, railways, power grids, pipelines, and other needed infrastructure. That vision invited broad international cooperation, but under circumstances where China could serve as a strategic catalyst and a beneficiary, in both economic and geopolitical terms.

President Xi unveiled his continentalist policies, popularly known as "One Belt, One Road" (OBOR) during the fall of 2013, with two important and related speeches half a continent apart, in Kazakhstan and Indonesia.[65] As suggested in Map 2.2, the ambitious program—the details of which are only gradually materializing—will involve the comprehensive development of both land and maritime infrastructure. That will prospectively involve port facilities, superhighways, high-speed railways, and pipelines, linking China with nations to the west and south—in Southeast, South, and Central Asia, as well as the Middle East, Africa, Russia, and ultimately Europe also.

The OBOR initiative, referred to in English since 2015 as the BRI, has two clearly distinct components, as enunciated in President Xi's Kazakh and Indonesian addresses.[66] One (the "Silk Road Economic Belt," presented in Kazakhstan) is overland, nominally following the historic Silk Road itself from China's ancient capital of Chang'an (today's Xi'an in Shaanxi province) through Central Asia, Iran, Turkey, and Russia, terminating finally in Western Europe. The other route (the "Twenty-First-Century Maritime Silk Road," presented in Indonesia) is maritime and also has historical antecedents in the classical voyages of Ming-era seafarer Zheng He, venturing out from Fuzhou in Fujian province, as well as overseas Chinese emigrants to Southeast Asia and beyond of more recent times.

The Maritime Silk Road initiative proposes extensive port construction and overseas development assistance in support of nations along the South China Sea, Bay of Bengal, and Indian Ocean. Two already apparent priorities of the initiative are large-scale port development projects in Bangladesh and Sri Lanka, with the east coast of Africa likely to benefit also. The new PLA Navy facility at Djibouti, announced in early 2016, and the expanded China Ocean Shipping Company (COSCO) presence at Piraeus, the port of Athens in Greece, link the BRI initiatives closely to China's deepening relationship with Europe as well.

Reflecting recent advances in intermodal transport technology and customs clearance, there are important prospective synergies between two distinct elements of the BRI: the overland Belt and the maritime Road. Shifting from rail or road transport to maritime traffic and back again is growing cheaper, faster, and more efficient. These developments, accelerated by cooperative ventures like the China-Singapore Internet of Things project in Chongqing and the rapid evolution of e-commerce, are making transcontinental supply chains in electronics, precision machinery, and fine chemicals increasingly plausible, giving BRI powerful new transcontinental geo-economic stimulus.[67]

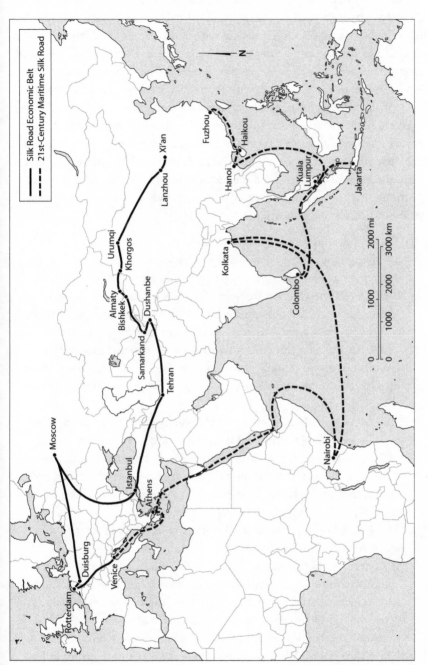

Legend:

——— Silk Road Economic Belt
- - - 21st-Century Maritime Silk Road

Cities labeled: Moscow, Rotterdam, Duisburg, Venice, Athens, Istanbul, Tehran, Samarkand, Dushanbe, Bishkek, Almaty, Khorgos, Urumqi, Lanzhou, Xi'an, Nairobi, Colombo, Kolkata, Hanoi, Haikou, Fuzhou, Kuala Lumpur, Jakarta

Scale: 0 1000 2000 mi; 0 1000 2000 3000 km

MAP 2.2   China's Belt and Road Initiative

Since Xi Jinping unveiled the BRI in general terms, other Chinese leaders and analysts have worked to clarify details of the initiative and to situate the BRI in global context.[68] One spectacular demonstration of this effort was the first Belt and Road Forum, convened in May 2017 and attended by leaders of twenty-nine member nations, excluding President Xi, and representatives of fifty-six countries in all, together with their technical advisors.[69] Top representatives of all the key global intergovernmental organizations (IGOs), including the World Bank, the International Monetary Fund, the World Trade Organization, and the United Nations, were also in attendance and were pressed to integrate their efforts with those of China, accenting the PRC's nascent ambitions to transform the BRI into a "parallel structure" of global economic governance.

Among the key supplementary contentions made by Chinese commentators about BRI are the following:

(1) The BRI is a tolerant alternative to Western-style globalization, which has allegedly intensified global inequalities and suppressed civilizational differences, while failing to generate global prosperity. Like the Silk Road of old, the Chinese argue, BRI is cross-civilizational, showing respect for individual cultures. Some Chinese analysts use the term *globalization 2.0* to describe what they consider a culturally sensitive variant.

(2) The BRI thus allegedly presents a new developmental model, focusing on international public goods and sustainable development, while operating through mutual benefit, cooperative management, and win-win cooperation.[70]

(3) The BRI explicitly respects national sovereignty. It seeks to attain its ends by providing forums and incentives for developing ties among NGOs, IGOs, and corporations, while also aiding national governments and their affiliated think tanks. It thus exploits "post-Westphalian" trends in the global political economy, while nominally respecting the nation-state-centric Westphalian order.

(4) The BRI seeks to promote its objectives by enhancing the connectivity of Asia, Europe, and Africa.[71]

(5) In contrast to the American "pivot to Asia" pursued by the Obama administration or the Trump Indo-Pacific strategy, which have both had an explicit political-military character, the BRI focuses solely on economic development. If pressed, Chinese analysts do admit the potential geo-economic and geopolitical benefits to China, given China's centrality. Yet they do not stress those domestic gains, at least internationally, as a rationale for the BRI initiative.

In Conclusion

Land routes across Eurasia were the central thoroughfare of international commerce—such as it was—more than two thousand years ago. Indeed, it is almost 2,150 years since a Chinese imperial envoy, Zhang Qian, first voyaged to the west, into the Fergana Valley of Central Asia, searching for military alliances and markets for his silk. Both the abstract concept and the physical reality of the Silk Road have thus been around for a long time, although there has been enormous variation in the popularity of the Silk Road concept itself.

Throughout their long history—from Zhang Qian up to and including China's BRI—the Silk Road and its permutations have never been based on contemporary Western paradigms. They have consistently been rooted in alternative modes of governance, involving multiple levels of authority, and ascriptive rather than universal principles of individual treatment. Transparency has typically been low, and the power of money has often been high. Prosperity, however, has often correlated with political stability.

A recurring complex of responses to the formidable political-economic challenge of governing Eurasia suggests the heuristic value of calling these responses a "syndrome." Structurally, the Silk Road has persistently found itself politically decentralized, with only loose, often personalistic sinews of transnational integration. There have been remarkably few periods, prior to the recent past, when individuals have been physically or politically capable of traversing the Silk Road as a whole. Middlemen—of all varieties—thus loom large over the classic history of the Silk Road, as do the challenges of ungoverned spaces and overlapping jurisdictions. At the individual level, traders, innkeepers, and priests, who ran the way stations and places of refuge where travelers took shelter along the way, were always important. At the broader sociopolitical level, city-states and empires have been central in furthering trade and information flows, with entities configured like the Holy Roman Empire, the Hanseatic League, and the Venetian commercial complex being far more typical as intermediaries across the ages than today's nation-states.

The Silk Road was generally most coherent when centralizing forces held sway in major parts of Eurasia. It flourished, for example, under Mongol rule in the thirteenth and fourteenth centuries, during which Marco Polo made his epic voyage. The reigns of the Han in China and the Romans in the West, as well as the Tang in China and the Sassanids in Persia, were other eras of unusual vigor for the Silk Road. It atrophied following the arrival of Vasco da Gama in India by sea, at the end of the fifteenth century, and did not begin to revive for nearly five centuries, until the explosive growth of China and the collapse of the Soviet Union began giving it a compelling logic again during the 1990s.

In modern days, several of the major Eurasian nations have begun to grasp the potential of continentalism, albeit from subtly divergent perspectives. The first was arguably czarist Russia, as Nicholas II and his advisor Sergei Witte began contemplating the Trans-Siberian Railway in the early 1890s. In more recent years, Mikhail Gorbachev, Vladimir Putin, and various Korean leaders have also actively entertained notions of Eurasian continentalism and considered how their nations might benefit, both in economic and in geopolitical terms, since the Silk Road emphatically has never included the United States. Their interests, and those of Japan and Mongolia to some degree, in energy development and an Iron Silk Road across Siberia have run parallel to one another. Turkey has also recently begun to consider the merits of continentalism, albeit from a competitive standpoint to Russia. The most systematic and operational concepts, however, have come from China. Xi Jinping's BRI, in particular, shows promise of fundamentally transforming both China and Eurasia, in China's own distinctive interest, moving the world palpably closer to a fateful global transformation that reorders the Washington-centric world prevailing since 1945.

3

Eurasia in the Making

"CUMULATIVELY, EURASIA'S POWER VASTLY overshadows America's," as Zbigniew Brzezinski noted in 1997, less than six years after the Soviet collapse. "Fortunately for America," he continued, "Eurasia is too big to be politically one."[1] Brzezinski's observation encapsulates the challenge of Eurasian integration for both the continent and the world. A simple glance at the world map brings home the potential significance of Eurasia in world affairs. It is by far the largest continent on earth, sprawling across thirteen time zones from east to west, and occupying over one-third of the world's entire land area. Beneath its earth lies over 80 percent of the proven natural gas, and almost 60 percent of the proven oil on earth. Eurasia is also home to over half the world's people. It is, in short, a potential Super Continent.

Yet despite its vast scale, and the potential geopolitical returns to its cohesion, Eurasia has rarely considered itself a coherent entity. As we just saw in Chapter 2, visionaries of multiple pedigrees have seen the potential importance of regional cohesion and even expounded prescriptions for its progression. Yet Silk Roads of the past have always been incomplete.

Politics, across Eurasia's long history, has always held the continent back. The key nations of Eurasia, in a fractious world, have lacked the energy or capacity to cohere. Larger globalist forces have often also stood in the way.

The history of Eurasia's early twentieth century is instructive. It began with incipient integration—the coming of the Trans-Siberian Railway, widespread transnational migration, and rising Western investment, albeit often in a colonial context. The continent was, however, abruptly divided, beginning in its second decade—by war, revolution, nationalism, partition, and the pervasive emergence of autarkic states that cared little for systematic interchange with their neighbors. By 1976—following Stalin's "socialism in one country," World War II, India's partition, the Chinese Revolution, the Cold War, and the Chinese Cultural Revolution—the nations of Eurasia were estranged, mutually suspicious, autarkic, and economically stagnant, save on their Western European and Asia-Pacific rims.

The empirical base for Brzezinski's pessimism regarding Eurasia's capacity for political cohesion was thus quite compelling during the mid-1970s, as he entered the White House to become Jimmy Carter's national security adviser. The world, however, began to change profoundly in succeeding years, in ways that presaged the rebirth of a more cohesive Eurasia. First the economic forces were unleashed, in the form of China's modernizations and the continent's rising energy demand, that began stimulating interdependence. Then the political reorientations and financial crises of the post–Cold War world, combined with the heavy infrastructure spending of the past decade, began driving new forms of cohesion, facilitated by a Logistics Revolution. As we shall see in the following pages, a new Eurasian transcontinental world is being born—through unanticipated crisis even more than rational intent—that is arguably more integrated than at any time in the past five or six centuries, finessing the political divisions of the recent past. Through a series of political-economic earthquakes, in short, a Super Continent that radically revises the political-economic patterns of the recent past is being reborn.

China's Four Modernizations and Continental Transformation

"When China wakes," Napoleon astutely predicted, "it will shake the world." Modern China, the most populous nation on earth, has encountered many fateful transformations across its recent history, including the Republican Revolution of 1911 and the Communist Revolution of 1949. Yet the most fateful development for global political-economic affairs, and indeed ultimately for the deepening of China's ties westward and southward to both Europe and the Strait of Malacca, was the economic liberalization known as the *Four Modernizations* (agriculture, industry, national defense, and science and technology). That fateful declaration was enunciated by Deng Xiaoping at the Third Plenum of the Eleventh Central Committee of the Chinese Communist Party in December 1978.[2]

The importance of the Four Modernizations, for China and the world, as well as the forces that inhibited China's transformation until it finally took place, becomes much clearer when we consider the situation ex ante. China, from May 1966 until the death of Mao Zedong in September 1976, had been in the throes of the Cultural Revolution. Economic growth and any form of international relationship had been subordinated to ideological purity and xenophobic revolutionary fervor. Even though the neighboring Soviet Union had emerged from the autarkic days of "socialism in one country" under Joseph Stalin, sharp geopolitical differences and lack of market incentives rendered Moscow's economic relations with China—and those of its satellites further west—static and stagnant.

Other Chinese leaders—notably the visionary, veteran premier Zhou Enlai—had thought of rationalizing the Chinese economy and opening it to the world long before Deng Xiaoping. Zhou himself actually introduced the term *Four Modernizations* two years before the Cultural Revolution, in December 1964.[3] Zhou also, in one of his last public acts, repeated the proposal in January 1975 at the Fourth National Peoples' Congress. Yet domestic opposition, notably from Mao's wife Jiang Qing and her Gang of Four compatriots, made realization impossible.[4] Only after Mao's death did a more favorable environment emerge.

By August 1977, ten months after Mao's passing, Deng had been reinstated and soon thereafter delivered a speech to the Eleventh Party Congress stressing the Four Modernizations, which he specified as meaning "electricity in the rural areas, industrial automation, a new economic outlook, and greatly enhanced defense strength."[5] In February 1978, Chairman Hua Guofeng, who had been advocating individual liberalization steps for nearly a year, approved a ten-year plan for the period 1976–1985 including many of the same notions, albeit with a more pronounced emphasis on heavy industry (steel, coal, electricity, and transportation infrastructure).[6] Deng, who was more pragmatic, market oriented, and politically sensitive, then made the definitive reformist pronouncements that reshaped modern Chinese history, in December 1978.[7]

The Impact of Critical Juncture

The declaration of the Four Modernizations might be considered a critical juncture for three basic reasons. First, it involved a pronounced *crisis* in the Chinese political economy following the turbulence of the Cultural Revolution, centering on agriculture and heavy industry. In agriculture, the per-capita output of grains was no higher in 1977 than it had been two decades earlier, despite rising demand.[8] Steel production in 1976 was less than 21 million tons—down from 25.5 million in 1973, and a net gain of only 10 percent over 1960 levels.[9] Rather than being a source of profits, state enterprises were absorbing large subsidies that required large transfers from agriculture. Oil fields like those of Daqing in the northeast, whose workers once served as a model for the Cultural Revolution, were stagnating, while electric power infrastructure was steadily deteriorating. Meanwhile, on the military front, a Soviet challenge was rising, giving Maoist China's economic vulnerability major national security implications. The Soviet Union had just signed a friendship treaty with Afghanistan's new communist government, and seemed to Chinese leaders bent on further expansion, generating in Beijing a deep sense of international threat to China.[10]

Second, there was major *political stimulus for change* in the China of the late 1970s. The country had undergone tremendous socioeconomic dislocation during the Cultural Revolution, with many, especially among more established groups, desperately hoping for a return to normalcy. Following the death of Chairman Mao, reforms that might redress the ravages of the Cultural Revolution at last became a possibility.

Third, there was intense *time pressure* during this period in implementing reforms. Part of the perceived urgency flowed from fear of Soviet machinations. Within China itself, Maoist remnants were still strong, and the national political situation remained fluid. Cosmopolitan economic and cultural interests were as yet not well represented in China. It seemed quite possible that China could revert to the perverse, parochial practices of Cultural Revolution days. In this situation, Deng Xiaoping and his allies felt it crucial to consolidate a forward-looking set of economic policies.

The overall design of the reforms was presented almost as soon as Deng took power, with initial implementation following soon thereafter. The early emphasis, and an important precondition for later steps, was the agricultural reforms. Market reforms in the countryside increased productivity there, and thus freed up much of China's massive rural labor force to work in the secondary and tertiary sectors of the economy.

Reforming heavy industry was Deng's next priority, with building the $2 billion Baoshan steel mill near Shanghai as a first major step.[11] China also put strong priority, however, on technical education. It increased its scientific and technical workforce from 60,000 when the modernization began to 400,000 less than five years later.[12]

With political conditions increasingly stable, Deng's approach steadily broadened beyond an initial emphasis on national self-reliance to include substantial foreign borrowings. In December 1978, for example, China arranged a $1.2 billion sovereign loan from a consortium of British banks; by mid-April the People's Republic (PRC) had received or arranged for $10 billion in foreign loans.[13] Five Special Economic Zones, or SEZs, (Shenzhen, Zhuhai, and Shantou in Guangdong, plus Xiamen in Fujian and the entire island of Hainan) were established, each of which had power to negotiate with foreign firms on the Yugoslav-Romanian model, thus blending socialist and capitalist systems.[14]

Although never officially designated as an SEZ, Tianjin was picked as a "coastal development area" and opened in the mid-1980s. Over the ensuing decade of the 1990s, the Chinese government switched definitively from SEZs to a new model of economic reform, opening "new areas" for which Pudong, across the Huangpu River from the traditional core of the Shanghai Municipality, received the first national-level new area designation. Tianjin's Binhai district became China's second new area in 2009.

One of Deng's important early initiatives, which magnified both the domestic and international impact of the Four Modernizations, was to reach out to overseas Chinese, particularly in Southeast Asia. In the late 1970s there were, after all, some 8.2 million descendants of Guangdong natives and an additional 5 million descendants of Fujian natives living outside mainland China, excluding Taiwan.[15] Many of them became favored partners in the new SEZs, several of which were established in their ancestral home areas along the coasts of Fujian and Guangdong provinces, as noted above. These zones became socioeconomic experiments in "marketization" and springboards for light manufacturing and international commerce with developing nations, thus paving the way for bolder future ventures, as capitalist Hong Kong also did for Guangdong.[16]

China's Four Modernizations, as suggested above, transformed China itself in many fundamental ways. Due especially to the explosive growth they unleashed at the center of Eurasia, the Modernizations set in motion powerful catalysts for change in the political economy of the continent as a whole. Those changes culminated in the increasingly integrated and interactive transcontinental chessboard that we see today.

The birth of a Eurasian Super Continent, however, involves much more than the rise of China alone. In this chapter, we chronicle several other critical junctures, synergistic with China's rise but separate from it, that are collectively triggering a second Crossover Point of fundamental importance for international affairs today. That transition is the rise of a Eurasia with increasing coherence and potential on the world stage. The ascent of China is a major part of that transition, to be sure. Yet as we shall see, the emergence of a more integrated Eurasian chessboard both predates and transcends China's Belt and Road Initiative, far-sighted and substantively important as it is. To grasp the true potential for Eurasian reconnection, those deeper origins, transcending China, need to be specified concretely.

These historic continental turning points that together make up Eurasia's Crossover Point include the 1991 collapse of the Soviet Union, which opened the post-Soviet space; the 2008 Lehman Shock, coupled with China's massive stimulus in response, which deepened the gap between Western and Eurasian contributions to global aggregate demand growth; and the 2014 Ukrainian crisis, which encouraged deeper Chinese ties with both Russia and Eastern Europe. Collectively, these regional critical junctures have transformed Eurasia into an increasingly interactive chessboard, amplifying the importance of intra-Eurasian developments for the broader world. Eurasia's transformation, to repeat, involves much more than simply the rise of China. It also prefaces the emergence of a much larger, increasingly interactive regional chessboard, whose deepening integration critically alters yet also enhances China's significance for the broader world.

The Collapse of the Soviet Union

The Silk Road over the centuries has oscillated between openings and closings—the erection of mercantilist political barriers to commercial intercourse and their later demolition. The twentieth century was no exception, and the reconnections of the past three decades, after six previous decades of autarky, are of truly continental significance. The collapse of the Soviet Union, a sudden critical juncture, opened the Soviet successor states as a transit corridor. That has led to a dynamic political-economic interdependence between China and Central Europe, including both Germany and the Visegrad 4, as we shall see later in this volume, with dual synergistic and competitive aspects.

Under the czars before 1917, travelers moved quite freely across the great steppes and deserts in the heart of Eurasia—even across Russian frontiers. During Stalinist days, however, most frontiers of the Soviet Union, including those in Central Asia, were hermetically sealed. Stalin built "socialism in one country" with little regard for broader continental developments.

The collapse of the Soviet Union in late 1991, transforming Central Asia from an isolated backwater within the communist bloc into a potentially dynamic, volatile zone of transnational economic intercourse and global geopolitical competition, radically changed the situation. That momentous development flowed from forces that had been culminating for a decade and more, yet the dramatic climax was completely unexpected until only a few months prior to its occurrence. The Soviet collapse demolished long-standing barriers to economic intercourse and political communication, many dating from Stalinist days, thus allowing Eurasia's remarkable growth and energy-demand equation of recent years to play itself out on a continental scale.

This abrupt collapse of the Soviet Union was actually in the making for a decade or more, with its roots in Soviet economic stagnation, failed attempts at reform, and the USSR's own overextension.[17] The costly war in Afghanistan (1979–1989) was a major factor, both in bleeding the Soviet Union physically[18] and in triggering Western sanctions. Those sanctions deprived the Soviets of valuable foreign exchange, by preventing construction of major energy pipelines from the USSR to the European Union (EU) and Japan.

Mikhail Gorbachev, taking power in 1985, understood the structural problems of the Soviet Union, responding with his *glasnost* (openness) and *perestroika* (restructuring) campaigns. Political turbulence intensified, however, following the Afghan withdrawal in early 1989, even though the withdrawal extinguished what had been a significant cause of previous dissatisfaction. In November 1989 the Berlin Wall went down, without a decisive Soviet response, deepening a sense—both in the Soviet satellites and within the USSR itself—that fundamental change was impending.

The Impact and Implications

While Gorbachev was vacationing in the Crimea, on August 19, 1991, his vice president, prime minister, defense minister, KGB chief, and other senior officials suddenly attempted a coup. Boris Yeltsin rapidly condemned the attempt and rallied popular support for himself. He was not arrested by the organizers, however, and after three days the coup collapsed. Gorbachev resumed his prior formal positions, but with his political position fatally compromised. Pressed by an ambitious Yeltsin, he rapidly lost legitimacy, generating both the crisis so often requisite for major policy change and the time pressure that so often shapes resultant outcomes.

Less than a month after the coup attempt, the Soviet state finally recognized the independence of the Baltic states, declared in Lithuania over twenty months before. Three months further on (December 1), Ukrainian independence was confirmed in a provincial referendum, attracting 90 percent support.[19] On December 21, the Alma-Ata Protocol was signed by all of the

Soviet republics except Georgia and the three Baltic republics, confirming the dissolution of the union, followed by Gorbachev's personal resignation on December 25. As 1991 expired, all administrative organs of the USSR ceased functioning, opening a new post-Soviet era in Eurasian history.

Merge Impact and Implications

As the Soviet Union collapsed, many of the classic autarkic elements of Stalinist practice also disappeared, despite their long pedigree from the days of building "socialism in one country." Acting as his own prime minister, on January 2, 1992, Yeltsin ordered a sweeping liberalization of foreign trade, prices, and currency. Following on these declarations, Yeltsin's market-oriented lieutenants, headed by Yegor Gaidar, also moved to encourage foreign investment. Gaidar's initiatives focused on market-oriented measures like price liberalization and financial stabilization, designed to promote a more favorable environment for capital inflows and deepened interdependence with the industrialized West.[20] In other parts of the "near abroad," officials likewise pursued policies supportive of foreign investment and expanded international trade.

New Linkages and Deepened Ties

In the more advanced western regions of the former USSR, the major short-term impact of the USSR's collapse and the sudden new market orientation was to deepen interdependence between Russia and noncommunist Europe, especially Germany. In the first two decades following the fall of the Berlin Wall, six former members of the Warsaw Pact and three former republics of the USSR itself joined the EU. This post–Cold War expansion of the EU—the direct consequence of Soviet collapse—had major implications for the nature of Europe itself as well as for Europe's ties to the broader world. It shifted the geographical center of the EU close to a thousand miles east— from France deep into Germany. It reoriented the supply chains of Europe inward, away from the Atlantic. And it gave birth to a dynamic new manufacturing zone, spanning Germany and the four Visegrad nations, that now produces 20 percent of the world's autos and auto parts.[21]

The emergence of this New Europe in the East provoked a substantial acceleration of the continent's economic growth. Indeed, as of 2017, nine of the ten fastest growing countries in the EU were post-2004 accession countries—six of them former members of the Warsaw Pact.[22] The other, Ireland, was a relatively small, internationally exposed nation where growth was accelerated by tax arbitrage.

Merge Linkages and Ties

The New Europe—former members of the Warsaw Pact, including East Germany, together with the three Baltic republics of the former Soviet Union—had strong, long-standing ties with Communist Asia (China, Vietnam, North Korea, and Mongolia) dating from the Cold War. The Soviet Union had been central in creating and monitoring these transcontinental ties, which included extensive trade, educational exchange, guest workers, and foreign assistance. For instance, tens of thousands of Vietnamese arrived in Poland, Czechoslovakia, Hungary, and East Germany during the Soviet years as "guest workers."[23] The European and Asian communists, however, established deep ties of their own, apart from the Soviet connection, made stronger by their desire to balance the Soviets and to enhance their own autonomy within the socialist bloc. All this helped stimulate Eurasian continentalism following the Soviet collapse, although at times tempered by local political backlash.[24]

In Central Asia and the Russian Far East, however, market forces naturally exerted an even stronger pull toward Asia than elsewhere in the former USSR or Eastern Europe, due to geographic proximity, especially as Asian growth accelerated over the 1990s and beyond. China, India, Iran, Turkey, Japan, and Korea all deepened ties with the component parts of the former Soviet Union substantially as a result of the Soviet collapse, supporting a revival of classic Silk Road relationships, and pulling Russia also to the east.

The Role of Energy

This time the new Eurasian continentalist interdependence was emphatically driven at first by energy demand. Importantly, the collapse of the Soviet Union led to unprecedented new ties between the PRC and Central Asia, with energy as a key driver. This new reality began emerging with the opening of multiple transcontinental pipelines from Turkmenistan to China's east coast during 2009–2014. Today those pipelines supply around half of Shanghai's local gas supplies.[25] There are now three pipelines conveying natural gas between Central Asia and urban China, with others also in planning.[26]

Just as the USSR was collapsing during 1990–1992, trade between Kazakhstan and China expanded tenfold.[27] Central Asian trade with both China and Turkey also intensified for years following the collapse of the Soviet Union, as indicated in Table 3.1, sharply outpacing the still substantial trade with Russia and gradually reorienting the region in new directions. In less than two decades, by 2010, the volume of Chinese trade with both Kazakhstan and

TABLE 3.1

Expanding Central Asian trade with Russia, China, and Turkey

Trade with Russia (million USD)					
	1995	2000	2005	2010	2015	2015/1995
Azerbaijan	187.2	347.6	1,002.6	1,918.6	1,854.7	9.9
Kazakhstan	4,265.5	4,190.6	9,518.4	7,761.0	15,076.8	3.5
Turkmenistan	162.6	1,283.8	310.0	902.0	1,037.8	6.4

Trade with China (million USD)					
	1995	2000	2005	2010	2015	2015/1995
Azerbaijan	4.6	28.0	273.0	926.5	565.1	123.7
Kazakhstan	331.7	824.7	3,675.8	14,084.1	10,567.9	31.9
Turkmenistan	14.8	24.0	113.8	1,523.8	8,247.1	557.0

Trade with Turkey (million USD)					
	1995	2000	2005	2010	2015	2015/1995
Azerbaijan	167.0	233.5	589.0	942.3	1,475.7	8.8
Kazakhstan	193.9	206.3	556.9	1,855.5	2,017.5	10.4
Turkmenistan	310.0	439.3	342.9	1,572.7	2,495.1	8.0

SOURCE: International Monetary Fund, *Direction of Trade Statistics*, accessed October 22, 2018.
NOTE: Data as reported by Azerbaijan, Kazakhstan, and Turkmenistan.

Turkmenistan was significantly greater than the trade of those two former So-viet republics with Russia itself, as the Central Asian states exchanged rapidly growing amounts of oil and gas for Chinese manufactures. By 2015, this gap had expanded still further in the case of Turkmenistan. Meanwhile, Turkish trade with Kazakhstan, Turkmenistan, and Azerbaijan also expanded steadily, consistently exceeding Russian trade with Turkmenistan and surpassing Rus-sian trade with Azerbaijan in 2016.[28]

The Soviet collapse at the end of 1991 triggered a wave of opportunis-tic responses across Eurasia. Within months, an annual Urumqi Trade Fair, with heavy Central Asian participation, was initiated in the PRC. In Octo-ber 1993, President Nazarbayev of Kazakhstan visited Beijing, and only six months later, in April 1994, Premier Li Peng reciprocated with a return visit to Almaty, Kazakhstan's capital. Their concrete discussions in Almaty regard-ing cross-border infrastructure came on the heels of a boundary agreement between the two countries.[29]

Ultimately this high-level Eurasian diplomacy led to transcontinental rail-roads, pipelines, and an SEZ established in Xinjiang's Ili Valley near the Ka-zakh frontier to encourage cross-border exchange.[30] By 2010 pipelines trans-ported 200,000 barrels of Kazakh oil exports daily, in addition to 10 billion cubic meters annually of Turkmen gas, from deep in Central Asia 7,000 kilometers across China to Shanghai.[31] In the same year China likewise began sharply expanding both cargo and passenger facilities at Urumqi International Airport as well as the nearby SEZ, in an effort to expand airborne trade with Russia and the neighboring Islamic world, collaborating with both Turkish and Iranian interests.[32]

Following the Soviet collapse, ties between Central Asia and large Islamic neighbors to the south and southwest—especially Turkey and Iran—rapidly expanded. Turkey, with ethnic bonds to the 100 million Central Asians, took a special interest, being the first country to recognize the newly independent Central Asian states. Prime minister Süleyman Demirel visited all the Central Asian states soon after the Soviet collapse, inaugurating a series of joint annual summits that established important new political and business networks transcending Cold War boundaries. President Erdoğan, Turkey's principal leader since 2003, has also used ethnic ties as a vehicle for developing closer relationships with Central Asia.[33] In 1996 Turkey, resisting pressure from the United States, concluded a $23 billion, twenty-three-year gas deal with Iran, which also opened a major gas pipeline northward to Turkmenistan in the same year.[34] In 2010 a second gas pipeline was opened between Turkmenistan and Iran.[35]

Japan and South Korea also broadened and deepened their ties with the former Soviet Union—both Russia proper and the neighboring states known as the near abroad—following the USSR's sudden collapse. Japan, in particular, invested heavily in Sakhalin Island's energy reserves, taking major positions in the Sakhalin I and Sakhalin II natural gas deals of the early 1990s. Both Japan and Korea also invested in Central Asia, with the Korean commercial position strengthened by strong ethnic ties with both Kazakhstan and Uzbekistan, ironically due to Stalin's deportation of Koryo-saram, literally "Korean people," who originally lived along the Pacific coast, to Central Asia during the 1930s. Japan and Korea both committed themselves to Central Asian uranium, even though vast continental distances from their homelands inhibited the kind of explosive pipeline-based hydrocarbon trade that emerged between Central Asia and China following the 2008 global financial crisis.

Western firms are substantial investors in Central Asia and to a lesser degree in the Russian Far East, especially through large energy projects such as Tengiz, Kashagan, and Sakhalin II.[36] Asia itself, however, is the ultimate market for former Soviet energy, as well as the low-cost supplier of most manufactures required in the Asian regions of the former Soviet Union. With East Asia growing, needing more energy, and extending economically westward across Eurasia, that intracontinental relationship might naturally be expected to deepen on market grounds. The collapse of the Soviet Union, Central Asian openness to foreign investment, and subsequent Yeltsin laissez-faire policies within Russia itself in the early post-Soviet days all deepened the realization of underlying Eurasian complementarities, bringing the continent together in unprecedented new ways, transcending Soviet-era ties, and reviving the classic Silk Road.

The Indian Outlier

India, like China and the former Soviet Union, underwent sharp, sweeping, and historic changes in the early post–Cold War period that helped prefigure the nascent Super Continent that is emerging today.[37] The sharp foreign-exchange crisis of 1990–1991, provoked by the repatriation of Indian workers from the Persian Gulf following Saddam Hussein's invasion of Kuwait, led to sweeping Indian domestic reforms, orchestrated by Finance Minister Manmohan Singh, that led ultimately to higher economic growth and inbound foreign investment. In contrast to the Chinese and Russian cases, however, India's reforms have not as yet played a central role in the reconnection of Eurasia.

Democracy, ironically, also complicates India's reconnection with Eurasia—even with its South Asian neighbors. Ambivalence in Tamil Nadu state, for example, reportedly inhibited Indian intervention during the critical later stages of Sri Lanka's civil war, leaving the way open for enhanced Chinese influence. Political opposition from the governor of West Bengal also delayed border negotiations with Bangladesh for several years.[38]

For both domestic and geographic reasons, amplified by the economic power of rivals like China, India has thus so far been confined to a marginal role in the reconnecting of Eurasia. Regional organizations like the Shanghai Cooperation Organization or the Belt and Road Initiative do not allow much additional scope, as they are dominated by China. That does not mean, however, that India is lacking in dynamic alternative options on the global stage—especially given its strong service and technology sectors. New Delhi's fateful options are a subject to which we shall return. Indeed, it is precisely India's constraints within an otherwise reconnecting Eurasia that make it important for both Indians and globalists worldwide to reach out to one another.

Despite its proximity to Central Asia and its established relations with the region from Cold War days, India was the one major Asian nation that failed to benefit much from the breakup of the Soviet Union. Its commercial ties with Central Asian states like Kazakhstan grew significantly, but only modestly compared to the explosive growth that the Chinese experienced. Indian trade with Uzbekistan, the most populous of the Central Asian nations, grew from $16 million to $321 million between 1995 and 2017. Meanwhile, Chinese trade grew twice as fast, on a larger base—from $116 million to $4.3 billion.[39]

The seismic shifts that reconfigured continental Eurasia in the 1990s and 2000s ironically hurt rather than helped India. New Delhi had maintained an intense and profitable relationship with the Soviets since the mid-1960s, but that was disrupted rather than furthered by the collapse of the USSR, in sharp contrast to the Chinese case. Similarly, the rise of the ayatollahs in Iran complicated rather than aided Indian ties with a traditional ally. India is geographically close to Central Asia, but highly volatile Islamic nations, including Pakistan and Afghanistan, stand in between. Both the Afghan conflict, continuing since 2001, and China's deepening ties with Pakistan have also made Indian overtures to the nations further west frustratingly difficult.

Consequential Indian relationships with energy-rich Central Asia make economic sense, and could well manifest themselves in coming years, if political relationships in the turbulent region stabilize,[40] and if the TAPI pipeline, already under construction, is finally completed. Indian energy ties with the Russian Far East have also grown stronger. India's Oil and Natural Gas Corporation (ONGC) has participated in the Sakhalin I project; in 2008 it also acquired British interests in Russia's rich west Siberian oil fields.[41]

India's broader future reconnection with Eurasia depends, however, on the degree to which Iran itself is integrated into continental affairs. And that depends in part on forces beyond Eurasia. The 2015 Iran nuclear agreement did have a positive impact on the relationship between India and Central Asia, but its future is in doubt. Expansion of the heretofore poorly developed Chabahar port just inside Iran's eastern frontier and only 550 nautical miles from Indian prime minister Narendra Modi's home Gujarat province in western India, which began after the agreement, opened an important new route from India across Iran to Central Asia and Europe, circumventing Pakistan. Normalized international ties with Iran, a traditional friend of India, could also help meet India's rapidly increasing energy needs, if ethnic tensions in Balochistan or linkages to the Saudi-Iranian rivalries do not complicate that equation.[42]

The Lehman Shock: Financial Crisis in the West, the Rise of China, and the Eurasian Crossover Point

The emergence of a Grand Chessboard across Eurasia, characterized by deepening yet volatile interdependence, was laid by the two critical junctures outlined above—China's Four Modernizations and the collapse of the Soviet

Union. Although these junctures set the basic trajectory, through the historic transformations in continental political-economic structure that they provoked, the fateful long-term global implications remained muted for more than a decade. China, which emerged only minimally affected by the Asian financial crisis of the 1990s due to its extensive capital controls, continued to rise gradually in economic terms following the crisis, powered by heavy and rising exports to the United States.

The pace of China's ascent, however, was slower than during the 1980s and early 1990s. Meanwhile, the US and Europe also grew steadily, powered first by the dot-com boom of the late 1990s, and later by the steady housing construction of the early 2000s, as well as the expansion of government spending entailed by the Afghanistan and Iraq conflicts. Chinese growth was much more dependent on the US market than it had been before the early 1990s, although declining slowly from its Asian financial crisis peak.

Quietly, however, the seeds of major change in the economic trajectories of the United States and China, major protagonists of the Crossover Points, were being laid. America's government debt, fueled by post-9/11 spending on two ongoing conflicts, was rising.[43] Increased welfare spending, inspired demographically by the retirement of the Baby Boomer generation, was compounding the fiscal challenge.

The US-Centric Financial Crisis

George W. Bush had been elected in the contentious presidential election of 2000, with arguably the narrowest and most disputed victory in American history. He and his political lieutenants realized that the path to reelection in 2004 could be narrow and lay through appealing materially to the middle class, especially in swing states such as geriatric Florida, which had been decisive in 2000. High on the Bush policy agenda were thus the Medicare prescription drug benefit, enacted in 2003, and favorable housing-finance policies, which appealed especially to the lower middle class.[44] The latter had been a mainstay of sustained conservative rule in Britain under Margaret Thatcher and attracted the Bush administration as well.[45]

The financial world of this period was also in transition, fueled by the repeal in 1999 of the Glass-Steagall separation of commercial and investment banking functions. This transformation, coupled with new, computer-oriented financial technology of the day, facilitated the emergence of powerful credit-default swaps that sharply boosted both profits for financial firms and bonuses for their savvy and technically sophisticated employees. The derivatives were arcane but blessed by AAA-rated insurance companies such as AIG, turning them into marketable commodities that foreign as well as American firms traded with confidence, to their later chagrin.[46]

The confluence of political incentives to make housing affordable with the potential of the new financial technology led to loosened restrictions on new forms of housing finance. It also led to the marketing of new, innovative financial products, such as credit default swaps. The newly deregulated environment led initially to a housing boom, just as America entered the 2004 electoral season. George W. Bush, who had struggled so desperately in 2000, carried Florida by a solid 52–47 margin over John Kerry and was triumphantly reelected.[47]

As inflation began rising during the 2005–2006 electoral aftermath, the US Federal Reserve Board began raising interest rates, despite stagnation in middle-class incomes, thus raising pressures on overextended borrowers and setting the stage for a deeper financial crisis. On July 31, 2007, the Bear Stearns securities firm liquidated two hedge funds and filed for bankruptcy protection. Only a week later, on August 6, American Home Mortgage Investment also filed for bankruptcy.

Early in 2008, another election year, it looked at first as though the crisis was subsiding. On January 11 Bank of America announced that it would buy Countrywide Financial for $4 billion. On March 16 the Federal Reserve guaranteed $30 billion of Bear Stearns's assets in preparation for its sale to JP Morgan Chase. And on August 15 the Soros Fund, previously known for its farsighted appreciation of global economic trends, increased its stake in the troubled Lehman Brothers investment banking firm from 10,000 to 9.47 million shares.

Within weeks the financial crisis, quietly deepening amid the massive risks posed by new derivatives such as credit default swaps, boiled dramatically into the open. On September 7, 2008, Fannie Mae and Freddie Mac, two of the most important dealers in mortgage-backed securities, were placed in conservatorship by the federal government. Just three days later, on September 10, Lehman Brothers posted a $3.93 billion third-quarter loss, after write-downs on toxic mortgages of $5.6 billion, and put itself up for sale the next day. Its shares dropped precipitously, by 42 percent, to $4.22, in a single day.[48]

Two Asian firms—the Korean Development Bank and an unnamed Chinese bank—together with London's Barclays courted Lehman Brothers as potential suitors. They terminated discussions, however, on sensing the magnitude of its troubles, including exposure to the US housing crisis.[49] Lehman looked to Bank of America as a potential buyer, but on September 15 BOA agreed to purchase Merrill Lynch instead, for $50 billion. Lehman Brothers, without a white knight, collapsed into bankruptcy with $613 billion in debts, precipitating the largest US corporate bankruptcy ever. One day later, on September 16, the Federal Reserve announced an $85 billion rescue package to save AIG from bankruptcy, out of fear that its bankruptcy, following on from Lehman, would result in all-out Wall Street chaos. Yet aftershocks continued: on September 25, Washington Mutual Bank, also a major home-mortgage lender, was officially closed by federal regulators, resulting in the greatest commercial banking failure in history.

In the face of deep commercial unease, all eyes turned to Congress to authorize large-scale federal backstopping. On September 29, however, Congress declined to approve the $700 billion Troubled Asset Relief Program (TARP). The Dow Jones industrial average promptly tanked by 778 points, the largest single-day drop in twenty years. Only when Congress passed a revised TARP as the Emergency Economic Stabilization Act on October 3 did the financial earthquake begin to subside. Based on the new legislation, financial authorities bailed out Citigroup on November 23. General Motors and Chrysler filed for bankruptcy in the summer of 2009, subsequently receiving TARP loans to aid their reconstruction.[50] Beginning in the spring of 2009, the US stock market gradually began to recover, and by early October 2018 the S&P 500 had risen over 400 percent from early March 2009 levels.[51]

Amid the financial uncertainty, which extended across the Atlantic and the Pacific to all of the liberalized players in the interdependent global economy, economic growth dropped precipitously into negative territory across the G-7 nations as well as much of the developing world. Only a few of the closed economies on the continent of Eurasia, preeminently China, were spared. Indeed, China, benefitting from its financial isolation as well as strong public finances at the national level, was able to launch a massive government stimulus program that proved to be a major engine of global recovery.

China's Powerful 2008 Stimulus and Its Global Impact

The two-year, 4 trillion yuan ($586 billion) stimulus package was the largest in Chinese history.[52] It involved coordinated central and local government spending in ten strategic sectors, focusing on transportation, housing, and infrastructure. The package fortuitously emerged just before the December 2008 inaugural G-20 summit and was previewed by Hu Jintao and George W. Bush only a day before its formal announcement. The package played a key role in allowing China to become a key stabilizer for the world economy in a period of extraordinary post–Lehman Shock turbulence. China, after all, maintained a GDP growth rate of nearly 10 percent during 2008–2009, as the world's third largest economy, while the rest of the globe was desperately struggling.

China's massive stimulus of 2008–2009 centered on huge road and railway infrastructure projects linking far-flung areas of China domestically while also strengthening transport links to the broader Eurasian continent, powerfully leveraging China's rise as a major power within both Eurasia and global affairs more generally. China's double-digit GDP expansion continued and then accelerated as G-7 growth fell below zero, sharply increasing China's share of global production. China also gained acclaim from influential Western financiers, including Tim Geithner, Hank Paulson, and Roger Altman, for its role in stabilizing the world economy as a whole.[53] China's day as a major global player, and as the principal driver of Eurasian continentalism, had arrived, with its GDP in purchasing-power parity terms passing the US in 2013.

The Ukraine Crisis and the Making of Eurasia

Kiev is a long way from Beijing, Tokyo, Seoul, and New Delhi. One might legitimately wonder what Ukrainian developments have to do with Eurasian integration, especially as the Ukraine has shrunk economically under the impact of domestic political uncertainties and the protracted conflict with Russia. The indirect effects of the Ukraine crisis have been quite important, however, and demonstrate concretely the steady reconnection of Eurasia across the past decade.

The Ukrainian crisis, including Russia's abrupt March 2014 annexation of Crimea—the first unilateral revision of European boundaries since World War II—virtually eliminated the prospect of a revived, cohesive Soviet successor state, depriving Moscow definitively of industrial and agricultural resources as well as human capital that would be needed. The crisis also created new security challenges for Russia, which has a 1,400-mile border with Ukraine; parts of Ukraine are less than 300 miles from Moscow. The crisis, finally, complicated Russian ties with important interlocutors in the West, including Germany, forcing Russia increasingly into the arms of China and transforming Russia increasingly from a powerful independent actor into a transit state between China and Central Europe.

The Ukraine was thus, improbably, a catalyst for reconnecting Russia and Northeast Asia, and stimulating emergence of a Super Continent. Russia and

Asian powers such as China and Japan, not to mention the Mongols, have eyed each other suspiciously for centuries. And it is only half a century since the Sino-Soviet border clashes on the Ussuri brought Moscow and Beijing to the brink of war. Even following the collapse of the Soviet Union, those atavistic mutual suspicions did not abate. Indeed, it was just in 2008 that outstanding border differences between the two Eurasian giants were finally resolved. And despite grand talk of massive bilateral cooperation, actual progress on economic matters was for many years exceedingly slow.

The Ukraine crisis of 2013–2014, it is becoming increasingly clear, has begun to fatefully reshape this political-economic equation, and Eurasia itself as a consequence. As we shall see, the sharp Russian response to regime change in Kiev has deeply alienated Moscow from Europe and the United States, precipitating Western sanctions. East-West tensions in Europe, now extended to Syria, have led Moscow to reach out to Beijing and altered the bargaining relationship between those Eurasian powers. Deepened Sino-Russian interdependence has been leveraged, ironically, by Moscow's attempts at increased autarky within Eurasia, in the form of the Eurasian Economic Union. The EAEU and the rising economic power of China, coupled with a technical revolution in supply-chain logistics, have also made transcontinental economic ties to Europe far more realistic than previously. A new transcontinental Eurasian political economy is being born, with the Ukraine crisis providing a powerful catalyst.

What sort of critical juncture actually transpired in the Ukraine to generate these fateful new political-economic pressures across the continent? It is important to understand the details of Ukrainian developments to know. As with other critical junctures, the key events occurred in a remarkably short period of time—roughly four fateful months late in 2013 and early in 2014.

Profile of the Ukraine Crisis

Relations between Russia and the Ukraine are innately both intimate and conflicted. The Ukraine, after all, is a large nation of 45 million people, the cradle of Russian civilization, and deeply linked industrially with Russia itself, yet possessed of a diverse population, much of which bitterly resents Moscow's traditional dominance. It is also strategically located in Southeastern Europe and a tempting target for intervention from both East and West. After independence in August 1991 as the Soviet Union was collapsing, the Ukraine underwent the Orange Revolution of 2004, involving a tilt to pluralist democracy, followed by a tilt back toward Moscow during 2010–2013 under Viktor Yanukovych, culminating in massive protest demonstrations involving 800,000 people; violence in which over 100 people died; the ouster of Yanukovych; and a contentious Westward orientation, from February 2014.[54]

In response to what was widely viewed in Moscow as an illegitimate, Western-inspired coup threatening fundamental Russian security interests, Russian president Vladimir Putin signed legislation passed by the Duma annexing the Crimea, where major Russian naval bases were located, on March 18, 2014. Violence also broke out elsewhere in the eastern Ukraine. On May 2 over forty people, mostly pro-Russian activists, died while trapped in a burning trade-union building in Odessa. Armed conflict exploded in the eastern Ukraine, while in June the Ukraine, Georgia, and Moldova all signed partnership agreements with the EU, deeply angering Russia.[55]

The United States and its allies responded to the situation in the Ukraine with a gradually broadening and intensifying set of economic sanctions.[56] In the first wave starting in March 2014, the EU and the US introduced travel bans and asset freezes against sixteen Russian government officials and members of Putin's inner circle linked to the military violence in the Ukraine.[57] In April 2014, seven additional Russian officials, including Rosneft executive chairman Igor Sechin, as well as seventeen Russian companies, were also targeted in a second round of US sanctions.[58] The EU added fifteen people to its own sanctions list.[59]

International tensions escalated further when Malaysian Airlines flight MH17, flying across the Eurasian continent from Amsterdam to Kuala Lumpur, was shot down by a Russian Buk 9M38 missile on July 17, 2014, resulting in the deaths of all 298 people on board the plane.[60] The third wave of sanctions that followed the incident was the most extensive, covering major financial, defense-industrial, and energy transactions.[61] Among the new measures, Russian state banks were banned from raising long-term loans in the sanctions-participating nations. Exports of dual-use military equipment to Russia were banned, along with all future EU-Russian arms deals. The US and the EU also banned exports of certain oil industry technology and services, although parallel technology with respect to natural gas was unaffected.

The EU also targeted Russia's access to overseas capital markets by preventing EU nationals and companies from buying and selling new bonds, equity, or similar financial instruments issued by state-owned Russian banks. The EU and the US also continued to target Putin's confidantes in the business world, including Gennady Timchenko (Novatek), Arkady Rotenberg and Boris Rotenberg (SMP Bank), Igor Sechin (Rosneft), Sergei Chemezov (Rostec), and

Yuri Kovalchuk (Bank Rossiya).[62] Asset freezes and travel bans were weapons of choice. In March 2018, the US extended sanctions for another year;[63] meanwhile, EU economic sanctions continued to June 2019, while individual asset freezes and travel bans persisted as well.[64]

Shock Waves across Eurasia

Western sanctions triggered compensating economic realignment elsewhere in Eurasia. The Ukraine crisis led, for example, to deepened and diversified ties between Russia and China bilaterally; between China and other nations of Eastern Europe and Central Asia; and between China and Europe. In May 2014 Russia and China signed a massive $400 billion energy deal, providing for unprecedented Chinese equity participation in the Russian energy sector itself.[65] Actual energy trade also began to deepen. Defense technology ties have also deepened, as is recounted in more detail in Chapter 7.

In the wake of the Ukraine crisis, China's ties with Eastern Europe, including the near abroad, have also begun to deepen. In August 2015, President Xi Jinping greeted Kiev on the Ukraine's independence day, emphasizing Chinese respect for Ukrainian independence and territorial integrity.[66] China and the Ukraine agreed to jointly build the Antonov AN-225, prospectively the largest plane ever built.[67] Xi also visited Belarus, Serbia, Poland, and Uzbekistan, as well as Russia, during 2015–2016, extending substantial assistance under the Belt and Road Initiative along the way. Particularly notable were the June 2016 visits to Poland, China's largest trading partner in the region, and to Serbia, where China has invested more than $1 billion in energy and infrastructure, including a high-speed rail line from Belgrade to Budapest.[68]

In Conclusion

Eurasia's geography itself harbors powerful potential synergies, including the close juxtaposition of large populations and huge natural-resource reserves. In global context, the continent's massive scale also endows it with fateful potential influence in world affairs. Yet in contrast to classical geopoliticians such as Halford Mackinder, we are skeptical of the notion that geography is destiny. Potential needs to be unlocked through conscious political-economic action. Super Continents are made, and not simply born.

This chapter has explored the political-economic actions that have given birth to a reconfigured Eurasia, a matter of continental and ultimately global consequence. These actions have collectively made Eurasia an increasingly interactive Grand Chessboard, with rising strategic significance as a continent in world affairs. The chapter has argued that a small number of critical junctures—short periods of high-stakes crisis decision making—are primarily responsible for the reconnection of Eurasia, transforming isolated countries into a larger, more interactive entity. Three such critical junctures, in particular, have been identified, apart from China's Four Modernizations: (1) the collapse of the Soviet Union at the end of 1991, (2) the Lehman Brothers global financial crisis of 2008, and (3) the Ukraine crisis of 2014.

China's Four Modernizations provided the catalyst for a broader process that is now beginning to transform both Eurasia and the world. Due to the PRC's scale and centrality in Eurasia as well as its catalytic role, China's critical juncture deserves to be considered also as the first Crossover Point. The latter three critical junctures, taken together, have transformed the continent of Eurasia more broadly, responding to the initial Chinese catalyst and creating a Grand Chessboard transcending any one nation. They have also created new incentives for economic growth and interaction throughout the Eurasian continent. The last two junctures, occurring after the domestic institutional changes, have accelerated the economic growth of the continent as a whole, relative to the rest of the world, and redirected it within. In combination, the critical junctures have, over a short four decades, released preexisting political constraints on Eurasian continental interdependence and created incentives now driving the continent both to deeper integration and to an expanding collective role in world affairs. The critical junctures and the forces they unleashed have, over a generation, thus driven Eurasia toward a reconnection with fateful long-term implications, that transcend even the leverage China enjoys with its new, connectivity-oriented BRI.

4

The Logic of Integration

LITTLE MORE THAN A CENTURY AGO, the notion of Eurasian centrality in world affairs seemed compelling, with only North America as a peer competitor, based on broad acceptance of geopolitical logic. Eurasia was recognized as by far the largest continent on earth, covering over one-third of the world's entire land area. It was seen as a veritable storehouse of raw materials needed in the industrial age then dawning; czarist Russia was, for example, the largest oil producer in the world. Eurasia was home to well over half of the world's population. And its internal lines of communication were rapidly developing, as symbolized by the progress of the Trans-Siberian Railway, completed in 1916 in an era when the technology of land transport was rapidly gaining on that of the sea. Eurasia's potential as a Super Continent seemed undeniable.

Halford Mackinder, a director of the London School of Economics, suggested in a landmark address to the Royal Geographical Society in January 1904 that Eurasia constituted "the geographical pivot of history."[1] The notion that Eurasia represented a "heartland" around which the fate of global affairs could potentially turn was firmly supported not only by Mackinder but also by myriad European and Japanese geopolitical analysts for close to half a century thereafter.[2] In recent years support for Eurasian centrality has been less prominent, although backed by prescient analysts such as US national security advisor Zbigniew Brzezinski.[3]

Consciousness of Eurasia, and of geopolitics generally, has waned in recent years. Yet the geographic fundamentals that convinced Mackinder and other classic geopoliticians before him of Eurasian centrality naturally remain unchanged. Static classical conceptions of how geography and world affairs immutably relate may need revision to account for changing political-economic circumstance. Yet geography does dictate many basic parameters of geo-economic competition, and one needs to be clear about what those parameters are.

The logic of Eurasian integration begins with geography. Eurasia is by far the largest continent in the world and dominates the land surfaces of the earth. Its interior lines of communication are short and potentially efficient. Its politics are complex but growing more coherent and complementary in the post–Cold War world, with China, Southeast Asia, Russia, the Middle East, and Europe all growing more interdependent, compared to three or four decades ago. Political crisis, as we saw in the last chapter, has played a paradoxical yet functional role in driving this deepening structural integration.

Although Eurasia's physical geography has an inherent logic, its political geography, remarkably malleable of late, requires concrete economic catalysts to generate the incentives for deeper integration. This chapter identifies three such catalysts: energy, logistics, and finance. Together, changes in these areas are creating new economic pressures and opportunities that enhance prospects for unprecedented political coordination as well.

Enduring Geophysical Traits

One reality that Mackinder continually stressed: the heartland of Eurasia has strong geographical coherence. The nations of Africa, he noted, are separated by the Sahara, as India and China are divided by the Himalayas. Between Europe and Asia, however, there are only modest slopes like the Urals, and narrow straits like the Dardanelles and the Bosporus.[4] Given the relative ease of geographic access, cultural flows in areas such as religion and the arts have been frequent since antiquity between Europe and Asia, enhancing their coherence as one continent still further.[5]

In Eurasia, geography thus privileges intracontinental relationships, as opposed to unfettered global associations, in three important ways. First of all, as just noted, there are relatively easy routes of access between Europe and Asia. Second, Eurasian geography generates potential internal lines of transport and communication across the continent—as Mackinder also stressed—that are manifestly shorter overland than circuitous routes by sea around the continent's periphery. As Map 1.1 suggested, the overland distance between major East Asian centers such as Shanghai, and European counterparts like Rotterdam, is more than one-third shorter than by sea.

A third immutable advantage that geography confers on internal transactions within Eurasia is the proximity of natural resources and population. Eurasia has over 80 percent of the world's proven natural gas reserves,
and nearly 60 percent of its oil. Most of those resources are concentrated
in the Persian Gulf and Russia, remarkably close to the largest—and generally energy-insecure—population centers in China and India. Eurasia is also
home to over half of the world's population.

Accessibility, overland lines of communication and the propinquity of resources and population are all immutable geographical features with enduring
relevance to Eurasia's future global role. Their actual geopolitical importance
at any one point in time does, of course, depend on broader technological
and economic factors, as we shall see. The geographic parameter, however,
is unchanging and fated to become more supportive of integration as Eurasia
grows and infrastructure becomes more sophisticated and cost-effective.

Realities of Political Geography

Political boundaries, of course, are not strictly geographic, and hence less
immutable. Their broad configuration, however, tends to be stable in the
nuclear age, and Eurasia's current political geography has three important features worth noting here:

1) *China lies in a geo-economically pivotal position on the continent.* It is not
   at the exact geographic center, but it does lie at the heart of the most
   populous and economically active region, flanked by Korea and Japan
   on the east, Southeast Asia to the south, and South Asia to the southwest.

China is surrounded, to be sure, by some formidable geographic barriers,
especially by the Himalayas to the southwest. Yet there are access routes, such
as through Myanmar and Pakistan, that finesse those barriers. And directly to
the west, across Central Asia, China faces largely deserts and flat, arid steppes,
which present little obstacle to transit in the machine age, despite the formidable Tian Shan, Pamir, and Kunlun mountain ranges, which limit transit
to the southwest. Strengthening its incentives for interdependence, modern
China extends deep into the Eurasian continent—two-thirds of the way to
the Strait of Hormuz, and one-half the distance to the borders of European
Union, as noted in Map 4.1.

2) *Despite their centrality on land, China and Russia both have constrained access
   routes to the southern seas*, as indicated in Map 4.2. These geopolitical

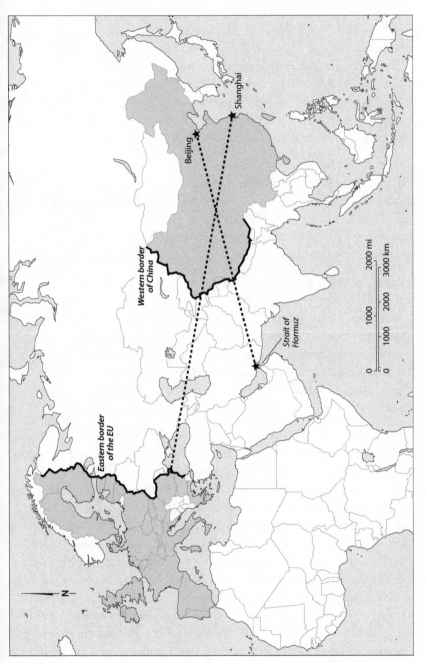

MAP 4.1 China dominates continental overland routes to the West

realities give them a dual incentive—to develop overland associations while also cultivating "amphibious" states with maritime access,
such as Turkey, Pakistan, and Myanmar. This basic reality lies behind
the geopolitics of China's Belt and Road Initiative (BRI), with its
dual continental and maritime dimensions, within which the China-
Pakistan Economic Corridor, the China-Myanmar Economic Corridor
Initiative, and relations with Turkey's Erdoğan administration loom
large. Alternatively, an Asian continental power like China can attempt
to become "amphibious," as the BRI itself proposes.

To be sure, the Strait of Malacca and the states that surround it—
Singapore, Malaysia, and Indonesia—are also important in the maritime geopolitical calculus for China. The Strait of Malacca, after all, is a critical way
station from East Asia to the Middle East. And 70 percent of China's oil
imports—from Africa as well as the Gulf—flow that way. In all these cases,
geography has vital geopolitical as well as geo-economic implications.

3) *India, in contrast to China and Russia, has commanding maritime access in
the Indian Ocean, but very difficult overland access on routes to Europe,* as
indicated in Map 4.3. India lies directly east of Pakistan, a bitter rival
with whom it has fought three bloody wars since partition in 1947 and
whom it continues to confront in Kashmir. Just as Pakistan provides
China with Gulf access, it denies India a viable overland path north-
ward toward Central Asia and ultimately to Europe. India's best option
for overland contact with Russia and Europe is thus via Iran.

Iran's southern port of Chabahar, dating from the 1980s, is located just 330
nautical miles east of the Persian Gulf and 550 nautical miles west of Indian
prime minister Narendra Modi's home state of Gujarat. Chabahar, a potential
gateway for European access via Iran, is thus of major geo-economic interest to India. So is stability in Iran's relations with the broader world, and the
prospect of improved north-south transport infrastructure across Iran.

Current Eurasian political geography, in sum, leverages the latent geographic incentives that a large, populous land power on that continent has to
seek greater connectivity across the continent. These incentives for the land
power are especially pronounced when its economy, resources requirements,
and need for markets are all strong. The prescription fits admirably well for
China in the twenty-first century. That is why the BRI, as grand strategy,
makes eminent sense for Beijing. Indeed, many analysts, such as Germany's

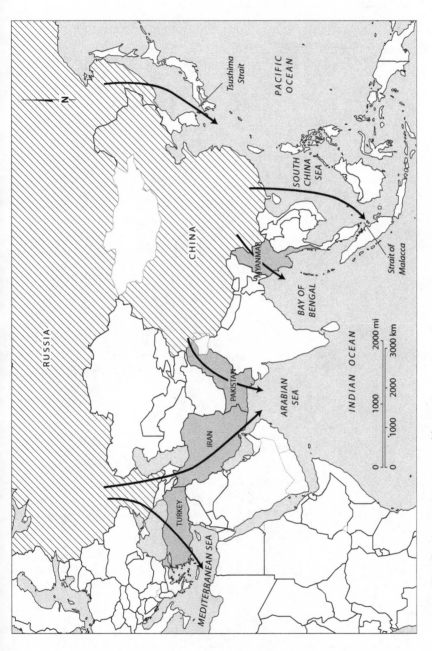

MAP 4.2 Sino-Russian maritime access dilemmas

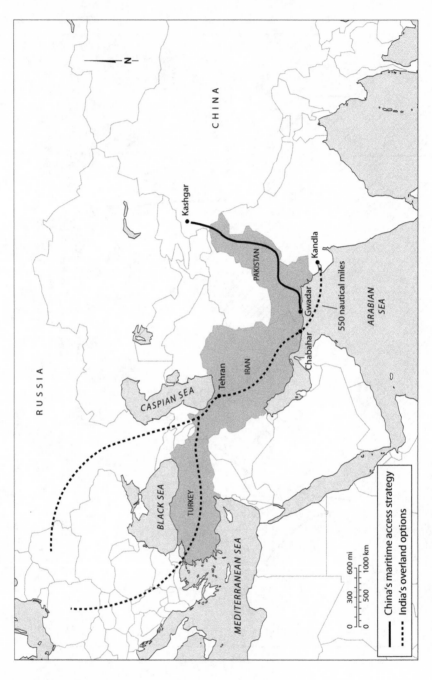

MAP 4.3 India's tortured overland options

recent foreign minister Sigmar Gabriel, argue that the BRI may be the one coherent large power grand strategy operative in world affairs today.[6]

The Forces Propelling Eurasia's Reconnection

Geography, as we have just seen, dictates many basic parameters of political-economic competition. It conveys certain latent, potential advantages in the Eurasian context to a centrally located power promoting overland connectivity. It also enhances the likelihood that continental interdependence itself will move forward when the centrally located nation is growing and politically influential. How strong today are these forces for integration, and where might they lead the continent? Those are the central questions that we now confront.

The balance of this chapter considers the three most basic and dynamic sectoral catalysts for Eurasia's deepening integration: energy, transit trade, and finance. Animating all three are even more elemental forces—economic growth and technological change. Both of these latent transformative agents have been unusually vigorous across the continent over the past three post–Cold War decades, with the Logistics, AI, and 5G Revolutions accelerating connectivity still further.

Energy as a Force for Eurasian Transformation

Eurasia is blessed, in the aggregate, with the largest energy reserves of any continent on earth. It also is home to well over half of the world's population. And the energy reserves are located remarkably close to the massive populations, as indicated in Map 4.4. So energy naturally has innate geo-physical potential to support deeper integration of the Eurasian continent, should propitious economic and political preconditions exist.

Energy supports Eurasian integration not just through the way it supplies direct economic needs but also due to the trade flows that it generates. Eurasian energy-surplus nations such as Russia, Kazakhstan, and Iraq export oil and gas, which generates the foreign exchange for them to buy Chinese, Korean, Japanese, or European manufactures. Energy is thus a trade generator, providing liquidity for trade in other sectors. If energy supply and demand complementarities did not exist within Eurasia, it would be hard for manufacturing and transport interdependence to emerge—a point sometimes lost on otherwise astute analysts of Eurasian interdependence.[7]

It is useful analytically to think of Eurasia as a unit for the purposes of energy analysis, in order to understand the potential synergies that complementary demand and supply patterns within the continent are beginning to create. It is also, however, important to recognize that geography decrees somewhat different supply patterns for Europe and East Asia—the principal energy markets on the continent. East Asia's energy markets—especially the large yet mature markets of Japan and South Korea—are most easily supplied from the Persian Gulf by sea. Europe is more easily supplied overland from Russia. Both Russia and the Central Asian republics of the former Soviet Union, however, also have the ability to readily supply major parts of China overland, as Map 4.4 suggests.

A brief review of global oil and gas reserves and the prominent position of Eurasia in both categories makes clear the potential of Eurasia for continental autarky in energy. As indicated in Table 4.1, nearly half of the proved oil reserves on earth are concentrated in the Persian Gulf, while an additional 8 percent are in the former Soviet Union (FSU).[8] If the high costs and political risks of extracting Canadian tar sands and Venezuelan heavy oil respectively are taken into consideration, the Persian Gulf and the FSU loom even larger.

A similar picture prevails in natural gas, with some important additional nuances. The Persian Gulf dominates, in terms of proved reserves, with close to 40 percent of the global total, although the Gulf's share in gas is not quite as large as in oil. The FSU controls a larger share of gas than oil, with more than a quarter of global reserves.[9] Many of those reserves lie in Central Asia, beyond Russia's current frontiers.

Energy trading patterns, of course, flow from national domestic supply-demand relationships, geographical proximity, and quality of needed infrastructure. As our figures suggest, the United States is a massive hydrocarbon producer, in the era of the shale revolution.[10] It has recently become the world's largest producer of both oil and natural gas. Yet it remains a marginal exporter in both categories, despite slowly rising exports to Asia.[11] US domestic demand was too large, and the combined geographic and infrastructural challenges are still too great for the US to be a major energy partner to Eurasia.

The natural energy partner for Eurasian consumers, as Tables 4.1 and 4.2 also suggest, is Eurasia itself. As the tables indicate, large exporters in the Persian Gulf, including Saudi Arabia, Iran, Iraq, Kuwait, and the United Arab Emirates (UAE), all generally send over two-thirds of their oil exports to Asia, although there are some country-specific fluctuations, partially due to political instability.[12] Some of the large gas exporters of the Gulf, such as the UAE and Qatar, send over half of their exports to Asia, in the form of liquefied natural gas (LNG). Turkmenistan, one of the FSU's largest exporters, also does so, in the form of piped gas. Indeed, there are now three major pipelines—all

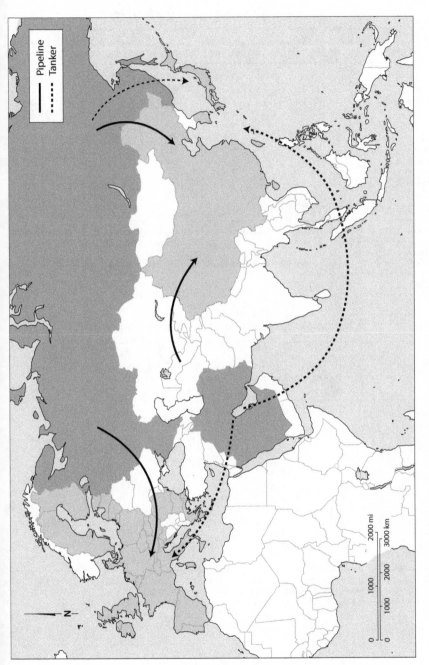

MAP 4.4 Contrasting energy supply options for Europe and East Asia

TABLE 4.1
Oil reserves, production, and exports (2017)

	Total Proved Reserves (billion tons)	Share of Total Reserves	R/P Ratio	Total Production (million tons)	Asia Share of Total Exports
United States	6.0	2.9%	10.5	571.0	32.1%
Canada	27.2	10.0%	95.8	236.3	0.4%
Venezuela	47.3	17.9%	393.6	108.3	40.3%
Russia	14.5	6.3%	25.8	554.4	29.0%
Iran	21.6	9.3%	86.5	234.2	64.5%
Iraq	20.1	8.8%	90.2	221.5	53.8%
Kuwait	14.0	6.0%	91.9	146.0	80.4%
Saudi Arabia	36.6	15.7%	61.0	561.7	67.9%
UAE	13.0	5.8%	68.1	176.3	98.8%
Libya	6.3	2.9%	153.3	40.8	12.4%
Nigeria	5.1	2.2%	51.6	95.3	28.3%
Total Persian Gulf	105.2	45.5%	–	1,339.7	70.3%

SOURCES: BP, "Oil: Proved Reserves," "Oil: Production—Tonnes (from 1965)," and "Oil: Inter-area Movements," *Statistical Review of World Energy*, June 2018; OPEC, "Table 5.1 OPEC Members' Crude Oil Exports by Destination," *Annual Statistical Bulletin*, 2018.
NOTES: 1) Venezuela, Iran, Libya, and Nigeria oil export data from OPEC; 2) Countries selected have at least 2 percent of global proved reserves.

TABLE 4.2
Natural gas reserves, production, and exports (2017)

	Total Proved Reserves (tcm)	Share of Total	R/P Ratio	Total Production (bcm)	Asia Pacific Share of Total Exports (pipeline)	Asia Pacific Share of Total Exports (LNG)
United States	8.7	4.5%	11.9	734.5	–	40.9%
Venezuela	6.4	3.3%	170.2	37.4	–	–
Russia	35.0	18.1%	55.0	635.6	–	99.2%
Turkmenistan	19.5	10.1%	314.1	62.0	94.2%	–
Iran	33.2	17.2%	148.4	223.9	–	–
Qatar	24.9	12.9%	141.8	175.7	–	67.3%
Saudi Arabia	8.0	4.2%	72.1	111.4	–	–
UAE	5.9	3.1%	98.2	60.4	–	93.4%
Algeria	4.3	2.2%	47.5	91.2	–	5.3%
Nigeria	5.2	2.7%	110.2	47.2	–	31.2%
China	5.5	2.8%	36.7	149.2	–	–
Total Persian Gulf	72.1	37.3%	–	571.5	–	69.1%

SOURCE: BP, "Gas: Proved Reserves," "Gas: Production—Bcm (from 1970)," "Gas: Trade Movements Pipeline," and "Gas: Trade Movements LNG," *Statistical Review of World Energy*, June 2017.
NOTE: Countries selected have at least 2 percent of global proved reserves.

completed since 2009—supplying China's east coast with piped gas out of Central Asia.

Given the huge reserves of the Persian Gulf, the low cost of extraction, and the rapid economic growth of East Asia, it is not surprising that East Asian oil dependence on the Gulf is both high and, in several countries, steadily rising. Japanese, Korean, and Chinese dependence on the Persian Gulf for oil supplies in 2017 was in each case higher than during the early 1990s.[13] Only in India was the Gulf percentage reliance falling.[14]

Significantly, Asia's rising dependence on the Persian Gulf for oil supplies contrasts to a *declining* reliance by both the US and Europe. US dependence on the Gulf fell from around 30 percent of US oil imports in 1991 to less than 25 percent in 2017.[15] Import shares also declined in the major EU nations, albeit from a lower base—from 16 percent in 1991 to only 13 percent in 2015.[16]

More than 11 million barrels of oil flow east from the Persian Gulf to Asia *every day*.[17] That represents over one-quarter of the oil flowing in international trade.[18] The largest national consumer is China, which takes nearly 2.4 million barrels daily—or roughly one-fifth of the Gulf crude exports that flowed to the Asia-Pacific region. Japan also imports 2.3 million bbl/day from the Gulf, with a much higher national percentage reliance on that region for its supplies than China sustains. Japan, however, faces rising long-term competition for Gulf supplies, not only from China, but also from Korea and the Association of Southeast Asian Nations (ASEAN). Those three actors take most of the flow eastward from the Gulf that does not go to Japan.

Asia's overall share of Persian Gulf exports, which is close to twice what any other region of the world procures, has risen considerably since the Asian financial crisis of 1997–1998—from 50 percent in the depths of the crisis to over 70 percent two decades later.[19] Asia's share of Gulf energy exports fell, to be sure, during the crisis itself, dipping slightly from 56 percent of regional exports in 1996 to less than 52 percent by 1998–1999. Yet Asia's share rebounded thereafter, as local economies began to recover, exceeding 60 percent of the Persian Gulf's total exports by 2003. That portion has since risen substantially, to 65 percent in 2009, and to over 70 percent in 2017, fueled by the rapidly rising demand of China and India. Persian Gulf exports to Asia appear likely to rise even higher in future, given the region's massive reserves, as demand in populous, high-growth China and India continues to rise.

By 2030 China is expected to pass the US as the world's largest oil consumer, with a larger long-term natural gas market than that of the EU. By 2040 China's total energy demand will likely be twice that of the US.[20] China is thus evolving into the world's preeminent energy market, albeit one chronically deficient in domestic supplies. Prospects for India are in some ways even more portentous. As oil production there declines relative to demand, Indian oil import dependence is expected to rise over 90 percent by 2040. That nation could then well become the world's fastest growing consumer of crude.[21] And it will likely have an even greater reliance on the Gulf than today.

In natural gas there is a pattern of deepening Asian interdependence with the Persian Gulf that parallels trends with respects to oil. Japan, China, and South Korea are by a substantial margin the largest LNG importers in the world, accounting for over half of global imports among them;[22] all three are heavily dependent on the Gulf, albeit receiving significant supplemental imports from Southeast Asia and Australia. India is also emerging as a major LNG importer, with significant Gulf reliance—all these nation-specific trends are deepening overall interdependence between East Asia and the Gulf.

For their part, the Gulf nations are also heavily reliant on Asia as an LNG export market—as in oil. Qatar, the largest Gulf LNG exporter, sends two-thirds of its gas exports to Asia, as indicated in Table 4.2. The UAE is almost 100 percent reliant on Asia—particularly on Japan. Oman is also heavily reliant on Asia, with half of its exports going to Korea and one-third to Japan.[23]

Asia and the Persian Gulf thus have a powerful new interdependence in both oil and gas that represents one sturdy pillar of the deepening Eurasian energy relationship. A second important dimension is the longstanding tie between Europe and Russia, dating from the dawn of the twentieth century, when czarist Russia was the largest oil producer in the world, drawing heavily on the bountiful Caspian Sea reserves of Baku.[24] Between 1904 and 1913, Russia's share of global petroleum exports fell from 31 to 9 percent due to domestic political turmoil,[25] and they did not recover until the late 1950s, when the Soviet Union, successor to the czars, emerged as the world's second largest oil producer.[26] Russia, of course, continued to have massive reserves of both oil and gas that underpin its formidable position as a potential Eurasian energy supplier.[27] As Tables 4.1 and 4.2 indicate, it holds the largest natural gas and the sixth largest oil reserves in the world. Russia's proved reserves-to-production ratio of 55 years is comparatively high in one of the world's most crucial resources.[28] And much of Russia's vastness remains geologically unexplored.

Although Russia's energy ties with Europe date back well over a century, they deepened sharply during the latter stages of the Cold War. The Soviet Union, drawing on both Caucasian and West Siberian reserves, built massive pipelines connecting gas fields deep inside the USSR with its Eastern European satellites, as far as central Germany. For Moscow, energy became an important vehicle for strategic control.

Following the Cold War, Russia continued, and actually expanded, its exports to the West. Major new east–west pipelines were built, including the two parallel pipelines of Nord Stream, completed in November 2011 and October 2012. These projects piped gas directly from Russia to Germany under the Baltic Sea, preventing Eastern European transit nations such as Poland and the Ukraine from gaining leverage by threatening to obstruct or compromise the natural gas flows.[29] By 2017 three-quarters of Russian gas pipeline exports were going to Europe, although the overall European market was not growing rapidly.[30] LNG exports to Asia, however, have been substantial and rising, totaling almost 15.4 bcm in 2017.[31] This compared to only 7.1 bcm in US LNG exports to Asia during the same year.[32] Gazprom's Power of Siberia project will also begin pipeline gas exports to China in December 2019.[33]

The third pillar of the deepening transcontinental Eurasian energy integration is the rapidly developing hydrocarbon relationship between the various constituent units of the former USSR and East Asia. This includes two supplier elements: (1) Russia, with its huge reserves, the bulk of which lie east of the Urals; and (2) Central Asian and Caucasian suppliers, including Turkmenistan, Azerbaijan, and Kazakhstan. These latter nations rank fourth, twenty-first, and twenty-fifth respectively in global proved gas reserves.[34] Kazakhstan also ranks twelfth in oil, partly on the strength of its mammoth Kashagan and Tengiz fields, followed by Azerbaijan at twenty-first.[35]

There is a powerful potential symbiosis between rapidly rising Chinese demand for natural gas and the ample reserves of the former USSR. Russian gas is particularly attractive to China due to its proximity, energy efficiency, and attractive environmental qualities. Two thorny problems complicate the seemingly natural relationship, however: price and the absence of infrastructure. Price is an issue for Sino-Russia energy trade because China's fallback option, in the absence of agreement, is low-cost coal. China has over 13 percent of world coal reserves,[36] and production costs are low. Additionally, the Russian gas most accessible to China—located northwest of Lake Baikal—cannot be extracted without substantial infrastructure investment.

For decades, the absence of infrastructure, particularly pipelines, stood as a formidable barrier to the flow of energy eastward and southward from Siberia and Central Asia to the markets of China, Japan, and South Korea. Hyundai in the early 1970s, together with Mitsubishi and Itochu in the mid-1990s, had ambitious plans for Eurasian gas extraction that foundered on the lack of infrastructure financing. Ultimately, however, the Chinese government stepped in, funding first the West–East Pipeline from Xinjiang to Shanghai during the early 2000s, and then two more ambitious gas pipeline projects from Turkmenistan and Kazakhstan to China's east coast.

Today Turkmenistan exports nearly all of its gas to East Asia—primarily China. Shanghai gets about half of its gas supply from Central Asia. This deepening Sino–Central Asian interdependence, epitomized in the building of three large transcontinental pipelines from Central Asia during the 2008 – 2014 period, has stirred competitive pressures encouraging Russians to move forward in supplying China on competitive terms also. Economic incentives flowing from China's post-2008 stimulus and political pressures for Sino-Russian collaboration flowing from the 2014 Ukraine crisis have aided as well in encouraging Russia to be tractable on energy-contract terms with China. In 2014, soon after the crisis erupted, a pipeline deal was signed; the Irkutsk Baikal-to-Daqing gas pipeline is scheduled to open at the end of 2019.[37]

In 2014 China and Russia also signed a massive $40 billion, thirty-year, long-term deal for comprehensive collaborative energy-sector development.[38] Driven by broader transcontinental geopolitical pressures, Russian president Vladimir Putin and Chinese president Xi Jinping agreed to use government subsidies to address the infrastructure challenges. That, and more recent initiatives, should go far in deepening the integration of Russian and Chinese energy sectors, thus leading to a broader reconnection of Eurasia as well.

A final dimension of deepening Eurasian energy ties is in renewable energy. Europeans have led the world in seeking alternatives to hydrocarbon fuels and were early—together with Japan—to support China's ambitious efforts to diversify into such sectors as solar and wind power, partially through Kyoto Protocol environmental credits. Firms like Denmark's Vestas were also supportive with technical assistance and export of capital goods.

China, of course, has become a dominant producer of solar panels in its own right, overshadowing the Europeans and the Japanese. Its energy demand has risen so rapidly as to lend credence to another Eurasian alternative energy vision—that of the Northeast Asian Super Grid proposed by Japanese entrepreneur Son Masayoshi.[39] This would utilize solar energy collected from the Gobi Desert, together with Russian hydropower and other regional sources, to address the energy deficiencies of China, Japan, and Korea. If realized, the project could be another important step toward Eurasian reconnection.

*The Logistics Revolution, "Continental Drift," and Deepening
Transcontinental Interdependence*

Energy, as we have seen, has been a major driver for Eurasian interdependence for half a century, building on the profound latent complementarity between Asia's massive population and the formidable hydrocarbon reserves of the Persian Gulf and the former Soviet Union. Over the past two decades, however, an important new transportation-based driver of deepening Eurasian interdependence has arisen to complement the powerful energy stimuli outlined above. That historic watershed is the Logistics Revolution—a radical change, due to the application of digital technology, in the way goods are transported and distributed. This transformation greatly simplifies, speeds up, and cheapens the cost of intermodal travel, thereby magnifying synergistically the impact of other geo-economic factors.

The Logistics Revolution has uniquely powerful implications for Eurasia, for at least four reasons. First, land routes between major European and Chinese manufacturing centers, for which logistical connections have heretofore been chronically underdeveloped, are much shorter than sea routes. Second, Eurasian transport involves an unusual variety of intermodal transfers, leading to a distinctively sharp decline in transport costs due to recent technological change. Third, Chinese domestic infrastructure—a critical variable as close to half of the transcontinental overland journey lies inside China—has radically improved over the past decade, reflecting strong Chinese sensitivity to the Logistics Revolution. The advent of business-to-business (B2B) e-commerce leverages these infrastructure improvements, making long-distance, just-in-time supply chains increasingly feasible. And finally, the direct connection between Northeast Asia and Europe, the two major poles of the global economy and global technological progress apart from the United States, is deepened by these technological and economic changes. Such deepened connections could ultimately pose a fundamental economic challenge to the global political-economic order as presently configured, with broader potential geopolitical ramifications.

The Logistics Revolution has its origins in the containerization of international trade, which began in the mid-1950s and accelerated during the Vietnam War. Today the majority of international shipments, apart from bulk commodities, travel in such containers, an innovation that radically reduces the cost of shipping. Containerization does, however, complicate security and reporting requirements, while posing new challenges for customs procedures that have inhibited containerization from attaining its full trade facilitation potential for several decades.

Containerization transformed shipping into an increasingly standardized process, holding out the promise of major new efficiency advances, especially as digitalization also gained momentum. Some of the related areas for innovation were insurance, customs clearance, freight forwarding, and intermodal transfer. Although containerization was an earlier development, technologies in the latter areas, especially intermodal transfer, have been evolving rapidly over the past decade and promise to evolve still further with the introduction of Internet of Things (IoT) and 5th-Generation (5G) wireless network technology, giving promise of further disruptive innovation in the coming years. IoT allows, for example, the real-time monitoring of goods as well as assets from individual cases to the whole company. It also allows organizations to automate procedures that were previously manual and to optimize how multiple logistics systems work together. Such innovations lead to higher utilization of existing assets, smart inventory management, and high-quality predictive maintenance, as well as accurate end-to-end tracking of high-value goods.

East Asian countries, especially China, Singapore, and South Korea, were the early pioneers in containerization, due to their growing economies and to aggressive capital investments just as containerization was emerging as a logistics option.[40] Although the first significant use of containerization came in the Atlantic, its major impact on the world economy came through East Asia. Japan was also a pioneer, with massive government support for the shipbuilding industry combined with the need to protect the fragile and high-value electronics exported by Japanese firms like Sony. More generally, containerization had an important facilitating impact on international trade, by lowering insurance costs and reducing the time needed to transfer goods.

Although East Asia was the pioneer on the transportation and manufacturing side, Europe was the pioneer in the political and financial dimensions of containerization, including insurance and customs clearance. Europe's steady march toward economic integration, from the Treaty of Rome (1957) to Maastricht (1992) and the advent of the common currency (1999), naturally encouraged such logistical advances as well. The rich geography of European transport, involving complex transfers among rail, road, river, and sometimes air, made intermodal transport innovation a high priority.

Digitalization has synergistically amplified the potential efficiency gains available through trade liberalization. These gains showed up first within the European Community early in the twenty-first century. They spawned the dynamic expansion of new logistics providers such as Deutsche Post DHL, formed by Deutsche Post's acquisition of DHL in 2002 and Airborne Express in 2003. By 2013 this postal-based European firm was drawing 53 percent of its total revenue from logistics alone.[41]

China is the world's largest manufacturer and naturally, like other large manufacturers such as Germany, is preoccupied with improving transportation efficiencies for physical goods. As in Germany, the digital revolution is creating powerful incentives to create or control state of the art digitalized distribution networks, by introducing the most advanced equipment and achieving optimal economies of scale. China now has one of the largest railway companies in the world, the largest container-shipping ports, one of the three largest maritime-shipping companies, and one of the two largest e-commerce firms on earth, with much of this distribution scale being created through mergers since 2015.

Artificial intelligence (AI) and IoT advances—both inspired by rapid progress in digital, computing, communications, and storage technology—lie behind recent progress in the Logistics Revolution. An explosive expansion in the use of transponders, combined with AI advances, are allowing computers to automate and track logistics as never before. These developments have especially dramatic consequences for intermodal transport and storage, making it possible for firms to effortlessly track shipments and to anticipate delivery. Blockchain technology can also enhance this predictability, by reducing errors from manual data entry, increasing data transparency, and helping track supply-chain sourcing more effectively.

The Logistics Revolution has fateful implications for producers, distributors, and consumers. For producers, it opens prospects for more efficient and predictable B2B supply chains, making long-distance production networks among manufacturers—including trans-continental networks—more and more feasible. For distributors, the Logistics Revolution intensifies competition, and privileges those, like Amazon and Alibaba, with intimate Big Data consumer understanding.[42] For consumers, this disruptive change means faster delivery, broadened consumer choice, and—at least in the short run—lower prices.

The Logistics Revolution has particularly substantial implications for the reconnection of Eurasia—arguably greater than for any other part of the world. First of all, Europe and East Asia have unusually strong manufacturing bases in China and Germany. These neighbors across the continent are, after all, the first and fourth largest manufacturers in the world, generating around 25 percent of the world's industrial production between them.[43] Their strengths in precision and labor-intensive manufacturing are also complementary, although as the Mercator Institute points out, China's manufacturing advances could well pose increasingly serious challenges to both Northeast Asian and European competitors, especially Germany and Korea.[44] Second, Europe and China are both leaders in logistical innovation, albeit in different areas (infrastructure versus custom clearances/finance) that are potentially complementary. Third, Europe and China lie across the Eurasian continent from one another, allowing them to benefit disproportionately from gains to both land-based and intermodal trade. Much of this intermodal trade will combine maritime and land-based elements. Finally, Europe and Asia lie on a continent where autarky and overregulation have been especially conspicuous, allowing that dynamic duo to enjoy disproportionate gains from the deregulation and rapid technological change now in progress worldwide.

One graphic manifestation of how the Logistics Revolution is propelling the emergence of a Super Continent is the so-called Land-Sea Express Route being promoted by China's COSCO and the Greek railway carrier Train OSE. These firms have begun to offer block train services to Central Europe for multinational firms that have established their logistics centers in Piraeus, the Greek port purchased by COSCO in July 2016. This route makes it possible to reduce the traditional maritime route from China to the EU by around 4,500 kilometers, and the total duration of transcontinental transport by about 8–12 days.[45] Streamlining of intermodal connections and customs-clearance procedures are key elements in making this Land-Sea Express Route possible, efficiently linking China and Europe.

China's Domestic Transport Revolution: Catalyst for Transcontinental Trade Half of the distance from China's east coast to the eastern border of the European Union is inside China, as has been noted, and China is by a considerable margin the largest economy on the Eurasian continent. Changes in China's internal rail and road infrastructure, together with their logistics, thus have major implications for Eurasian transit economics as a whole. And those changes have been sweeping over the past fifteen years.

The most important change has been in high-speed rail (HSR). During the first decade of HSR development (2006–2015), the Chinese government invested an estimated 2.4 trillion yuan in railways and is planning to invest a further 3.5 trillion during the 2016–2020 period.[46] Since 2015 the pace has slowed, but by the end of 2017 China had 127,000 kilometers of rail lines, of which 25,000 were HSR.[47] This represented over 65 percent of the HSR track laid in the entire world.[48] In 2017 this HSR network carried 1.7 billion passengers—roughly half of the global total, and more than twice the share of Japan.[49] China plans to increase its railway infrastructure by 2025 to over 175,000 kilometers, of which 38,000 would be HSR.[50] Freight traffic is also growing steadily, although not as rapidly as infrastructure is expanding.[51]

China's program of infrastructure-centric development has also naturally seen massive investment in roads as well. Between 1997 and 2015, China constructed close to 120,000 kilometers of expressways—a massive effort involving annual investment exceeding rail by a considerable margin. This network has fostered not only passenger and truck traffic but considerable intermodal transport as well.

China has also put considerable effort over the past decade into improving intermodal connections—an effort strongly synergistic with its massive domestic infrastructure program. Under a November 2015 agreement between President Xi and Singapore prime minister Lee Hsien Loong, China and Singapore have been pursuing the Chongqing Connectivity Initiative, building an IoT industrial base in Chongqing that has a strong intermodal logistics dimension, inspired by BRI.[52] China is also working on IoT projects oriented to improving BRI logistics with French affiliates of Foxconn, the world's largest contract manufacturer, and Microsoft of the United States. Although the e-commerce dimension of BRI is as yet not well recognized, it has important geo-economic implications for the future.

Deepening Linkages between Northeast Asia and Europe As logistics grow more technically efficient, and as border clearance becomes smoother, interdependence across Eurasia has deepened: the overland routes from Northeast Asia to Europe, depicted in Map 4.5, show these conduits clearly. These routes are geographically much more direct that the circuitous sea lanes around the southern rim of Asia, with their numerous chokepoints. And these routes are strategically much more attractive to the heartland powers. In the era of high-speed rail and expedited border clearance, overland routes are also potentially speedier and more economically efficient than they have heretofore been.

The contrasts in transit time among the emerging transcontinental transport options are dramatic. The southern sea voyage, from Shanghai through the Strait of Malacca, Indian Ocean, and Suez Canal to northwest European ports such as Rotterdam, is 23,000 kilometers long and takes 45–60 days to complete.[53] The Chongqing-Duisburg overland route, by contrast, which is presented in Map 4.5, is only 10,769 kilometers long and can be completed in 15 days.[54] A southern overland route across Turkey, totally avoiding Russian territory, can be completed in 20–23 days.[55] Cities marked in Map 4.5 can be grouped into three categories: (1) political drivers (e.g., Beijing or Berlin); (2) key terminals (e.g., Chongqing-Duisburg, Yiwu–London/Madrid); or (3) crossroads (e.g., exits to China).

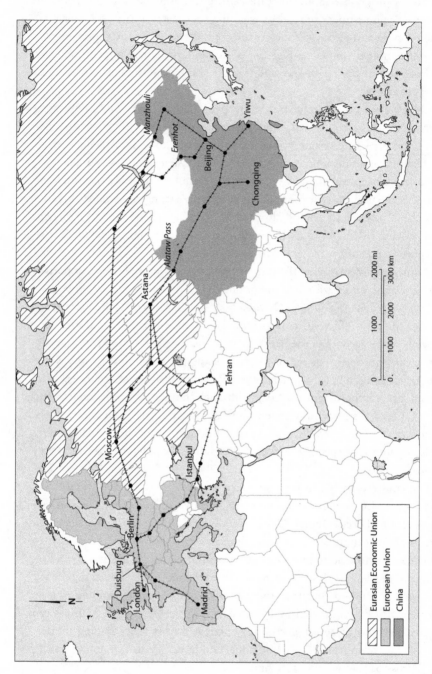

MAP 4.5 Deepening East-West railway routes across Eurasia

SOURCE: Author's illustration based on National Development and Reform Commission, "China Railway Express Construction and Development Plan for 2016–2020," released on October 17, 2016.

As transit times decline, especially on the shorter yet heretofore impractical overland and intermodal routes, the cost of such overland travel comes closer and closer to that of slow and circuitous yet cost-effective routings by sea. Rail transport is naturally attractive for places that are farther from the sea, such as central Europe and central China. Between Chengdu and Warsaw, for example, shipping costs by land for a container were in late 2017 already only 10 percent higher than by ship, while shipping time was just one third as long.[56]

Political constraints on transcontinental interaction are declining, just as economic constraints are, partly due to Russia's declining leverage over transcontinental interactions. In contrast to the situation prevailing before the late 1991 Soviet collapse, it is thus now quite possible for overland transport to bypass areas of Russian control and still proceed efficiently across Eurasia between China and Europe. Aside from a "100 percent overland alternative" via Iran, as illustrated in Map 4.5, there are also "intermodal alternatives," such as Kazakhstan-Caspian Sea-Azerbaijan-Georgia-Turkey. The Baku-Tbilisi-Kars railway, a key component of this intermodal route, was opened in October 2017 by the leaders of Azerbaijan, Georgia, and Turkey.[57] Even when small portions of Russia are crossed, as on the most expeditious trans-Eurasian routings, overland transportation is far less "Moscow dependent" than in Cold War days. Kazakhstan is becoming far more central, both to China-Europe transport and to the increasingly important traffic between China and the Middle East.

In the new world of Eurasian transport, Russia is being transformed from a hegemonic demandeur into at best, from Moscow's perspective, a transit stop. As is apparent from Map 4.5, there are only three nations between the western borders of China in Xinjiang and the eastern frontiers of the European Union in Poland—Kazakhstan, Russia, and Belarus. All these are members of the Eurasian Economic Union, inaugurated at the beginning of 2015, ironically intended to constrain the economic inroads of China. The customs union among these three former components of the Soviet Union has actually had the unintended consequence, however, of simplifying and accelerating transit trade between China and Europe.[58] It has thus deepened the consolidation of Eurasian continentalism as a whole, even as it disadvantages the Russian Far East. The most geographically efficient routes between Europe and China's major manufacturing sites, as well as the best infrastructure, lie largely across China and Kazakhstan. They generally transit small portions of Russia, but there are alternate southern options through Azerbaijan and Turkey as well, including rail-road-maritime intermodal variants traversing the Black and Caspian Seas, that give Chinese and European logistics firms increasing leverage in relation to Russia.

China and continental Europe, both densely populated in their industrial cores, have become, over the past two decades, two of the principal manufacturing bases, or "foundries" of the world economy. Between them, they produce nearly half of the manufactured goods on earth, in product lines that are increasingly complementary and that increasingly rely on transcontinental production networks. The European Union and China are also two of the three largest markets on earth. Both have grown sharply in economic scale over the past three decades—China through prodigious internal growth and the European Union through expansion from nine to twenty-eight members.

Unlike China and the United States, or Europe and the United States, China and the EU connect over land. Throughout most of recorded history, that has made little difference, as transportation and logistics across the continent were traditionally inefficient—compounded by the complexities of contentious continental politics. Over the past two decades, however, revolutionary, synergistic, and as yet little-noticed developments at the microeconomic level have laid the basis for much deeper transcontinental economic interaction between Northeast Asia and Europe than ever before. These disruptive changes are occurring in three interrelated areas: (1) geographical locus of production chains, (2) intermodal transport logistics, and (3) e-commerce. In the aggregate, they are drawing the manufacturing-oriented political economies of China and central Europe together as never before, tearing them away from previous transoceanic moorings, in an accelerating process of epochal geo-economic integration.

Most importantly, the manufacturing centers of continental Europe and China are drawing geographically closer, through the geo-economic process of "continental drift" discussed in Chapter 1. Since the end of the Cold War, German manufacturing production chains have reoriented to the east, driven by lower labor and real-estate costs in the Visegrad countries of central Europe (Poland, the Czech Republic, Hungary, and Slovakia).[59] Meanwhile, Chinese manufacturing has slowly begun to migrate westward, from coastal centers around Shanghai, Tianjin, and Guangzhou to interior provinces such as Sichuan and Shaanxi. As infrastructure and logistical connections have improved and transcontinental investment has surged, transcontinental supply chains have become more extensive and coherent—a tendency that could be greatly leveraged in future by e-commerce.

Auto and electronics firms operating in Germany and surrounding countries, especially the Visegrad nations, now produce over 20 percent of the world's automobiles. This dynamic Central European industrial complex is becoming a key global manufacturing base, focusing on precision machinery and chemicals as well as autos and electronics, that generates 42 percent of the European Union's entire manufacturing value-added exports.[60] This competitive cluster, drawing investment from throughout the world, is sourcing increasing quantities of components in China, while Chinese firms move up the value chain into Central Europe by acquiring German *Mittelstand* (small and medium-sized) manufacturers and robotics firms as well.[61] German logistics firms like DHL and DB Schenker Logistics, as well as massive Chinese intermodal transport conglomerates like COSCO and China Railway Corporation, compete to control railways and ports, with the BRI conferring major strategic advantages on the Chinese.[62]

Arctic Transit Routes There are, finally, also the transit routes from Northeast Asia to Europe across the Arctic seas, recently termed the "Polar Silk Road" by the Chinese government.[63] These routes are also shorter than the traditional maritime routes around the southern rim of Eurasia, and could be efficient if only frigid conditions did not block the way. Since 2011, there have been periodic commercial voyages—escorted by icebreakers—across the northern seas from Northeast Asia to Europe, with the first bulk carrier completing the passage in 2013.[64] As global warming proceeds across the Arctic, there are prospects that these Arctic routes could assume more importance in linking Europe and Asia, as discussed in Chapter 7. They may well give Russia leverage that it finds lacking in other sectors of trans-Eurasian transport, since roughly two-thirds of the most passable trans-Arctic route between Northeast Asian and Europe runs close to the Russian coastline, and Russia has by far the most experience and the best equipment for pursuing the Arctic route.

Finance as a Catalyst

Energy and the Logistics Revolution are clearly reconnecting the disparate parts of continental Eurasia in myriad new ways, facilitated by the explosive growth of China, the transformation of Europe, and the collapse of the Soviet Union. Yet even as these economic drivers open new potential forms of interdependence, physical realities of the vast Eurasian continent constrain the amount of actual commerce that can transpire. To reduce the tyranny of distance, there is a powerful need for new railways, pipelines, highways, and power grids that span the continent. Indeed, the Asian Development Bank (ADB) in 2017 estimated a need for $26 trillion in new infrastructural investment across Eurasia over the 2016–2030 period, or $1.7 trillion annually, with much of it falling in this transcontinental category.[65] The advent of China's BRI has intensified expectations for large-scale infrastructure spending still further.

The bottleneck—and potential catalyst—is finance. How can the resources be mobilized to provide the capital needed for Eurasia's growth? What new politics and institutions would be necessary to achieve this? Can existing institutions be expected to carry this burden, given the geopolitical implications involved?

A major start was made by multilateral institutions long before China's BRI appeared on the horizon. The ADB has been funding major regional connectivity projects since 1966, such as the Greater Mekong Subregion Southern Coastal Corridor Project[66] and the Turkmenistan-Afghanistan-Pakistan-India Natural Gas Pipeline (TAPI) Project.[67] The ADB's Central Asia Regional Economic Cooperation (CAREC) program, founded in 2001, is a partnership of eleven Eurasian developing countries, including China, as well as six multilateral development institutions. It has made $31.5 billion of investments across Central Asia, one-third of them funded by the ADB itself.[68] CAREC's focus is on electric-power transmission, multimodal transport networks, and border-clearance procedures, which can be negotiated more smoothly by multilateral institutions than national governments.

The World Bank, co-financing many of Eurasia's key infrastructure projects with CAREC and BRI-affiliated institutions, currently devotes 35 percent of its total lending to East and South Asia—a larger share than directed to any other global regions.[69] And the European Bank for Reconstruction and Development (EBRD), founded in 1991 to ease the post–Cold War transition, has also been active in promoting transcontinental connectivity within the successor states of the Soviet Union, including Central Asia, for nearly three decades. It is currently financing, among other projects, Kazakhstan's $7.5 billion Southwest Roads Project, to upgrade the International Transit Corridor between Western Europe and China, in cooperation with the World Bank, the ADB, the Islamic Development Bank, and the Kazakh government.[70]

There still, however, is a geopolitical dimension to international project finance in Eurasia that must be recognized, in order to understand the sea change now underway across the continent that has been giving Eurasia's reconnection unprecedented momentum since 2013. The principal policy lender globally has since the early post–World War II years been the World Bank, and the main regional lender since the mid-1960s has been the ADB—both dominated by the United States and secondarily by Japan. There have been attempts, such as the 1991 Northeast Asian Development Bank proposal of former Korean prime minister Nam Duck Woo, informally backed for years by the Korean government, to supplement this "Washington Consensus" structure.[71] Yet these revisionist proposals for many years invariably failed due to quiet opposition—or at least lack of enthusiasm—from traditionally dominant institutions, who pointed to potential dangers of moral hazard.

It is in this connection that the proposals by China (the Asian Infrastructure Investment Bank, AIIB) and the BRICS countries (the New Development Bank, NDB) are so interesting. These initiatives are grounded in the massive foreign-exchange reserves of China, totaling over $3 trillion when the proposals were formally made and supported by over $1.3 trillion in Chinese sovereign wealth funds and informal reserves.[72] Yet they also involve substantial cooperation from outside China, which will be crucial to the ultimate success of the BRI, given the ambitiousness of its developmental goals.

Questions remain about the transparency of the new institutions and their lack of working-level expertise. Their headquarters locations, in cities like Beijing and Shanghai as opposed to Hong Kong or other established global financial centers, may not be ideal in terms of market-oriented syndications, which could also ultimately be important in raising the huge sums that BRI in principle involves. Yet top leadership at these new institutions appears to be highly professional and dynamic. Indeed, three of the five vice presidents of the AIIB, including the corporate secretary, chief financial officer, and vice president for policy and strategy, are experienced European financiers.

Importantly, China's new initiatives have attracted the broad global support that earlier regionalist efforts, such as Korea's NEADB proposals of the 1990s, were unable to obtain. The acceptance process, however, was a tortuous one, which offers insights into how the global political economy is changing. The five-year evolution of the AIIB concept, so important now in stimulating the reconnection of Eurasia, is a revealing case in point.

The need for a multilateral institution based in Asia that would focus on infrastructure finance was first stressed by Prime Minister Wen Jiabao in his keynote to the Boao Forum for Asia in April 2009 as an internationally constructive way for China to use its massive foreign-exchange reserves to aid regional recovery in the shadow of the 2008 global financial crisis. Wen also concretely proposed a $10 billion China-ASEAN Fund on Investment Cooperation to support regional infrastructure cooperation.[73] Four years later, during the 2013 Boao Forum, former Chinese vice premier Zeng Peiyan reiterated the proposal for a multilateral development bank based in China, in the presence of US ambassador to China Gary Locke, who indicated casual personal interest. US Treasury officials reportedly discouraged Australia and South Korea informally from endorsing the concept, but President Xi of China proposed it formally in his Maritime Silk Road speech before the Indonesian parliament in October 2013. Chinese prime minister Li Keqiang reiterated that China was ready to intensify consultations in his April 2014 Boao keynote.[74]

The decisive international breakthrough came in early March 2015, when British chancellor of the exchequer George Osborne announced that the United Kingdom had decided to apply to join the AIIB. Within a few days Germany, France, Italy, and South Korea also applied.[75] On March 28, President Xi affirmed China's resolve to strengthen connectivity through the AIIB.[76] On January 16, 2016, the AIIB began actual operation, headquartered in Beijing with an initial capitalization of $100 billion, including $50 billion contributed by China.[77] During its first year, the AIIB funded nine projects in seven countries, worth over $1.7 billion.[78] By March 2017, the AIIB had received membership applications from all of the G-7 industrial nations except the United States and Japan, together with most of the developing world.[79] And Japan was growing increasingly conciliatory.

China has played a central role in realizing the originally Indian concept of a BRICS Development Bank, proposed in March 2013 at the fifth BRICS summit, in Durban, South Africa. A formal agreement to establish this bank, renamed the New Development Bank (NDB), with headquarters in Shanghai and holding an authorized capital of $100 billion, entered into force at the seventh BRICS summit in July 2015. A year later, in July 2016, the NDB board of governors held its first annual meeting in Shanghai.[80]

China has been active directly, of course, in equity investment and development finance, as well as through multilateral banking. Indeed, its own national contribution under BRI, a classic expression of "distributive globalism," is the most important single financial catalyst for the deepening integration of the Eurasian continent. Although at times criticized for furthering Chinese geopolitical interests and loading developing countries with excessive debt, it is undeniably transforming Eurasia, in both its overland and maritime dimensions.

At the end of 2014, China inaugurated the $40 billion Silk Road Fund (SRF), a state-owned investment entity, which pools resources from a variety of Chinese public and private institutions to support promising Eurasian infrastructural, industrial, and resource-development projects.[81] Seventy percent of its promised investments are in BRI participant countries and regions, focusing on energy, electric power, and communications; over 70 percent of these promised investments represent equity stakes.[82] The SRF cooperates closely with a panoply of Chinese domestic financial institutions, discussed in Chapter 5, including the China Development Bank, the Export-Import Bank of China, Sinosure, and the four major commercial banks, to support the BRI and thus connectivity across Eurasia. In 2018 the activities of these Chinese domestic consortia began drawing increasing international criticism for lack of transparency and for opportunistically exploiting local political-economic vulnerabilities. Such criticism came not only from predictable Western sources but also from Asian political leaders, such as Malaysia's Mahathir Mohamad.

Xi Jinping added further to the momentum of China's development finance initiatives at the inaugural Belt and Road Forum convened in Beijing during mid-May 2017. He announced that China would contribute an additional 100 billion yuan ($14.5 billion) to the infrastructure-oriented Silk Road Fund, and that the China Development Bank, together with the Export-Import Bank of China, would set up special lending plans worth 250 billion yuan and 130 billion yuan respectively to support BRI cooperation on infrastructure and industrial capacity.[83] World Bank president Jim Yong Kim also indicated that his institution would cooperate, potentially leveraging the BRI's financial initiatives still further.[84] In the scale of financial resources it deploys, the BRI already compares to the Marshall Plan of the late 1940s.[85] And due to the greater interdependence and sophistication of financial markets today, the ability of BRI to leverage its own resources and serve as catalyst for large, globally stimulative efforts is arguably even greater than that of the Marshall Plan seven decades ago, although it appears to operate much more narrowly in the interest of domestic firms than did its predecessor.

The story of Eurasian developmental finance is of course far from complete. In its first three years of operation, the AIIB began establishing itself as a credible multilateral institution, but one with a naturally more Eurasian continentalist bias than any predecessors. Its policy direction, supported by the NDB, the Silk Road Fund, and other China-related institutions, helped encourage other mainstream financial institutions, including the ADB, to focus more and more on Eurasian connectivity.[86] Project finance is thus now enabling the logic of Eurasian reconnection, already enhanced by the Logistics Revolution, to realize itself in unprecedented new ways.

In Conclusion

Eurasia has undergone a profound transformation over the past quarter century, becoming an increasingly integrated and interactive chessboard, albeit one on which important political, social, and economic differences still remain. The three most important drivers of this transformation have been energy, transit trade, and finance. Together, they have fostered deepening economic interdependence across Eurasia, including more concentrated transit trade and production networks linking China and Europe. These networks potentially hold long-term significance for global geopolitics, and for global governance as well.

In hydrocarbons, there are three important dimensions to Eurasian transcontinental interdependence: (1) between Asia and the Persian Gulf, (2) between Russia and Europe, and (3) between Asia and the FSU (both Russia and Central Asian energy producers like Turkmenistan and Kazakhstan). The deepening mutual interdependence of Asia and the Gulf has been the most dynamic. At the beginning of the twenty-first century, roughly half of the Gulf's oil flowed to Asia; by 2015 that ratio had risen to nearly 75 percent, due to rapid demand increases in China and the Gulf's vast capacity to supply. Asian dependence on the Gulf is also steadily rising—from around 30 to 50 percent in China as well as by smaller increments in Japan and Korea.

Asian growth, Gulf reserves, and compelling geographic logic will likely intensify this Persian Gulf-Northeast Asian interdependence in future, mitigated only by a potentially greater role for Russia in the Eurasian energy equation. Meanwhile, energy ties between the United States and Eurasia are complicated by the Shale Revolution, geopolitics, and geographical distance. Geography and geopolitics also complicate energy ties among the Gulf, Russia, and Europe.

Transit trade has become an important driver of Eurasian interdependence since the Lehman Shock, with new technology radically subverting the tyranny of distance. A geo-economically mandated "continental drift" that brings the locus of China's political economy westward, even as Europe's manufacturing center moves eastward, lays the groundwork for deeper east-west interaction. The growth of China, improved transcontinental infrastructure, deregulation, and the digitalization of logistics have all accelerated this process. Since the 2008 global financial crisis, overland transit trade as well as intermodal combined rail/air/maritime transport have begun to grow explosively. Total Kazakhstan rail freight trade, for example, totaled 12.6 million tons in 2008, but rose to 16.5 million in 2012, only four years later. By 2020, that rail traffic is expected to reach 30 million tons. Half of rail transit trade in 2020 will likely be westbound trade from China—nearly three times the share recorded in 2012.[87] And intermodal trade, exploiting the cost-effectiveness of maritime transport, as well as the geographic efficiencies of overland, is expanding also.

Innovations in finance have accelerated the integration process still further. Establishment of the Silk Road Fund in 2014, followed by the New Development Bank and the AIIB during 2015–2016, provide fresh sources of capital to fund the estimated $26 trillion of needed infrastructural investment for the 2016–2030 period, as noted above. Announcements at the May 2017 Belt and Road Forum expanded Chinese and multilateral commitments. Flows from global capital markets, through London, Hong Kong, and elsewhere, accelerate this process still further. In the political-economic sphere, transcontinental relations are additionally intensified by the 16+1 Forum, an initiative by China established in 2012 and aimed at intensifying cooperation among China, eleven EU member states, and five Balkan nations, in the fields of investment, transport, finance, science, education, and culture. This forum, involving an annual summit, provides China and the Central and Eastern European Countries (CEEC) with a useful platform for discussing common trade and regulatory issues generated in the process of deepening interdependence.[88] Financial transparency, especially regarding commercial dealings of Chinese domestic institutions abroad, remains an issue in countries like Malaysia, Sri Lanka, the Maldives, and Pakistan, but whether it will have substantial impact on actual BRI connectivity efforts remains to be seen.

Deepening energy ties, improved intermodal transport, and new financial institutions are thus enhancing prospects for Eurasian political-economic interdependence. New transcontinental political-economic networks are also facilitating that process. In the pages to come, we explore concretely how ties between China, on the one hand, as well as Russia and Europe, on the other, are deepening, followed by an assessment of what these deepening transcontinental ties mean for the world more generally.

5

Quiet Revolution in China

CHINA, AS OUR GEOGRAPHICAL ANALYSIS has suggested, has the latent potential to play a catalytic—although not exclusive—role in the political-economic reconnection of Eurasia. Half the distance from Shanghai to the eastern border of the European Union lies inside China, as does two-thirds of the distance from the Bohai Gulf to the Strait of Hormuz. China has also, across most of recorded history, been home to more people, a larger economy, and a more sophisticated material culture than any other Eurasian nation.

As early as the Han dynasty—over two thousand years ago—Chinese artifacts were finding their way to Europe, as we noted in Chapter 2. Yet remarkably few Chinese people ventured out along the Silk Road. China played no role at all in building elaborate thoroughfares abroad, as the Romans did. And few Chinese armies ventured abroad, except to subdue unruly barbarians threatening China itself. It was the Mongols—not the Chinese—who felt the lust for international power projection and conquest.

The dimensions and drivers of China's role in the broader world are much different today. What is distinctive this time is that twenty-first-century China has both the ability and the incentive to pursue regional *connectivity* with an intensity and an international intrusiveness that it has never exhibited before. China is now much larger economically than it has previously been. And it is reaching out, at last, to grasp the geo-economic potential implicit in its central position within Eurasia. Promoting connectivity through the panoply of distributive tools implicit in the Belt and Road Initiative (BRI) program both enhances China's role in Eurasia and bootstraps prosperity for the broader region. "Distributive globalism," in short, builds on the PRC's own recent economic success and encourages a proactive Chinese role in international affairs that the world has rarely seen before.

This chapter explores, from a historical perspective, the domestic forces that have driven China to pursue with increasing vigor and effectiveness Eurasia's reconnection over the past four decades. It begins by considering the impact of that great critical juncture, the Four Modernizations, on both Chinese growth and domestic interest group structure. It shows how China profoundly changed—from a static socialist economy through the 1970s to a growing export juggernaut in the 1980s and 1990s, with an expanding private sector. It then chronicles the subsequent transformation of China since the global financial crisis of 2008 into a much more internally driven infrastructure builder. In today's China, the Communist Party of China (CPC), the Peoples' Liberation Army (PLA), and state-owned heavy industrial firms in particular have strong incentives to pursue the reconnection of Eurasia, epitomized in the BRI of Xi Jinping.

The epic policy changes orchestrated by Deng Xiaoping, beginning at the climactic December 1978 CPC meetings, represented a historic directional shift in China's political-economic course. They provoked a quantum leap in the country's economic magnitude, with fateful implications for the broader world. Such changes could not, of course, reorient China overnight. It was, instead, the economic growth unleashed through the incentive shifts created by the Four Modernizations, combined with policy fine-tuning over three decades and more, that finally converted Deng's creative new policy line into the sharply more proactive, continental, influential, and increasingly globalist China that we encounter on the world stage today.

The Four Modernizations were national objectives first set out definitively by Deng Xiaoping to strengthen four sectors of the Chinese economy: agriculture, industry, national defense, and science/technology. These goals had their origins well before the Cultural Revolution—actually around 1964—in the development-oriented pronouncements of Zhou Enlai, who reiterated their importance again in 1975 shortly before his death.[1] The Four Modernizations were far sighted and visionary—designed to make China a major global economic power, but only by the early twenty-first century.

By the early 1980s, Chinese economic growth was already surging into double digits—a pattern fated to persist for three decades and more. China's economy jumped from twelfth largest in the world in 1980, according to World Bank nominal GDP calculations, to second by 2010.[2] Over the three decades from 1980 to 2010, China's overall economy expanded more than

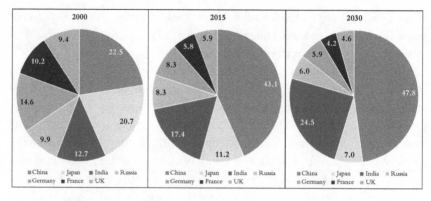

FIGURE 5.1   China's rising share among major Eurasian economies

SOURCES: World Bank, "GDP, PPP (Constant 2011 International $), *World Development Indicators*, accessed September 28, 2018; and PwC, "The Long View: How Will the Global Economic Order Change by 2050?" February 2017, Table 2: Projected Rankings of Economies Based on GDP at PPPs (in Constant 2016 $bn).
NOTE: Figures are for shares of the total GDP, expressed in PPP terms, of the major Eurasian economies—China, Japan, India, Russia, Germany, France, and the United Kingdom.

thirty-fold. This expansion has sharply outpaced economic growth elsewhere in the region, leading to steady growth in China's share of the total economy. As indicated in Figure 5.1, China's portion of the Eurasian economy in purchasing power parity (PPP) terms rose from 22.5 percent of the whole in 2000 to 43.1 percent in 2015, with that share expected to increase further— to 47.8 percent by 2030.

The Changing Profile of Chinese Growth

For the first two decades, in particular, much of this high-speed growth was export led, as indicated in Figure 5.2, and focused on coastal provinces like Guangdong, to which Deng Xiaoping and Xi Zhongxun gave special attention in reforms surrounding Deng's fateful 1992 Southern Tour. During the three decades after Guangdong and Fujian were granted special status, Chinese exports had multiplied over one hundred times, from less than $10 billion annually in 1978 to more than $1 trillion in 2007—more than one-third of which originated in Guangdong.[3] There was a heavy initial emphasis on exports to Japan and Europe that spread during the 1990s to the United States as well. The Association of Southeast Asian Nations (ASEAN) also emerged during the 2000s as a major Chinese export destination, passing Japan in 2009 as China's largest export market in Asia.

Foreign multinationals, which handled more than half of China's exports, also played a major initial role in spurring Chinese growth. After the mid-2000s,

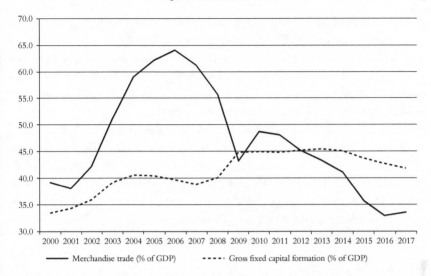

FIGURE 5.2 From exports to a domestic driver—changing demand structure in the Chinese economy (2000–2017)

SOURCE: World Bank, "Merchandise Trade (% of GDP)" and "Gross Fixed Capital Formation (% of GDP)," *World Development Indicators*, accessed October 22, 2018.

however, this foreign dimension gradually declined in relative importance, as the geographic sphere of China's growth broadened westward, beyond eastern coastal areas into China's vast interior, with domestic demand gaining greater salience. In 2006, the share of merchandise trade in China's GDP peaked at 64 percent. Since then, this share has steadily declined, to below 35 percent by 2017. Conversely, gross fixed capital formation's share in GDP has steadily risen—from 33 percent in 2000 to 42 percent in 2017, highlighted by a sharp 5 percent increase in 2009, as China's mammoth stimulus package came on stream.

The Rise of Private Enterprise

Across the first four decades of China's economic reforms, the role of private firms and collectives in the economy steadily continued to expand. State-owned enterprises (SOEs), to be sure, continued to dominate the commanding heights of the economy in strategically important sectors such as shipping (COSCO), rail transport (CRRC and CR), energy (CNPC), and telecommunications (China Mobile). Collective enterprises with a mixed public-private character, such as Huawei in mobile communications, played important public policy roles. Such government-favored companies enjoyed preferential access to both equity markets and bank lending; indeed, they continue to dominate such markets for capital.

Purely private firms, to be sure, are steadily continuing to grow—even more rapidly than the SOEs. As much as 70 percent of firm-level investment in China is financed by retained earnings, since private firms do not enjoy the access accorded SOEs to capital markets.[4] Such Chinese firms, however, dramatically outperform SOEs in return on assets, as Nicholas Lardy points out. Indeed, between 2010 and 2014 the gap between the rate of return achieved by private firms and that recorded by SOEs was almost 3 to 1.[5]

Dynamic private and semiprivate firms, such as Alibaba, Huawei, Tencent, and JD.com are thus an increasingly important part of the domestic political economy. Their profitability gives them a measure of economic independence. Several have growing global competitiveness, and their relationship to Chinese industrial strategy and the BRI will be a matter of worldwide interest in the years ahead.

Industrial Policy as a Driver

Even as the Chinese political economy has moved away from socialism and private interests have grown stronger, a more strategic and dirigiste variant of state action has also appeared, especially since the mid-2000s. In 2006 China announced its new "Indigenous Innovation" policy to promote local research and development, together with technology-intensive industries. This dirigisme rapidly led to a confrontation with Japan and the United States, as China escalated demands on foreign firms, stepping up antimonopoly enforcement and discriminatory procurement practices against those who did not comply.[6] At the same time, China continued to maintain strict controls on international data and financial flows to and from the PRC, preventing US internet firms such as Facebook and Google from operating freely in the country. The Chinese government thus pursued a mixed strategy that both exploited market dynamism and protected strategic or politically sensitive sectors.

In 2015 China's State Council released "Made in China 2025," the Ministry of Industry and Information Technology (MIIT)'s blueprint for strategically upgrading its manufacturing industry. This plan focused on the development of ten industries, including next-generation information technology, robotics, and automobiles powered by alternate energy.[7] The program, recently deemphasized formally in the face of foreign criticism, is supported by subsidies from government-run investment funds.[8] It is in many ways synergistic with the ambitious connectivity programs embodied in the BRI, especially in the transportation and telecommunications areas.[9] Another key element of recent Chinese industrial policy has been providing a favorable environment for "new economy" enterprises in e-commerce.[10]

Finance: Enhanced Fire Power for Connectivity

However desirable Eurasian connectivity might be for China from a long-term geostrategic or geo-economic standpoint, market mechanisms do not naturally generate such an outcome. Government financial support, in concert with industrial policy, has played a central role in generating that connectivity. To understand the immense potential of China's ambitious connectivity programs like BRI—and their vulnerabilities—it is therefore crucial to grasp the financial base on which they stand, and to see that base from a comparative perspective.

Four aspects of China's financial situation today are crucial. First, the PRC is a huge country—the second-biggest economy in the world in nominal terms, and now the largest in PPP GDP, at $21.2 trillion.[11] Growing at over 6 percent annually in real terms, it continues to have massive developmental needs, but also huge potential.[12]

Second, China's fiscal situation is quite good at the national level. Its public debt in 2017 was only 47.8 percent of GDP, compared to 82.3 percent in the United States, or 236.4 percent of GDP in neighboring Japan.[13] And China's prospective national-government revenue growth over the next decade is likely much higher than either. To be sure, transparency is relatively poor in China, while local governments and SOEs may have some large concealed debts. Yet China appears to have both fiscal slack and the largest foreign-exchange reserves in the world, which can and are used flexibly to support government strategic objectives, at home and abroad.[14]

Third, China has more effective means of raising revenue for state purposes than any other major nation, for both structural and political reasons. On the structural side, it relies heavily on value-added taxes (VAT)—like the Europeans and increasingly Japan, but in contrast to the United States, which relies much more heavily on income taxes. VAT raises huge amounts of revenue in small increments. They can be difficult to adjust for political reasons in democratic systems, as Japan's efforts of the past four decades have shown, but China is a soft-authoritarian system of more limited transparency, where VAT adjustments should be easier to implement.

Finally, China has a variety of institutions well suited to state-led economic action, many of which Europe and Japan—not to mention the United States—abandoned years ago. China has, for example, the off-budget financing mechanisms such as postal savings, a state-controlled fiscal investment and savings program that Japan largely abandoned during the Koizumi years (2001–2006). To be sure, such systems have weaknesses in a volatile, market-oriented world, which will be discussed shortly, but the reality that the Chinese state has massive resources to deploy, both at home and abroad, must not be forgotten.

One of the key institutions for explicitly furthering interdependence is the China Development Bank (CDB, founded 1994), which now has provenance of a quarter century. CDB, with total assets close to RMB 16 trillion (around $2.3 trillion), is now the largest development lender in the entire world, substantially exceeding the World Bank.[15] China's major government and semigovernmental banks, as well as sovereign wealth funds, have strongly supported these new investment vehicles. Indeed, the CDB alone has loaned more than $110 billion to BRI countries.[16] And the Big Four state-owned commercial banks have lent at least $150 billion more.[17] In addition, the China Securities Regulatory Commission has approved applications from seven domestic and foreign companies to issue a combined 50 billion yuan of "Belt and Road" bonds through the Shanghai and Shenzhen stock exchanges.[18]

Since the advent of the BRI, there has also been a further rapid proliferation of new institutions to support connectivity, including the Silk Road Fund (SRF, 2014) and the Asian Infrastructure Investment Bank (AIIB, 2016). Several targeted regional investment funds have also been established, most of them financing equity investments by Chinese firms. The first two of these, the China-Africa Development Fund and the Russia-China Investment Fund, had their start before the BRI's formal inauguration, but several others have emerged since. These investment vehicles include the China-Central and Eastern Europe Investment Fund (November 2013), cosponsored by the Export-Import Bank of China and the Hungarian Export-Import Bank, as well as the Russia-China RMB Cooperation Fund (July 2017), jointly funded by the China Development Bank and the Russian Direct Investment Fund.[19]

The two conspicuous risks that the Chinese state-dominated financial system presents to global finance are the converse of its strengths. The system is, precisely because it is a creature of the Chinese state, vulnerable to moral hazard. Japan saw the consequences of such a system in the late 1990s, amid the Asian financial crisis, after its administered credit system was opened to the world. For related structural reasons, the contemporary Chinese financial system is not good at credit assessment—a problem sometimes compounded by political pressures for problematic lending, both within China and in host nations. Such pressures have led to a rash of credit scandals, sometimes involving favoritism to host governments to undertake economically dubious projects, as recently revealed in Malaysia, Sri Lanka, Pakistan, and elsewhere.

Western and Japanese banks do seem to have continuing interest in the BRI, despite the obvious risk that some projects may present. Foreign banks focus on providing foreign exchange, trade finance, interest-rate swaps, and cash management to multinational firms working on BRI projects. Citigroup, for example, had led large bond issues for the Bank of China and Beijing Gas to finance their BRI plans. It has also landed cash management and foreign-exchange hedging contracts for several Fortune 500 companies operating on BRI projects. Standard Chartered has similarly won twenty BRI-linked financing deals over the past four years, including a $200 million loan for a Bangladeshi electricity utility being built by a Chinese consortium and a $42 million export-credit facility for a Sri Lankan gas terminal guaranteed by China.[20]

Toward Continentalism and Distributive Globalism

Many nations, including Japan, Korea, and even the United States, have pursued industrial policy in various dimensions, often relating it to national security. What is distinctive about today's China is the way it has systematically related such strategic efforts to infrastructure development on a continental scale. This pattern has flourished under Xi Jinping through the BRI, but it has much deeper roots—at least two decades before Xi came to power.

Another distinctive aspect of the Chinese approach is the way it resolves the inherent tension between industrial policy, by its nature nationalistic, and the broader imperative of international coexistence. China strives to do this by retaining explicit barriers in some strategic sectors such as IT, Internet services, and finance, while allaying foreign opposition by providing distributive benefits to partner nations, in the form of infrastructure, target loans, and strategic purchases—in a word, through "distributive globalism."

Distributive globalism only emerged as conscious policy in China quite recently, as the country's deep involvement with the international economy necessitated a policy response to liberal globalism. Yet active public works spending has a long history as a valued policy approach. Measures to accelerate domestic demand through construction of roads, railroads, dams, and electric-power grids became important supplements to the export drive of Deng's early Four Modernizations, beginning in the mid-1990s. In 1994, for example, important tax policy changes initiated by the State Council centralized most tax collections to the central government, save income from land rentals, while continuing to hold local governments responsible for the bulk of social welfare provision.[21]

This historic expansion of unfunded mandates rendered local governments increasingly dependent on real estate development for the revenue needed to satisfy local needs. That powerful incentive to increase revenue gave them strong motivation to build infrastructure and also to demand that the central government expand infrastructure spending, which could in turn inflate local land prices. The basis was thus laid for a construction-oriented engine of economic growth, also operating in high-growth Asian economies like Japan and Korea of an earlier age. That public-works bias has morphed since the 2008 global financial crisis into the massive, infrastructure-driven stimulus programs epitomized in the BRI of Xi Jinping.

The rise and transformation of the Chinese steel industry from the 1990s to the present shows graphically the political-economic forces that have transformed the maritime, light-industrial China of the early Four Modernizations into the more muscular, ambidextrous, and continentalist China of the BRI era. In 1978, China produced only one-third as much steel as either the US or Japan, amounting to just 4.4 percent of the global total.[22] Before the Asian financial crisis, China had reached par with both, becoming the largest steel producer in the world during 1996.[23] By 2015, China was producing nearly *eight times* as much steel as Japan, and close to *ten times* as much as the US.[24] Indeed, China today accounts for half of the entire world's crude steel production, at around 49.6 percent; Japan is second, but with only 6.5 percent of the global total.[25]

China's shift from deficit to surplus in its steel trade with the world was even more dramatic. As indicated in Figure 5.3, China was a net importer of 35 million tons annually as late as 2003. By 2005, however, it had become a net exporter, and in 2006 it passed Japan to become the world's largest steel exporter.[26] By 2015 the PRC was exporting over 110 million tons/year, accounting for nearly a quarter of the entire world's steel exports.[27] At least half of this export total was flowing to other destinations in Asia—particularly Korea and Southeast Asia—with less than 1 percent going to the United States.[28] China's steel exports are thus a significant global issue, but exports to the US only appear to be a small piece of the overall picture.

Policy changes *within* China—related to, but following incrementally from the Four Modernizations—have played a central role in the explosion of Chinese steel production, and ultimately exports, since the 1990s. First of all, there were national government subsidies to steel, defined as a strategic industry in National Development and Reform Commission documents. Local governments, however, greatly magnified the impact of original national policy by provision of energy and land at sharply below-market prices.[29] And

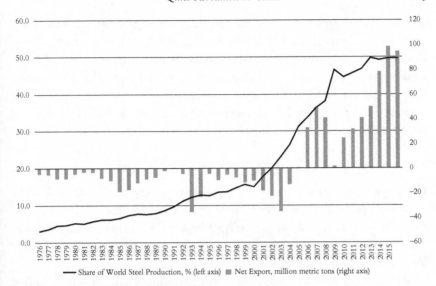

FIGURE 5.3 China's steel overcapacity

SOURCES: World Steel Association, "Total Production of Crude Steel," "Exports of Semi-finished and Finished Steel Products," and "Imports of Semi-finished and Finished Steel Products," *Steel Statistical Yearbook*, 1986, 1996, 2006, 2016, and 2017 editions.

the steel producers were SOEs, uninhibited by potential losses due to over-expansion.

The local tax system in China, as described above, gives local governments strong incentives to lure industry to their jurisdictions and to build related infrastructure for industrial parks. Steel, given the large scale of investment involved, the jobs provided, and the traditionally bright market prospects due to infrastructure demand, was for years a favored local-government target. The same incentive structure makes consolidation of capacity among conflicting jurisdictions difficult, even as overcapacity clearly emerges within China as a whole. In 2002 China's steel industry capacity utilization ratio was 95 percent; by 2015 it had fallen to under 71 percent.[30]

Excess capacity in China—a deepening problem since the early 2010s—perversely intensifies pressure on individual firms both to expand production domestically and to export. It also increases incentives to export in policy-supported fashion to non-Western markets, as under the BRI. China today has around four million steel workers—over 60 percent of the global total. Removing 200 million tons of overcapacity in China—which the PRC argu-ably has—could result in job losses of 800,000 workers and a negative eco-nomic impact of over $150 billion, according to one 2013 Morgan Stanley analysis.[31] The impact would likely be concentrated geographically in northern Rust Belt provinces like Hebei, Shanxi, and Liaoning, located close to Beijing. Quite clearly, an expansionist, neo-Keynesian approach to this overcapacity, involving accelerated global construction activities under the BRI, is politically preferable inside China to retrenchment—for related sectors like mining, nonferrous metals, and machinery production, as well as for the steel sector itself.

Microperspectives on Eurasian Reconnection

Geography endows China with a latent opportunity to reconnect Eurasia. Economic growth, as we have seen, sharply enhances that capability in historically unprecedented ways, leveraged by China's growing financial power and ability to access international financial markets. Yet whatever the *capability*, the *intentions* are also crucial.

We have already noted the deepening intentions of government industrial strategists to pursue Eurasian connectivity. We will, of course, soon consider the role of national leadership in the following section, and have just seen the powerful *sectoral* incentives that prevail in the steel industry. There are also important drivers among interest groups and business firms, as we shall see below.

Interest Group Pressures

Beyond heavy industry and local governments themselves, other growth-oriented yet politically conservative establishment groups have gained powerful stakes since the 1990s in a continentalist, domestically driven growth path for China. The PLA has naturally supported improved national infrastructure, including high-speed communications and transportation linking Beijing to outlying areas of the country and beyond, on national security grounds. Given China's geo-economic prominence in south-central Asia and its rising political-economic leverage, deepened continental and maritime connectivity with surrounding nations naturally has strategic attractions for the PLA. The historical role of paramilitary units such as the Xinjiang Production and Construction Corps (*Bingtuan* in Chinese) in the economic development of Xinjiang, where construction battalions were important in the early post-revolutionary days, no doubt deepens the attraction.[32] The ruling CPC—like the veteran ruling parties of neighbors like Japan—also sees large distributive expenditures on roads, rail, and air transport as attractive tools for reinforcing domestic stability as well. Broadly speaking, the ordered, organized,

state-dependent environment prevailing in many parts of China's interior, especially during its developmental phase, is congenial to established political
groups in China, inclining them to be supportive of the continentalist policies
pursued continuously by Chinese leaders since Jiang Zemin.

National Champions and Eurasian Connectivity

Individual firms are both the agents and the drivers of government policy,
including Beijing's current campaign to reconnect Eurasia, epitomized by the
BRI. Due to China's complex transition from socialism to a mixed economy
over the past four decades, business firms take a broad variety of organiza-
tional forms, exhibiting varied incentives. To understand the grassroots forces
that are animating Chinese business as it confronts the challenge of Eurasian
reconnection, it is useful to consider the behavior and incentives of various
types of firms.

We consider here three varieties of Chinese national champion—all currently involved in supporting the BRI. China Ocean Shipping Company
(COSCO) is an old-school state-owned enterprise. Huawei is, formally
speaking, a collective, ostensibly owned and managed by its employees. Alibaba is a private company. They operate in complementary ways and sub-
scribe to different strategic goals, yet all support the Chinese government in
promoting the reconnection of Eurasia.

The Chinese government employs a variety of specific tactics to encourage
cooperation by these individual firms. One approach, especially important for
"new economy" firms, is protection against foreign competition. A second is
subsidies in targeted areas, such as batteries, electric vehicles, and telecommunications. A third tool is manipulation of corporate vulnerabilities. Alibaba,
for example, is listed on the New York Stock Exchange through a complex
shareholding structure of questionable legality.[33] Were it to run afoul of the
Chinese state, the company would be highly vulnerable. Beijing's selective
use of anticorruption policy also forces successful private entrepreneurs to
stay on their toes.

Broadly speaking, the Chinese government offers national champions—
both public and private, whose interests it considers promoting—a strategic
bargain. The firms are protected against foreign entry into one of the largest markets in the world, in return, first of all, for conformity with Beijing's
domestic political agenda. Those firms are expected to invest domestically in
strategic sectors while also investing overseas in strategic locations that are of
special interest to national policy. Thus, these national champions are offered

prosperity in return for dynamically serving broader governmental interests—
in the current context, that means support for the BRI.

Of the three enterprises, COSCO's involvement with the reconnection of
Eurasia is clearest and least ambiguous. The firm is a venerable state-owned
enterprise, founded in 1961, that has achieved massive scale through policy-
driven mergers. Its current form dates from 2016, when COSCO and China
Shipping, the two largest SOEs in mainland China's shipping industry, were
merged. In 2017 the merged company, with roots in Beijing and Shanghai
respectively, acquired Orient Overseas International, the large shipping line
of Hong Kong's well-known Tung family.[34] COSCO is now the third largest
container shipping company in the world, with both powerful political ties in
Beijing and Hong Kong's cosmopolitan business expertise.[35]

COSCO has become one of the most prominent cornerstone enterprises
of both the Belt and the Road. It famously acquired, in 2016, the Port of Piraeus in Greece, which once home-ported a US aircraft carrier, and in 2017
also purchased a 24.5 percent stake in the massive Khorgos dry-port on the
border of Xinjiang and Kazakhstan.[36] COSCO likewise owns a controlling
stake in Spanish terminal operator Noatum,[37] as well as a 35 percent stake in
Rotterdam's Euromax port.[38] It has also invested $400 million in the expansion
of Abu Dhabi's Khalifa port, giving the UAE central government based in Abu
Dhabi a competitive alternative to Dubai.[39] COSCO's operations clearly facilitate maritime, overland, and multimodal trade throughout Eurasia, helping
make the continent's reconnection a deepening reality by both land and sea.

COSCO is representative, but by no means the only major state enterprise
involved centrally with the BRI. Another big player is China Communications Construction Company (CCCC), the BRI's largest contractor, involved
with 700 projects in more than 100 countries, at a value of more than $100
billion.[40] CCCC also ranked in 2017 as the largest transportation infrastructure construction company in the world.[41] Its projects range from Chinese
military bases in the South China Sea to the Hambantota Port and Colombo
Port City projects in Sri Lanka. They are heavy consumers of the Chinese-
made steel that now accounts for half of global production.

Another major BRI-related SOE, increasingly active outside China as well
as within, is China Railway Corporation (CR), the most heavily used rail
company in the world, servicing more than 1.7 billion passengers in 2017.[42]
CR, with more than two million employees, operates over two-thirds of the
world's high-speed rail track, and carried more than half of the world's HSR
passengers by 2015.[43] The company also carries freight to fifteen European
cities, including Madrid, Hamburg, and London, and is supplied with trains

by CRRC Corporation Limited (CRRC), the largest rolling-stock manufacturer in the world, and also a Chinese SOE.[44]

A second variety of Chinese national champion, Huawei, was founded in 1987 and is officially structured as an employee-owned collective It is considered close to the Chinese military, which has led to complex relations with US regulators. Formally, Huawei is a fairly straightforward private company, controlled by its founder and his hand-picked managers. It has, however, risen to become the largest telecommunications equipment maker in the world and the third-largest cell-phone producer,[45] with the strong support of the Chinese government, and is a key player in China's digital-communications connectivity efforts. Despite controversies regarding its international role, the firm nevertheless recorded revenues of $92 billion in 2017, 50 percent of which came from outside China.[46] Large loans from the leading state-owned banks as well as government subsidies for research have been central to its development.

Huawei has focused single-mindedly in its business strategy on building transcontinental mobile telephony relations with Europe.[47] Indeed, over 35 percent of its total sales in 2017 were in Europe, representing three-quarters of its international total, with a special concentration in East and Central Europe, where it outsells Apple.[48] Huawei operates large research centers in Sweden and Russia, and an innovation center for supercomputing in Poland.[49] In total, it has over 10,000 employees in Europe, including 1,570 across its eighteen R&D centers there, and plays a central role in the increasingly important "Digital Silk Road" across the continent.[50]

These European research ties helped make Huawei the second-largest filer of patent applications in the world during 2016.[51] Since 2009 it has placed special emphasis in its European research on advanced 5G technology, where together with Qualcomm, Nokia, and Ericsson it is one of the world leaders.[52] It also collaborates closely with the Europeans in setting telecommunications equipment standards, complicating the task of US majors through such trans-Eurasian collaboration.[53]

Alibaba, a third variety of national champion, was founded in 1999 by Jack Ma, a former English teacher with extraordinary vision and drive.[54] From the start, it had significant foreign support, particularly through investment by Goldman Sachs and Softbank.[55] The Chinese government indirectly supported it in its early struggle with eBay, which supported its payments system, while at times placing obstacles in the way of eBay's alternative. This state backing apparently represented, however, more a broad government policy of limiting foreign access to the financial sector rather than targeted support for Alibaba. This firm succeeded in the Chinese market in the face of fierce domestic competition through creative corporate strategies. Indeed, its innovative Alipay system of e-based credit, as well as its Yu'ebao money market fund with attractive consumer deposit rates, undermined the UnionPay system of the state-owned banks and is leading China into a cashless credit age.[56]

Alibaba, one of the world's preeminent e-commerce firms, is intrinsically in the business of interconnection. Its core e-commerce business still provides 86 percent of its revenue, and only 8 percent comes from international markets.[57] It is, however, expanding rapidly in Southeast Asia and India and will likely be a powerful figure in reconnecting the Eurasian continent in future years. Indeed, Alibaba's international commerce retail business expanded 94 percent in fiscal 2018, primarily due to the acquisition of Lazada (as part of Alibaba's Southeast Asian expansion strategy) and AliExpress (Alibaba's global online retail service).

Given Alibaba's ambiguous international legal standing and heavy reliance on Chinese government regulatory discretion, it can be expected to cooperate closely with Beijing suasion, despite being an innovative private firm. Domestically, Alibaba is already one of the firms trialing a government-initiated "social credit" system for assessing the behavior of individuals, while its work on big data and cloud computing has major potential for boosting government surveillance and data collection capabilities. Internationally, Alibaba founder Jack Ma, although not involved in any formal Chinese political activity, has been a prominent international spokesman for President Xi's global economic initiatives, including the BRI. Ma met with president-elect Donald Trump just before Trump's inauguration, for example, to discuss ways of promoting US small-business exports through e-commerce.[58] And he spoke again in support of President Xi's initiatives at the 2018 Davos World Economic Forum meetings.[59] Through its e-commerce activities, Alibaba is continually promoting a next-generation version of the BRI.[60]

Taken together, the three types of Chinese national champions—SOEs, government-supported private firms, and employee-owned collectives—all play central, if varied, roles in deepening Eurasian connectivity. COSCO is a dominant transcontinental player in shipping, both by sea and increasingly on land. China Railway and CRRC play complementary roles in passenger rail and rolling-stock supply, with CRCC providing railroad design and construction. Huawei and Alibaba focus on enhancing digital connectivity. Through its national champions, China thus occupies many of the commanding heights in the deepening economic interaction that is finessing cultural and political barriers to quietly give concrete substance to an emerging Super Continent.

Regional Dimensions and Related Constraints

Across the first two decades of China's reforms (1978–1999), economic growth was heavily concentrated along China's east coast, particularly from Tianjin south to Guangdong. Even today, over 80 percent of China's exports, as well as close to half of its industrial production and total output are concentrated in only five coastal provinces and three municipalities.[61] These coastal areas were the primary beneficiaries of export-oriented industrialization and the emergence of a market-oriented economy in China, although the massive post-2008 public-works programs including the BRI have redressed the balance marginally in favor of inland areas.

Climate also imposes some natural constraints on a continentalist orientation in China. More than 90 percent of China's people live east of a 15-inch annual rainfall line, stretching diagonally from northeast Manchuria to the Myanmar border. Some economically promising noncoastal areas such as Sichuan, eastern Gansu, and Yunnan lie east of that line, but more than half of China's territory in the west does not. Climate thus poses important material challenges to China's westward expansion that cannot be ignored.

A Struggle for Strategy

Despite climatic constraints and private-sector preferences, however, Chinese public policy has stressed western development ever since enunciation of Jiang Zemin's western policy in 1999, both for national-security reasons and to reduce rising income differentials between the coast and the interior. Domestic pressures from inland local governments and heavy industry have reinforced this bias, as suggested above. Western development policies have also attracted support from the PLA and the CPC, who both play more central roles in interior western provinces than in coastal, more market-oriented local economies. The PLA-N, China's navy, has been energized, however, by a renewed emphasis on maritime issues under President Xi Jinping in both the South China Sea and under the Maritime Road proposals initiated in late 2013. All these considerations have amplified domestic support for the BRI in both its continental and its maritime dimensions.

The Road builds on China's existing strengths in maritime trade and among the extensive ethnic Chinese community of Southeast Asia. It supports the economic agenda of important export-heavy areas of Southeastern China, like Guangdong and Fujian, which themselves have had longstanding historical trade ties with Southeast Asia. Over the past several hundred years, those ties have been much more consistent than China's relations with

Central Asia and across the Eurasian continent. The Belt, by contrast, is the more geopolitically visionary of the two programs, and arguably the more forward looking. It builds on a powerful complex, not only of party and military ties, but also of new SOE and corporate drivers that have emerged with considerable momentum since the global financial crisis of 2008, as we have seen.

The Catalytic Role of Leadership

A series of far-sighted leadership initiatives, building on the Four Modernizations, and the tax policy changes of the 1990s reflected the foregoing logic and intensified the Eurasian continentalist dimension of the Chinese political economy across the first two decades of the twenty-first century. First, Jiang Zemin initiated his infrastructure-based western development policies in 1999, intended to offset regional imbalances with the coast that had previously emerged. Hu Jintao, who had served in Tibet and other depressed inland regions including Gansu and Guizhou, continued along this line during his tenure (2002–2012), supported by Wen Jiabao, who had also served in Gansu. Hu's massive $586 billion stimulus plan, launched in the shadow of the 2008 global financial crisis and heavily oriented toward developing inland infrastructure,[62] was an especially powerful stimulus to both domestic growth and trans-Eurasian continentalism, as we shall see more extensively in the following chapter.

The most energetic and visionary continentalist initiatives, however, have been taken by Xi Jinping, building on the increasingly intricate and technically advanced domestic infrastructure initiated under his predecessor Hu Jintao. In September 2013, as is well known, Xi announced the Silk Road Economic Belt initiative, followed by his visionary Twenty-First-Century Maritime Silk Road address in Indonesia the following month. During 2014–2016, China followed up with a series of institutional initiatives—most notably establishment of the AIIB in January 2016—that gave concrete political-economic substance to Xi's pronouncements in both their continental and maritime dimensions. At the end of 2016, the BRI involved almost $300 billion in outstanding loans or equity investment—roughly three times the scale of the Marshall Plan in 2016 dollars.[63] Of this total, around $150 billion, or nearly half, was provided by China's Big Four state-owned banks, $110 billion by the China Development Bank, and only smaller amounts as yet by the new BRI-related policy institutions.[64]

Following the accession of most European nations to the AIIB in 2015, and even Canada in 2017,[65] Xi's initiatives began to have not just regional but ultimately global implications. These were dramatically manifest in the Belt and Road Forum for International Cooperation of May 14–15, 2017. It was attended by leaders of twenty-nine nations, in addition to the host, Xi Jinping.

The visitors included many Eurasian heads of government as well as prominent figures from Africa, Latin America, and the major global multilateral organizations. From the industrialized world, there was a special concentration of top leaders from Central, Eastern, and Southern Europe, including heads of state and government from Serbia, Greece, Italy, the Czech Republic, and Hungary. Seven of ten ASEAN governmental leaders, as well as three of five from Central Asia, also participated. UN secretary general Antonio Guterres, president of the World Bank Jim Yong Kim, and IMF managing director Christine Lagarde also attended the forum.[66]

At the May 2017 Belt and Road Forum itself, China announced several new deliverables. First, the China Development Bank is to introduce a Belt and Road Multicurrency Lending Scheme for Industrial Cooperation (RMB 100 billion equivalent) and an additional credit line for overseas financial institutions (RMB 50 billion). In addition, the Export-Import Bank of China is setting up parallel facilities to those of the China Development Bank, with almost equivalent scale.[67]

Implications for Eurasian Interdependence

Before the Four Modernizations, China was an island unto itself—massive but economically static and self-absorbed. The modernizations and the ensuing growth surge that they inspired radically transformed this equation, laying the basis for a domestic Chinese Crossover Point. With high-speed development, China—like Japan before it—began to rapidly outstrip its substantial domestic resource basis and grew at once increasingly import dependent and simultaneously more export oriented. That export orientation in turn shifted from a maritime, regional focus to an approach much more ambidextrous, continental, muscular, and ultimately global.

The initial international impact of the Four Modernizations, as noted above, was to deepen interdependence with Southeast Asia and with the United States—both traditional Chinese export markets—in preference to other parts of the world. Dependence on the US market rose higher, to its peak in 2002. Then gradually the dependence of other nations on China grew increasingly salient, even as the trade dependence of China and other nations on the United States began to wane.

China's prominence is also advancing steadily through its major bilateral relationships in Asia, including those with several of America's principal allies. This trend is especially pronounced in South Korea, which in 2017 traded more with China than it did with the United States and Japan combined.[68] China has become the largest trading partner of such US Pacific allies as Australia, New Zealand, Japan, the Philippines, and Thailand. This pattern has recently been extending still further across the Eurasian continent—to Saudi Arabia, and—in 2016—to Germany, Europe's largest economy. As noted in Figure 5.4, the US-China volume gap in trade with virtually all these countries has widened sharply since China's accession to the WTO in 2001.

A secondary effect of the Four Modernizations was energy-driven interdependence with continental Eurasia. This intensified greatly after 2000,

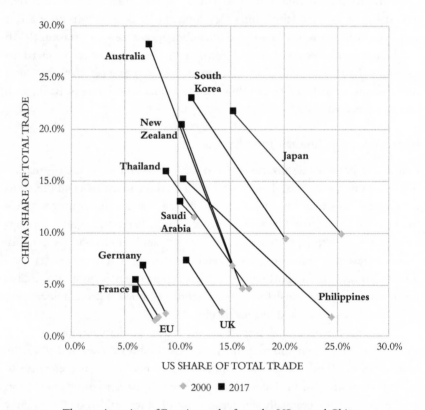

FIGURE 5.4 The reorientation of Eurasian trade: from the US toward China

SOURCE: International Monetary Fund, *Direction of Trade Statistics* (2000, 2017), accessed June 11, 2018.

NOTE: This figure compares trade shares of selected Eurasian partner countries with the US and China (2000 vs. 2017).

becoming central to China's subsequent relations with the world, even as dependence on America began to wane. Since late 1993, China's previous long-standing oil export surplus has evolved into a massive deficit of over 8 million barrels of oil per day, surpassing the US as the largest crude oil importer in the world for 2017.[69] Nearly 70 percent of all the oil that China consumes is now imported, and prospects are strong that China will import 80 percent of its oil needs by 2040.[70] The US Department of Energy forecasts that the United States will be a net energy exporter by 2022 or earlier.[71] This historic transformation has propelled a spiraling and unprecedented Chinese hydrocarbon dependence on continental Eurasia—the Middle East, Russia, and Central Asia—that is being complemented by broadening nonenergy relationships with these Eurasia neighbors as well.

A third crucial long-term implication of China's Four Modernizations for Eurasia's collective future concerns is the political context within which they were achieved. Unlike the Soviet Union, China pursued economic reform without engaging in political reform, through a process of gradualism, administrative decentralization, and particularistic contracting.[72] The PRC's special brand of communism—less institutionalized and more decentralized than that of the USSR, yet still adhering to CPC leadership—also facilitated this outcome. China thus emerged as a high-growth yet soft authoritarian power—only partially open and shallowly integrated with the world.[73] As a consequence of its distinctive critical juncture, dominated by the fear of resurgent anarchy through the Cultural Revolution, the leadership that emerged oriented the PRC toward a soft authoritarian alternative to the classical Western pattern of "liberty under law."[74]

Most recently, the economic dynamism generated by the Four Modernizations, including the gradual broadening of development westward from China's coastal regions, improved infrastructure, relaxed customs procedures, and increased complementarity with post–Cold War Europe. These changes have led to a surge of Eurasian transcontinental commerce. Between the launch of the first China-Europe freight train in January 2011 and the end of June 2016, approximately $17 billion of cargo was shipped by rail between China and various European and Central Asian destinations.[75]

Transcontinental manufacturing supply chains in electronics, auto parts, and precision machinery are likewise growing increasingly intense, as overland and intermodal transport grows increasingly convenient, as infrastructure improves, and as logistical costs steadily decline. The China of the early Four Modernizations—dynamic in light industry on the coast, with the heavy involvement of multinationals, leaving an impoverished and isolated interior—has morphed into a more powerful and self-sufficient nation of broader geo-economic diversity. China is rapidly growing both more assertive and more globally active in such areas as service trade, logistics, overseas investment, overseas lending, and absolute volume of exports. China is thus approaching a domestic Crossover Point with fateful implications for Eurasia and beyond.

Shadows on the Future?   •

By some economic measures, the Crossover Point to a new global system may already have begun. The World Bank recently concluded that, in PPP terms, China now has the largest economy on earth. Less felicitously, China is also now the world's greatest contributor to CO_2 emissions, accounting for 27.3 percent of worldwide emissions in 2016, compared to 16.0 percent for the United States and 10.4 percent for the European Union.[76]

The PRC is likewise the largest manufacturer and exporter in the world. It also has the largest market for oil, motor vehicles, smartphones, Daimler-Benz products, and even Kentucky Fried Chicken, while likewise serving as the largest importer of oil.[77] Since 1996, China has also been the world's largest crude steel producer. It follows in the steps of Germany, with its *Wirtschaftswunder* (economic miracle) of the early postwar years; Japan, which became the largest shipbuilder on earth during the late 1950s; and Korea, whose firms are still among the largest semiconductor producers in the world.[78] China thus now stands in the vanguard of a broader process of rising Eurasian industrial prominence and connectivity that was pioneered by other neighboring countries in a previous generation, and that continues to include them in a fundamental way, since production value chains across the region are highly integrated.

In Conclusion

Although China played a surprisingly minimal role in configuring the classic Silk Road, despite its standing as the most consequential nation of antiquity, its contemporary role in reconnecting Eurasia is inevitably much more central. It sprawls across half the distance from the East China Sea to Eastern Europe, as well as two-thirds of the distance from the Bohai Gulf to the Persian Gulf. And it has become one of the two largest economies on earth, with a high savings rate, the world's largest foreign-exchange reserves, and considerable political-economic potential to amass additional funds for global development. The PRC's future role in reconnecting Eurasia and in turn the broader world must continue to depend on its economic vitality, together with the inclination of domestic interests to prioritize the building and maintenance of needed infrastructure. Yet the momentum in support of both these objectives appears strong.

We have found in this chapter that China over the past four decades has both amassed the economic scale and gained the political-economic inclination to reconnect Eurasia through an aggressive program of infrastructure building. These capabilities and inclinations began emerging under the Four Modernizations of Deng Xiaoping, which catalyzed the historic acceleration of Chinese growth. The emphasis on infrastructure and continental reconnection did not become explicit until much later, however.

Throughout the 1980s and 1990s, Chinese growth was export driven, and private interests grew increasingly important in the political economy as a whole. The critical juncture inspiring China to move decisively back toward infrastructure building and domestic demand expansion was the global financial crisis of 2008 and the massive $586 billion infrastructure program that flowed from it. The BRI of Xi Jinping has doubtless amplified and intensified China's efforts at reconnection, supported by the CPC, PLA, and heavy industrial and recently maritime interests, although the efforts at reconnection began much earlier. Through its sustained efforts at enhancing connectivity, leveraging its geopolitical centrality, and increasing economic weight, China is playing a central role in welding fractious Eurasia slowly and at first quietly, but surely, and ever more visibly, into a veritable Super Continent, with global implications.

6

Southeast Asia
The First Experiment

CHINA IS LITERALLY THE MIDDLE KINGDOM, lying in the geo-economic heart of the largest continent on earth. From Beijing and Shanghai Eurasia stretches westward, across the steppes of the former Soviet Union, toward Europe. Yet the potential Super Continent also stretches southward, across the tropical greenery of Southeast Asia, toward the Strait of Malacca. Continentalism and China's prospective geopolitical reach thus have two distinct geopolitical dimensions, increasingly synergistic, and both fundamental to Eurasian reconnection.

Beyond China to the northeast lie Japan and Korea. Japan remains the third largest economy in the world, with sophisticated technological capabilities and deep, historically rooted strategic interests, especially in maritime Asia, to the Strait of Malacca and beyond. Korea—both North and South—likewise has continuing involvement to its southwest, with China, as always, looming in between.

On the far side of Eurasia Europe too, of course, has its own Southeast Asian connections. Many of these ties—between Britain, France, Portugal, and the Netherlands, on the one hand, and all the nations of ASEAN except Thailand, on the other—have colonial origins. Other ties, especially with Vietnam, date from Warsaw Pact days. Yet China and the overseas Chinese of the region, 30 million strong, play a persistent political-economic role as an intermediary, to both Europe and the broader world. Numerous other Eurasian powers, including India, Russia, Japan, South Korea, Germany, and Singapore, are also involved.

Three-quarters of a century ago, Japan explicitly declared a Greater East Asian Co-Prosperity Sphere, with Southeast Asia as a central element. Those days are gone. Yet as we shall see, a dynamic, interactive relation with Eurasian powers has arisen once again—this time with China in the ascendancy, albeit in less coercive fashion. All major parts of the Super Continent are represented, with the synergy propelling growth even as geopolitical tensions also slowly rise.

The Heritage of History

China's westward Silk Road ties are classical, dating from the Han dynasty even before the Christian era. China's southern relationships are also venerable. Southward territorial expansion of the Han Empire in the second century BC was followed by emergence of a maritime trade network along the coastline that would eventually develop into the so-called Maritime Silk Road. Funan, a historical Cambodian kingdom from the first to the sixth centuries AD, played a key role as a trading hub. By the seventh century AD, the Srivijaya kingdom on Sumatra had also established itself as a new international trading center.

Despite its early maneuverings to the south, ancient China had felt little need to trade externally, possessing a huge and well-integrated internal market. To the extent that it did venture abroad, China in classical times was more of an "overland continentalist" country, favoring trade to the west across the classical Silk Road. Periodic external pressure from the northern nomads, however, which cut China off from its traditional overland trade routes to Central Asia, did encourage the Chinese state periodically to promote maritime commerce, as during the Song dynasty. After the fall in 1127 of its capital at Kaifeng on the lower reaches of the Yellow River, the Song court fled southward and relocated to present-day Hangzhou, where the globally oriented Internet giant Alibaba, a catalytic force in Eurasian connectivity, is based today.

With overland trade blocked, seaborne commerce became China's only option during the late Song period. Between 1056 and 1127, income from maritime trade jumped over tenfold, from 1.7 to 20 percent of Chinese imperial revenues.[1] Following the Mongol invasion of Java in 1293, Chinese Muslim traders frequented coastal towns of Indonesia and Malaysia during the fourteenth and early fifteenth century. The mariner Zheng He, among others, passed through Surabaya, Palembang, and other Southeast Asian ports during his seven voyages to the region between 1405 and 1433.[2]

From the earliest days of China's interaction with Southeast Asia, overseas Chinese (*haiwai huaren*) have been a central part of the equation—building cultural bridges, but often stirring antipathies and fears as well. The first wave came as merchants arrived, becoming central figures in such trading centers as Palembang and Surabaya in the course of the fourteenth century, although they were largely assimilated into the local population over the following two hundred years.[3] The second and most numerous wave of migration arrived in Southeast Asia at the high tide of European colonialism during the late nineteenth century, with many being driven from China by the poverty and ruin caused by the Taiping rebellion (1850–1864). In Southeast Asia, the Dutch, French, and British colonizers used these new migrants not only as laborers on plantations but often also as tax collectors and low-level administrators of colonial rule. This socially complex work earned them not only modest wealth but also frequently the enmity of indigenous populations such as the *pribumi* of Indonesia. The turbulence of early twentieth-century China, the revolution of 1949, the Cultural Revolution, Hong Kong's 1997 reversion, and the Chinese globalization that followed all produced new waves of migrants from China to Southeast Asia. Yet it was the migrations of the late nineteenth century, complicated by the conflicted intermediary roles into which the overseas Chinese were forced by colonial rulers, that most significantly colored Southeast Asia's relations with both China and the broader world.

The overseas Chinese of Southeast Asia—now almost 30 million strong, making up over half of the Chinese living permanently abroad, and blessed with extraordinary global networks—are a crucial intermediary between a rising China and the world, as well as a major force in the political economy within their adopted part of the world. History has been kindest to the overseas Chinese in Thailand, which has the second largest *haiwai huaren* population in the region, as indicated in Table 6.1. Chinese immigrants were fortunate at an early stage to be befriended and highly evaluated by Thai royalty; indeed, King Rama I, who founded the present Chakri dynasty in 1782, was partly Chinese.[4]

For over four hundred years, Thai and Chinese elites have thus intermingled and assimilated, without the complexities of colonial rule that set Chinese and indigenous peoples against one another across the rest of Southeast Asia. History thus provides a solid platform for a major Chinese political-economic presence in Thailand, centering on the massive overseas Chinese community of Yaowarat, Bangkok's Chinatown, which constituted over half of the capital's population until the 1950s.[5] Even today, overseas Chinese make

TABLE 6.1

The varied patterns of overseas Chinese presence in Southeast Asia (2011)

Country	Overseas Chinese Population (thousands)	Total Population (millions)	Overseas Chinese Share of Total Population (%)	Assimilated?
Indonesia	8,010.72	248.00	3.23	No
Thailand	7,512.60	64.26	11.69	Yes
Malaysia	6,540.80	28.73	22.77	No
Singapore	2,808.30	5.26	53.39	N/A
Philippines	1,243.16	95.83	1.30	Yes
Myanmar	1,053.75	62.42	1.69	No
Vietnam	992.60	89.32	1.11	No
Laos	176.49	6.56	2.69	No
Cambodia	147.02	14.43	1.02	No
Brunei	51.00	0.41	12.44	No
Total	28,536.44	615.22	4.64	

SOURCE: Dudley L. Poston Jr. and Juyin Helen Wong, "The Chinese Diaspora: The Current Distribution of the Overseas Chinese Population," *Chinese Journal of Sociology* 2, no. 3 (2016): 348–73, doi: 10.1177/2057150X16655077.
NOTES: 1) Figures for Singapore include the guest-worker population, which includes few Overseas Chinese. Around three-quarters of Singaporean citizens are ethnic Chinese. 2) Singaporean Chinese are in a numerically dominant position, making the "assimilation" comparison difficult.

up 10 percent of the entire Thai population, own 90 percent of all invest-ments in the commercial sector, 90 percent of all investments in the industrial sector, and 50 percent of all investments in the financial sector.[6] More than 80 percent of the forty richest people in Thailand are Thai of full or partial Chinese descent.[7] The political-economic influence of a local Chinese com-munity that is well accepted and highly regarded also provides China with a stable diplomatic platform in Bangkok for its broader regional operations.

Malaysia and Indonesia are polar opposites of Thailand—cases where the heritage of history is not so kind to the relationship with China. Malaysia, in particular, has a very large local Chinese population—the third largest in the region numerically, after Indonesia and Thailand, constituting nearly a quar-ter of the local population. Yet the Malaysian Chinese community is not well assimilated into local society, partly due to the controversial enforcement role that the British forced the Chinese to assume during colonial days. The gov-ernment has systematically worked to marginalize overseas Chinese political-economic influence ever since independence, giving Malays systematic pref-erence in government employment and in public corporations, for example.

In Indonesia, the historical heritage is similar. The Dutch systematically favored the Chinese, using them as tax farmers and petty officials who were widely disliked by the general *pribumi* populace. After independence, many Chinese grew wealthy and influential behind the scenes, but resentment and antagonism against them grew. In 1965, after an abortive coup resulted in the death of several Indonesian generals, the military closed its eyes to sweeping pogroms that led to the deaths of between 500,000 and 1 million former communists, as well as many ethnic Chinese.[8] This backlash also inhibited the reestablishment of active diplomatic relations between China and Indonesia until the 1990s; many Indonesian elites remain fundamentally suspicious of China to this day.

A third pattern of relations between China and Southeast Asia, also deeply immersed in history, is the Singapore model. Singapore, of course, is the one Southeast Asian nation with an ethnic Chinese majority. That does not mean, however, that it is reflexively pro-Chinese. Its leadership emerged through a struggle with the Communist Party, deeply suspicious of a communist China, and has from the country's inception been highly sensitive to the resentment and suspicion of China that is historically pervasive among its Malay neighbors. Consequently, Singapore has traditionally named Indians as foreign minister, despite the local ethnic Chinese majority, and was the very last ASEAN nation to recognize the People's Republic of China (PRC), in 1990.[9]

Although Singapore has kept discreet diplomatic distance from Beijing over the years and has carefully cultivated the United States in political-military matters, it has also actively aided China's economic development in a variety of ways. Most significantly, the Singaporean government has cosponsored four important pilot projects with key institutions in China—each designed to impart valuable development skills to Chinese colleagues. These projects dealt with (1) promoting foreign investment in manufacturing (Suzhou, from 1994), (2) eco-urban development (Tianjin, from 2008), (3) knowledge-intensive economic development (Guangzhou, from 2010) and (4) Internet of Things (Chongqing, from 2015).[10] Beginning with Lee Kuan Yew and his intense interaction with Deng Xiaoping, Singaporean leaders have also served as sophisticated confidantes to China's leadership on issues of global importance, although this role may be of declining importance as China's own global contacts steadily expand. Local Singaporean business firms and investors have also made use of their cultural and familial ties to particular regions and districts within China, such as Fujian and Sichuan provinces.

Southeast Asia's Importance for China

In an era when China is facing outward—as in the fifteenth century, and in the twenty-first as well—Southeast Asia continues to hold substantial geopolitical and geo-economic importance for China, along two dimensions.

Most importantly, it borders China directly, raising both security challenges and economic opportunities for the PRC. Three Southeast Asian countries—Vietnam, Laos, and Myanmar—are China's direct neighbors to the south; continental Southeast Asia as a whole (including Thailand, Malaysia, and Singapore) is geographically appended to China's southern provinces of Yunnan and Guangxi. Security challenges from Vietnam date back two millennia, continuing into the late 1970s when Vietnam and the PRC fought a bloody four-week border war in early 1979 that generated at least 20,000 fatalities.[11]

Chinese economic ties with Southeast Asia are also deep, rapidly growing, and interrelated with Beijing's security concerns. Southeast Asia, after all, is the third largest supplier of Chinese imports in the world, centering on electronic components and raw materials.[12] In the first decade of the twenty-first century, bilateral trade between China and ASEAN grew by an explosive 640 percent.[13] Nearly 60 percent of the computers China imported in 2016 and more than a third of its integrated circuits came from Southeast Asia, with imports from Malaysia being particularly notable.[14] Chinese investment in the region rose nearly thirtyfold, from $1.3 billion in 2005 to $38.6 billion in 2017.[15] So Southeast Asia lies within China's natural and continuous sphere of regional concern along several dimensions.

Southeast Asia is also important for a growing, outward-oriented China due to its positioning along the sea lanes to the broader world to the west. The Malay Peninsula, comprising peninsular Malaysia, the southern tip of Myanmar, and southern Thailand, serves as a formidable geographic barrier, and the Strait of Malacca as a chokepoint, controlling China's westward maritime access. The sea lanes outward from China, stretching through the South China Sea, through the Straits of Malacca, Sunda, Lombok, and Makassar, into the Bay of Bengal and the Indian Ocean, as indicated in Figure 2.1, carry fully a third of all maritime traffic by volume that flows in international trade worldwide. They also carry 70 percent of China's oil imports, together with an increasing variety of raw materials and food.[16] Southeast Asian entrepôt centers along the sea lanes, including Penang, Malacca, and particularly Singapore, provide commercial services, technology, and strategic intelligence that leverage an increasingly global China in broader ways as well. Southeast Asia is thus a central element of that venerable Ming-era thoroughfare, most recently known as the Maritime Silk Road.

Beyond purely economic considerations, the South China Sea has special strategic importance to China for four basic reasons. First, it serves as a natural shield for the security of the PRC's southern regions—among the most densely populated and economically developed regions of the country. The South China Sea also serves as a strategic hinterland that channels US Navy transit around Asia, as a vehicle for potentially breaking the straitjacket of the US-dominated first island chain (the Japanese home islands, Okinawa, Taiwan, and the Philippines), and as an important long-run source of energy, close to China's own domestic shores.[17] As noted above, Chinese mariners have been traversing the South China Sea regularly for over six hundred years. So there is ample reason for a rising China to think of that strategic waterway possessively, as the United States has historically regarded its own nearby Caribbean.[18]

Several nations in Southeast Asia, including Vietnam, Malaysia, and the Philippines, have traditionally taken a very different view, supported by the United States.[19] In January 2013, the Philippines instituted arbitration proceedings against the PRC under UNCLOS Annex VII with the Permanent Court of Arbitration (PCA) in The Hague. China adopted a position of nonacceptance and nonparticipation in the proceedings.[20] China also responded with land reclamation in the Spratlys, including the construction of artificial islands for military purposes, and by erecting oil rigs in the Paracels.[21] In July 2016 the PCA rendered its ruling in favor of the Philippines. The tribunal rejected China's historical rights claims and said that China had instead violated the Philippines' sovereign rights. China rejected the ruling.[22]

Following the PCA's early 2016 judgment, however, a Philippine presidential election in May 2016 brought Rodrigo Duterte to power. In October 2016, Duterte visited China, established substantial rapport with Chinese leaders, and signed a total of $24 billion in intergovernmental and private-sector deals with China.[23] Two months later, Duterte announced that he would "set aside" the tribunal ruling.[24] Subsequently, under Philippine chairmanship the ASEAN summit of April 2017 dropped references to "land reclamation and militarization" from the chairman's statement.[25] Vietnam has also been subdued in its recent bilateral response to China, although its past disputes with China in the area, dating back to 1975, have occasionally been violent.

The dual, historically classic geo-economic challenges for China that Southeast Asia inherently poses—border security and commerce, as well as control over westward sea routes to the Indian Ocean and beyond—have grown more and more intense over the past three decades as China's economy has grown and globalized. Until the fall of 1993, China was an oil exporter. In 2017 it imported over 8 million barrels a day, 70 percent of which flowing through the Strait of Malacca.[26] By 2040, the International Energy Agency projects that China will be importing 80 percent of its oil, or roughly twice the volume of the present, largely along the same energy sea lanes through Malacca, the Bay of Bengal, and the South China Sea.[27]

A growing China naturally needs, and will continue to need, enormous volumes of raw materials. Southeast Asia, especially Indonesia, is a major supplier in that regard—38 percent of Indonesia's exports to China are minerals, particularly oil, natural gas, and coal.[28] An increasingly industrial China also needs huge volumes of industrial components. Notably, machinery (mainly electronic and automobile components) constitutes the largest single element of exports from the Philippines, Malaysia, Singapore, Vietnam, and Thailand to China, reaching 76, 63, 42, 53, and 35 percent respectively of each nation's totals.[29] Malaysia, China's largest trading partner in Southeast Asia, is one of the largest suppliers of low-cost consumer electronics worldwide to Chinese consumers, flowing from huge Chinese, Japanese, and Western factories in Penang and other sites along the Strait of Malacca.[30] Electronics production and trade has expanded rapidly since the early 2000s, due to efficient, low-cost labor; a stable business environment; and quality infrastructure. Malaysian electronics production has become an important input to many of Eurasia's industrial centers, as well as the United States.

As the Chinese economy expands and China grows more affluent, the country has also begun to invest beyond its borders. Southeast Asia—close by, and with copious resources as well as low labor costs—is a natural destination. Large local ethnic Chinese communities, especially in Thailand, Malaysia, and Singapore, help to facilitate business transactions, despite intermittent ethnic frictions. Not surprisingly, between 2005 and 2017 fully 12 percent of China's total overseas investment went to ASEAN countries, despite the relatively small scale of the region in global economic terms, with Malaysia (21 percent), Indonesia (19 percent), Vietnam (11 percent), and Singapore (18 percent) the major recipients.[31] The largest share of Chinese investments in Southeast Asia (46 percent) is going to the energy sector.

The second largest share of Chinese investments in ASEAN (17 percent during 2005–2017), and the most rapidly growing component, is devoted to transport. Fifty-six percent of that transport investment has gone to rail and 16 percent to shipping.[32] This reflects an increasing Chinese investment emphasis worldwide, dating back about a decade, on acquiring distribution networks into which both imports and exports can be channeled. The Belt and Road Initiative is only the latest expression of this strategic geo-economic thrust.

Over the past few years, local Chinese firms, often in cooperation with Taiwanese and foreign capital, have begun to create consciously integrated production and logistics chains between China and Southeast Asia, to facilitate intraindustry trade. In Guangxi province next to Vietnam, for example, total import-export value from processing trade grew at an average annual rate of 33 percent from 2010 to 2016.[33] Such trade, in sectors like electronics, food processing, and pharmaceuticals, was typically conducted through tax-advantaged industrial zones close to the sea or the Vietnamese border, often relying on low-cost guest workers.[34] These China-centric export-processing zones also cut costs by subcontracting low-end processes to Cambodia while retaining mid- to high-end functions, including skills training, within China.

China and Malaysia are also working to systematically coordinate value-chain development, through their "two countries, twin parks" initiative. This program, whose foundations were laid in 2012, involves two jointly built industrial parks in Qinzhou in Guangxi province and Kuantan in Malaysia. Both are port cities with access to the South China Sea. In the Qinzhou Industrial Park, six industrial clusters are being built up for coordinated development, including healthcare, marine industries, and food processing. One special niche is bird-nest and halal food processing, building on Malaysian traditional industries, for product distribution in China and neighboring countries.[35] While Chinese infrastructure projects in Malaysia have come under review following the election of China critic Mahathir Mohamad, joint commercial projects in China like the Qinzhou industrial park are unlikely to be affected.[36]

Deepening China–Southeast Asia Transportation Networks

China is separated from its immediate neighbors in continental Southeast Asia (Vietnam, Laos, Myanmar) by mountainous terrain and at times by impenetrable jungles as well. The border areas of China, including Guangxi and Yunnan provinces, have been poor and underdeveloped, with large populations of minority border tribes. This combination of logistical difficulty and limited economic incentive has meant that most economic and cultural intercourse between China and Southeast Asia, apart from Vietnam, has historically been by sea.

Despite the operational difficulties, there is a powerful economic and strategic logic for China to be more connected overland with its neighbors to the south. And as China grows, its ability to create such connections—all the way to the Strait of Malacca and beyond—is clearly growing. The most concrete manifestation is the so-called Singapore-Kunming Rail Link (SKRL), connecting Kunming in Yunnan with Singapore along three separate lines.

Bits and pieces of this network have been in existence since French and British colonial days, although the project was first announced as a systematic regional venture at the fifth ASEAN summit convened in 1995.[37] For many years after that, the railway was largely just aspirational.

The SKRL network is projected to operate along three main routes from Kunming to Bangkok, and thence in consolidated fashion to the already operational, although not fully upgraded, Thailand-Singapore line. As indicated in Map 6.1, this Southeast Asia–centric network also links into the Eurasian transcontinental transport network to Europe via Chongqing, creating the prospect of tighter integration across Eurasia as a whole. The three main proposed routes between Kunming and Bangkok are: (1) an Eastern Route via Vietnam and Cambodia, (2) the Central Route via Laos, and (3) the Western Route via Myanmar.

With the advent of the Belt and Road Initiative in late 2013, the Central Route of the SKRL network has gained momentum. Construction of the China segment (Yuxi-Mohan) started in November 2016 and is scheduled for completion in December 2021. Construction of the Laos portion

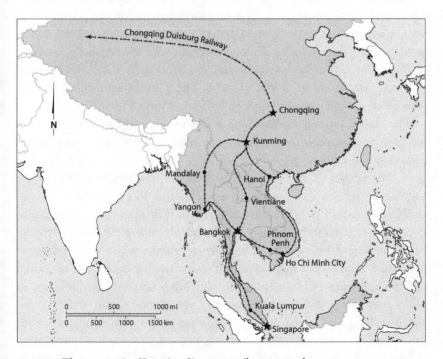

MAP 6.1 The prospective Kunming-Singapore railway network

(Boten-Vientiane) also started in late 2016, and is scheduled to launch in late 2021. The Laos-China Railway Company, a joint venture where the China side holds 70 percent, is responsible for the $6 billion project. The Laos government has borrowed $470 million from the Export-Import Bank of China at 2.3 percent interest rate with a 35-year maturity.[38] Together, the Chinese and Laotian segments would take the railway half the distance from Kunming to Singapore.

After repeated delays due to disagreement on financing terms, the construction of the Bangkok-Nakhon Ratchasima section of the Thai segment is beginning. Construction on the section between Nakhon Ratchasima and Nong Khai on the Thai-Laos border is scheduled for 2019.[39] The rail link between Thailand and Laos is projected to be completed in 2023.[40]

The southern half of the SKRL between Bangkok and Singapore is primarily a matter of refurbishing. Questions, however, linger about future prospects for the line linking Kuala Lumpur and Singapore. The multibillion deal was signed by former Malaysian prime minister Najib Razak in 2016. Najib was defeated in the May 2018 general election by Mahathir Mohamad. The new 93-year-old prime minister announced cancelation of the project right after winning the election, arguing it a necessary step to consolidate Malaysia's massive national debt. He later agreed to negotiate a delay, as cancellation would entail a high amount of compensation under the original agreement. In September 2018, the two countries agreed to defer the high-speed rail project for two years, up to May 31, 2020. The Kuala Lumpur-Singapore express service is now expected to open by January 2031.[41]

The eastern route from Kunming across Vietnam to Ho Chi Minh City has been operational intermittently since colonial times, and a modernized version of the Chinese segment, from Kunming to Hekou, was finished in 2014. The ravages of war and neglect, however, have rendered most of the Vietnamese section functionally inoperable, and Vietnam's National Assembly rejected a $56 billion plan to upgrade it in 2010.[42] The Vietnamese government has recently regained interest in the project. The plan currently being considered by authorities proposes to construct the 1,545-kilometer north-south high-speed railroad in two stages: the two sections from Hanoi to Vinh and from Nha Trang to Ho Chi Minh City will be built first in 2020–2030 and open in 2032, while the rest of the railroad will be completed and become operational by 2040–2045. The new estimated cost is $58 billion.[43]

Finally, the railroad between Phnom Penh and the Cambodian-Thai border, which was destroyed during the Cambodian civil war, has recently been rebuilt. Reconstruction of the forty-two-kilometer segment was founded by a $13 million loan granted by the ADB in 2009.[44] A proposed segment from Ho Chi Minh City to Phnom Penh, however, remains largely missing.

As the Chinese and Southeast Asian markets, totaling two billion consumers in all, continue to expand, the economic logic of linking them grows more and more powerful. The SKRL will also have geopolitical attractions for China, as it will reach the Bay of Bengal, connected to the Indian Ocean, in southern Thailand and the western Malay Peninsula. Such a route could create an overland alternative to the vulnerable sea lines of communication (SLOCs) running through the Malacca Strait, although it does face periodic political challenges, such as the 2018 ambivalence of Malaysian prime minister Mahathir Mohamad.

Compared to other ambitious projects connecting China to South and Central Asia, the SKRL is a particularly appropriate platform to demonstrate China's technical capabilities in high-speed rail technology. China now has the largest high-speed rail network in the world, providing valuable, saleable production experience. And it has begun exporting its HSR technology to overseas markets, recently including Indonesia and Turkey.[45] Unlike lines in those countries, which are geographically separated from China, the SKRL will be able to interconnect directly with China's own massive existing network, enhancing the overall economic value of both in synergistic fashion.

The SKRL also presents unusually favorable conditions for high-speed rail technology, although both the Laos section and the recently revived Vietnamese section are likely to be medium-speed rather than high-speed for cost reasons. Although the total prospective length of the SKRL is over 3,000 kilometers, much longer than the ideal operational range of between 200 and 1,000 kilometers, several sections, such as the Kuala Lumpur-Bangkok segment, fit the optimal operational ranges.[46] Those cities, and others along the way, also have buoyant local economies that will likely provide growing markets for Chinese goods.

Some coordination issues remain with Malaysia, despite heavy Chinese investment in the Malaysian rail industry.[47] China's rising geo-economic leverage, however, seems likely to produce, at last, a coordinated outcome, with an operational SKRL line likely within ten to fifteen years.

One of China's classic and enduring geo-economic challenges in dealing with Southeast Asia, as noted above, has always been the way that the Malay Peninsula blocks access from eastern China to the Indian Ocean and beyond. The SKRL would help to address that problem, but the challenge for China of finessing the SLOC chokepoint at the Strait of Malacca still remains. For this reason, China has quietly yet persistently pressed—for more than two decades—for the building of a canal across Thailand's Isthmus of Kra, to connect the Gulf of Thailand and the Andaman Sea directly.[48] The advent of the Belt and Road Initiative raises the prospect that this canal proposal might be realized at last, although huge prospective costs, political uncertainties within Thailand, and differences within ASEAN continue to cloud the outlook.

Southeast Asia and China's Domestic Transformation

As noted in Chapter 5, China is changing domestically along two fundamental dimensions. Its economy is growing much larger, which means greater domestic demand for resources and more importance as a market, as well as greater political and military leverage in relation to the outside world. At the same time, however, the PRC is also changing within. Its economic center of gravity is shifting to the west and to the south, a tendency accelerated by the massive national public works projects undertaken in China since the 2008 global financial crisis. The country is also growing more integrated, enhancing its attractiveness abroad.

Inland areas such as Sichuan and Yunnan provinces have been among the most rapidly growing in all of the PRC over the past decade, with inland growth rates reaching double digits even as coastal growth has slowed. Inland demand for energy and other resources, as well as consumer goods, has also risen, together with the capacity of such areas to produce for markets beyond China itself. These inland regions have incentives for interaction with the broader world beyond China that are not necessarily best served through traditional entrepôt ports on the east coast such as Shanghai and Hong Kong. Their rise thus stimulates pressures for a more flexible, less centralized Eurasian continentalism.

Peripheral Chinese Cities as Catalytic Regional Hubs

The inland regions have rising incentives to establish direct overland regional connections with nearby parts of Southeast and South Asia such as Myanmar and Bangladesh, which are intensified by rapid growth in those populous neighboring areas as well. This is leading to the creation of dynamic transportation and logistics in regional Chinese cities, replete with high-quality airports and Special Economic Zones that serve as bridges to surrounding nations.

Kunming, for example, has developed such a complex. It is within two hours' flying time of countries with close to two billion consumers, across China, Southeast Asia, and South Asia, which have copious raw material reserves also. Furthermore, Kunming is less than eight hundred miles north of the Bay of Bengal, which provides access to the Indian Ocean.[49]

Deeper in China's interior, regional cities with superior logistical capabilities are coming to play central roles in the burgeoning continental trade between Southeast Asia and Europe. Preeminent among them is Chongqing, where roads and rail from the north, south, east, and west meet the Yangtze River in China's most populous province, 900 miles up the Yangtze from Shanghai but only 550 miles from the Gulf of Tonkin at Qinzhou. Chongqing is also the eastern terminus of the most widely used trans-Eurasian railway, with its western terminus at Duisburg in Germany's Ruhr industrial heartland. Since the initiation of regular two-way freight service on this line in 2014, volume has increased from three trains a week to over twenty-five.[50]

Chongqing's connections with Southeast Asia, and similarly with Europe, have several dimensions. Three road-freight routes connect Chongqing with Southeast Asia—through to Vietnam (in service), Thailand (in service), and Myanmar (via Yunnan, under construction). Regular road freight services to Southeast Asia began in April 2016, exporting auto parts while importing fruit, rice, and timber.[51] Regular sea-rail freight service between Chongqing and Singapore also started operations in September 2017 via Guangxi, shortening transport times to one week compared to three weeks down the Yangtze and via Shanghai.[52]

The prospect is strong that transit trade between Southeast Asia and other parts of Eurasia via Chongqing will grow even more efficient in future. Through the Chongqing Connectivity Initiative, established by Xi Jinping and Singapore prime minister Lee Hsien Loong in November 2015, Singapore is working with China to set up a single electronic platform for data and information sharing in order to speed up customs clearance. The objective is to further shorten freight times between Singapore and Chongqing to five days.[53]

The rising prosperity and geo-economic importance of inland China has led to multiple construction projects involving Southeast Asia, which will likely proliferate in future under the Belt and Road Initiative. In October 2013, for example, a long-distance natural gas pipeline went into operation between Kyaukphyu on the Bay of Bengal in Myanmar and Kunming. The same pipeline also supplies Middle Eastern LNG in large quantities to rapidly growing parts of Guizhou and Guangxi.[54] An oil pipeline from the Bay of Bengal to Kunming also became operational in 2017.[55] Kunming itself has likewise opened a "national economic and technological development zone" near its newly refurbished, multi-billion-dollar airport to promote enhanced trade in high-value-added products with Myanmar, Bangladesh, India, and other rapidly growing areas immediately to the south.[56] Plans are also developing for a high-speed rail link between Kunming and Kolkata as part of the Bangladesh-China-India-Myanmar economic corridor element of China's Belt and Road Initiative.[57]

Southeast Asia's Special Cultural and Political-Economic Utility

Classically, Northern and Eastern China have traditionally been the center of the Sinic world, with Southeast Asia—and even the outlying southern areas of China itself, from whence the ancestors of most Southeast Asian Chinese originated—a substantially less-developed region. Since the 1970s, however, as China has opened so dramatically and remarkably to the broader world, Southeast Asia has come to play a much different and highly dynamic new role. It has become a source of capital, technology, intelligence, and policy advice, as well as diplomatic mediation that has greatly facilitated China's remarkably smooth emergence as a responsible Eurasian continental power. The region has also become a source of information and advice regarding China for the broader world, including Europe, the United States, and Russia. Southeast Asia has thereby aided China's stable emergence on the global stage as well.

Southeast Asia, particularly Singapore, has been able to support and mediate China's international emergence. That the region has still retained credibility with Western powers and Japan, which collectively remain deeply suspicious of Beijing itself, is no mean diplomatic feat. Yet it has been a task successfully achieved. That success is a tribute to the shrewdness and diplomatic skills of Southeast Asian leaders as well as the pragmatism of their Chinese interlocutors. It may also have been facilitated by timing. The important role of Southeast Asian leaders, beginning with Lee Kuan Yew, in triangular US-China-ASEAN relations arose amid a Vietnam War that deeply involved all three parties in the task of risk reduction and deepened during a Cold War when the strategic interests of the various parties were broadly aligned as well.

Southeast Asia, and particularly its ethnic Chinese community, has had a powerful stake in China's peaceful international emergence of the past forty years. There are nearly thirty million ethnic Chinese across Southeast Asia, but they are a majority only in Singapore. Elsewhere they are invariably influential economically, but as wealthy minorities in a frequently vulnerable political position.[58] To the extent that China inspires fear or anger in the broader populations of the nations in which they reside, overseas Chinese can suffer as they also did during the Japanese occupations of World War II. And China's actions can powerfully affect the way that these overseas Chinese are treated and regarded within their own home nations.

In the earliest days of China's Four Modernizations, Southeast Asia played a crucial role. Lee Kuan Yew met with Deng Xiaoping at length in Singapore, a month before Deng's historic announcement of the Modernizations and just two months before the United States shifted diplomatic recognition from Taiwan to the PRC.[59] On several occasions he played a key mediating role between US leaders, including Richard Nixon, Jimmy Carter, and their key advisors (Kissinger and Brzezinski), and the Chinese.[60] Lee also helped to mediate Cross-Straits relations, as did his successors; it is no accident that the Cross-Straits dialogue began in Singapore (1993) and that its most important formal manifestation, the meeting of Xi Jinping and Ma Ying-jeou, was also held there in 2015.

China and Southeast Asia in the Broad Eurasian Context

Southeast Asia, as noted earlier, has deep historical and economic relations with both Europe and Japan, as well as China. Indeed, the EU remains Southeast Asia's largest foreign investor, with Japan second.[61] Both are wary of Chinese dominance in Southeast Asia, although Japan has recently begun collaborating with China on some infrastructure projects in the region.[62]

Southeast Asia has also played a role in supporting China's integration within a broader Eurasian context that includes both Europe and Northeast Asia. Singapore's former prime minister Goh Chok Tong, for example, was instrumental in establishing the Asia-Europe Meeting (ASEM), in which both China and Japan were to play central roles. Virtually all Southeast Asian nations, including Singapore, have also joined China's BRI program, including the AIIB, as have most European states as well.

Although Singapore has in reality played a central role in mediating Southeast Asia's relationship with China, and even at an early stage China's emerging ties with the United States, Singapore has maintained an extremely low profile diplomatically in dealing with China. Singapore has rarely named an ethnically Chinese foreign minister, and most of its most senior diplomats, like the first foreign minister, S. Rajaratnam, have been ethnically Indian. Shortly after ASEAN was formed in 1967, Singapore committed to be the last ASEAN member to establish active diplomatic relations with the PRC, and honored that pledge, waiting until October 1990—a quarter century after its own independence—to formally recognize China.

Southeast Asia's role in China's global emergence has not been limited to the diplomatic sphere. China's first Special Economic Zones under the Four Modernizations were mainly located in the ancestral homelands of Southeast Asian overseas Chinese, scattered along the coasts of Fujian and Guangdong provinces; those expatriates invested heavily in the zones during the 1980s and 1990s, thus contributing heavily to China's early modern economic development. Since 1994 Singapore has also undertaken a series of five pilot projects, cosponsored by Chinese partners, designed to transfer expertise in planning and project management to the Chinese side. The first was a foreign-investment park in Suzhou; others dealt with city planning (Tianjin), environmental management (Guangzhou), and Internet of Things (Chongqing).[63]

In Conclusion

Southeast Asia has broad historical and economic relations with other parts of Eurasia, including both Europe and Japan, but with a deepening recent China concentration. All of the Southeast Asian nations except Thailand were once European colonies; virtually all were occupied by Japan as well; and Vietnam, with the most complex foreign ties, also had deep Cold War ties links to the Soviet Union, as well as to the United States. The geographical and economic fulcrum for Southeast Asia's continental ties, however, has almost invariably in recent years been China—the formidable geo-economic presence looming to the north.

China's relations with Southeast Asia are venerable, dating back to the Han period. Yet they have always been subject to major geo-economic and geo-political challenges. Southeast Asia is a southern neighbor to China, which shares land borders with three Southeast Asian nations. The region also lies across China's sea routes to the west, through which around half of its oil and a substantial fraction of its manufactured exports must flow.

Economic relations between China and Southeast Asia have deepened rapidly since the Four Modernizations began during the late 1970s. Today ASEAN is China's second largest source of imports, surpassing both Japan and the United States. Although raw material imports are important from Indonesia, electronic components and other varieties of machinery are dominant from most other Southeast Asian nations, with Malaysia occupying the largest share due to its buoyant electronics industry. Chinese investment in Southeast

Asia is also substantial and growing, particularly in the energy and transportation sectors.

Several large-scale transportation projects are making much of Southeast Asia as a central participant in the new Eurasian continentalism. The SKRL, involving the construction of a dedicated high-speed rail line between Singapore and southern China, is the most important of these and likely to be completed in the 2020s. As the center of gravity in China's domestic political economy moves inland to the west and the south, provinces such as Sichuan and Yunnan are seeking increased access to seaborne trade, leading to pipelines, roads, and railways across Myanmar and Bangladesh between these inland Chinese provinces and the sea.

As China has emerged actively into international affairs since the late 1970s, Southeast Asia has played a unique role in mediating that historic transition. Overseas Chinese from throughout the region have invested heavily in Special Economic Zones within their ancestral homelands along the coasts of Fujian and Guangdong, fostering complex production chains extending throughout the world. Singaporean leaders, in particular, played key roles in mediating relations with the United States during the 1970s and 1980s and in supporting the Cross-Straits Dialogue from its inception in the early 1990s up through the historic Xi-Ma summit of late 2015. Overall, Southeast Asia has played a central role in China's steady global emergence, regional conflicts like those in the South China Sea notwithstanding, and will likely be important in supporting, informing, and mediating that growing international role in coming years. Its historic ties with Europe—still vibrant, both economically and politically—are broadly synergistic with those Chinese relationships. Following the advent of the Trump administration, with its harsher trans-Pacific trade policies, collaboration among Southeast Asia, China, and the Northeast Asians (Japan and Korea) intensified as well, thus contributing to broader connectivity and co-prosperity across Eurasia as a whole.

Russia

An Unbalanced Entente

EURASIAN CONTINENTALISM HAS MANY DIMENSIONS. One of the most consequential from a global strategic perspective is how the relationship of the continent's two largest military powers, also sophisticated producers of defense technology, will evolve. Deepened intimacy between them clearly raises strategic concerns of the US and its allies. And the relative leverage of Russia and China in their partnership has major consequences for world affairs also, including for the flow of defense technology and the profile of mutual concessions in trade, investment, and international finance. In both economic and military dimensions, Sino-Russian relations thus can fatefully determine the profile of Eurasia's emerging Super Continent.

China and Russia are at one level radically vulnerable to one another. They share one of the longest land borders in the world—over 2,200 miles, from the Pacific deep into the heart of Eurasia, longer than the US-Mexican frontier.[1] In Soviet days, the Sino-Soviet frontier was rivaled only by US-Canada as the longest land border on earth. Unlike US frontiers, the Sino-Russian border has been fraught with political tension and actual conflict across most of its modern history, and was conclusively delineated only a decade ago.[2] The two countries are also unbalanced demographically, especially in the Far East, where a Russian population of considerably less than seven million confronts six times that number in the adjoining Chinese province of Heilongjiang which is geographically much smaller.[3]

Across the first three centuries of the Sino-Russian relationship and more, however, Russia was persistently dominant. Russians reached the Sea of

Okhotsk, bordering on the Pacific, as early as 1639. Conflict between the Russians and a newly established Manchu (Qing) Dynasty began less than a decade later,[4] while an otherwise ambitious Qing China was expanding in different directions. China's northernmost provinces, after all, were the sacred ancestral home of the ruling Manchu rulers themselves, who did not encourage settlement or commercial activity by other Chinese in the vicinity. So, a vast terra incognita initially separated the two sides. After intermittent conflict across the seventeenth century, centering on control of the Amur Valley, Manchu sovereignty there was confirmed by the Treaty of Nerchinsk (1689), the first ever concluded between China and a foreign power. For 170 years thereafter, peace prevailed along the Sino-Russian frontier.[5]

Russia had never reconciled to loss of the Amur Valley, however. When the Opium War (1839–1842) between China and Britain dramatically revealed the weakness of the Qing Empire, Russian viceroys and adventurers in the East saw their opportunity to capitalize.[6] During the 1850s Russian traders, encouraged by Eastern Siberian governor-general Nikolay Muravyev and supported by Cossack troops, advanced aggressively down the Ussuri to the Pacific, through areas traditionally Manchu. China, in its weakened state, could not resist. It resentfully ceded the land between the Stanovoy Range and the Amur River of Manchuria, also known as the Primorsky district, to the czar under the 1858 Treaty of Aigun. Two years later, under the Treaty of Peking (1860), China ceded the entire region between the Ussuri and the Pacific to Russia. In 1860 also, Vladivostok was founded; by the end of that momentous year around forty thousand Russian colonists had arrived in the Pacific region, where numerous dockyards and military bases were constructed, to hold the territory for the czar.[7]

Soon thereafter, during the Dungan Revolt of 1862–1877, the Russians occupied Xinjiang. They did, however, withdraw under the Treaty of St. Petersburg (also known as the Treaty of Ili) in 1881, which returned the eastern part of the Ili Basin to China. Considerable Sino-Russian interdependence did nevertheless continue. Over the ensuing half century, Qing China transferred extensive railway rights within the Manchu ancestral homeland to the Russians—rights not fully rescinded until the Japanese imperialists assumed them following their own Manchurian occupation of 1931.

The Russian Revolution of 1917 brought temporary improvement in tense Sino-Soviet relations, with the Leninists in China, led by Mikhail Borodin, initially making common cause with Sun Yat-sen against European imperialism.[8] In 1927, however, when Chiang Kai-shek fell out with the communists and suddenly tried to destroy them, a cautious and cynical Stalin stood passively by. During the bitter and precarious years of the Long March,

Yan'an, and even beyond into the post-1945 era, Mao Zedong and the Chinese Communist Party made revolution with their own hands. And Soviet passivity stirred enduring resentments, despite significant Soviet support during the 1946–1949 civil war.

Within four months of revolutionary triumph, in February 1950 the People's Republic of China (PRC) and the Soviet Union did, to be sure, sign an early treaty of alliance and friendship, directed particularly at Japan. The Soviet Union sent thousands of advisors through the 1950s to help China rebuild and modernize.[9] Yet unease continued to pervade the relationship on both sides. Mao's meetings with Stalin were tense. Fearing World War III, the Soviets failed to actively support China's costly intervention in the Korean War.[10] The Soviets only grudgingly withdrew from Port Arthur and other bases in Manchuria, confirming Chinese perceptions of them as rank imperialists.

Ultimately Moscow withdrew its experts during the summer of 1959, and Sino-Soviet relations spiraled further downward. A decade later, in March 1969, the two countries engaged in mortal combat atop ice floes in the frigid Ussuri River.[11] Soon thereafter, the Soviet Union approached the Nixon administration in the United States about a coordinated preemptive strike to destroy China's newly acquired nuclear weapons.[12] In a striking defensive response, China even went so far as to implant US-made intelligence devices in Xinjiang's borderlands, to monitor Soviet Central Asian nuclear tests for the Pentagon.[13]

From the late 1980s, the Soviets under Mikhail Gorbachev began to seek rapprochement, initiating negotiations on a bilateral Sino-Soviet border treaty in 1987. Yet Sino-Russian reconciliation was a long time coming—a treaty formalizing the boundary and agreeing on military frontier force reduction was not concluded until 1997. The final agreement on border islands only came in 2008.[14]

The collapse of the Soviet Union sharply shifted the dynamics of bilateral relations in China's favor, although the asymmetries, obscured by the energy factor, were slow to become evident. Political transition in Moscow delayed the border reconciliation process and reduced its urgency for China. The two continental giants, suddenly strange bedfellows with contrasting political systems, found coordination difficult. The diplomatic uncertainties generated by neoliberal Russian reforms during the 1990s were greeted with considerable skepticism in a still-communist China. Even some of Vladimir Putin's early policy steps, such as the demolition of Yukos during the 2005–2007 period, complicated Sino-Russian relations;[15] Yukos chairman Mikhail Khodorkovsky, whom Putin purged and arrested, had been one of China's closest economic confidantes in Moscow.

Underlying Economic Synergies

Since the late 1990s, Sino-Russian trade relations have expanded and deepened remarkably, with a stagnant Russia increasingly ceding preeminence to a rising China. Bilateral trade only passed $10 billion in 2001. Yet it exceeded $21 billion in 2004, and more than quadrupled from there, to $95.2 billion in 2014. Bilateral trade value dropped in 2015 and 2016 due to Russia's economic downturn, but recovered in 2017.[16]

Since the Ukrainian crisis exploded in December 2013, Moscow has actively sought expanded access to Chinese credit and technology, with Beijing responding positively to some degree.[17] This improvement has its roots, of course, in the underlying complementarity of the Russian and Chinese energy economies: Russia is a major energy exporter, with nearly one-fifth of the world's conventional natural gas reserves and substantial oil, as shown in Tables 4.1 and 4.2, while China is the world's largest energy consumer and rapidly becoming one of its largest energy importers as well. By 2017 China had in fact already overtaken the United States as the world's largest crude oil importer.[18]

The potential for energy symbiosis between Russia and China is especially pronounced with respect to North China, directly adjacent geographically to Russia itself. As Map 7.1 indicates, Beijing and Tianjin, two of China's six largest cities, are little more than a thousand miles from the large natural-gas deposits around Lake Baikal.[19] The major economic centers of Manchuria, such as Shenyang and Harbin, are even closer. The Daqing and Shengli fields of northeastern China supplied these pillars of Chinese industry with fuel throughout the second half of the twentieth century.[20] Yet their local resources are now approaching exhaustion, making supplies from Russia increasingly attractive for the future, especially for China north of Shanghai. And supplies from Russia obviate the need for precarious sea transport more than 6,000 nautical miles from the Persian Gulf, across sea lanes dominated by the US Navy.[21] Even energy imports from the south, by pipeline across Myanmar from the Indian Ocean, must pass through waters of the Indian Ocean and the Bay of Bengal, over which China has little control.

With rapid economic growth propelling rising levels of energy demand, China—particularly its northern regions—has ever more economic reason for energy interdependence with Russia, provided that mutually agreeable pricing arrangements can be negotiated and financing is available. As Russia becomes more and more of a consumer society, Moscow also has increased reason to accommodate China's cost-effective manufactures. These complementarities, synergistic with geographical proximity, create a foundation for economic interdependence with a more substantial economic rationale than in earlier periods of bilateral détente, such as the 1950s. Ironically, market forces, based on a trade-off between energy and manufactured goods, are thus a growing catalyst for bringing these two traditional pillars of the communist world together, in unprecedented new ways.

In May 2014, Russia and China agreed to cooperate on the 3,000-kilometer Power of Siberia gas pipeline, running from the Yakutia and Irkutsk gas-production centers north of Lake Baikal to the border of China.[22] Siberian energy development is a major element of Eurasian continentalist activity in the North. The Power of Siberia project would deliver 38 bcm of gas annually, amounting to 40 percent of China's annual 2014 consumption and 60 percent of its imports from Russia's Gazprom to China's CNPC, beginning around 2019–2020.[23] On the Russian side, the project involves $70 billion in overall exploration and construction, including $35 billion for the pipeline itself, $20 billion for field development, and $15 billion for a gas-treatment

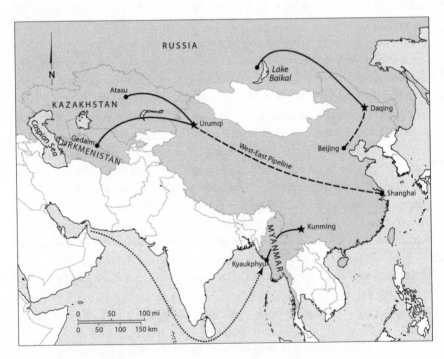

MAP 7.1 China's multiple pipeline options

plant at the Chinese-Russian border, in partnership with the Russian chemical company Sibur.[24]

Converging Interests in the Arctic

Throughout the previous history of Sino-Russian relations, including the fraternal interlude of the 1950s, the Arctic has been largely irrelevant. Russia, of course, has been a central geographic presence in the Arctic throughout its modern history. Yet China does not border the Arctic Ocean and has traditionally held no significant economic or strategic interests there.

Since 2010 this situation has begun to change quite dynamically. In contrast to the Antarctic, where thousands of feet of ice stand atop a solid continent, the area surrounding the North Pole has been covered only with pack ice, obscuring open seas beneath. Over the past half century the Arctic has been steadily warming at twice the global rate, and recently open water has begun to appear. Global warming has suddenly made Arctic circumnavigation from Northeast Asia to Europe possible[25] and opened the prospect of resource extraction as well.

The Arctic Ocean, over half of which fronts on Russia, including the most passable routes, is increasingly attractive to China on three counts. First, polar transportation sea routes from China to Europe are much more direct than those through the Strait of Malacca and the Suez Canal, as suggested in Map 7.2. Indeed, traversing the Arctic Ocean cuts 6,000 kilometers off the nautical distance from Shanghai to Hamburg.[26] From northern Chinese ports like Dalian, travel time to northwestern Europe during the July-to-November open season is potentially 25 percent shorter via the Arctic than via the Suez Canal.[27]

Second, whatever the remaining technical difficulty of navigating in frigid waters, Arctic sea lanes are potentially more strategically accommodating for China in a strategic sense than those of the southern seas, given the PRC's emerging geostrategic differences with the United States. Travel to the south, as indicated in Map 7.2, involves navigating numerous narrow choke points, most of them dominated by the US Navy. Travel along northern routes, by contrast, involves less of these narrow byways, and traverses waters dominated by Russia rather than the US.

The Arctic is increasingly important to China, finally, due to the region's yet-untapped potential as the globe's last resource frontier. The Arctic is estimated to hold 30 percent of the world's entire undiscovered supply of natural gas and 13 percent of its untapped oil, not to mention substantial stores of

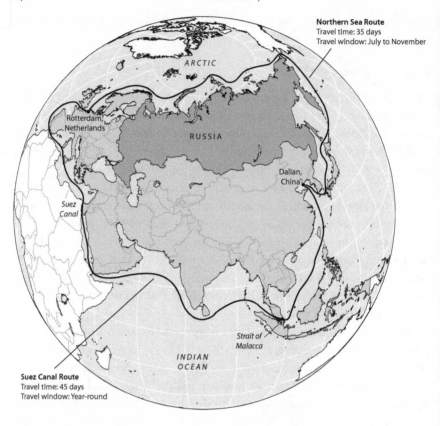

MAP 7.2 The new Eurasian Arctic shipping frontier

coal, iron, uranium, gold, copper, and fish.[28] China is not an Arctic nation, and an estimated 88 percent of Arctic resources fall within 200 miles of the coastlines, where they can be claimed by the five littoral nations (Russia, Canada, the US, Norway, and Denmark).[29] Yet over half of this entire coastline is indisputably Russian, creating natural opportunities for Sino-Russian cooperation, provided that global warming intensifies, China's growth continues, and Arctic resource development proceeds as expected. In September 2012, a Chinese merchant vessel, the *Snow Dragon* (*Xue Long*), traversed for the first time the increasingly navigable Northern Sea Route between Asia and Europe, travelling from Qingdao to Iceland.[30]

The Arctic has deep national symbolic and strategic significance for Russia, which for many years was reluctant even to admit observer states into the Arctic Council. Moscow only relented in May 2013, when China became one of the first observer members.[31] Since then, however, China's involvement in the Russian Arctic has rapidly deepened. One week after China joined the Arctic Council, Rosneft and CNPC signed an agreement to undertake joint exploration and production in the Barents Sea; three months later CNPC acquired a 20 percent stake in Russia's giant Yamal LNG project.[32]

In December 2017 the first stage of the massive, $27 billion Yamal LNG project in the Arctic came on stream. The project has been jointly financed by Russia's Novatek (50.1 percent stake), CNPC (20 percent), Total (20 percent), and China's Silk Road Fund (9.9 percent).[33] The first shipment of LNG from Yamal to China was made in summer 2018.[34] Yamal, with 16.5 million tons of annual LNG capacity when complete, is the first, but unlikely to be the last, major energy project undertaken under the Belt and Road Initiative (BRI). It provides access to both China and Europe, across the Russian portion of the Arctic Ocean.

Although some geopolitical wariness no doubt remains between the two Eurasian giants, unprecedented cooperation in the Arctic is clearly aligning their interests more clearly. This has been especially true since the advent of Ukraine-related sanctions in 2014, with over two-thirds of the offshore drilling equipment Russia needs in the Arctic subject to Western sanctions in which China is not participating.[35] As sanctions ease, China, with its rapidly rising demand, will be the natural market for expanding Russian Arctic energy production.

Increasingly Congruent Geopolitical Concerns?

The Arctic is clearly one area where Chinese and Russian geostrategic as well as economic interests are converging, under conditions that offer leverage for both. Russia has resources and transit routes in the Arctic that China values. And China has a market that, especially in the wake of Ukraine sanctions, Russia also needs. The Arctic will thus be one likely catalyst for deepened Sino-Russian bilateral interdependence.

Yet there are many other promising arenas for Sino-Russian cooperation further to the south on the Eurasian continent as well—many animated over the past two decades by an intrusive American continental challenge. Until the 1990s, the heart of Eurasia was effectively an exclusive Sino-Soviet preserve. Following 9/11 and the US Afghan intervention in October 2001, however, well over 100,000 American troops were deployed in Central Asia, with bases in Kyrgyzstan and Uzbekistan, as well as Afghanistan itself.[36] They remained within the borders of the former Soviet Union and a few hundred miles from

China's western frontiers as late as June 2014, when the US returned its last Central Asian base, the Manas Transit Center, to Kyrgyzstan.[37] And American military advisors and special forces have continued their Afghan presence, directly adjacent to China, to this very day.[38] The US also engages in joint military exercises with Mongolia,[39] sandwiched directly between Russia and China, which would have been unthinkable thirty years ago.

The immediacy of American military presence on the Eurasian continent is thus one common, and continuing, geopolitical concern that draws Russia and China together in unprecedented new ways. So does the new post–Cold War sociopolitical uncertainty and turbulence of Central Asia itself. Until 1992, for example, China's Xinjiang province bordered only on the Soviet Union; Mongolia, a Soviet satellite; and Kashmir. It had a predominantly Uyghur population. Today, however, Xinjiang borders on seven independent countries, most dominated by Turkic populations with compatriots across the common border, in a world swept since the Iranian revolution by a rising tide of ethnic and religiously inspired violence.[40] And the solid Uyghur majority appears to have disappeared, especially in large urban centers, even as the local population grows increasingly urban and affluent, with rising expectations. Meanwhile, across its own borders, Russia contends with extremist violence as well, in Chechnya as well as major urban centers. The specter of both terrorism and broader ethnic tensions thus draws Beijing and Moscow together.

External Crisis and Deepening Bilateral Collaboration

Clearly Russia and China have had a variety of deepening long-term incentives for collaboration, especially over the past decade, that had not prevailed during the 1960s, 1970s, and 1980s. Some of these, such as the US Central Asian presence, had never occurred previously at all. Deepening ties have also been steadily ratcheted upward by periodic spasms of political-economic crisis.

Four post–Cold War crises have been especially important in spurring a deepening of Sino-Russian relations. First, in 1999, there was the Kosovo War and the bombing of the Chinese embassy in Belgrade. Then, in 2002, the United States withdrew from the Anti-Ballistic Missile Treaty (ABM), deepening the specter of intensified US-Russia strategic competition. In the early 2000s there were the Color Revolutions in Russia's near abroad—the Rose Revolution in Georgia (2003), followed by the Orange Revolution in Ukraine (2004–2005). These sudden political shifts raised the specter of domestic provocations inspired from abroad.

Finally, and most importantly, there was the Ukraine crisis of 2013–2014, precipitated by what was, for a paranoid Russia, another abrupt and especially painful political change in its "near abroad." This crisis led, as has been noted, to an intensification of Western sanctions on Russia and an increasing institutionalization of Sino-Russian ties, accelerated by a decline in the traditional importance of Euro-Russian economic relations. In each case, as we shall see, Sino-Russian relations deepened and ratcheted upward to a new level of intensity, with fateful geopolitical implications.

A Radically Shifting Sino-Russian Geo-Economic Balance

Russia and China, as we noted from the outset, share a long, vulnerable frontier, and have been deeply suspicious of one another across the ages. Yet much has happened since the early 1990s to alter their traditional bilateral equation. Energy interdependence has arisen. Trade ties have deepened. Common strategic challenges from the US have arisen. And most importantly, the geo-economic balance between them has *radically* shifted—in China's favor.

In 1992, just after the political collapse of the Soviet Union, the Russian economy was slightly larger than China's, as indicated in Figure 7.1. By 2017, the Chinese economy was nearly six times Russia's. Even South Korea, with

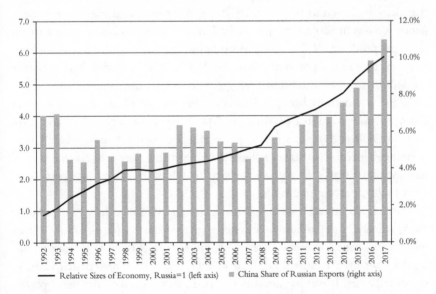

—— Relative Sizes of Economy, Russia=1 (left axis) ▪ China Share of Russian Exports (right axis)

FIGURE 7.1 China's rising economic scale relative to Russia (1992–2017)
SOURCES: World Bank, "GDP, PPP (Constant 2011 International $)," *World Development Indicators*, accessed October 22, 2018; and International Monetary Fund, *Direction of Trade Statistics*, accessed October 22, 2018.

little more than a third of Russia's population, was larger economically in nominal terms. The bulk of the shift in the relative economic fortunes of the two nations came after the two most recent critical junctures that we emphasize in this volume: the global financial crisis of 2008 and the Ukraine crisis of 2013–2014.

In 2008 and shortly thereafter, the shift in the relative economic circumstances of China and Russia was due primarily to the rise of China, powered by the PRC's massive economic stimulus amid the global financial crisis. After 2013, by contrast, the shift was intensified particularly by Russia's declining fortunes, although Chinese growth continued to be a consideration. Three factors were at work: demography, declining energy prices, and Western sanctions.

Demography was already a problem for Russia in 2008, but the challenge has continued to intensify since then. Roughly 18 percent of Russia's population in 2008 was over age sixty-five, and that share has since risen to around 20 percent. By 2030, however, fully 30 percent of all Russians will be above what is conventionally considered retirement age.

Energy export dependence has recently been an even more serious obstacle for the Russian economy, in an era of volatile energy prices. In 1998 oil and gas represented only 40 percent of Russia's total exports, but by 2014 that share had risen to 70 percent.[41] Much of the increased energy-export dependence was in natural gas, just as the United States was emerging as a major shale gas producer. Rising global gas supplies and increasingly liquid markets, as the impact of the post-Fukushima nuclear backlash subsides, have seriously eroded Russian geo-economic leverage, both with China and globally.

Western sanctions brought Russia's economic troubles to a crisis point following the invasion of Crimea in March 2014. Between 2013 and 2016 Russian GDP and exports fell 44 percent and 46 percent respectively.[42] Real household income had been falling, as of 2017, for four consecutive years.[43] Meanwhile, Russia's reliance on exports to China rose from 6.8 percent in 2013 to 10.9 percent in 2017.[44]

Russia is also losing leverage in next-generation distribution. In September 2018, Alibaba, the Chinese e-commerce giant, signed a joint-venture agreement with several Russian partners, including the Russian sovereign wealth fund, to set up a Russian branch of its retail site AliExpress, to sell Chinese goods in Russia. Russia has never before had a major local e-commerce player, and the venture will likely be the largest in the country when it opens in 2019.[45]

A final factor eroding Russia's leverage in the Eurasian context has been the shifting pattern of international trade across the continent. Two decades ago the principal source of transit goods was the Northeast Asian capitalist economies—Japan and secondarily South Korea. And the Trans-Siberian Railway across Russia was the only means of overland access to Europe, although these countries traditionally shipped most of their Europe-bound freight by sea.

Today the major source of transit goods from the east is China, and there are multiple routes across the continent. Some, such as Turkey's "Middle Corridor" from Istanbul to China, *totally* circumvent Russia. Most traverse mainly Kazakhstan, with only minor Russian transit in western Siberia. Russia has thus lost substantial leverage with China in transport logistics, as in most other areas of Eurasian affairs.

Deepening, Asymmetrical Eurasian Entente under Xi and Putin

During the last years of the Cold War and beyond, both China and Russia reached out actively to the Western industrialized nations, including the United States. Deng Xiaoping normalized relations with Washington in 1979 and spoke later of "hiding our capabilities and biding our time."[46] Gorbachev spoke during the late 1980s of "our common European home" and sought disarmament understandings with Ronald Reagan at Reykjavik and beyond.[47] Yeltsin, Medvedev, and the first Putin administration in Russia, as well as Hu Jintao in China, took a similar relatively conciliatory line.

In 2012 Vladimir Putin began his third term as Russian president, after a four-year interlude as prime minister.[48] And in 2012 Xi Jinping also assumed power in China. Both are expected to continue as leaders of their respective nations for many years—in the case of Xi indefinitely. And both Putin and Xi have, from the beginning of their respective terms, adopted complementary grand strategies that are both distinctive in comparison with their predecessors and also arguably competitive with the foreign policy of the United States.

In contrast to the Eurocentric Russian policies of previous years, Putin began drifting toward the Pacific soon after assuming office for his second term as president, driven by a combination of "push" and "pull" factors. The 2010 European debt crisis as well as deepening hostility in Brussels toward future EU expansion convinced Putin, and Russian elites more generally, that prospects for a productive Russian future in a "common European home" were bleak.[49] At the same time, the rising economic power of China, the Obama administration's own "pivot to Asia" in the United States, and the advent of new, empathetic Chinese leadership convinced Moscow to itself give increased priority to the East. The continuing hostility of the US Congress toward Moscow, conciliatory gestures by the Trump administration notwithstanding, also no doubt discourage the Kremlin from expecting major changes in US policy.

One major symbolic watershed for the second Putin administration's "pivot to Asia" was the Vladivostok Asia-Pacific Economic Cooperation summit of September 2012, which Xi Jinping attended, as presumptive Chinese leader, but which Barack Obama did not. A follow-up move was the launch of 2015 launch of the Eastern Economic Forum, which is to be held in Vladivostok every September. In 2018 this forum was attended by Putin, Xi, Japan's Abe Shinzō, Mongolia's president Battulga Khaltmaa, and Korean prime minister Lee Nak-yon.[50]

Russia's pivot to Asia has had five major dimensions: (1) economic development of the Russian Far East; (2) expanded energy exports to Asia, including higher value-added products such as petrochemicals; (3) increased capital flows from Asia, especially China, into Russia; (4) expanded defense cooperation with key Asian nations, including China, India, and Vietnam; and (5) expanded Asian recognition of Russia's great-power status, through Moscow's expanded participation in high-level Asian conferences and multilateral gatherings, such as the BRICS (Brazil, Russia, India, China, and South Africa) conference, the Shanghai Cooperation Organization, and the East Asia Summit. Russia under Putin has reinforced its deepening interest in Asia with increased military deployments and a search for new bases in the region, such as Cam Ranh Bay in Vietnam, where it once held sway.[51]

Shortly after Putin began his intensified push eastward, Xi Jinping formally came to power in China. From the beginning Xi began proactively building bridges to Russia and surrounding states, making his first presidential visit overseas—to Moscow—in late March 2013. The first overseas foray of Chinese prime minister Li Keqiang was to Berlin, declining an appearance at a trilateral China-Japan-Korea summit conference in Tokyo to do so. In the succeeding months, Xi held three summit meetings with Vladimir Putin and also visited four of the five Central Asian nations.[52] In September 2013, he unveiled the Silk Road Economic Belt Initiative at Nazarbayev University in Almaty, Kazakhstan. Only a month later Xi announced, before the Indonesian parliament, the Twenty-First-Century Maritime Silk Road and the Asian Infrastructure Investment Bank (AIIB)—other central elements of his signature BRI.

The BRI, a major expression of the "new continentalism" that is transforming the international relations of Eurasia,[53] focuses on the provision of infrastructure—high-speed rail, electric power transmission lines, superhighways, and port facilities. These link China with nations to the west and south, across the Eurasian continent and into Africa. The infrastructure is to be provided cooperatively by the nations of the region, with new financial institutions initiated by China, such as the AIIB and the Silk Road Fund, as the catalyst. Geographically, the BRI has, as noted above, two dimensions: (1) the Silk Road Economic Belt, a transcontinental transport and communications network across the Eurasian landmass; and (2) the Maritime Silk Road, a series of port facilities around the southern periphery of Eurasia, across the South China Sea, Bay of Bengal, and Arabian Sea, to the Persian Gulf and the east coast of Africa.[54]

After two years of sustained interaction as leaders of neighboring great powers, intent on ending two decades of American unipolar hegemony since the collapse of the Soviet Union, Xi Jinping and Vladimir Putin had by the end of 2013 drawn politically and personally close to one another. Their entente was consolidated further by the Ukraine crisis, which exploded in November 2013 with the antigovernment demonstrations in Kiev and the overthrow of the pro-Russian Yanukovych administration. Three months later, after Russia annexed Crimea, the G-7 nations imposed stiff sanctions on Moscow, giving it more incentive to prioritize relations with Beijing.

These historic developments in Ukraine and in Russo-European relations led to a quantum intensification of the Sino-Russian entente, along many lines. The close preexisting relationship between Xi and Putin greatly facilitated this intensification. In May 2014, less than two months after the West's Crimea-related sanctions, Putin and Xi met in Shanghai for extensive bilateral talks. They announced a mammoth $400 billion bilateral energy deal, involving the construction of a new, $70 billion "Power of Siberia" pipeline from the Irkutsk-Baikal area of Siberia to the vicinity of Beijing, and the continuous supply of natural gas from Russia to China to total 38 billion cubic meters/year.[55] In October 2014 they concluded another technical agreement on still further expanded pipeline development, which outlined the parameters for design, construction, and operation of the Power of Siberia pipeline.[56]

The multiple seventieth anniversary commemorations of World War II events during 2015 helped to bring the two Eurasian superpower leaders even closer to one another. In May 2015 Xi Jinping visited Moscow, together with his wife Peng Liyuan, as one of the principal international guests at Russia's

Victory Day ceremonies, commemorating V-E Day in Europe. During more extended official travel across Eurasia, he also visited Kazakhstan and Belarus. While in Moscow, Xi concluded a major agreement with Putin, symbolically integrating China's new Silk Road Economic Belt concept with the Russian-inspired Eurasian Economic Community notion, intended to create a common political-economic space stretching from China's western frontiers to the eastern borders of the European Union.[57] China also agreed to invest $5.8 billion in the Moscow-Kazan high-speed railway, as the first stage of an extension to China.[58] In June 2015, China actually signed a contract with Moscow to build a Russian domestic high-speed rail line between Moscow and Kazan, ironically the site of Ivan the Terrible's historic victory over the Mongols on the Volga.[59] This segment was to be the first stage of an ambitious Moscow-to-Beijing high-speed railway.[60]

Four months later, Putin reciprocated as a main guest at China's September 3 Victory Day commemorations, further consolidating the Sino-Russian entente. During his Beijing visit, Putin also held a bilateral summit with Xi, to discuss signing over twenty cooperative agreements dealing with transportation, finance, and natural gas cooperation.[61] After making two trips to China during 2016, including the G-20 summit in Hangzhou,[62] Putin repeated this practice in 2017. He returned to Beijing once again in May 2017, as a principal foreign guest among twenty-eight international leaders at Xi Jinping's elaborate Belt and Road Forum, before attending the 2017 BRICS summit in Xiamen and the 2018 Shanghai Cooperation Organization (SCO) summit in Qingdao as well. As Donald Trump withdrew from the Iran JCPOA agreement and escalated his economic confrontation with China in the summer and fall of 2018, Putin and Xi continued their close collaboration.

The Profile of Deepening Sino-Russian Political-Military Interdependence

Deepening coincidence of economic interest and leadership interaction between Russia and China, in the context of rising Chinese leverage, has had consequences in the political-military sphere also. Since the collapse of the Soviet Union at the end of 1991, Russia has continuously served as China's largest source of imported weaponry, filling the important gap left by the Western embargo on arms exports to China imposed after the 1989 Tiananmen massacre. Russia's share of overall Chinese arms imports has averaged around 70 percent for over two decades. It declined significantly from around 2005 to 2012, falling from over 80 to around 40 percent of China's total.[63] Russia and China signed several major new arms agreements during 2013–

2014, however, as tensions between Russia and the West, as well as Chinese leverage with Russia, began to rise. The technological level of weaponry that Russia provides to China has significantly improved even as the number of contracts declines, with Chinese leverage rising particularly since the onset of the Ukraine crisis.[64]

In April 2015, for example, Russia sold the advanced S-400 air defense system to the PRC in a $3 billion arms deal, despite intellectual property concerns and years of previous ambivalence.[65] Moscow's leverage against China was waning in the face of Western sanctions against Russia following the March 2014 Crimea annexation, helping to account for this apparent shift in Russian policy.[66] The S-400 SAM system has a range of over 400 kilometers, which would put all of Taiwan's air space within the range of mainland-based SAM batteries.[67] It could also potentially be used to enforce the PRC's East China Sea Air Defense Identification Zone (ADIZ), and potentially the northern segment of a South China Sea ADIZ, should one be announced in the future.[68] The first unit was delivered in May 2018.[69]

Since the Ukraine crisis erupted, Moscow has also contracted to supply advanced Sukhoi-35 (Flanker E) fighters to Beijing, which would represent another quantum advance in Sino-Russian defense-procurement collaboration.[70] This deal could potentially expand China's air superiority over Taiwan and also aid China in enhancing the capabilities of its J-20 stealth fighter close to those of the US F-22.[71] In December 2016, four of these Su-35 fighters were delivered; another ten were delivered in December 2017; and the remaining ten were delivered in late November 2018.[72]

Chinese arms imports from Russia have moved in cycles. They rose sharply during 1999–2005, before falling during 2005–2010, and then stabilizing during the 2010–2015 period, when some strategically important deals like the S-400 contract were also finalized. These fluctuations, driven particularly by oscillations in air-defense missile and aircraft procurements, appear to correspond to political-military crises that Russia and China have confronted together, such as the 2002 US withdrawal from the ABM treaty, as well as the Ukraine crisis of the post-2013 period.

Although Chinese levels of dependence on arms imports from Russia, as opposed to other nations, have been remarkably consistent, there have been occasional sharp fluctuations. Import reliance on Russia declined significantly, for example, in 1994 and 1998. The two countries also experienced continuing mutual wariness on intellectual-property grounds.

Despite the cyclical pattern and the rising magnitude of transfers compared to 2010, the number of recent Sino-Russian arms transfer contracts is significantly less than in the mid-2000s. This appears to be due partly to the rising technical level of the Chinese domestic defense industry, based to some degree on reverse engineering, which has made the Russians more reluctant to license to China. The PRC reportedly reverse-engineered the Su-27 fighter in order to develop its own domestic Shenyang J-11 aircraft. China received the license to build the Su-27s from Russia in 1995 for $2.5 billion, to cover 200 J-11A aircraft. Russia, however, terminated the contract in 2006, when it realized that China had created a reverse-engineered variant, the J-11B. Although China became the first importer of Russia's Su-35 fighter, questions remained as to whether China might again reverse-engineer the aircraft.[73] It appears, however, that China may well have other routes as well.[74]

Apart from Russian fears of Chinese reverse engineering, geopolitical considerations also complicate Sino-Russian defense-technological ties to some degree. Russia apparently strives to countervail Chinese leverage by diversifying its defense exports—including supplies to several of China's traditional rivals. While Russia exports large quantities of weapons to China, it also exports to countries with which China has territorial disputes, including India and Vietnam. In some cases, Moscow actually exports more advanced defense technology to India, with which it has longstanding defense-technology ties, than it does to the PRC.

There is, however, also a rising institutionalization of the bilateral Sino-Russian defense relationship since the 2014 introduction of Ukraine sanctions, with potential long-term global geopolitical consequences. The two countries are planning maneuvers, for example, in much more systematic fashion than heretofore, and consciously picking notably strategic venues such as the South China Sea in coordinated fashion. This structural shift is also manifest in the rising importance of defense-industry licensing contracts. As of late 2015, China and Russia had signed nine licensing contracts, including Russian assistance in China's production of fourth-generation Sukhoi-27 fighters as well as sea and air search radars. Five were signed in 2015, including the $2 billion deal for 24 Su-35s.[75] China has also been allowing Russia to pay off debts with weapons, acquiring advanced Su-35 related missiles and surplus engines, while collaborating selectively with Russia in defense electronics, cyber security, missile defense planning, and Internet management.

Strategic Implications

The strategic implications of Sino-Russian defense cooperation, operating within an increasingly asymmetric overall Sino-Russian relationship, have come in three main areas, with some especially important developments since the 2013–2014 Ukraine crisis. The first has had to do with antiaccess/area denial, specifically aimed at prohibitively increasing the potential cost of outside military support for Taiwan. During the late 1990s and early 2000s, while Lee Teng-hui and Chen Shui-bian were in power in Taiwan, Russia's most important arms supplies to the PRC appear to have been KILO-SS and Petersburg-Lada class submarines, the latter group of which were jointly designed and developed.[76] Russia also supplied 150 SS-N-27 anti–surface vessel cruise missiles during 2005–2009.[77] All this weaponry could be construed as strengthening China's antiaccess/area denial capabilities against US carrier battle groups, in a period during which China was particularly determined to inhibit what it considered provocative political-military steps by Taipei.[78]

In more recent years, Sino-Russian defense cooperation appears to have focused on a second area: air defense and aircraft development, with potentially broader geopolitical implications. To be sure, Russia has been balancing its arms sales to China with periodic sales of advanced hardware to potential Chinese rivals, as noted above. Moscow has, for example sold diesel submarines to Vietnam and more advanced Sukhoi-30 fighters to India.[79] Since the onset of the Ukraine crisis, however, Moscow has clearly enhanced its defense-technology support of Beijing to levels not provided to India.

A third area of cooperation has been military exercises, which have broadened substantially in both geographical and technical scope while increasingly reflecting the strategic interests of the two sides in turn.[80] Even as the Chinese and the Russians have institutionalized defense-technology cooperation to levels far beyond even those of the 1950s, they have also engaged in ever-more-complex and far-ranging joint exercises, recently including missile defense, and increasing the interoperability of their forces to unprecedented levels. Such joint exercises, which had been common in the 1950s, resumed only in 2005. Yet they have grown increasingly common over the past decade.

In Peace Mission 2005, a bilateral exercise conducted during August of that year at Vladivostok, the two countries practiced joint amphibious assaults, maritime blockade, and neutralizing antiaircraft defenses, against a "third-party" target resembling Taiwan.[81] Between January 2003 and December 2018, China and Russia held thirty joint military exercises, including seventeen bilateral and eleven within the SCO multilateral framework, mostly focusing on counterterrorism.[82] Since 2012, however, with Putin and Xi in leadership positions in their respective countries and with the specter of sanctions clouding Russian relations with the West, the character of joint exercises has changed.

In April 2012, the "Joint Sea" series of naval interactions was inaugurated, with enhanced geostrategic implications. In May 2014, this involved joint Sino-Russian maneuvers involving surface ships, submarines, and marine commando units in the East China Sea.[83]

In May 2015, the navies of Russia and China undertook a joint passage through the Dardanelles to begin the first-ever Sino-Russian joint exercise in the Mediterranean.[84] The second, conducted in August 2015, was equally ambitious in geopolitical terms, involving joint maneuvers in the Sea of Japan (East Sea) within days of the seventieth anniversary of Japan's surrender in World War II. This exercise also involved the first joint Sino-Russian amphibious maneuvers, uniquely relevant to Taiwan and East China Sea territorial issues, in fully a decade. The two countries also undertook major exercise together in the South China Sea during September 2016, following the ruling at the Permanent Court of Arbitration in The Hague against China's expansive South China Sea claims.[85] In 2017 they exercised in the Baltic and in 2018 in the Yellow Sea, thus continuing a pattern of alternating between areas of Russian and Chinese strategic interest that has continued at least since 2014.

In the fall of 2018, they conducted their largest joint exercise ever, in eastern Siberia, Vostok 2018, reportedly involving 300,000 Russian troops and over 3,000 from China.[86] In an additional step toward deeper Eurasian integration, Mongolia also participated. Vostok 2018 was the largest military exercise on Russian territory since 1981, and the first post–Cold War exercise to openly advertise an interstate-conflict scenario. Previous exercises were designed only to counter nontraditional security threats.

In Conclusion

Moscow is a natural, albeit junior, economic partner for a growing China—less than one-fifth its economic size—and an attractive strategic partner as well. Russia and China share a 2,200-mile border in the heart of Eurasia and have distinctly complementary resource endowments. China has provided the bulk of the increment in global energy demand for more than a decade, and for the foreseeable future will be the largest energy consumer in the world. Russia conversely has a quarter of the world's conventional natural gas reserves and substantial amounts of oil and other raw materials. In 2016 and 2017 it was also China's largest oil supplier.[87]

For most of the two centuries that Russia and China have been in close contact, the two Eurasian giants have had delicate and often explicitly conflictual relations. There has been a quantum transformation, however, over the past decade. The emergence of an increasingly durable Sino-Russian entente, we have seen here, is a function of four factors: (1) a deepening Russian estrangement from the West, intensified by the Ukrainian crisis and broader tensions over the post–Cold War expansion of NATO; (2) economic complementarities in the energy and manufacturing spheres; (3) a confluence of strategic interests between two global actors intent on undermining US unipolar hegemony; and (4) rising Chinese leverage in the bilateral relationship. Since the outbreak of the Ukrainian crisis, this entente has increasingly operated on Chinese terms.

As we have seen, the deepening Sino-Russian entente, in which China holds leverage, has had a series of dramatic manifestations since the Ukraine crisis erupted full-scale in early 2014. On the economic side, there has been the May 2014 Sino-Russian energy agreement and the May 2015 agreement to consolidate China's Silk Road Economic Belt and Russia's Eurasian Economic Union. On the security side, Russia is significantly expanding the range of defense equipment and technology it provides to China, including the advanced S-400 air defense system and the Sukhoi-35 fighter, Russia's latest fighter in actual production.[88] The two countries are also engaging in increasingly elaborate and geopolitically meaningful joint exercises. Post-Ukraine political-economic developments within the Sino-Russian relationship, in combination, are bringing Russia and China closer together, and in more durable institutionalized ways, than at any time since the Sino-Soviet split of the late 1950s. Their deepening entente is a major dimension of Eurasia's nascent transformation into a Super Continent; it intensifies, in particular, the insecurities of Taiwan, and the challenges of pariah states, while also providing China with greater access to Europe—an interlocutor of rising importance to Beijing, as we shall see in the chapter to follow.

The New Europe
Deepening Synergies

EUROPE AND CHINA STAND HALF a world apart: they lie at the antipodes of Eurasia. The two represent the core of contrasting civilizations; their relationship suffers from a complex heritage of both cultural distance and past imperialism. Yet they share a common landmass, and a history of important if intermittent contact, with few geophysical barriers between them. As the two largest manufacturers and technology centers on earth outside the United States, they also share compelling mutual economic attractions. For a Eurasian Super Continent of global consequence to arise, Europe and China would need to be its sustaining pillars.

As transatlantic tensions rise in the era of Trump, Europe and China grow steadily closer, building on interdependence fostered a decade ago by the Lehman Shock, and deeply synergistic with even more recent technological advance. That rising trans-Eurasian intimacy has social, economic, and even political dimensions, with potentially fateful long-term implications for the broader structure of world affairs. Europe and China, after all, despite their differences are the two core components of the global political economy with the greatest collective potential to challenge the preeminent global role of the United States and to provoke major structural changes in the international system.

Europe and China matter greatly for world affairs, because they are decidedly the largest entities in the international system, apart from the United States. The European Union, with a GDP of over $16 trillion in nominal terms, generates about 22 percent of the global product, while China adds another 15 percent. Together, they thus generate 37 percent of worldwide output, compared to only 25 percent for the US.[1] Both produce highly sophisticated technology. And given the huge population, rapid economic growth rate, and still low per capita income level of China, as well as the substantial growth potential of Europe, it is likely that the Sino-European aggregate will wield increasing weight in world affairs over the years to come.

A Checkered Path to Reconnection

China and Europe have been remote from one another in political-economic terms throughout most of recorded history and have not been well acquainted culturally. They once, however, nevertheless often experienced the fascination with the exotic that flows from distance. And that infatuation has recently rekindled once again.

The interaction between China and Europe, intimately entwined with the Silk Road's history, dates back at least two thousand years to intermittent trade between Han China and the Roman Empire. This commerce was especially vigorous following the pacification by Augustus of the entire Mediterranean region and his settlement with Parthia in 20 BC.[2] It lapsed as the Roman Empire disintegrated, revived during the Middle Ages, and atrophied once again with the voyages of discovery, as we shall see.

As noted in Chapter 2, trade between Europe and China along the Silk Road over the past two millennia has ebbed and flowed in intensity, conducted generally through intermediaries. For the first half and more of Silk Road history, Europe and China knew each other only quite indirectly, through the stories of Sogdians, Parthians, and other traders. One of the first Europeans who actually seems to have experienced China at length personally and popularized his views was Marco Polo, writing in the thirteenth century.[3]

Polo had the rare opportunity of travelling freely from Europe to China and back due to the unusual political stability and openness provided, ironically, by the brutal Mongol Empire, which invented the passport and inhibited the numerous brokers and middlemen who more normally limited Silk Road transactions and long-distance travel. Following the expulsion of the Mongols from China with the collapse of the Yuan Dynasty in 1368, direct intercourse between Europe and China became much more difficult. It was not until the sixteenth century that direct European relations with China began to revive once again, this time through the efforts of Jesuit missionaries, who saw in the huge Chinese population a bountiful potential harvest of souls for the Christian faith.

Among the most active and articulate of these Jesuits was another Italian, Matteo Ricci, who lived in China from 1583 to 1610.[4] Ricci, as Jonathan

Spence points out, "admired the industry of China's population, the sophistication of the country's bureaucracy, the philosophical richness of its cultural
traditions, and the strength of its rulers."[5] His meticulously detailed journals
provide one of the best early European accounts of classical China, albeit
from the laudatory perspective that was quite standard in Europe until at least
the mid-eighteenth century.

The French Jesuits, who dominated Christian interaction with China during the early Qing period (late seventeenth century), were even more effu-
sive about Chinese practices and potential than their Italian counterparts had
been. Behind this approach was a clear appeal to the "Sun King," Louis XIV,
to back their efforts with more money and personnel.[6] The French Jesuits
highlighted, in particular, the Confucian Classics, whose ethical content, they
argued, showed that the Chinese were a profoundly moral people who at one
point had practiced a form of monotheism so close to the Judeo-Christian
tradition that they should be natural converts to Christianity.

For two centuries and more the works of the Jesuits on Chinese government and society were the most detailed available in Europe. They profoundly shaped European views of China, even as Jesuit influence waned in
Europe, with the order being suppressed altogether by the papacy itself in
1773. As the eighteenth-century Enlightenment era dawned on the continent, Europe's view of China remained very much the positive one that Ricci
and the French Jesuits had espoused.

The German philosopher Gottfried Wilhelm von Leibnitz, his French
contemporary Voltaire, and French physiocrats like Francois Quesnay all read
and reflected on Chinese works in detail, admiring the Middle Kingdom particularly for rejecting feudal aristocracy and for embracing bureaucratic rule.
Voltaire euphorically suggested that China was the one country in the world
where the ruler was at the same time a philosopher, thus emulating Plato's
political ideal.[7] His vigorous advocacy ultimately helped inspire the birth of
the European civil-service tradition.[8] The anticlerical Voltaire did, however,
brilliantly reinterpret the Jesuits' laudatory view of Chinese moral probity,
contending that it demonstrated clearly why Christianity need not be the
basis of a moral society, since the Chinese were not Christians.[9]

Voltaire's fascination with China reflected the broader European cultural
sympathy of his age that evoked another common trait in transcontinental
Euro-Chinese relations: a tendency to view the Other through the prism of
one's own frustrations and hopes for the future. Europe in the mid-eighteenth
century was both opening to the world and teetering on the verge of revolu-

tion, seething with the frustrations of social transition—in some respects like the Europe of the 1960s, two centuries later. China presented a large and distinct alternative paradigm, whose attraction lay precisely in its ambiguity and freshness.

A cult of China, literally chinoiserie, spread broadly across Europe— far beyond the sociopolitical sphere. "In prints and descriptions of Chinese houses and gardens, and in Chinese embroidered silks, rugs, and colorful porcelains," as Spence points out, "Europeans found an alternative to the geometrical precision of their neoclassical architecture and the weight of baroque design."[10] Chinese aesthetics powerfully influenced everything from French rococo design to the pagodas that were erected in public parks, the sedan chairs that the wealthy used for transport, and the latticework surrounding ornamental gardens.

With the Enlightenment, however, also began an anguished sociopolitical debate over China's nature and the implications for Europe's relations with that enigmatic nation, which continues to be a hallmark of the Eurasian transcontinental relationship to this day.[11] Although Voltaire and Leibnitz were generally complimentary toward China, Rousseau and Montesquieu, by contrast, were sharply critical. They argued that, for all their cultural sophistication, the Chinese did not enjoy true liberty; that their laws were based more on fear than on reason; and that their elaborate educational system could well lead to the corruption of Chinese morals rather than to its improvement.[12] The Enlightenment debates of the eighteenth century thus eerily prefigured the intellectual confrontations that continue to roil Sino-European relations today.

However intimate Europeans and Chinese felt their relationship to be in the Age of Enlightenment, it evolved by quantum leaps in succeeding years, at an accelerating pace from the 1960s on that has—since 2015, when most European nations joined the Asian Infrastructure Investment Bank (AIIB)— taken on some dimensions of entente. The European Union today is China's largest trading partner, and China is the EU's number two, following only the United States. Cross-border investment is surging, with the Eurasian continent and even the Arctic beginning to offer increasingly attractive transit potential.[13] European and Chinese leaders hold annual summit conferences, and the Europeans shocked Washington in March 2015 by eagerly agreeing to join an AIIB organized by China that did not include the United States.[14]

To understand where the Sino-European relationship stands today and where it will go in the future, it is useful to recall where it has been in the recent past. After the cultural intimacy of the Enlightenment, China and Europe fell into a more distant and ambivalent relationship with the rise of European imperialism. In 1842, as a result of the First Opium War, the British annexed Hong Kong; unequal treaties with continental Europe and even Japan were to follow.

In 1949, in the words of Mao's historic address to the Chinese People's Political Consultative Conference, "The Chinese people stood up." Europe responded more favorably than the United States to the revolution, with Britain recognizing the People's Republic of China (PRC) in early 1950[15] together with several smaller European nations, such as Denmark, Finland, Sweden, and Switzerland. The large states of continental Europe, however, were slower.[16] One landmark development was Sino-French cross-recognition in 1964, followed by the triumphal visit to Beijing of French minister of culture Andre Malraux, whose seminal work *La Condition Humaine* (*Man's Fate*) had sympathetically portrayed the early Chinese Revolution.[17] Once again, France was leading Europe's intellectual engagement with China.

Despite superficial parallels to the past, today's Sino-European relationship is qualitatively different from that of the pre–Cold War period in ways that profoundly enhance its potential for the future. First of all, there is a sophisticated institutional structure for interaction that facilitates political-economic contacts, gives them predictability, and helps to insulate them from the anguished intellectual debates over China's political system that have wracked Europe since Voltaire and Rousseau. The central actor is the European Commission, founded in 1958. This supranational actor transcends the politics of individual nations, especially on economic issues, providing a technocratic, apolitical dimension that helps to stabilize the relationship and leads the EU-China Dialogue, which is composed of an annual EU-China Summit (since 1998), a High-Level Economic and Trade Dialogue (since 2008), and a High-Level People-to-People Dialogue (since 2012).[18] The unanimity rule at the international level in EU decision-making also inhibits rapid policy shifts in response to economic and financial flows.

The Asia-Europe Meeting (ASEM), inaugurated in 1996, also provides a broader "Track 1.5" structure for interaction among government officials, academics, and NGOs. The European Bank for Reconstruction and Development (EBRD) supplies an additional counterpart in the financial realm; China became the EBRD's sixty-seventh shareholder in January 2016.[19] In the security sphere, the North Atlantic Treaty Organization (NATO), based in Brussels, provides another technocratic contact point, albeit one with sensitive geopolitical implications.

EU Expansion: How It Deepens EU-China Relations

Over the past three decades, the European Union has changed internally in fundamental ways, with major, albeit heretofore little noticed, implications for the evolution of EU-China relations. Most importantly, it has expanded greatly in geographic terms to include two new groups of countries, with internal political-economic traits and historical experiences that contrast significantly to those of the original Cold War West European Six[20] and Nine.[21] Those two new entrant groups, depicted clearly in Map 8.1, were (1) Mediterranean countries, including Spain, Portugal, and Greece, which joined during the 1980s following their democratization;[22] and (2) nations of the "New Europe" (Eastern and Central European former satellites of the USSR) that entered the EU following the collapse of communism in the early 1990s.

The first group of post–European Nine—the new southern democracies—expanded the EU's presence in the Mediterranean for the first time since Italy's accession in 1958 at the European Community's (EC) initial foundation. Greece, Spain, and Portugal were nominally democratic—a condition of entry into the EU. Yet they were still fragile democracies, with traditionally interventionist militaries, strong labor unions, weak bureaucracies, and a rich civic tradition of governmental distrust. Not surprisingly, in later years these southern states fell into economic difficulties that made them notably amenable to economic support from rising outside economic powers like China.

Fresh EU entrants from the New Europe, indicated in Map 8.1, who entered the EU nearly two decades later than their Mediterranean cousins, have in turn fallen into three categories: (1) former Warsaw Pact members, such as Poland, the Czech Republic, and Hungary; (2) former constituent parts of the Soviet Union itself until the early 1990s; and (3) elements of the former Yugoslavia. The first group has broader and more stable relations with the world, due to their more established international standing. The second includes the Baltic states (Estonia, Latvia, and Lithuania), which had been independent for over two decades prior to being absorbed into the Soviet Union by Stalin in 1940.[23] And integration of Yugoslav components remains incomplete, with only Slovenia and Croatia having joined the EU so far.

The New Europe members of the EU share two distinctive traits deriving from Cold War days: (1) longstanding and generally positive traditional relations with China, a longtime fellow socialist state with whom they traditionally balanced to increase autonomy from the former Soviet Union; and (2) delicate, often hostile, relations with Russia, their former imperial master,

MAP 8.1 Expansion of the European Union (1957–2013)
SOURCE: Author's illustration based on European Union, "EU Member Countries in Brief," https://europa.eu /european-union/about-eu/countries/member-countries_en.
NOTE: The United Kingdom will be leaving the European Union during 2019.

dominated by a fear of renewed Russian geopolitical assertiveness.[24] The New Europe thus provides distinctively strong geopolitical support for deepened relations with China, apart from the economic motives often stressed, even as it also introduces a pronounced cautionary note into the EU's relations with Russia. Indeed, the very ambivalence about neighboring Russia's renewed assertiveness under Vladimir Putin intensifies the New Europe's interest in having far-off China as a balancer; the more threatening Russia becomes, the more attractive China therefore seems to be.

In 1992 the Maastricht Treaty committed the core members of Europe to currency integration, which sharply intensified their trade and financial interdependence. The treaty also mandated an increased level of fiscal and regulatory coordination. Following the actual birth of the Euro in 1999, with eleven members, monetary integration initially led to a spurt of growth in the new member nations, including those of the Mediterranean, as governments, businesses, and consumers all rushed to avail themselves of the lower interest rates and expanded borrowing opportunities that flowed from the union.[25] With the growth spurt, however, also came a steady expansion of debt, which cast a deepening shadow over the viability of the monetary union in succeeding years.

Increasing *diversity* is thus a hallmark of the New Europe, which has emerged over the past quarter century, together with a much higher level of regional and global interdependence than had previously prevailed. Some— but certainly not all—of the New Europe welcomes deepening economic interdependence with China. Crucially, however, the European Union operates on decision rules of *unanimity*. Thus, individual states that benefit from deepened interdependence with China, such as poorer states of Eastern and Southern Europe, like Hungary, the Czech Republic, and Greece, are in a position to block efforts to constrain a forceful response to China in many areas, even when core Western members may consider it justified.[26]

The Security Dimension of Europe's Transformation

The North Atlantic Treaty Organization (NATO) has a provenance even longer than that of the European economic integration process. Formed in response to the Czech coup and Berlin blockade of 1948, it was constituted nearly a decade before the EC was established in 1957. Like the EC, NATO expanded thereafter in several waves, especially following the fall of the Berlin Wall and the collapse of the Warsaw Pact in the 1990s. During the 2000s, it grew still further to include even three former republics of the Soviet Union—Estonia, Latvia, and Lithuania. It includes a few nations, such as Albania, Montenegro, and Turkey, that are not members of the EU, and excludes some neutral countries, like Austria, Finland, Ireland, and Sweden, that are conversely part of the EU. In general, however, the memberships of the two multilateral bodies are similar and have expanded in similar directions over the past several decades.

NATO's expansion has significance for the Sino-European relationship for three reasons. First, it intensifies the deepening tensions and estrangement between Russia and much of Europe—especially in the East. This naturally enhances the role of China as a strategic balancer—a role the PRC often also played during the Cold War from the late 1950s on. Second, NATO's eastward expansion, beginning in the 1990s, introduced nations into Western ranks with long experience in and personal contacts with China that have since facilitated European economic and diplomatic relations with Beijing. Third, NATO's expansion mutes the ambivalence of the United States about expanding Sino-European ties, due to the felicitous impact that such ties have on NATO's deterrence capabilities vis-à-vis Russia.

Rising Chinese Trade and Investment in Europe

The deepening Sino-European relationship flows both from developments within China as well as the historic changes in Europe outlined above. On the trade side, China's explosive growth of the past four decades, coupled with a degree of trade liberalization after China joined the WTO in December 2001, have naturally made China a larger and larger market for European firms, as indicated in Figure 8.1. The pace of expansion in trade reliance on China has flattened since 2010, however, as China's growth has slackened and penetrating the Chinese market has grown more difficult, for a variety of reasons.

The most dynamic element of recent Sino-European economic relations has been Chinese investment in Europe. Chinese investment flows into the EU first exceeded the converse in 2014. Between 2014 and 2017, Chinese

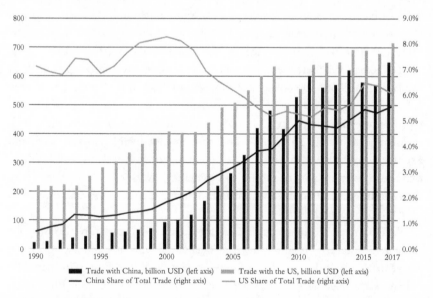

FIGURE 8.1 Rising EU reliance on the Chinese market (1990–2017)
SOURCE: International Monetary Fund, *Direction of Trade Statistics*, accessed June 26, 2018.

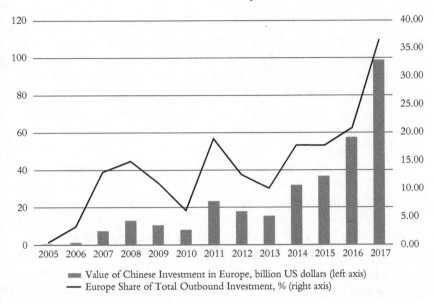

FIGURE 8.2 Rising Chinese investment in Europe

SOURCE: American Enterprise Institute and the Heritage Foundation, *China Global Investment Tracker*, updated January 2018.

foreign direct investment (FDI) into the EU outpaced EU investment flows into China by a factor of three, bringing the stock of Chinese FDI in the EU to the same level as EU investment in China by 2017.[27] Chinese investment within the Union *doubled* in 2016 alone, to around $40 billion, constituting fully a quarter of the PRC's global total.[28] China has also been investing heavily in European countries such as Serbia and its western Balkan neighbors, that are not yet members of the EU, but are included in the data presented in Figure 8.2. As indicated in Figure 8.2, which includes data for all European countries except Russia, such investment has soared, particularly since 2010. In 2010, Europe as a whole shared only 6.4 percent of total Chinese outbound investment. By 2017, however, Europe's share had risen to 36.8 percent.

Two Recent Critical Junctures Catalyze a Redefined and Deepened Interdependence

Throughout the 1990s and 2000s, Sino-European relations continued to deepen in trade, investment, and cultural relations. Yet so too, under the pressures of globalization, did China's relations with North and South America, as well as Africa, not to mention Europe's ties with Southeast Asia and with

South America as well. The general pressures of globalization were propelling transregionalism throughout the world, with deepened Eurasian ties just one manifestation of a broader globalizing trend.

Two critical junctures in the late 1970s and early 1990s, however, gave birth to an increasingly integrated geo-economic playing field within Eurasia specifically. These junctures included China's Four Modernizations (1978) and the collapse of the Soviet Union (1991). The second of these relates profoundly to the geo-economics of both Europe and Asia, with a special corollary in Europe. The Soviet collapse was in fact part, in the European theater, of a broader post–Cold War transformation that really began with the fall of the Berlin Wall in November 1989 and also involved the wholesale collapse of communism across Eastern Europe. That in turn allowed the EU and NATO expansions that have so profoundly transformed Europe in recent years.

Since 2008 two new critical junctures—one an economic phenomenon and the second a security development—have accelerated the pace of Eurasian regional integration and the deepening of Sino-European relations in particular, as noted in Chapter 3. The first of these fateful recent developments was the global financial crisis (GFC) of 2008, which shook the Western industrial world to its foundations on both sides of the Atlantic. Meanwhile, China launched a massive stimulus program, which rapidly enhanced Chinese political-economic influence in the ravaged West. The GFC led before long, in a weakened Europe, to a related crisis of the Euro.

This crisis of the south, largely divorced from the dynamic post–Cold War forces at work in Germany and the Visegrad nations, has bubbled on episodically since 2010. It affected all of the Mediterranean countries (Spain, Portugal, Italy, and Greece), but came to a head in the protracted Greek financial difficulties since 2009. As with the Ukraine crisis to follow, the Greek crisis has its roots in an ambitious structural attempt to bind the nations of Europe together that ran into difficulty. A rapidly rising China—the largest creditor nation in the world, with over $3 trillion in foreign-exchange reserves—looms as an important and empathetic potential stabilizer for Europe, in contrast to the impotence or perverse intentions of Russia, and the reticence of the United States.

In relation to the crisis of the Euro, however, China's potential role is also quite direct. The Eurozone has expanded, for geopolitical reasons, to include nations, many of them Mediterranean, that find it difficult to adjust sociopolitically to the austere, frugal policy standards of Northern Europe. The result of this disjunction has been periodic financial crises in the southern-tier Euro members as they struggle with chronic budget deficits and with structural reform. These were the focal points of financial crises in 2010 and 2014–2015. This pattern could easily reemerge in future, given the Mediterranean's intractable fiscal problems.

With the introduction of the Euro in 1999 and its steadily broadening usage across the continent, the fates of the stronger economies of northern Europe became increasingly linked with the success of the weaker ones to the south. Mediterranean Europe has expanded its trade with China very rapidly since 2000, even as Japanese trade with the Mediterranean has been declining. And the Mediterranean—particularly its eastern portion—has special geo-economic attraction for Beijing, given its proximity to major shipping routes to and from China. Thanks to Chinese growth and eagerness to engage, each of the Mediterranean nations has grown increasingly dependent on China over the past five years, even as dependence on Japan has significantly fallen.[29]

Direct foreign investment has followed a similar pattern. Capital outflows from China to Europe as a whole have accelerated substantially in the past five years, as previously indicated in Figure 8.2. And relative to the size of struggling local economies, the flows to the nations of the Mediterranean—Europe's vulnerable southern tier—have been particularly large, even though these southern countries have also experienced lower growth and higher inflation than their brothers to the north and a sharper decline in overall foreign investment.[30] Interestingly, Chinese investment flows have been sharply less to Ireland—a target of the 2010 financial crisis, but not on the Mediterranean—than to the southern tier. China, in short, has been increasingly important in propping up the weaker nations of the European Union, such as Greece—a role that naturally brings it more importance not only in the weaker nations themselves but with EU authorities in Brussels as well. Japan, by contrast, has not actively assumed as decisive a stabilizing role.

The second of these fateful developments affecting Sino–European relations was the Ukraine crisis, erupting first in November 2013. The Russia-oriented Yanukovych administration rejected the prospect of affiliation with the European Union, provoking sustained protests on the Maidan, Kiev's central square. These spiraled upward into violence and ultimately revolution. The pro-Moscow regime was deposed, replaced by a militantly anti-Putin coalition, with whom an escalating conflict ultimately provoked Russia's March 2014 annexation of Crimea and subsequent Western sanctions. Those in turn led to intensified East-West military confrontation—not only in Ukraine but also involving increased Russian pressure on the Baltics and other recalcitrant parts of the former Soviet Union.[31]

East-West tensions over Ukraine have conversely enhanced Sino-European relations in several ways, as noted in both Chapters 3 and 7. These tensions have seriously alienated Russia from much of Europe, thus forcing the Russians into the arms of the more welcoming Chinese. This shift in the Sino-Russian relationship has given China more leverage in Central Asia, long a Russian preserve, as well as in Belarus, making it easier for the Chinese to use the entire former Soviet Union as a transit platform to Europe. Tensions over Ukraine have also made China more geopolitically attractive to the Europeans than previously, as a prospective balancer against an increasingly aggressive Russian bear.

Looking forward, it appears that the tensions unleashed in the Ukraine crisis, on both the Russian and Western European sides, could be quite fundamental. They call into question the longstanding concept of a "common European home" from the Atlantic to the Urals, espoused by Russian and European leaders since the late Cold War days of Mikhail Gorbachev.[32] Coupled with expanded Russian military pressures against the Baltic states and Poland—now members of NATO—Russian tensions with Europe also call into question the credibility of the Western alliance itself. The West cannot easily back down in the face of Russian pressures. And the Russians, themselves threatened by the strategic dangers that they perceive from a Western alliance intruding into the heart of the former Soviet Union, cannot easily avoid pressuring the West to withdraw.

China, in contrast to Russia, is hardly challenged by the new strategic reality epitomized in the Ukraine crisis. A NATO ensconced in the heart of the former Warsaw Pact, and indeed increasingly in the heart of the former Soviet Union itself, does not challenge Beijing the way it does Moscow. To the contrary, this new reality presents expanded leverage for China, since it can remain on good terms with both Russia and Europe even as they feud with one another. And since the new reality of a NATO expanded eastward is structural, this situation is quite basic and likely to institutionalize Russo-European tensions—as well as related Chinese opportunities in Eastern Europe—for some years to come.

Special Chinese Complementarity with Central Europe

Chinese trade and investment in Europe has been rising with particular speed and intensity of late toward the industrial heart of Europe: Germany and the so-called Visegrad 4 countries (Poland, Hungary, the Czech Republic, and Slovakia). Together, these five countries—the so-called German-Central European Manufacturing Core, or GCEMC—account for close to half of all the European Union's manufacturing value-added exports, a share that has risen significantly since the 2008 GFC.[33] This GCEMC regional manufacturing complex, which emerged powerfully during the 1990s on the ashes of Europe's Cold War divisions, replaces earlier and less dynamic supply chains linking West Germany with Italy and France. Its strength is buttressed by short and efficient production networks across one-time Cold War boundaries in Central Europe that combine technology and labor cost synergies due to the fortuitous geo-economic proximities that are clear in Map 8.2.

The post–Cold War GCEMC is now among the most competitive industrial bases in the world for production of precision machinery, automobiles, and fine chemicals. It has a geo-economic logic, reflected in short, efficient supply chains, that is second to none. Thanks to the GCEMC's productivity, Germany is today the fourth largest industrial producer in the world, exceeded only by China, the United States, and Japan.[34] The PRC itself has strong strategic interest in precisely these sectors of GCEMC industrial strength, as indicated in the "Made in China 2025" ten-year plan, unveiled in 2015.[35]

BMW's interaction and deepening cooperation with China illustrates the synergies at work. China is now BMW's largest, and one of its fastest growing markets.[36] The firm operates both component and final assembly facilities at both ends of Eurasia, including several in the GCEMC, and sends 3-7 trains weekly to China.[37] It is also cooperating with Chinese firms in its movement into electric-vehicle markets, as we shall see later in this chapter.

The scale and future potential of the industrial symbiosis between China and the GCEMC, with Germany at its core, is graphically clear from recent trade and investment figures. China is the largest market in the world for German industrial machinery. Between 2002 and 2015, German trade with China grew 326 percent, as opposed to an average of 32 percent for German trade with the EU as a whole.[38] Overall, by 2016 German exports to China had risen to almost 45 percent of all EU exports to China, or 6.4 percent of all German exports—the highest ratio in the EU.[39] In 2016, China became the largest source of German imports worldwide, with bilateral Sino-German trade as a whole approaching $200 billion annually.[40]

Investment trends have paralleled those in trade, with Chinese investment in Central Europe, like Chinese trade there, rising with particular intensity since the 2008 Lehman Shock. Chinese investment and construction contracts in Germany between January 2005 and June 2018 totaled over

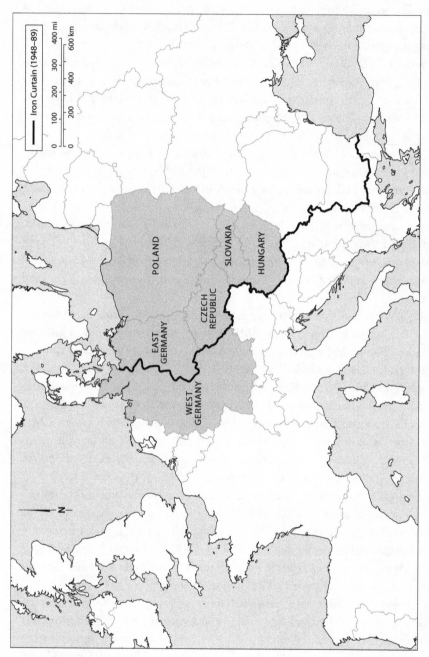

MAP 8.2 Germany, the Visegrad Four, and the shadow of Cold War divisions

$37 billion, second only to Britain, and around 11 percent of China's total for the EU as a whole.[41] Chinese investment in Germany and the Visegrad nations was concentrated strongly in automobiles, electrical machinery, chemicals, industrial machinery, and construction—areas of special German competitiveness. Corporate acquisitions have included the German robotics manufacturer Kuka, one of the world's leading suppliers of intelligent automation solutions, and Kraussmaffei, a world leader in the production of robotic automated tools and engineering plastics. Geely, the Chinese owner of Volvo, also acquired 9.7 percent of Daimler in February 2018.[42]

Cooperation between German and Chinese firms is also deepening in the strategic realms of electric vehicles and battery development. In July 2018, for example, China's CATL, the world's largest maker of battery cells for electric vehicles, signed an agreement with BMW to source 4 billion Euros ($4.7 billion) of battery cells from CATL over the next few years. 1.5 billion Euros worth are to be produced by CATL at a site in Erfurt, eastern Germany.[43]

The Rising Importance of Infrastructure

The sectoral composition of recent Chinese investment in Europe is as interesting as its magnitude. There are, of course, the luxury investments in Bordeaux vineyards. Chinese firms, however, also bought controlling interests in Swedish auto manufacturer Volvo, Norwegian offshore oil exploration firms, key Portuguese banks, and even Club Med.[44] Also notable are the substantial investments in infrastructure, with energy, construction, and real estate being three areas of significant Chinese investment in Europe.[45]

Recent trends in Chinese infrastructural investment within Europe, including the massive Belt and Road Initiative (BRI) expenditures since 2013, have a complex yet compelling logic. That logic can be understood only in the context of both post–Cold War European economic transformation, discussed above, and the related revolution in Eurasian infrastructure, considered below. With the Iron Curtain division of Europe from the Baltic to the Adriatic ended, locational economics and infrastructural imperatives on the continent have radically shifted.

With the dynamic core of European manufacturing moving to the Central European access routes noted above, routes to that core have become increasingly important. Several such routes are illustrated in Map 8.3. These alternatives have included rail networks into the Visegrad nations from the east, across Belarus; access overland from Turkey or Greece by rail; and Central Europe. China has been particularly active and strategic in promoting a construction route up through the Western Balkans, from Greece through non-EU former Yugoslavian states to Budapest, known as the Land-Sea Express. Its project, already under construction, upstages the EU Commission's proposed TEN-T Orient/East Mediterranean Corridor project, still on the drawing board, which is scheduled to run through Romania and Bulgaria, both EU member states.

Infrastructure, of course, has an increasingly important high-tech dimension, which could bind Europe—especially emerging East and Central Europe—more closely to China in future. High-speed telecommunications, including so-called 5G linkages, combined with IoT technology, have the potential to link production processes smoothly over long distances, if politics

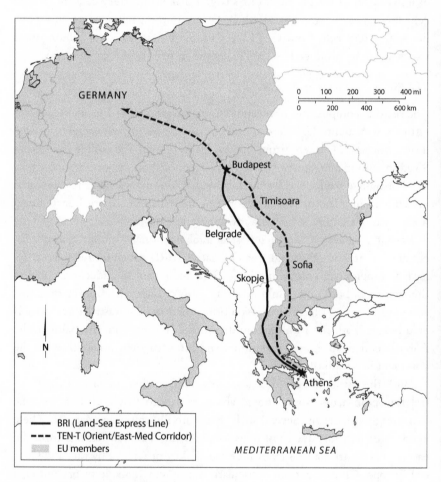

MAP 8.3 The Orient/East-Mediterranean corridor

and regulatory barriers do not interfere. Communications is thus synergistic with physical infrastructure, creating the potential for major improvements in B2B e-commerce, as well as supply-chain development, in coming years. The digital dimension of transcontinental relations, a veritable "Digital Silk Road," will doubtless grow increasingly important in the future, although thorny issues relating to standards policy and investment transparency remain.

BRI-related investments within the EU, especially its central and eastern portions, could well thus lay the groundwork for still deeper Chinese political-economic involvement with Europe, while enhancing Chinese geopolitical influence as well. A clear example of how Chinese investments can lay the basis for greater future influence, corresponding to China's changing geo-economic needs in Europe, is the port of Piraeus, directly adjacent to Athens, where the US once concluded an agreement to homeport one of its eleven aircraft carriers.[46] There COSCO, China's largest shipping company and a government-affiliated firm, has invested nearly $5 billion since 2009. COSCO now owns two of the major piers at Piraeus as well as a 67 percent stake in the Piraeus complex as a whole.[47] The complex itself, thanks to refurbishing and the rising importance of intermodal trade from China via the Suez Canal and Indian Ocean, is now the seventh busiest container port in Europe and the thirty-eighth busiest worldwide.[48] China is also financing railways northward from Piraeus into the Balkans, including the trunk railway line through Macedonia, as well as the principal Belgrade to Budapest high-speed rail link.[49] The hybrid rail and maritime inter-modal route which these new facilities make possible takes half the time of the closest purely maritime alternative, at less than half the price of a purely overland routing.[50]

Growing Ambivalence in the West and North

Chinese investment in Europe started in Britain. It has risen rapidly of late in Europe's central industrial core, as well as in infrastructure leading to the continent's economic heart. Such investment has been much less vigorous in Scandinavia, Ireland, and several other nations in the west and north of the continent. And that investment has often privileged the creation of Chinese-dominated production chains, providing only limited opportunity for non-Chinese workers and corporations.

The potential synergies between China and Europe as a whole are substantial and deepening, as we have seen, especially in the technological sphere. Yet they are skewed geographically and sectorally. The multilateral and supranational institutions of Europe are consensus based and generally supportive of open trade and investment regimes, and so will be slow to grow protectionist.

Yet an ambivalence to Chinese inroads in Europe and to Chinese protectionism at home is rising, especially in the north and west. It should not be
dismissed.

Steel has been the major recent political flashpoint. In 2016 EU lawmakers
voted against China's application for "market-economy status" under WTO
law, which if granted would reduce penalties in antidumping cases.[51] Their
reason was steel: China's huge production capacity has been flooding world
markets and threatening the robust industrial base that the European Commission identifies as essential for jobs, growth, and competitiveness.

Some influential West European think tanks have also been ambivalent
about China's deepening involvement in Europe. Prominent among them has
been MERICS, which has warned that China's industrial policies, epitomized
in "China 2025," could have serious negative implications, especially in the
high-technology sphere, for European manufacturers, particularly German.[52]

In 2014–2015 Western European leaders, beginning with British prime
minister David Cameron, welcomed China's AIIB initiative and rapidly
agreed to join. By mid-2017, however, due to deepening trade and investment concerns, several were more hesitant. The prime ministers of Spain,
Hungary, and Greece, together with the Polish president, all participated in
China's May 2017 Belt and Road Forum, chaired by Xi Jinping, and made
laudatory speeches about BRI. None of the major West European leaders, the
EU president, or the EU Commission's director attended, however. On her
eleventh official visit to China, German chancellor Angela Merkel in May
2018 stressed the need for reciprocal access, especially in high-tech sectors
where Chinese capacity is rising, warning of potential European backlash if
such reciprocity were not forthcoming.[53] Both the EU's unanimity rules and
the responsibility of individual states for implementation of common rules
within the union, however, inhibited a proactive actual policy response to
rapidly deepening Chinese involvement in sensitive high-tech sectors.

The Rising Geo-Economic Importance of Central and Southeastern Europe

As noted earlier, during the early post–Cold War years an important new
transnational manufacturing complex, the GCEMC, was born across previous Cold War boundaries in Germany and neighboring Visegrad nations and
subsequently began developing dynamic new geo-economic ties with China.
A second new area of interaction, as we have seen, was in the Mediterranean.
Most recently, since 2012, China has established a still broader and more
formal cooperation framework in the region, with sixteen Central-Eastern

and Southeastern European nations. This is known as the 16+1 Cooperation Framework. It has rapidly become a priority of Chinese policy overtures with respect to Europe, due no doubt to the geo-economic importance of long-term Sino-European cooperation to the countries involved, the complementarity of their economies with China, and the rising ambivalence to Chinese inroads in Western Europe, as noted above. The 16+1 has become quite formalized, with a secretariat, national coordinators, and regular meetings. The forum geographically includes the Visegrad 4, but also encompasses a much broader region east of Germany and stretching from the Baltics to the Black Sea, as indicated in Map 8.4.

The 16+1 framework has both trade and investment dimensions, with a particularly strong focus on infrastructure relating to the BRI and directed toward making eastern Europe a strategic gateway for two-way trade between China and Europe. The forum has already established a $10 billion special credit line, used mainly by Balkan nations outside of the EU, provided by a consortium of Chinese banks; an investment cooperation fund between China and the European members; economic and technological zones in each member country, to facilitate cooperation with China; and a dedicated China–Central European Fund, unveiled by Chinese prime minister Li Keqiang at the November 2016 meeting of the forum, to finance infrastructure projects in relation to a new connectivity initiative. Chinese exports to Albania, Bosnia-Herzegovina, Montenegro, Serbia, and Macedonia—the non-EU members of the forum—have grown especially rapidly: China's exports to these nations more than doubled between 2004 and 2014 while its imports increased sevenfold.[54]

Building the Economic Highways across Eurasia to Europe

There is no question that Chinese trade with and investment in Europe itself is rapidly expanding, both absolutely and relative to Chinese economic involvement in most other parts of the world. This is true even though Europe is a formidably long distance from China, across a Eurasian landmass that traditionally has been neither economically nor politically hospitable to transit travel. Beijing, after all, lies well over 6,000 miles from the eastern borders of the EU, and the western reaches of the continent in the Iberian Peninsula are close to a thousand miles further still.

Despite the raw distance, however, intermodal transit trade from China, across Eurasia, to Western Europe and back has begun to accelerate rapidly since around 2013, following its inauguration in 2011. This trade typically

MAP 8.4 The 16+1 Cooperation Framework Nations

involves multiple means of transport—not just rail or ship, but road and
sometimes air as well. A strategic European logistics hub at Duisburg and its
Chinese counterpart in Chongqing have been linked in similar, systematic
fashion since January 2011.[55] Regular freight service opened between the two
destinations in 2014. Scheduled overland shipping routes from the massive lo-

gistical hub of Yiwu in China's Zhejiang province[56] to Madrid have also been operating since December 2014.[57]

Many transcontinental rail services remain highly subsidized,[58] but there is no question that they are rapidly expanding, especially from the Chinese side and, within China, from inland economic centers. Such services grow more and more economically efficient, of course, as the volume increases. The value of total overland trade using these routes exceeded $17 billion in 2015.[59] In January 2017, a demonstration rail freight service between China and Britain also began, leaving Yiwu on the seventeen-day voyage to London and returning to Yiwu three months later.[60] By the end of 2018, over 10,000 transcontinental cargo trips by rail between Europe and China had been taken, with well over 3,000 in 2017 alone.

China's National Development and Reform Commission (NDRC) in October 2016 announced a "China Railway Express Construction and Development Plan for 2016–2020" that is expanding Europe-China rail service still further. The plan aims to connect more cities from more regions across China to the long-distance trunk service and to consolidate the transcontinental network outside China, by building railway hubs in Central-Eastern Europe as well as Central-Western Asia under the BRI. The NDRC aspires to see three corridors open systematically to connect China and Europe, as indicated in Map 4.5.

Cargo flights between China and Europe have also been rapidly expanding. Helsinki and Chongqing are now extensively linked. So are Shanghai, Amsterdam, and Frankfurt. Large new transit air-cargo facilities like Navoi in Uzbekistan are also being erected to accommodate the increased air freight across the continent, mainly from Europe to China, Korea, and back.[61] Interestingly, the UK and China responded to the Brexit vote by removing all limits on the number of cargo flights between the two countries, suggesting the future potential of Britain as a catalyst for transcontinental trade.[62]

Cargo traffic is rising across Eurasia, between China and Europe, in part due to the rising scale of transcontinental trade, including bulky items such as machinery and some electronics that travel easily by rail. Rising Chinese plant investment in Europe—as well as European investment in China—is also inspiring greater movement of capital goods for building and equipping new factories. China has, after all, rapidly become the manufacturing hub of the entire world over the past two decades, with its share of global industrial production more than quadrupling during 2000–2016 to nearly 25 percent of the entire world's total.[63]

Trade between China and Europe, however, has been substantial for well over three decades. Little of it until recently, however, moved by land, despite the clear geographical benefits of doing so. The overland route from Shanghai to Hamburg is around one-third shorter than the alternative distance by sea, with the differential even greater for inland locations.[64] Yet until recently the land alternative was little used.

What one really needs to ask is why the recent growth of overland and intermodal transport between Europe and China—or from Europe to Northeast Asia more generally—is at last occurring. This has five central aspects. First, transport technology is changing, radically reducing the cost of intermodal transport, which can include a cost-effective combination of overland and maritime. Second, customs clearance is growing more transparent and efficient due to computerization. Third, infrastructure itself is physically improving. Fourthly, in the case of Eurasia, geographical distances in question are simply much shorter overland—roughly 40 percent in the case of key economic locations on both sides. And finally, reflecting the foregoing, multinational firms are finding transcontinental supply chains to be cost effective.

Technological change is doubtless reducing transport costs. Container shipping is growing cheaper and more efficient. Shifting from one means of conveyance to another is growing cheaper due to computerization. Meanwhile, cargo trains are growing faster and more powerful, although clearly not approaching the quickness of high-speed rail. On the consumer side, new service innovations, such as Alibaba's Alipay credit-purchase system, now ubiquitous in Europe as well as China, are also facilitating transcontinental commerce.

An even greater catalyst for transcontinental transit trade, however, comes from increasingly efficient border clearance procedures. Massive clearance centers like Khorgos on the Chinese-Kazakh frontier have arisen, fostered by multilaterals like the Asian Development Bank and supported by computerization. These transportation and logistics nodes process cargo more rapidly and much more transparently than even a few years ago.[65]

The inauguration of the Russian-inspired Eurasian Economic Union in January 2015 now means that there are effectively only two land frontiers to be crossed—the newly streamlined China-Kazakh border and the frontier between Belarus and the EU.[66] This administrative simplification enhances still further the efficiency of transcontinental land and intermodal transport. With increased investment, facilitated by rising economic attractions and improved relations between China and Europe, the quality of both rail and road connections is also improving. And companies like BMW and Hewlett Packard are capitalizing on the new political-economic environment, now including increased latitude for corporate control of China-based subsidiaries, by creating and expanding transcontinental production networks.[67]

Taken together, these four important changes in the political economy of overland transit trade between China and Europe, plus the underlying geographical advantages, are accelerating the attractiveness of interdependence across the continent itself. So, from a long-term perspective, are developments around the northern rim of the continent along the long-neglected but increasingly promising Arctic transit route. Like overland transit across Eurasia, the northern sea route between China and Europe has substantial geographic attraction, cutting as much as 40 percent off the distance between Shanghai and Hamburg, for example.[68]

Due ironically to the generally perverse consequences of global warming, the northern seas from the Bering Strait to Murmansk and beyond are growing passable, albeit still only with icebreaker support. In 2012 the first commercial vessels traversed the northern sea lanes, initially between Korea and Norway.[69] In 2013 the number of commercial passages along the full Arctic sea route more than doubled. More recent trends suggest that full commercialization of the Arctic routes will take time. Yet some 200,000 tons of commercial cargo was still transported between Asia and Europe on the Arctic route during 2017.[70]

In Conclusion

Historic changes in transport, finance, and industry over the past two decades have created a natural space for steadily deepening Sino-European relations, especially in Central and Eastern Europe, grounded in historical networks from Cold War days. Meanwhile, new transit routes across and around Eurasia between China and Europe are growing more numerous, more cost-efficient, and easier to use, thus amplifying political-economic supports for deepening Sino-European interdependence, and the gradual emergence of a Eurasian Super Continent. Rapidly developing new transport options are just as rapidly drawing Europe and China closer together and are synergistic with financial, industrial, and e-commerce complementarities. Structural transformations of early post–Cold War days in Europe, newly including the expansion of NATO and the birth of the Euro, intensify serious, fundamental strategic tensions between Russia and much of Europe. Deepening American provincialism under Donald Trump, together with differences over security and environmental matters, are complicating Europe's traditionally central transatlantic ties.

Europe's relations with China are not without shadows, especially for the northwestern side of the continent, which is growing less rapidly and remains more challenged industrially by China than the south and the east. On trade, steel is a flashpoint, with high-tech sectors as a rising concern. Demands for both trade and investment reciprocity are rising, as Chinese global competitiveness steadily rises. Yet unanimity rules within the European Union inhibit a coherent policy response, despite the marked frustrations with the status quo.

For much of Europe, especially Germany, the Mediterranean, and former socialist states in the East, China looms as an attractive partner, despite some long-term misgivings. Deepening Sino-European ties across Eurasia, leveraged by new technologies eroding the tyranny of transcontinental distance, give the continent the sheer mass and integrity in global geo-economic terms that Mackinder foresaw a century ago. Sino-European reconnection leads both Eurasia and the world ever closer to the fateful era of a broader, worldwide systemic transition point, a Crossover Point, raising the specter of historic transformations in global political-economic governance that remain only dimly and vaguely understood.

Shadows and Critical Uncertainties

OUR EMERGING TWENTY-FIRST-CENTURY WORLD is a complex mosaic of multiple, intertwined transformations at the national, regional, and global levels. The globalization that has grown ever more pervasive since the 1970s is creating clear winners and losers at every stage. And these changes in political-economic standing are occurring with a speed that can easily leave analysts with outdated paradigms, while rendering their leaders devoid of relevant, effective tools for response.

Political-economic ties across Eurasia have been deepening steadily in the post–Cold War world, as we have seen. Both Europe and Russia have forged dramatically closer relationships with China than was true five or even three years ago. These new alignments hold strong promise of creating a new, more multipolar order in the uncertain new world of multiple domestic transitions that is now emerging. These transitions, beginning with the epic changes in China and coupled with the approaching Eurasian and global Crossover Points, show prospect of dramatically changing the face of world affairs.

From the early pages of this volume, we have stressed the pervasive theme of transformation; the world, and Eurasia within it, have recently entered an unprecedented era of structural change at multiple levels. Momentous national, regional, and even global reconfigurations are transpiring. Domestic transformations in China, Russia, and Central Europe, in particular, are provoking broader Eurasian continental changes replete with global significance.

Shadows on China's Transformation

China is the world's largest economy in purchasing power parity (PPP) terms and also the largest in population, situated at the very heart of the world's largest continent. This Middle Kingdom has been the driver behind Eurasia's remarkable growth for over a generation. Its internal transformation from a maritime into an increasingly continental power has also been a critical stimulus to the deepening Chinese interdependence with Russia and Central Europe—a globally significant development that we have documented in the past two chapters. China's own domestic Crossover Point thus has profound significance for global affairs more generally.

Although China has remained remarkably stable for more than four decades since the end of the Cultural Revolution in 1976, it is crucially important to remember the monumental challenge that the problem of simple governance presents in a nation of nearly 1.4 billion—well over four times the population of the United States. In contrast to democratic India, with over 1.3 billion people itself, China lacks the "safety valve" of political pluralism—it cannot easily legitimate its leaders through the ballot box or readily jettison on electoral grounds those who have lost popular confidence.

The PRC has traditionally been governed through the Communist Party of China (CPC), supported by the People's Liberation Army (PLA). The rise of civil society and a vibrant middle class, driven by globalism, has rendered CPC rule less secure. Deepening economic inequality, flowing from disproportionate economic growth dividends to entrepreneurs and social elites, has intensified the challenge of party legitimacy. The CPC has responded with nationalist assertions, particularly against Japan, which have in turn deepened regional tensions. The East China and South China Seas have emerged as arenas for unprecedented conflict with Vietnam, the Philippines, Japan, the US, and others.

The problem of domestic governance has been a major catalyst for the continentalist policies that have over the past two decades become an increasingly pronounced dimension of Chinese foreign policy as well as local government strategy. Over the first two decades of Chinese post-1978 development, the transpacific export surge and the influx of multinational corporations into the PRC quietly fueled the rise of China's middle class. Yet such cosmopolitan forces arguably also undermined the relative standing of entrenched interests dating from the Maoist era, including the PLA, the CPC, and smokestack industry.

These established groups have all depended, in different ways, on continentalist policies of infrastructure building, manufacturing, and real estate development that have been given increasing prominence over the past decade, culminating in the Belt and Road Initiative (BRI). Local governments, eagerly seeking to expand their tax base, have also found persistent, ever-expanding development of inland areas attractive, even when frenetic construction defies economic logic. Since 1994, due to Zhu Rongji's tax reforms, local governments have lacked adequate revenue through income and value-added taxation, becoming ever more dependent on the sale of land-use rights. Reflecting a deepening real estate and infrastructure emphasis, during 1991–2008 the importance of land-leasing fees rose dramatically, from 5.7 percent of total local budgetary revenue in China to 43.5 percent.[1]

China's recent continentalist political-economic bias has been the driver for over three decades of high-speed national Chinese economic growth. That growth is steadily transforming the Eurasian continent as a whole, as we have seen. This type of stimulus does, however, generate political-economic risks—not least in the massive and often nontransparent liabilities of public-works related projects, especially those generated by local-government-related entities. Indeed, by the end of March 2018, local government debt in China—much of it land related—had reached RMB 16.6 trillion ($2.6 trillion), amounting to 36 percent of GDP.[2] Much of this debt is nontransparent, compounding the potential systemic danger it poses, especially if China's growth were to dramatically slow.

China's recent macroeconomic growth, like Japan's high-speed expansion of the 1950s, 1960s, and early 1970s, has been leveraged by a mountain of debt, secured mainly by real estate. The structural disequilibria in the Chinese political economy have, like those of Japan before 1980, been insulated from global pressures by foreign exchange controls, preventing the outflow of capital. The uncertain consequences for the Chinese domestic political economy if exchange controls were substantially liberalized are an imponderable that must be haunting Beijing. In Japan, financial liberalization led, after an interval of powerful countervailing stimulus during the 1980s, to an economic dislocation from which that country has still not fully recovered, nearly three decades later. The prospect is not negligible that something similar could happen in China as well.

Chinese SOEs, collective enterprises, and private firms are also expanding rapidly abroad, supported in many cases by BRI initiatives. They have lent heavily to local enterprises, in such nations as Pakistan, Sri Lanka, and Malaysia, with the debt burden becoming a widespread issue, aggravated in 2018 by rising global interest rates, as the United States withdrew from quantitative easing. How debt problems in the developing world might affect China at home, as its overseas economic stakes expand, is a deepening issue for both China and the broader world.

As China's economy has grown and begun to globalize, it has acquired rapidly growing assets and human entanglements abroad. In the volatile world of the early twenty-first century, that has meant threats to Chinese nationals abroad that have provoked Chinese military intervention, and the gradual expansion of Chinese military deployments abroad.[3] Amid the Arab Spring and resulting turbulence in Libya, China's military was forced to evacuate 35,000 citizens. Soon thereafter, it also undertook similar operations in Syria, Iraq, and Lebanon. China also confronted hostage situations in Egypt and the South Sudan, while also facing expanding confrontations with its Uyghur minority around the world. China is facing new security challenges and opportunities as it globalizes that are transforming its international political-military role, with uncertain consequences.

Shadows on the Eurasian Continental Future

Today's world is decidedly an uncertain place. As powerful as the new continentalist trends may be—far stronger, we feel sure, than conventional wisdom allows—the practical implications of those trends for world affairs itself remain difficult to foresee, and any predictions we might make are naturally probabilistic. There are inevitable shadows that cloud any confident forecast of Eurasian integration. And critical uncertainties could well confound predictions of a prosperous, cooperative future.

In this chapter we will review the important caveats that must qualify any reasoned speculation about Eurasian political-economic interdependence, in addition to the shadows on China's domestic future just discussed. Some questions relate to (1) the domestic systems of Eurasia, including especially China and Iran; and (2) interactions among the continent's subsystemic parts. Some further uncertainties qualify our general forecast of a deepening Eurasian integration, particularly between Central Europe and China, which if realized could transform the world as we know it today. There are also broader international uncertainties, however, on both the economic and political fronts. Global energy and food-price shocks, or the prospects of a major political upheaval in China, Russia, Britain, or even the United States, for example, could radically reconfigure prospects for Eurasian continental interdependence. Any of these developments could in turn significantly alter the impact of long-term trends even in such predictable areas as demography.

Predictable Dimensions

The Eurasian continent, as we know, is the largest land mass on earth, comprising 40 percent of the earth's entire surface. Much of that vast expanse consists of uninhabitable polar terrain, as in northern Siberia, or impassable deserts, such as the Gobi and Taklamakan of Mongolia and Xinjiang. Even though Eurasia includes an unusual share of unhospitable territory, the sprawling continent is nevertheless home to over 5 billion people, or nearly 70 percent of the global total.[4] It has many, many mouths to feed, and an inadequate amount of arable land on which to do so.

The Varied Challenges of Demography

To make matters worse, the demographic crisis that Eurasia confronts is intensifying, and doing so in very predictable, if bifurcated, fashion. In some parts of the continent—notably the Middle East, South Asia, Southeast Asia, and Southeastern Europe—population growth and administrative mismanagement are outpacing employment opportunity, even as economic growth and commodity prices both fluctuate violently.[5] The proliferation of people leads to frequent spikes in unemployment, especially among the young, and often becomes a major source of political instability. In India during 2017, for example, overall unemployment was only 3.5 percent, while youth unemployment was three times higher, at 10.5 percent.[6] In Egypt, total unemployment in the same year was 12.1 percent, but youth unemployment reached a disastrous 34.4 percent, even higher than the painful 28.8 percent recorded in 2010.[7]

Employment uncertainty can naturally become a breeding ground for nationalistic outbursts and ultimately for terrorism. Unemployment—born variously of economic stagnation and politically inspired migration, or both—has already sadly emerged as a powerfully destabilizing factor in Syria, Iraq, Egypt, the Palestinian Authority, Yemen, and at times Central Asia. Youth unemployment has recently (2017) reached 35 percent in Syria, 26 percent in Yemen, and 18 percent in Iraq.[8] In all three nations, it has been a dangerous catalyst for local instability. India, Indonesia, and the Philippines also face a similar challenge of rising youth population and inadequate employment opportunities.[9]

In other countries, notably Russia, predictable demographic trends have generated a different type of malaise—a downward cycle of stagnation and defensive nationalism, stemming from high death rates and a declining population trend. Between 1992 and 2008, Russia lost nearly six million people,

with its population falling nearly every year, and life expectancy for men declining precipitously to 65 —a full decade less than longevity for women.[10]
Despite a slight recovery over the past decade, Russia's population remains
below Cold War levels of a quarter century ago, and the demographic burden
on Russia's economy continues to be severe.

Aging also casts a deepening shadow on the long-term future of Northeast
Asia. Japan now has nearly 70,000 centenarians[11] and a population that has
been dropping since 2010.[12] Twenty-seven percent of its people are now over
65.[13] Korea is similarly steadily graying, with a fertility rate of only 1.2 babies
per woman (among the lowest on earth).[14] And China's demographic transition is impending, influenced by its longstanding one-child policy, only fully
abandoned in 2015.[15] By 2050 the number of births in China is projected by
the US Census Bureau to be 35 percent less than in 2000, with China's median population age rising close to 50.[16] China's total population will likely
begin declining around 2025, the working-age population will fall more than
100 million workers by 2035, and before 2050 China will likely have more
elderly than all the G-7 nations (North America, Europe, and Japan) combined.[17]

The Socioeconomic Impact of Globalization

The incorporation of three billion new active participants in the world economy over the past three decades has had many positive effects, as China, India,
Russia, and surrounding countries have at last begun interacting systematically
with global markets. This historic change has lowered labor costs, created vast
new pools of consumer demand, and taken vast populations out of poverty.
Over 700 million people have escaped from poverty in China alone.[18] Broadly
speaking, globalization has decreased income inequality *between* nations—
especially between newly industrializing economies and Western industrial
powers.[19]

Despite these felicitous developments, globalization has also generated a variety of predictably negative consequences that threaten global stability, and
that of Eurasia, from a long-term perspective. Most importantly, globalization seems to have deepened income inequality *within* nations—with the fruits
of global interdependence flowing disproportionately to urban professionals,
corporate executives, and in many cases government officials—particularly in
the financial sector. In China, for example, the net Gini index has risen over
fifteen points since 1990.[20] This perverse pattern prevails in both the G-7 nations and the developing world.[21] As Thomas Piketty has pointed out, returns

to capital have substantially increased relative to returns to labor over the three decades that globalization has recently intensified. And the prospects are strong that this general pattern of deepening intranational inequality will continue.[22]

Financial-sector globalization has also had a perverse, destabilizing potential impact, even as it has accelerated growth and enhanced economic efficiency. The rise of truly global, interrelated financial markets, together with a proliferation of financial instruments such as derivatives and options, has sharply increased the speed and intensity with which markets respond to unsettling phenomena. As the 1997 Asian financial crisis, the 1998 Russian financial crisis, and the 2008 global financial crisis all demonstrated, turbulence in one market can easily spread to others through contagion, thus greatly magnifying the impact of even seemingly minor and mundane developments in any one system.

A related trend is what Fareed Zakaria calls the "globalization of people."[23] "The world," as he points out, "has been transformed by the globalization of goods, services, and information, all of which have produced their share of pain and rejection."[24] This has, together with the related transformative forces of which he speaks, triggered unprecedented mobility, intensified further by political instability, such as the recent civil war in Syria. In 2017 there were 258 million international migrants and 25.9 million refugees and asylum seekers worldwide.[25]

Globalization has also created an increasingly complex constellation of transnational actors—interrelating in a broadening range of international settings. Joseph Nye has aptly characterized this as a "three-dimensional chess game," operating at military, economic, and amorphous cross-border levels.[26] Amitav Acharya, in another promising analogy, has characterized this as a "multiplex world," in which the making and management of order is increasingly decentralized, with economic interdependence and transnational elite networks providing some modicum of integration.[27]

The Scourge of Ethno-Religious Conflict

Demographically related problems, such as the challenge of high youth unemployment, often relate closely to another shadow on Eurasia's future: the scourge of ethnic conflict. The continent is a distinctive hodgepodge of intermingled civilizations—members of contrasting ethnic groups and religions living in close proximity to one another. Ethnic conflict can be a particular scourge to connectivity projects, such as many of those proposed under BRI, due to the intense, territorialist sentiments—often resulting in infrastructure-targeted violence—that they invoke.[28]

In India, to take a pronounced case of ethnic pluralism, there are fully 22 officially recognized languages, but more than 780 languages actually spoken, with 86 different scripts.[29] Nearly 80 percent of the Indian population is Hindú, but fully 14 percent, or close to 200 million people, are Muslim.[30] Neighboring Bangladesh and Pakistan are Sunni Muslim, Sri Lanka is largely Buddhist, and nearby Iran is primarily Shiite Muslim. Even China, while predominantly Han Chinese, has a large Uyghur Muslim population in Xinjiang and a substantial Tibetan Buddhist population in Tibet.

Particularly explosive is the bitter conflict between Sunni and Shiite Muslims across the continent. Stemming from a traumatic schism closely following the birth of Islam itself in the seventh century, this rivalry has spawned intermittent violence across the centuries throughout the Middle East.[31] The great majority of the world's over 1.5 billion Muslims—probably between 85 and 90 percent—are Sunnis, holding large majorities in such major countries as Egypt, Saudi Arabia, and Jordan.[32] Both Sunnis and Shiites, however, are broadly distributed across much of Eurasia.

There are less than 200 million Shiites worldwide, but they are heavily concentrated around the Persian Gulf. Iran, Iraq, Bahrain, Azerbaijan, and, by some estimates Yemen all have majority Shiite populations. There are also large Shia minority communities in Kuwait, Qatar, Saudi Arabia, Lebanon, Syria, Turkey, and Pakistan.[33] As can be inferred from this list, the confluence of sizeable Sunni and Shiite populations in the same nation correlates strongly with ethnic violence, as does the close juxtaposition of predominantly Sunni and Shiite nations also.

Since the Iranian Revolution of 1979, in which a secular monarchy was replaced in Tehran by a fundamentalist Shiite regime intent on supporting fellow Shiites abroad, the Sunni-Shiite conflict within Islam has assumed geopolitical implications, including deepened rivalries between Iran and Saudi Arabia as well as Iranian proxy support for Shia-affiliate groups in Lebanon, Syria, Bahrain, the Gaza Strip, Saudi Arabia, Yemen, and Afghanistan.[34] Sunni Saudi Arabia—government and civil society, in varying configurations—has conversely supported Sunni extremists around the region, in Afghanistan and elsewhere. The bitter civil wars in Syria, Yemen, and Afghanistan; the sporadic violence in places as far apart as Saudi Arabia, Uzbekistan, and Xinjiang; and the less violent regional blockade of Qatar all bear testimony to the destructive implications of Sunni-Shia conflict and related Islamic fundamentalism.

The clearest recent manifestation, of course, is Daesh, or the Islamic State (IS)—a radical Sunni sociopolitical incarnation emerging suddenly from the chaos of Syria and Iraq during 2013–2015. IS established a self-proclaimed caliphate at Raqqa in northern Syria and proceeded to dominate, through terror and decisive military victories against both Iraqi and Syrian troops, a cross-border segment of Iraq and Syria as large as the US state of Indiana until suppressed by the US-backed Syrian Democratic Forces in late 2017.[35] Parallel, albeit less institutionalized, Islamic terrorist groups with their roots in ethnic tensions have proliferated across the continent. These have included al-Qaeda, Hizb-ut-Tahrir (Liberation Party) in Central Asia,[36] and a complex agglomeration in Kashmir, Pakistan proper,[37] Myanmar, and Sri Lanka.

In Sri Lanka, Buddhist terrorism appears to have been deeply intertwined with racial tensions. Some Buddhists of the Sinhalese majority have expressed discomfort at both the Tamil population in the region and the rise of Muslim social conservatism; most Sri Lankan Muslims are Tamil, although the bulk of Tamils are Hindu. Tamil extremism has spurred the rise of a hardline Buddhist group, the Bodu Bala Sena, or Buddhist Power Force (BBS). While hardline Buddhism is not new to Sri Lanka, it has become more assertive in recent years, targeting Tamils, other Muslims, evangelical Christians, and even moderate Buddhists who advocate religious cooperation. Sri Lankan president Maithripala Sirisena has been working to undo many of the divisive policies of his predecessor, Mahinda Rajapaksa, who had been accused of supporting the rise of the BBS.[38]

Buddhist terrorism in Myanmar has parallels to that in Sri Lanka. The "969" movement there, for example, has incited widespread anti-Muslim violence. 969 leader Shin Wirathu has also been recently invited to Sri Lanka by the BBS.[39] Recently, attacks by separatists of the Arakan Rohingya Salvation Army in Myanmar's Rakhine state has led to harsh sectarian reprisals against Rohingya civilians by both Myanmar's army and by militant Rakhine Buddhists, leading to the tragic displacement of close to 700,000 civilians.[40]

Eurasian ethnic conflict at times does have significant geopolitical implications, generally by complicating otherwise plausible alliances and economic projects. A clear case in point is the Balochi tribal insurgency in western Pakistan. The Balochis, resentful of sustained dominance by nearby Sindh in Pakistani domestic politics, have taken to terrorism as a means of constraining broader regional integration that they fear could threaten them. The Balochis have, for example, reportedly blown up pipelines extending across their land from Iran toward India and killed Chinese construction laborers working to build infrastructure in Balochistan, such as the port of Gwadar near the Iranian frontier on the Persian Gulf.[41]

Among the most complex and geopolitically important ethnic conflicts in Eurasia are those involving the Uyghur people of Xinjiang, which is becoming an important transit region for Eurasian continental economic exchange. Once among the most prominent nomadic peoples of Eurasia, and still among the most culturally sophisticated, the Uyghurs supplied scribes to the illiterate Mongol armies of the thirteenth century and developed an alphabet that the Mongols later appropriated as their own. An Islamic people for over a thousand years since the arrival in Central Asia of Turkic Muslims, the Uyghurs today comprise around 46 percent of Xinjiang's total population, including as much as 90 percent of the total in southwestern areas of Xinjiang near the Pakistani border, around Kashgar.[42]

During the first four decades following the revolution of 1949, there were few reported incidents of ethnic violence, despite ongoing tensions flowing from substantial Han migration into Xinjiang. The revolution stressed the importance of respect for ethnic diversity, making such gestures as the establishment of the Minzu University of China (Minzu Daxue), formerly the Central University for Nationalities, and providing ethnic representation in the National Peoples' Congress to Uyghurs, Tibetans, and others. The CPC and the PLA spearheaded increased Han colonization in Xinjiang, but the numbers of Han immigrants in Xinjiang remained relatively small, especially in the Uyghur-dominant southwestern districts near the Pakistani and Tajik borders.

The political economy of Xinjiang began to change radically in the early 1990s, following the collapse of the Soviet Union. When the Soviet Union collapsed, Xinjiang was suddenly bordered by seven countries, where it has previously bordered only three. And two of the additional nations—Kazakhstan and Kyrgyzstan—were Turkic republics, inhabited by ethnic brethren of the Uyghurs.[43]

Rapid growth in China and the deepening integration of the devoutly Muslim Uyghurs into broader Chinese society also intensified ethnic conflict between Han Chinese and their Uyghur fellow citizens. In July 2009, following an attack by Han Chinese on Uyghur migrants in Guangzhou, large-scale retaliatory ethnic riots broke out in Urumqi, Xinjiang's capital. One hundred ninety-seven people, mostly Han, were killed, and 1,700 injured.[44] To prevent an escalation, the government enforced an Internet blackout, while China Mobile cut service to the region. Within three days, the city began to run again, but thousands of Han and Uyghurs fled the area; Urumqi mosques were closed for Friday prayers as well.[45]

The Urumqi riots were followed by sporadic Islamic violence in other major Uyghur centers, including Kashgar and Hotan in the southwest. Such violence spread during 2013–2014 to a broader domestic stage. In October 2013 there was a dramatic Uyghur car bombing in Tiananmen Square. This was followed in April 2014 by a knife attack at Kunming station that killed thirty-one people.[46] The Chinese worked to neutralize the violence through a threefold strategy: a tough crackdown, involving sustained military force; efforts at promoting economic development that integrated Xinjiang ever more tightly with China as a whole; and a diplomatic offensive directed toward neutralizing the Islamic resistance and its international legitimacy. Major elements of this new strategy included efforts to encourage sister-city assistance ties between Xinjiang cities such as Kashgar and metropolitan centers like Guangzhou; establishing special economic zones in Xinjiang, like the one in Kashgar; and diplomatic initiatives like China's approaches to Turkey, designed to cut off transnational support for the Uyghurs. Some of these diplomatic initiatives, such as Chinese approaches to Turkey, did strengthen continentalism, but in a larger sense could only neutralize the underlying sociopolitical tensions arising from the changing relationship of Uyghurs and Han in the ancestral Uyghur homeland.

Xinjiang is not the only part of Eurasia experiencing ethnic violence. The Fergana Valley of Central Asia is divided among several nations, peopled by a diversity of groups, and is a hub for illicit drug trade from Afghanistan. The Fergana part of Kyrgyzstan, where a local Uzbek majority considers itself discriminated against, experienced considerable ethnic violence in 1990 and again in May/June 2010, when 420 people were killed and 80,000 displaced.[47] Uyghur separatists also bombed the Chinese embassy in the Kyrgyz capital of Bishkek in August 2016, wounding three Kyrgyz staff members.[48]

In the case of Xinjiang Uyghurs, ethnic tensions can likely be neutralized with only minimal impact on broader national security, since China has a relatively strong state. Yet nation-state efforts cannot universally constrain such tensions. In failed states, such as Syria and Yemen recently, ethnic tensions run rampant, disrupting any broader social cohesion that could otherwise prevail.

Weapons of Mass Destruction

At the geopolitical level, weapons of mass destruction (WMD) remain an imminent, predictable danger, casting a dark shadow over continentalist prospects and indeed the likelihood of Eurasian stability itself. Virtually all the large nations of Eurasia—including China, Russia, India, and Pakistan, together with North Korea—are already declared nuclear powers, with most also retaining "poor-man's nukes"—chemical and biological weapons. The geographical prominence of WMD across Eurasia is graphically clear in Table 9.1. Iran also continues to retain potent threshold nuclear capabilities, the recent multilateral nuclear accord constraining its nuclear development notwithstanding.

Nuclear proliferation has been arrested over the past half century in many parts of the world, including Africa and Latin America.[49] Efforts to control the spread of WMD and WMD technologies have sadly *not* been quite as effective in Eurasia, as suggested in Table 9.1. India, Pakistan, and North Korea have gone explicitly nuclear since the late 1990s, while Israel has deepened its undeclared capabilities. The pariah states of Eurasia, including North Korea, Iran, and Syria, have conducted vigorous exchanges in both WMD and missile technology with one another, while also consorting secretly with rogue scientists and arms producers in transitional states like Ukraine.[50]

Recent developments regarding North Korea generate both hope and still deeper uncertainties. The dramatic June 2018 Singapore summit between Donald Trump and Kim Jong-un, preceded by an upbeat intra-Korean summit, produced a categorical yet vague commitment to denuclearization, that was not clarified by subsequent high-level meetings later in 2018.[51] If such efforts should finally lead to meaningful strategic progress, they could well

TABLE 9.1

WMD prominence across Eurasia

	Region/Country	Chemical	Biological	Nuclear
Asia	China	Yes	Yes	Yes
	India	Eliminating	Research?	Yes
	Iran	Yes?	Research?	Research
	Israel	Yes	Yes?	Yes
	Korea (North)	Yes	Yes	Yes?
	Korea (South)	Eliminating		
	Pakistan	Research?	Research?	Yes
	Syria	Yes		
Europe	Albania	Eliminating		
	France			Yes
	Russia	Eliminating	Yes	Yes
	United Kingdom			Yes

SOURCE: Joseph Cirincione, Jon B. Wolfsthal, and Miriam Rajkumar, *Deadly Arsenals: Nuclear, Biological, and Chemical Threats*, 2nd ed. (Washington, DC: Carnegie Endowment for International Peace, 2005), Table 1.6. The Fifteen Countries with Nuclear, Biological, or Chemical Weapons or Offensive Research Programs.

unleash major infrastructural projects, including transnational pipelines, railways, and electric power grids, that could link the entire Korean peninsula much more tightly to the Eurasian continent.

An immensely important lingering uncertainty remains the impact of continental Eurasian strategic developments on Japan, a grossly underestimated factor in the overall Eurasian political-military equation. Japan has long kept a low political-military profile, flowing from both its World War II role and the Hiroshima/Nagasaki tragedies. It does, however, have sophisticated technical capabilities, as well as over forty-seven tons of plutonium[52] and the world's third-largest economy, which would make extensive WMD programs and delivery-system development easily conceivable should Tokyo desire to pursue them. If ongoing arms control efforts in Korea leave either North Korea or a unified Korea with nuclear weapons or ambiguous capabilities, Japan would have strong incentives to hedge, possibly by developing parallel capabilities to those in Korea, casting another dark shadow over its neighborhood.

The Quest for Resources

Ultimately, the most troubling shadow over the dramatic emergence of Eurasian continentalism could flow precisely from the same source as its meteoric rise: namely, the huge number of ambitious, hard-working people that populate the continent. Eurasia, after all, is home to more than five billion people, or close to 70 percent of humanity. As nations of a continent with such huge populations continue to industrialize and grow, they naturally provide huge markets, both for aspiring citizens and for foreigners, even as they become a principal industrial foundry for the world. Their economies also naturally loom ever larger in the global calculus.

Even as Eurasia grows larger and larger in aggregate terms—and more influential globally due to its scale—it also grows more vulnerable. Somehow, somewhere, it needs to procure food and raw materials to feed and clothe those teeming masses. And Eurasia, in contrast to the Americas, does not have a bountiful supply of arable land to feed and clothe its growing and increasingly affluent billions.

Food and water challenges are clearly daunting in arid, heavily populated countries such as Pakistan, as in parts of India. They are also serious in Central Asia. In Tajikistan, for example, the World Food Program calculates that 80 percent of household income is spent on food.[53] Water supply is also uncertain there, and even more so in nearby downstream countries such as Turkmenistan and Uzbekistan, due to dam projects that monopolize scarce water resources upstream.[54]

For some Eurasian countries—the resource exporters—there is often the converse problem of overreliance. Especially when a resource is in persistently high demand, as has often been true of hydrocarbons, a country becomes specialized in its production, losing competitiveness in other areas. Russia, for example, has grown heavily dependent on oil and gas, with 70 percent of its exports concentrated in that area. When prices prove weak, as they cyclically were during the 1997–1999, 2008–2009, and 2014–2016 periods, the national economy suffers.

It is, of course, immensely difficult to accurately project long-term food and energy prices, which have proven volatile in the short run over the past two decades. We can, however, quite confidently suppose that long-term demand will be high in the Asian giants, given their huge populations, low per-capita consumption, and reasonable likelihood of sustained economic growth. According to recent International Energy Agency (IEA) forecasts, China will remain the world's largest consumer and producer of coal through 2030, with oil demand growing 44 percent, overtaking that of the US.[55] By 2040 the PRC will be importing 12 million bbl/d of oil—roughly 50 percent above current levels.[56]

Indian energy demand will also likely rise, even more clearly reflecting a younger demographic than that of China and achieving correspondingly higher rates of economic growth. By 2020 India is expected to be the world's largest coal importer. Its oil imports could double by 2030 and reach 90 percent of consumption by 2040.[57] Together, China and India will likely import nearly half of internationally traded crude oil—up from just over 25 percent today.[58] Their combined demand could thus put major upward pressure on world energy prices, unless equivalent alternative supplies are found—a globally significant uncertainty, since the capital costs—and attendant risks—of energy investment are so high.

Environmental Degradation

China and India are two of the most rapidly growing large nations on earth. They are also the two most populous nations in the world, with nearly 37 percent of the entire world's population between them. Both of them are also around 50–60 percent dependent on coal as a primary energy source.[59] And coal is so cheap that they, as countries with many poor citizens who lack without realistic alternatives, can only slowly reduce dependence, however perverse the environmental implications may be.

Not surprisingly, China is by a substantial and growing margin, the largest CO_2 emitter on earth—over 9.2 billion tons annually, compared to around 5 billion tons for the next largest polluter—the United States.[60] For most of the past decade, China's large cities have been among the world's most polluted. Since around 2015, however, conditions in much of urban China have slowly improved; Beijing, Shanghai, and Tianjin have ceded place to others. Major cities of South Asia, including Kanpur, Patna, and Delhi have taken their place, however, while Southeast Asia's environmental problems have also deepened. In 2018, according to World Health Organization (WHO) figures, fourteen of the twenty most polluted cities in the world were Indian and only one was Chinese.[61] And the number of deaths attributable to severe (PM 2.5) pollution in China peaked in 2005 at a tragic 1.14 million, while the number in India accelerated.[62] Overall, eastern Eurasia, with its massive population, rising material consumption, and heavy coal reliance, has the most serious environmental problems on earth, for reasons that are sadly predictable.

Critical Uncertainties

Clearly the future of global commodity supply and demand relationships stand among the most critical uncertainties that cloud Eurasia's future. If demand for food and energy are high and supply is limited, the great population centers of China and India will likely suffer unfavorable terms of trade with the commodity exporters such as Russia, the Persian Gulf states, Australia, and the United States. Conversely, if commodity demand slacks and supply is ample, Sino-Indian growth and savings rates will likely be higher, and trade balances of these Asian giants more positive.

Fragile States in the Developing World

Prospects for global exchange rates and interest rates, like commodity prices, are intrinsically uncertain. As the world retreats from quantitative easing, however, after a full decade of relaxation, interest-rate pressures on heavily indebted developing nations will likely increase. "Distributive globalism" has compounded the impulse of less developed countries to borrow when interest rates are low, as have domestic pressures, leading to serious, destabilizing debt problems in many nations. Pakistan, Sri Lanka, Laos, Tajikistan, Kyrgyzstan, the Maldives, Djibouti, Montenegro, to name a few, all have serious BRI-related debt problems that could be destabilizing.[63] Important nations of the Middle East, including Iran and Saudi Arabia, arguably confront instability on other grounds.

Intra-Eurasian Relations

Within Eurasia itself, as well as in Washington, the stability of Sino-Soviet relations were throughout the Cold War days considered to be an overriding

critical uncertainty. To some extent that logic continues to prevail among sea-
soned observers. We have argued here, of course, that Sino-Russian relations
are likely to remain stable and indeed to deepen, enhancing prospects for
a global Crossover Point leading from American hegemony toward a more
multipolar system of world affairs. The critical uncertainties in regional, as
opposed to global, relations lie elsewhere.

The most likely prospects for critical uncertainties must lie, almost by
definition, in relations among the major powers of the continent—China,
India, Russia, and Japan.[64] The most problematic of these all could potentially
be between China and Japan—the second and third largest economies on
earth in nominal GDP terms and two nations also of considerable technological sophistication. Precisely because these two giants are so finely balanced
and because they have no prior history of association as equals, their relationship is a delicate one that could provoke serious conflict in future, especially
if North Korea's failure to denuclearize should provoke Japan to rearm more
decisively. During 2018 there were short-term signs of reconciliation, correlated to escalating American trade pressures against both, and an exchange of
high-level visits related to historic anniversaries and Japan's 2019 G-20 chair-
manship.[65] Whether this détente was more than an "Indian summer," to be
followed by a harsh, chilly autumn of renewed tension, was difficult to foresee. Certainly a reconciliation would give further momentum to a Eurasian
Super Continent's emergence.

The future relationship between China and India is also important to the
future profile and stability of Eurasian continentalism. Because these two nations are so large—the two most heavily populated on earth, and the second
and seventh largest in nominal economic terms as well—the future of their
relationship is naturally consequential for global prospects. That said, Sino-
Indian relations seem less likely to be plagued by serious conflict than the
relations between China and Japan. Both of the emerging giants are growing
rapidly and have broadly complementary economies—manufacturing versus
services.[66]

Populism and the Western Industrial World

Income inequality *within* the major nations of the world is deepening, even
as income inequality *between* nations is generally falling, as noted earlier. Such
domestic inequality is felt more intensely in the West than in Asia, because
economic growth is lower in the West and competition between immigrants
and the native born is more intense. The tension is especially intense in Eu-

rope, both because growth is generally lower there than in North America and also because immigration is more extensive. More than 78 million migrants, for example, were resident in Europe during 2017—by far the largest number inhabiting any region of the world, relative to local population.[67] The periphery of Europe also houses a large number of refugees, due to continuing turbulence in the Middle East. These include over three million in Turkey, with the largest refugee population in the world,[68] and many of them are trying to enter the EU through the Balkan peninsula.[69]

Stagnant growth, income inequality, rampant unemployment, and surging immigration have together triggered a surge of local populism in many European nations that does introduce uncertainty into their otherwise deepening relations with Asia. Collectively, populist parties scored an average of 16.5 percent of the vote in national elections of sixteen European countries over the 2010–2015 period, and actually gained the largest share of parliamentary seats in six (Greece, Hungary, Italy, Poland, Slovakia, and Switzerland).[70] Populism has been particularly strong in Eastern Europe, strengthening the East-West divide within the region that has, as noted in Chapter 8, aided the rise of Chinese influence in the East.[71]

Recent European populism has come in two varieties, both catalyzed by income inequality, unemployment, and surging immigration, particularly from the Middle East and Africa.[72] On the left, parties like Syriza in Greece and Podemos in Spain have stressed an antiausterity theme but have embarrassingly been forced by financial need to accept many of the painful spending cuts and neoliberal structural reforms that they had previously pledged domestically to prevent. On the right, populists have been far more successful, by focusing on nationalistic, anti–European Union appeals.

Right-wing populism has dominated Slovak politics since the 1990s, while populist Viktor Orban has remained in power in Hungary since 2010. Britain's UK Independence Party and its Leave movement, which precipitated Brexit in the June 2016 British national referendum, had a similar character. Although France's National Front, led by Marine Le Pen, was defeated in the May 2017 French presidential elections, it polled close to 34 percent of the national vote[73]—nearly double what Le Pen's father polled in 2002.[74] And the German right-wing party, Alternative for Germany, won 13 percent of the vote in the September 2017 Bundestag elections, marking the first time in almost six decades that an openly nationalist party entered major German political assemblies.[75] The long-term trend thus seems to favor politicians capitalizing on mass frustration.

Europe's left-wing populists, due to the antiausterity nature of their appeals, have developed some surprisingly symbiotic relationships with Asian nations, especially those with deep pockets. The Syriza government in Greece, for example, has dealt realistically with China's shipping giant COSCO, concluding a privatization agreement for the Piraeus port in 2016 that afforded the beleaguered Greek government around $2 billion in return for 67 percent Chinese equity ownership.[76] How the European nationalist right-wing populists will respond to Chinese economic inroads in Europe in future, however, is more uncertain.

The United States and Eurasia

In the end, the most critical uncertainty of all for Eurasian continentalism could be the American response to developments on the world's oldest and largest continent. As the world's preeminent superpower for most of the past seventy years and more, the United States has long held the capacity to shape events and institutional developments at various levels throughout the world. And one significant consequence of its global sway was to reinforce a "hub and spokes" of alliance relations that arguably inhibited the evolution of competing intra-Eurasian ties.

Over the past forty years an America beset by globalization has begun to change in historic ways. Labor unions organize a smaller and smaller share of the American work force, with that share declining from 20 percent in 1983 to less than 11 percent in 2017.[77] Income inequality is also rising sharply—in 1980 the top 1 percent of Americans earned on average 27 times more than the bottom 50 percent. By 2014, however, they were earning 81 times more.[78] And the foreign-born share of the US population has risen from under 5 percent in 1970 to 14 percent in 2016.[79]

In responding to these sweeping social changes, the resources at Washington's command, however, are not infinite and its intentions are not immutable. In 1950, the US share of global GDP was 27.3 percent; by 1995 it had declined to 20.0 percent, and by 2015 to 15.7 percent.[80] US federal budget deficits, meanwhile, have nearly tripled over the last two decades, from $164.0 billion in 1995 to $665.4 billion in 2017, making it harder and harder for governments to proactively address socioeconomic needs or even national-defense concerns.[81]

Even as fiscal pressure increasingly constrains the ability of the American government to act, technological change and related globalization intensify pressures within the United States for structural change. Government, lacking resources, cannot easily cushion the social impact of the information revolution, or of new technologies that are making driverless vehicles possible. People like the three million truck drivers of America, to cite one painful example of a broader pattern, naturally become vulnerable.[82]

The American political economy in the second decade of the twenty-first century is thus beset by a variety of social pressures—rising income inequality and a sharp increase in social pluralism prominent among them. Predictably, these deep social changes produced a powerful backlash, concentrated in the economically distressed Rust Belt sections of America's Midwest. That backlash, more surprisingly, elected Donald Trump president of the United States. Trump focused heavily on revising liberal American trade policies during his 2016 campaign, and cancelled the Trans-Pacific Partnership during his first week in office. Trump did subsequently bargain pragmatically with Prime Minister Abe of Japan and President Xi of China, before opting out of COP-21 and then threatening trading partners throughout the world with massive tariff increases as well as offending NATO leaders, thus creating considerable uncertainty as to how US trade, financial, and security policies toward the Pacific, and toward the world more generally, would ultimately evolve.[83]

Uncertainty about American policies and capabilities has especially powerful implications at the global level today, because plausible alternatives to American hegemony are at last arising. As Amitav Acharya, among others, has noted, the era of an American world order may well be waning, even as the US itself continues to be a central world power.[84] As we have seen, China has steadily, over the past decade, been gaining economic strength, with more and more longstanding US allies becoming reliant on Beijing. And under Xi Jinping China has, since 2013, both enhanced foreign incentives to cooperate with Beijing and begun to suggest alternative paradigms under its BRI for global cooperation itself. This Chinese version of distributive globalism is particularly attractive in elemental political-economic terms, due to the way that it concentrates benefits so intensely and concretely for recipients while diffusing and externalizing costs.

How much attention and resources will Washington direct to Eurasian developments in coming years, and under what circumstances? That remains indeterminate, with the uncertainty compounded by US domestic political fluidity, including the populist surge that dismantled the Trans-Pacific Partnership and other supports for multilateral integration. If the deepening inequality of American society, including the erosion of the middle class, were arrested together with deindustrialization of its Midwest manufacturing core, protectionist impulses might be arrested. And if the pace of immigration slowed, without recrimination, ethnic tensions might ease. Yet all these trends have deep-seated economic origins and cannot easily be reversed. Critical uncertainties regarding Washington, DC, remain a shadow hanging heavily over Eurasia's future, and over conversely related prospects for a global Crossover Point that reconfigures global governance.

In Conclusion

As we have argued in earlier chapters of this volume, both China and Eurasia more broadly have changed profoundly since the advent of China's Four Modernizations in 1978. The pace of change has accelerated since the global financial crisis of 2008. Deepening relations are being forged between China on the one hand and Southeast Asia, Russia, and Europe on the other, epitomized in the BRI of Xi Jinping. These synergistic relationships, emerging across Eurasia, hold promise for changing the world more significantly than is generally perceived in the West, both due to their intrinsic attraction and the failure of the United States, in particular, to present a plausible alternative.

There are, however, important caveats to any forecast on global transformation driven by developments in Eurasia, which this chapter elaborates in detail. These caveats fall into two categories: (1) predictable elements of the future that cast shadows on the peaceful evolution of an interdependent Eurasia; and (2) critical uncertainties that render any confident future projections at all problematic. It is these critical uncertainties that ultimately determine probabilities for alternative future scenarios.

In considering the future of China itself, this chapter argues, it is critical to begin by recognizing the imposing challenge that governing a continental nation of 1.4 billion people without the "safety valve" that feedback-inducing political pluralism presents. The CPC and the PLA have been central actors in stabilizing China for around seventy years. Yet they now face increasing challenge in maintaining both prosperity and stability within a changing, increasingly mobile Chinese society, ever more interdependent with the world, that features both a rising middle class and growing economic inequality. The BRI, it is argued, helps to sustain the role of established political institutions and industries, therefore serving a central and predictable foreign policy function under President Xi Jinping. How financial or trade liberalization might impact the stability of this system is a critical uncertainty that will profoundly shape China's—and Eurasia's—future.

Predictable shadows on the Eurasian future include demographic change (the graying of Asian society), globalization, ethno-religious conflict, weapons of mass destruction, and possible conflict over natural resources, especially under high-growth scenarios. Critical uncertainties include the impact of excessive debt, intra-Asian relations (especially Sino-Indian ties), the impact of Western populism on Eurasia, and, in particular, the trajectory of US-China relations. Whether the US plays a constructive global leadership role, supporting causes that are broadly considered credible and important, with sensitivity to the fragile circumstances of others, will profoundly configure both Eurasia's prospects for autarkic continental cohesion and also Eurasia's own global profile and international leadership role in future years.

Toward a New World Order

OVER THE PAST SEVERAL CHAPTERS we have reviewed in detail the drivers of change in twenty-first-century international relations, leading toward deeper Eurasian continental interdependence, with potential global implications. We have also surveyed how some central bilateral pillars of the global system, including the Sino-Russian and Sino-European relationships, as well as Chinese ties with Southeast Asia, are themselves in fact shifting, as elements of that continental consolidation proceeds. We did stress the volatility of global affairs today and caution about the difficulty of prediction. We also noted, however, that it is possible amid this fluidity to identify certain critical uncertainties and shadows that could systematically transform and potentially qualify our forecasts of impending international systemic change.

We have so far focused mainly on the *forces* for global systems transformation, in such areas as energy, logistics, and finance, and *why* they are propelling us toward new systems of international affairs. We have not, however, spent much time speculating about what a transformed global system itself might concretely entail. To formulate such a vision, we need first of course to review the major structural features of the global political economy as we know it at present. That is the task to which we now turn.

Profile of the Current System of Global Affairs

The major structural features of our current global political economy grew out of the World War II peace settlement, and hence strongly reflect the overwhelming position of political, economic, and military strength that the

United States enjoyed at that time. The core was the Bretton Woods system of international finance, established at a gathering of distinguished financial specialists in July 1944, led by Lord Maynard Keynes of Britain and Harry Dexter White of the United States. It was quintessentially a *regulatory* system in Lowi's parlance—an elaborate, formalized structure of institutions and rules, with concentrated costs and diffuse, broadly distributed benefits. One single power—the United States—played a tortured hegemonic role.

The historic Bretton Woods conference, setting forth a plan to reconfigure the international financial system so as to avoid repeating the coordination failures of the Depression years, proposed establishing multiple multilateral financial institutions, in each of which the United States was to hold veto power. These included the International Monetary Fund (IMF), oriented toward providing emergency lending to keep sovereign borrowers solvent, and the International Bank for Reconstruction and Development (IBRD, the central element of the World Bank Group), intended to serve as the principal international supplier of development finance.

In later years, this basic structure, hegemonic to its core, was supplemented by the establishment of regional development banks, in most of which the United States also played influential roles. The Inter-American Development Bank, founded in 1959, was followed by the African Development Bank (1964); the Asian Development Bank, founded in 1966; and the European Bank for Reconstruction and Development, founded in 1991, as communism was collapsing in Eastern Europe. Four additional new multilateral auxiliary institutions, loosely affiliated with the World Bank Group, included the International Finance Corporation (1956), International Development Association (1960), the International Centre for Settlement of Investment Disputes (1965), and the Multilateral Investment Guarantee Agency (1988).

To forestall ruinous competitive devaluations like those that ravaged the 1930s, the new economic order proposed by White and Keynes included a system of fixed exchange rates that could only be altered through consultation with the IMF. Those rates were to be set by reference to the price of gold and the US dollar, the key currency of the entire system, whose value was to be fixed at US\$35/ounce of gold. Since the price of gold was to be fixed, nations were free to hold their international reserves in dollars, in gold, or in a limited number of alternative reserve currencies, most prominently the British pound sterling.

Lord Keynes and Harry Dexter White also envisioned a multilateral body to regulate global trade, christened the International Trade Organization (ITO), to obviate the rampant protectionism that had so painfully exacerbated the Great Depression of the 1930s. An ITO charter was actually agreed upon at the March 1948 Havana UN Conference on Trade and Employment, but never ratified by the US Senate and other key national legislative bodies, thus preventing implementation.[1] Parallel negotiations on a General Agreement on Tariffs and Trade (GATT) were, however, successfully concluded in October 1947, and GATT took effect on January 1, 1948, supplying a provisional framework for regulating tariffs and trading conditions.

Establishment of the World Trade Organization (WTO) was contemplated in the late 1940s but realized only in 1995.[2] It is nevertheless a logical piece, however, of the original Bretton Woods system, designed to prevent a relapse into the predatory trade and financial policies that spawned the Depression of the 1930s, in a vicious cycle ultimately leading to World War II. That classic structure of global economic management thus now rests on a troika: the World Bank, the IMF, and the WTO.

The United Nations, established formally on October 24, 1945, was the principal security pillar of the original postwar system. Like the IMF and the World Bank, its venerable institutional partners in the economic realm, the UN was created to forestall a post–World War II relapse into the chaotic and brutal patterns of the 1930s and 1940s. Yet the UN had a fatefully different governance structure from its financial brethren. Due to the permanent-member veto system, however, which rendered it a "concert of powers" rather than a unitary "regulatory order," the politically enmeshed United Nations has had more trouble since the Korean War than economic institutions like the IMF in responding to major threats to global peace and security. The UN has been effective in reducing tensions in some parts of the world, such as Africa, where the interests of major powers have not been so deeply engaged, and occasionally in monitoring fragile cease-fires in strategic areas of major-power interest such as the Golan Heights. Yet it has rarely been able to respond effectively in cases of great-power conflict or to provide effective representation for nations that rose to renewed international prominence from the ashes of World War II defeat, such as Japan and Germany.

Due in part to the inability of the UN to respond adequately to major global security challenges, the postwar security order also came, from the late 1940s on, to include a complex system of bilateral and multilateral alliances. In the Pacific, the US established a "hub-and-spokes" system of bilateral ties radiating out from its Washington hub, involving Japan (1951), Australia and New Zealand (1951), the Philippines (1951), and South Korea (1953).[3] Nationalist China and South Vietnam, representing the anticommunist protagonists in continuing civil wars, were also included in the original framework of bilateral ties, although those alliances later became defunct.[4] Thailand was incorporated multilaterally through the 1954 Manila Pact establishing the Southeast Asia Treaty Organization (SEATO) and bilaterally through a 1966 US-Thai Treaty of Amity and Economic Relations.[5] The Soviet Union and China also in February 1950 concluded a bilateral alliance with one another, nominally directed against Japan, which paralleled the emerging American structure.[6] North Korea and the Soviet Union concluded a mutual-assistance treaty in 1961, while Vietnam also signed a Treaty of Friendship and Co-operation with the USSR following its accession to the Council for Mutual Economic Assistance in 1978.[7]

In the Atlantic, the Middle East, and the Americas, the prevailing post-war security structure ultimately became multilateral rather than bilateral. In April 1949, following a procommunist coup d'etat in Czechoslovakia and the Berlin blockade, the United States and eleven partners established the North Atlantic Treaty Organization (NATO) to provide mutual collective security.[8] In the Middle East, the Baghdad Pact, and later the Central Treaty Organization, served a similar function.[9] In Southeast Asia, the Eisenhower administration in the United States inspired creation of SEATO to provide collective security in the wake of French withdrawal from Indochina—the one multilateral addition to the generally bilateral Pacific security architecture.[10] SEATO formally dissolved in June 1977 following the total US withdrawal from Indochina.[11]

Political-Economic Transformation Erodes the Prevailing Structure of Global Governance

The classic structure of global political-economic governance forged in the wake of World War II has persisted in its essence now for three generations and more. The permanent membership of the UN Security Council, for example, is precisely the same as it was in 1945. To be sure, voting rights at the IMF and the World Bank have shifted at the margins, but there is still an American president at the World Bank and a European managing director at the IMF, just as there were on the days of their foundations more than seven decades ago.

The locus of influence in the global system, however, has shifted radically over the past seventy years through four fundamental transformations. First, there was the economic rise of Europe and East Asia during the 1950s and 1960s, fueled by the recovery of the former Axis powers, especially Germany and Japan. Second, there was the rise of the oil producers during the 1970s, with the Persian Gulf, led by Saudi Arabia and Iran, coming into special

prominence. Third, the Soviet Union and its associated Warsaw Pact collapsed during the early 1990s, creating a "unipolar moment" for the United
States. And finally, the past decade has witnessed the rise of China and its
deepening interdependence with Russia, Central Asia, Africa, and the New
Europe, with an emerging Eurasia at its core.

These momentous global political-economic changes have naturally put
new pressures on the relatively rigid set of global institutions involving embedded Atlantic dominance that were established by the victor nations in the
wake of World War II. The UN, IMF, and World Bank have all been to some
extent accommodating, especially through their auxiliaries. Yet a serious and
intensifying disjunction between past structures and future capabilities clearly
remains.

Alternative Routes to Systems Transformation

If there is indeed a disjunction between the core governance institutions of
the global system and the power configurations of world affairs, how can the
conflict be resolved? Classical theory in international relations has suggested
that major changes in the global system are achieved through hegemonic
conflict—the Napoleonic Wars, World War I, and World War II among
them.[12] In the nuclear era hegemonic conflict, as between the United States
and China, would come at a prohibitive human and economic cost. Even the
process of mutual deterrence is growing ever more expensive and uncertain.
Is there any alternative mechanism for systemic transformation?

A generation ago, the United States and Japan spoke at the Palm Springs
summit of 1990 about a "new world order" to be forged in the wake of the
Cold War.[13] This formulation was echoed in multiple US-Russia summits following the collapse of the Soviet Union.[14] Despite the rhetoric, such summit
diplomacy did not produce any substantial change in global governance. Yet
it did popularize the promising notion—contrasting so strongly to the pessimistic realist vision—that there is indeed an alternative to armed conflict as
an agent of fundamental systemic change in world affairs.

Both academic research and post–Cold War diplomacy did give some
substance to the search for nonviolent alternatives to hegemonic conflict as
vehicles for systems transformation. Keohane, Nye, Vernon, and Yergin, to
name a few prominent international political economy specialists, all stressed
the role of multilateral regimes and transnational enterprise in structuring international affairs.[15] A series of international trade rounds, disarmament initiatives, and environmental conferences, not to mention security gatherings

convened to coordinate response to historic post–Cold War changes in Eastern Europe, all imparted momentum to multilateral diplomacy in the 1990s, 2000s, and 2010s. Yet by 2017, with the advent of the Trump presidency, this momentum had subsided.

The previous chapters have suggested that the underlying geography and resource endowments of Eurasia give the continent innate long-term potential for prominence in world affairs as a coherent unit. Given geopolitical and geo-economic substance by a series of critical junctures across the past third of a century, that potential is being gradually realized and creating prospects for a major transformation of the international system—a Crossover Point from the open, liberal order of the past seven decades to new forms of global governance and political economy, spurred by gradually deepening Eurasian relationships. As a consequence, China and the United States, in particular, will likely play somewhat different roles in the global system than at present, and the question is how that transition to new responsibilities can be peacefully achieved.

Many international relations theorists, such as Charles Kindleberger and Robert Gilpin, have insisted that stable international systems require a stabilizer, or hegemon, that serves as a lender, market, and defender of last resort. In their common conception, this stabilizer needs to be a unitary power in which other actors in the system can have confidence. The traditional notion is that the role of hegemon cannot be shared, and that "co-hegemony" is impossible. Coming years could potentially test that concept, with distributive globalism as a less conflictual alternative than the battles for supremacy that hegemonic transitions have traditionally entailed.[16] Why is it not possible for multiple powers to share governance responsibility, especially if doing so reflects the emerging reality of international affairs? Cannot multilateral institutions serve as a vehicle for this more collective and nonconflictual form of governance? Cannot the provision of new distributive resources with a public-good character be related to governance, especially in new institutions? And cannot existing global bodies be managed in a more pluralistic manner than in the past? A significant body of neorealist thinking in international relations affirms such a possibility.

What the Global Crossover Point Could Portend

Across the preceding pages, we examined in detail the forces that are eroding classical Atlantic-centered globalism, propelling a new continentalism within Eurasia, and enhancing the global significance of the new continentalist tendency. To understand the sheer scale of the changes in prospect and the need for new institutions to cope with them, it is crucial to grasp the concrete outlines of the global Crossover Point now impending and the prospects of a new Super Continent emerging within that broader global order. That means not only reviewing the central features of the current world order, as we have just done, but also understanding the subsystemic forces now quietly transforming the world in which we live.

A Steady Erosion of Multilateralist Globalism

From the early postwar years until the global financial crisis of 2008, global trade rose steadily while multilateral institutions for managing global affairs through rule-based procedures grew steadily stronger, especially in the economic and financial sphere. Both the IMF and the World Bank grew increasingly powerful and inclusive; in 1995 they were supplemented by a WTO that by 2016 boasted virtually global membership, including 164 member nations.[17] A series of global trade talks, including the Kennedy and Uruguay Rounds, led to progressively freer trade; average tariffs for manufactures dropped from almost 22 percent at the beginning of the 1947 GATT negotiations, to 14 percent during the Kennedy Round talks (1964–1967), to under 5 percent globally following the Uruguay Round.[18] The world seemed clearly moving toward freer and more open commerce.

All this began operating in reverse following the 2008 crisis, which led to deepening unemployment, income inequality, and working-class disaffection in the West. Since 2010, global trade has been growing at barely more than 2 percent, or just two-thirds the rate of increase in goods and services production.[19]

Faced with increased volatility, deepening inequality, and increased domestic parochialism, rule-based global trading systems grew increasingly difficult to expand and even sustain. The Doha Round of global trade negotiations, launched with optimistic fanfare in 2001, began floundering soon thereafter, culminating in a recession-induced 2008 gridlock before effectively ending at the 2015 Nairobi ministerial trade conference.[20] Ultimately, the regionalist Trans-Pacific Partnership (TPP) and Transatlantic Trade and Investment Partnership (T-TIP) frameworks, promoted assiduously by multiple US administrations in place of Doha, were repudiated by incoming US president Donald Trump on his first full day in office, late in January 2017.[21]

Even as the classic US-centric pattern of multilateralist economic governance has eroded, a more decentralized, region-centric pattern centered on

Eurasia, given coherence not by abstract rules enforced by a hegemon but by the distribution of material benefits through a less centralized leadership system, has begun to emerge. This new phenomenon is a geographically rooted regionalism with global implications, driven by—yet far transcending—the rise of China and the collapse of the former Soviet Union. Important changes in manufacturing logistics, rooted in revolutionary cost reductions in land, sea, and intermodal transport, are making Europe-China production networks ever more cost-efficient, even as transcontinental energy dependence rises, and financial flows accelerate. These economic trends are creating new forms of political-economic interdependence that are steadily eroding long-standing political constraints on interdependence.

The Economic Driver of Continentalist Political Change: A More Interactive Eurasian Playing Field

Geopoliticians often accord special precedence to geographic centrality. Eurasia is by far the largest continent on earth, with over 40 percent of the world's entire land area. And it is situated amid—and dominating—a "World Island" that also includes Africa and surrounding territories.

Although Eurasia has, of course, remained central in geographic terms across recorded history, the broader economic and geopolitical significance of that centrality was long masked by static economic and technological patterns within the continent, compounded by endemic political-economic divisions and geographic barriers that inhibited transnational dialogue. A poverty of transnational infrastructure, together with an underappreciation of the geo-economic importance of infrastructure itself in linking contiguous nations, have also conspired to obscure the latent potential of Eurasian economic interdependence. Only within the past half century has that static situation, pregnant with possibility, given way to significant change.

Eurasian Infrastructure

In contrast to Western Europe and North America, most of Eurasia has never enjoyed well-developed natural gas pipeline grids, transnational railroad networks, or cross-border networks of electric power transmission lines. As it develops such infrastructure, political-economic relations among Eurasia's constituent jurisdictions, heretofore quite distant, are growing steadily more intense. As we have seen, both the functional importance of Eurasian infrastructure to economic growth and the quality of infrastructure in prospect have been sharply improving in recent years, making infrastructural investment a central prospective driver of the political-economic transformation in Eurasia.

Infrastructure has special potential as a catalyst for growth in Eurasia, and particularly between its economic poles in China and Central Europe. This is because the two cores of the transcontinental political economy share three vital characteristics: (1) large population and high population density; (2) concentrated, complementary centers of manufacturing; and (3) a diversity of transport options (overland by road and rail, as well as maritime and air). These various socioeconomic traits maximize the synergistic potential of new infrastructure and logistics innovations for economic growth.

Economic growth in strategic areas of the Eurasian continent, fortuitously synergistic with technological changes such as intermodal transport that sharply reduce freight costs, have been sharply increasing the functional importance of new infrastructure for much of Eurasia over the past decade. This impulse to build new, state-of-the-art railways, power grids, and digitalized logistics management systems is intensified in particular by growth in China—especially its western reaches, far from the sea. There is a parallel dynamic in Central and Eastern Europe, likewise landlocked. Where infrastructure is antiquated and funds to renovate are available, as in countries like Belarus, much of the former Yugoslavia, and Kazakhstan, the incentives to build can be overpowering, especially with Chinese Belt and Road Initiative (BRI) financial support readily available.

In purely geographic terms, land transport should be a more efficient means of getting across the continent from Northeast Asia to Europe than taking circuitous sea routes, as we have noted. From coastal cities like Shanghai and Rotterdam, the overland distance across Eurasia is over 30 percent shorter than the most direct, currently feasible sea routes through the Suez Canal. For inland cities like Chongqing and Duisburg, the geographical logic of overland transport is even more geo-economically compelling, for three important reasons: (1) inland to inland geographical distances are shorter, (2) deregulation is making the cross-border procedures involved in land transport less onerous, and (3) digitalization of logistics is making intermodal transport via river, rail, road, and air dramatically faster and cheaper than ever before.

A core problem with land routes across Eurasia has always been political-economic, although geographic barriers like the Himalayas also tend to channel them across specific corridors. Tariffs and a host of regulations, from complex border-clearance procedures to differing rail gauges, have stifled trade. Finance has been difficult, while infrastructure and security over key transit sections has been substandard also.

Technological and macroeconomic developments of the past decade, as suggested above, have dramatically changed this equation. Since 2005, digital freight documents have begun replacing the classical paper versions, beginning with the air-cargo supply chain, thus radically improving technical prospects for streamlining customs clearance.[22] Recent trends in Internet of Things, big data, B2B e-commerce, and 3D printing have all helped shorten delivery times as well, enabling just-in-time sourcing that is also helping to rationalize trans-Eurasian production chains in the electronics, machinery, and auto industries, among others.[23]

Chongqing, for example, produced no personal computer laptops at all for foreign manufacturers as recently as 2009. Yet since then it has become a global center of PC manufacture, attracting investment in local manufacturing capacity by Hewlett Packard, Fujitsu, Dell, Acer, and other major international brands. By 2016 exports from Chongqing alone exceeded 45 million units annually, valued at nearly $15.9 billion due both to Chongqing's centrality in the massive, growing Chinese market and synergy with the ongoing Logistics Revolution, which allowed flexible and cost-effective component sourcing from around the world and particularly from across Eurasia.[24]

Deregulation in logistics has made transcontinental freight-forwarding dramatically cheaper and faster. The birth of the Eurasian Economic Union in 2015 also reduced the number of borders crossed by freight shipped between China and the European Union (EU) to just the China/Kazakhstan and Belarus/EU crossing points. And the digitalization of logistics has rendered transcontinental transport much faster and cheaper still.

Responding to recent technological developments that magnify the economic benefits of standardization, the European Commission and the Chinese government in 2015 inaugurated the EU-China connectivity platform. This intergovernmental arrangement facilitates transcontinental cooperation in setting infrastructural and equipment standards. It also promotes technical cooperation between China and Europe, while also establishing a forum for systematically discussing logistical and other constraints on deepened continental interdependence, especially in the transportation field.[25] These developments have created a powerful new logic to land transport where quality infrastructure is available. That logic applies particularly to intermodal transport by land, sea, or air, which before the days of digitalization was woefully complex. These sweeping political and technical changes are opening prospects for cost-effective economic interaction among a broad range of inland areas—from Belarus and Poland to Sichuan, Gansu, and Inner Mongolia—that had never been in sustained commercial contact before.

Transnational infrastructure holds promise of binding the often fractious nations of Eurasia in new and more cooperative ways, with positive geopolitical implications. Eurasian needs in this realm are massive—recent ADB estimates suggest US$26 trillion in new infrastructure is required over the 2016–2030 period.[26] Despite massive infrastructural spending across the continent already since the crisis of 2008–2009, particularly in China, the process of building the requisite superhighways, high-speed rail lines, electric power grids, electric power generators, dams, ports, airports, and communications systems across Eurasia has just begun.

Electric power transmission systems are growing capable of conveying greater and greater volumes of power over longer and longer distances, due to technical improvements in grid management as well as the progress of superconductivity.[27] Increasingly sophisticated electric power grids (smart grids) are becoming ever more capable of managing energy usage at the grassroots level, including inside the home, drawing on technical and financial support from both ends of the Eurasian continent. In electric power, telecommunications, and other areas, there is a new digital dimension that greatly intensifies potential for efficient interaction across long distances. The new transcontinental infrastructure, once in progress, sets in motion expectations of deepening economic interdependence between the powerful European and Chinese poles of Eurasia, placing fierce pressure in turn on national regulatory barriers while marginalizing the influence of protectionist forces in between.

One key dimension is just becoming clear: the central importance of logistics in creating efficient, cost-effective linkages among varied forms of delivery. If goods and services cannot be efficiently delivered, new physical infrastructure is meaningless. A synergistic combination of deregulation and technical change, driven by digitalization and innovations in intermodal transport, leveraged by Chinese market growth, has revolutionized the economics of Eurasian transcontinental commerce over the past few years, reducing transportation costs and intensifying pressures for still deeper interdependence. The impact is more powerful in Eurasia than elsewhere in the world, precisely because previous barriers have been so high, frustrating the otherwise compelling logic of geographic proximity.

The first crucial logistical development, which laid the technical basis for efficient transcontinental commerce, was the advent of containerized shipping. This allowed in turn for intermodal freight transport, with potential for ultimately linking road, river, rail, and air. Containerization began around 1956. During 1968–1970, at the height of the Vietnam War buildup, the size of containers operating internationally was largely standardized, allowing such standard-sized containers to be transported efficiently without repackaging the goods to suit alternative means of transport.[28] In 1992, the EU's intermodal initiative PACT abolished constraints within the EU by quota and administrative authorization while also decreasing taxes on intermodal vehicles. After that, intermodal transport within the EU took off, providing a model later to be applied transcontinentally as well.[29]

The second innovation underpinning deepened interdependence across the Eurasian continent was the rise of the container port, particularly in China. Between the early 1980s and 1999 the number of Chinese container ports rose from a handful to eighty-five, with their volume of trade soaring as well.[30] Government aided this expansion, through initiatives such as the 1995 central government decision to build the Shanghai International Shipping Hub, a cluster of twelve ports in central China. Outside China, governments in Korea, Singapore, the Netherlands, and the UAE, among others, took parallel steps to facilitate container trade. The increase in maritime trade through container ports proved to be synergistic with intermodal trade also involving road and rail. Revolutionary cost reductions in intermodal transport, intensified by computerization and the Internet of Things, thus exposed inland as well as port cities to transcontinental commerce and simultaneously facilitated transcontinental supply chains.[31]

A concrete example of this trans-Eurasian intermodal dynamic in operation is the production, distribution, and marketing of personal computers and their components between China and central-southern Europe. COSCO Logistics, a subsidiary of COSCO, for example, designed and implemented a system for transporting Hewlett Packard (HP) components from Foxconn factories in Chongqing, in central China, overland within China to Guangdong province. From there, the components are shipped by sea to Piraeus in Greece and thence onward by train to assembly plants in the Czech Republic, also owned by Foxconn. The final products are ultimately sold by HP all across Europe.[32]

COSCO Logistics has been instrumental in setting up this intermodal operation, including establishment of a cross-docking center at Piraeus for HP products. Because HP is the client, this new transport corridor has been more an initiative of private American and Taiwanese capital (Foxconn is a Taiwanese firm) rather than a purely Chinese initiative. It does rely on the Piraeus activities of COSCO Shipping Ports, another COSCO subsidiary, which are formally part of the "One Belt, One Road" (OBOR) initiative, but COSCO's role in fostering supply chains, and supplying logistics for these chains, is considerably greater.

If financial, technical, and political-economic obstacles to continental integration are beginning to erode, who are the beneficiaries, and what is the likely configuration of national, regional, and global power beyond the global Crossover Point? To grasp the broader implications of the massive infrastructural spending of the past decade across Eurasia, especially on digitalized facilities, and the potential escalation of spending on high-quality infrastructure in coming years, one need only glance at a map of the continent. Four conclusions readily occur: (1) China will be a huge beneficiary, due to its central geopolitical position, as literally the "Middle Kingdom" within the economic heart of Eurasia; (2) Continentalism is more than simply the rise of China and includes a variety of multinational firms as intermediaries, including those of G-7 nations; (3) Continentalism naturally deepens ties, both cooperative and conflictual, between China and Europe, which has been a central pole of the traditional transatlantic order; and (4) At the corporate level, firms with strong production bases, supply chains, distribution networks, and advanced logistical capabilities will be major beneficiaries.

Massive recent improvements in connectivity, rooted in transportation and communications economics, are drawing political and administrative systems closer as well. Together, the vitality of China and Europe, incorporating the former Soviet states in a more subordinate transit role, is generating a critical mass of geopolitical power, much less receptive to American influence than global regimes of the recent past, even though US-based multinational firms often play important roles as intermediaries. Recent signs are that Korea, and possibly Japan, are beginning to recognize the force of this continentalist dynamic also. The synergies between China and Europe—especially its central and eastern regions—are deepened by technological and financial change, centering on an intermodal transport revolution. Together, these changes, played out on an increasingly interactive Eurasian chessboard, have potential to create a Super Continent.

It is, of course, premature to say that such a configuration has emerged. Recent changes do, however, point to the need to rethink patterns of global governance. As a roadmap to the future, however, let us briefly sketch out four possible implications. And let us then assess the concrete challenges to global stability that they portend.

Geopolitical Uncertainties?

What, concretely, might the emergence of a Eurasian Super Continent with compelling global influence involve for world affairs? International relations theory is not optimistic about the stability of systems in geopolitical transition, an appellation that seems to describe today's volatile world. Robert Gil-pin has noted the correlation with hegemonic wars.[33] Charles Kindleberger has argued that every system needs a hegemonic stabilizer.[34] Aaron Friedberg and others have noted the dismal record of multipolarity in Europe over the past four hundred years and the prospect that such patterns could repeat in Asia as well.[35]

The US has, for more than seventy years, played a central role as global stabilizer. Developments of the past decade—under both Obama and Trump, in different ways—suggest that its willingness and ability to play that classical role may be declining. The macroeconomic foundations of that preeminence, in particular, show some initial signs of erosion, especially in relation to China. America retains formidable underlying strengths in technology, food, energy, and military power, but Chinese trade dependence on the US has measurably declined from the high levels of the 1990s, especially since the fall of 2017 as US-China trade tensions have intensified.[36] And new "continental-ist" ties with Europe, the Middle East, and Russia, embodied in Xi Jinping's BRI, give China important new geo-economic options, trending toward the emergence of a potential Super Continent, as we shall see.

What impact could a possible American retrenchment have on the future of global governance? To what extent will Beijing-inspired alternatives—either global or regional—fill the gap? Can India potentially come to the fore? And what are the prospects for rivalry and cooperation between alterna-tive US, Chinese, and other visions of world affairs?

Changing Role of the US Dollar?

The Bretton Woods system of 1944 established the US dollar as the primary key currency of world affairs, with the World Bank and the International Monetary Fund as the central global institutions. As a consequence, the US has enjoyed what Valéry Giscard d'Estaing enviously called the "exorbitant privilege" of a key-currency seigniorage that imposed only very limited fis-cal constraints of Washington's ambitious foreign policies. The United States was, as a consequence, able to intervene proactively in Korea, Vietnam, Iraq, and other hot spots across the world, confident of repaying the consider-able fiscal costs involved in its own currency without going to international financial brokers, as Britain had been forced to do during the Suez crisis of 1956. Washington has enjoyed the attractive option of intervening unilater-ally on a global basis, without the need in an extremity for special inter-national consultation. This invaluable ability lies at the core of US global leadership capacity.

The seigniorage role that the US enjoys as the issuer of a key global currency also has little-recognized but crucial political-economic implications at home. It allows the Federal Reserve to control domestic interest rates and to regulate them preeminently on the basis of domestic considerations. American homeowners no doubt enjoy more stable home mortgage conditions and rates, due to the dollar's key currency status, than would otherwise be true. A favorable interest-rate and monetary regime also clearly contributes to stable domestic employment and economic growth.

That the dollar's key currency role is not necessarily immutable is clear from past financial history. Before 1914, the dollar played almost no international role; the gold standard prevailed and the British pound was dominant as a currency of exchange. The combination of a geopolitical shock, coupled with institutional change, radically transformed this equation.[37]

The geopolitical shock that created strong pressure for systemic change was World War I. The conflict made it hard for neutral nations to engage with British banks and to settle their accounts in sterling. They consequently began looking for alternatives.

After World War I, economic growth slowed while unemployment erratically spiked in Britain.[38] The UK's troubled circumstances rendered the pound sterling less and less competitive vis-à-vis the dollar as a reserve currency. Home ownership also faced new financial challenges, as Britain worked desperately to defend the gold standard, generating political pressures to back away from the key-currency role.[39]

Meanwhile, as Britain faced mounting difficulties in maintaining its role, an alternative began to emerge across the Atlantic. The crucial precondition was an institutional change: the Federal Reserve Act of 1913. This historic legislation, ironically directed at domestic challenges rather than international, created a body that increased the liquidity of markets in dollar-denominated credit and enabled US banks to operate overseas for the first time. By the early 1920s, the dollar had become a significant vehicle of international financial transformation.

The sterling continued for some years in a parallel role to the dollar. Due to economic difficulties related to the role of sterling, however, Britain also could not easily respond to foreign-policy crises where its core interests were involved, ranging from the Greek and Turkish crises of 1947–1948 through the Suez crisis of 1956 to the Indonesian *Konfrontasi* against Malaysia and Singapore during the early 1960s.[40] Difficulties in financial management, such as the Harold Wilson administration's long and futile struggle to defend the pound sterling during 1966–1967, also eroded political legitimacy, leading to both leadership instability and short-sighted neglect of national strategic interests.[41] Clearly key currency standing had been beneficial in both economic and strategic terms for Britain, and its erosion conversely had painful costs, both foreign and domestic.

That the dollar will indefinitely continue as the world's key currency is not inevitable. Indeed, between 2006 and 2013, the dollar's share of global foreign-exchange reserves fell from 41 to 33 percent.[42] The dollar's share has since rebounded, but other long-term forces, including the rising economic role of China, show prospect of ultimately challenging the dollar's preeminence.

Aggressive American unilateralism could ironically be the catalyst that both creates the crisis and encourages the institutional developments that fatally undermine the dollar. In May 2018 President Donald Trump announced US withdrawal from the JCPOA agreement with Iran, in the face of strong opposition from the European Union, Russia, and China. Foreign firms were advised to reconsider their contracts with Iran to avoid exposure to US secondary sanctions, which were activated in the late fall. Such alternatives have encouraged many of the JCPOA backers to beginning to explore alternative financial frameworks.[43]

The dollar remains by a substantial margin the world's preeminent currency in virtually all dimensions—as a reserve asset, payments currency, and IMF basket currency. China's renminbi (RMB), however, has risen remarkably rapidly since the 2008 financial crisis as a potential challenger. As late as October 2010, the RMB ranked only 35th as the world's most widely used payments currency. A year later, it had moved up to the 17th spot. By December 2013 it had jumped into the 8th position. In November 2014, the RMB became one of the top five world payments currencies.[44] On October 1, 2016, the RMB also became the fifth currency in the IMF's special drawing rights (SDR) basket of currencies, enjoying third-ranking prominence after the US dollar and the euro.[45]

The European response to the RMB's inclusion in the IMF's SDR basket has been interesting, particularly in view of recent European cooperation with China on several other financial fronts, including establishment of the Asian Infrastructure Investment Bank (AIIB). The European Central Bank (ECB) was one of the first major global institutions to add RMB to its reserves; in June 2017 the ECB converted 500 million euro worth of US dollars into RMB.[46] In January 2018, Germany's Bundesbank also announced a decision to add RMB to its foreign-exchange reserves.[47] During 2018 the RMB's share of total foreign-exchange reserves slowly began to rise.[48]

Although the RMB's role has grown remarkably on a global basis since 2010, it has risen even more rapidly in trade-financial dealings with some strategic areas of the world—notably in those alternative corners of the Eurasian continent, Europe and the Middle East. A substantial share of payments between France and China (over 55 percent), for example, were denominated in RMB by 2017.[49] The UAE's use of RMB for trade finance was around 74 percent of payments by value in the same year.[50]

Within Asia, this trend toward RMB trade finance was even more striking. In Korea, the weight of RMB in payments with China/Hong Kong rose from 7 percent in 2012 to over 80 percent by 2017. In Taiwan, comparable ratios increased from 13 to 70 percent; and in Singapore from 22 to around 50 percent.[51] To be sure, the RMB's position as an international payment currency did weaken during 2015–2016, reflecting softness in the Chinese domestic economy, and a gradual depreciation of China's currency.[52] Cyclical strength in the dollar, as the US emerges from the aftermath of the financial crisis, could inhibit short-term expansion of the RMB's role. The rising scale of RMB reliance, however, could well increase further still in future years, both within Asia and beyond, and especially as Chinese financial instruments grow more sophisticated and the People's Republic's markets grow deeper.

A critical uncertainty, to be sure, is the future of Chinese capital controls—their removal or relaxation would no doubt increase confidence in the RMB still further. It is also possible, however, that China could further develop its hybrid system of continued domestic controls, coupled with expanded off-shore transactions through congenial markets like Hong Kong or London, to finance the extensive requirements of the BRI. Certainly there is little in the nature of China's distributive globalism, which operates heavily through state development banks and sovereign wealth funds, that intrinsically mandates full financial liberalization. The sobering Japanese experience since the late 1980s with financial liberalization, which has correlated with decline or at best stagnation in domestic asset prices, seems to give the Chinese pause. And their global leverage as the world's preeminent creditor makes it difficult for outsiders to forcefully compel full financial liberalization in China, if Chinese authorities themselves do not strongly desire it.

It is thus quite possible that, for a substantial period of time, the world could continue with a bifurcated financial system of liberalized/integrated and nonintegrated elements. If and when a basic transformation in the international key-currency system occurs, however, it is likely to have exactly the two drivers that created the dollar's ascendancy a century ago: (1) geopolitical crisis, and (2) institutional change. The geopolitical crisis could easily be generated by the dissatisfaction of key surplus nations/potential lenders with the behavior of the key-currency nation—Chinese and European opposition to US policies on Iran are a recent case, as noted above. Russia and China are already bypassing the dollar explicitly, while the Europeans are also creating a special-purpose financial vehicle to bypass SWIFT, the dollar-based clearance system.[53] In the long run assertive US unilateralism could seriously erode the dollar's role, especially as vigorous financial markets develop outside the United States.

Resource Insecurities?

Sustained growth in the heavily populated giants of Asia suggests the likelihood of sharply rising demand for food and raw materials. Technological changes, such as fracking, horizontal drilling, and advances in biotechnology, could help neutralize the economic impact of this demographically inspired increase in demand. Even so, the scale of the demand transformation as Asia's middle class grows could well intensify pressures worldwide on supplies of energy, raw materials, fish, and agricultural goods.

Asia's energy insecurities, in particular, are globally distinctive—huge populations, rapid economic growth, rising energy consumption, inadequate domestic reserves, inadequate energy infrastructure, and limited political-military capacity to ensure adequate resource flows. No other part of the world shares these challenges to the same urgent degree. The contrast is particularly striking to the United States, which enjoys resource abundance and the political-military strength to unilaterally control resource flows. Not surprisingly, much of Asia—especially China—would like to see changes in regional and ideally global governance that would accommodate the continent's distinctive interests with respect to resource security.

New Patterns of Multilateral Organization?

The rise of Eurasia is already creating new power centers in world affairs. As suggested earlier, that deepening global pluralism naturally creates the danger of deepening instability—so clearly manifest in arenas of conflict from Syria to the South China Sea. Established institutions like the United Nations have proved ineffective in handling global conflict, especially among large powers.

For many years after World War II, the United States stood as guarantor and enthusiastic promoter of multilateralist institutions, at both the global and the regional levels, ranging from the World Bank, GATT, and ultimately the WTO to the Asian and Inter-American Development Banks.[54] Recent developments, including the repudiation of the 2015 TPP agreement by both major candidates in the 2016 US presidential election campaign, suggest that the classical multilateralist era may be ending. The Trump administration shows distinctly limited enthusiasm for multilateralist approaches and a preference for more limited solutions reflecting sharply etched, and often parochial, American national priorities.

Charles Kindleberger has stressed that every system needs a stabilizer,[55] and this is especially true of multilateral organizations. If the United States, as appears increasingly evident, is not willing to serve as principal stabilizer—at some inevitable cost to its narrow interests—then who will play that role? That is a pressing question that the international system faces today.

Following the French Revolution, a multipolar concert evolved at the Congress of Vienna in 1814, based on compromise and accommodation.[56] In the post-post–Cold War world, a multipolar power configuration seems to be emerging, as China and India rise, Russia grows more assertive, and Europe develops new linkages that transcend the Atlantic. How these configurations relate to new multilateral bodies capable of stabilizing this complex world will be a pressing issue for the coming years, if the international system is to have coherent rules.

The Twenty-First-Century Challenge of Assuring Global Order

Henry Kissinger has acutely grasped the structural challenge of assuring global order in the twenty-first century, noting its four basic elements.[57] First of all, and most critically, the nation-state is losing legitimacy worldwide, eroding the intrinsic viability of state-to-state agreements. Second, global political-economic organization is at variance—the economy is organized on a global basis, while political organization, itself eroding in credibility, is preeminently national. Third, there is no serious global consultation mechanism, despite the rising complexity and vulnerability of international affairs. And finally, there is a global need for a transcendent conception of America's role in the world, which is conspicuously lacking in the Trumpian universe that we now inhabit.

China's Approach to Global Order

There is also, it should be added, a global need for a clearer picture of China's prospective relationship to global order, since China is the preeminent rising power of the twenty-first century and the only plausible current challenger to a US-centric global order. China starts, as Kissinger also points out, with a profound ambivalence about abiding by global rules that it did not make.[58] And to a greater degree than the United States, it is a relationship-based rather than a rule-based society in any case. Accordingly, it seems likely, at least in the short run, to seek to shape international relations indirectly through distributive tools such as infrastructure spending, or through the creation of new institutions, rather than to challenge established global norms, governance structures, and regulatory procedures directly.

China's underlying historical-geographical circumstances also help condition its response to global order. Across its long history, China has always had powerful adversaries next door, in sharp contrast to the US, which has rarely faced that challenge.[59] Given its underlying skepticism and distrust regarding the prevailing global order, China has put priority on evolutionary structural and conceptual departures from the status quo, rather than isolated, pragmatic solutions to individual problems—an approach that the US tends to prefer.[60]

Chinese analysts appear to place considerable emphasis, at least in theory, on normative aspects of international relations. Yan Xuetong of Tsinghua University, arguably China's foremost current international relations theorist, stresses, for example, the importance for China of promoting "humane authority" rather than hegemony, which he categorizes as the typical recent Anglo-American approach to international relations.[61] Ren Xiao, in a similar vein, stresses that China has not and should not focus on actual control of foreign societies, and should not consider reviving the tributary system, however much it may be justified in occasionally "righting the order" (reestablishing *li*) that has classically prevailed in China's foreign relations.[62] Wang Gungwu also stresses approvingly that *tianxia* ("all under the heaven") was invariably formed by "natural expansion" of the Middle Kingdom, in classical times, and not by conquest.[63] These prescriptions are congruent with the sort of voluntarist "win-win" approach, capitalizing on rising Chinese economic strength and geo-economic centrality, to generate political-economic influence that has been implicit in China's BRI since the fall of 2013. It is highly compatible with the "distributive globalism" underlying recent Chinese foreign policy, which is discussed later in this chapter.

Substantively, China's historic conception of global order (*tianxia*) had three key dimensions. As John K. Fairbank pointed out, it was built around "a sense of superiority and hierarchy without the concepts of sovereignty, territorially bounded nation states, or a balance of power," all of which were prominent in the West. Rather, *tianxia* was given "symbolic order and unity by the universal presence of the Son of Heaven."[64] China, in short, has endeavored to order the world by *awing* other societies with its cultural magnificence, economic bounty, and willingness to support constructive projects by others.[65] This munificent, often personalistic approach, frequently reflecting an inability or reluctance to pursue military resolution, has contrasted starkly to the much more legalistic US cultivation of shared principles, with leadership directed toward the pursuit of justice rather than demonstrations of benevolence. The distinction, in Lowi's terms, is clearly between a distributive and a regulatory approach.[66]

China's classical conception of world order seems remarkably well illustrated, as suggested above, in the BRI proposals of President Xi Jinping. The approach is voluntary rather than compulsory. It also hedges on broad issues of global governance, eschewing radical proposals for change in favor of incremental changes through establishment of new institutions like the AIIB that in turn can collaborate with established interests, through distributive activities like cofinancing, while also marginally shifting broader governance patterns in China's favor.

The BRI derived its persuasive power not from legal compulsion, but from the munificence that Beijing proposed to bestow on participants. This "distributive" globalism conveyed attractive material benefits without imposing onerous rules. It "rhymed" with, even if it did not repeat, the tribute systems of bygone years. At the same time, it also serves, even today, as a catalyst for broader transformations to China's advantage in the overall structure of international affairs.

Creating New Institutions

The creation of new institutions could well be a key element of peaceful transitions to a New World Order, based on connectivity globalism, beyond the global Crossover Point. Even if it is difficult to significantly change governance structures in established bodies like the IMF and the World Bank, those structures can be specified flexibly from the outset in newly created institutions. And new, rising actors with resources can determine operational rules in the new institutions that they sponsor.

China has been applying exactly this approach in the several new multilateral financial bodies that it has initiated since Xi Jinping came to power in late 2012. The collective purpose of these institutions seems to be promoting connectivity—first at the regional level, but increasingly at the global level as well. In the fall of 2013, for example, when China first proposed establishment of the AIIB, the PRC stipulated that 75 percent of the initial capitalization and voting rights would be allocated to Asian nations, and that subscriptions would be allocated in proportion to national GDP. This set of criteria automatically made China, as an Asian nation with the largest GDP in Asia, the largest shareholder in the bank, while also giving it veto power over major decisions. The arrangement also marginalized the United States, as a non-Asian nation, even though the US has the largest GDP in the world in nominal terms and is the largest shareholder in almost all other multinational financial institutions. China, finally, agreed to provide an initial subscription of around $30 billion to get the new institution started.[67]

Through these various gestures, the PRC was able to earn regional good-will by addressing the massive infrastructural needs of Eurasia, including rail, roads, ports, telecommunications, and electric power grids, in a cooperative way. Since the facilities being financed are divisible assets, China has been able to minimize zero-sum conflicts among recipients and to maximize local goodwill. It has also been able to gain enhanced geo-economic and geopoliti-cal influence by establishing a multinational financial institution from scratch in which Asia at last enjoys a dominant position. Connectivity has been an especially auspicious approach for China in relations with Eurasia, given its own geo-economic centrality on the continent.

In the process of establishing the AIIB, China was also to serve a num-ber of national geopolitical and economic objectives. Not only did it address Eurasia's imposing infrastructural challenges—which reportedly mandate at least $26 trillion in capital investment over the 2016–2030 period.[68] It also consolidated its relationship with capital-short Russia, suffering from Western sanctions. And it created fissures in Western solidarity by attracting major European nations, including Britain, Germany, and France, into membership, against the entreaties of the United States.

The AIIB is the most substantial of the recent Chinese multilateral initia-tives undertaken since the birth of the Xi Jinping administration, but several others have also been established on a similar pattern. There is the $40 billion Silk Road Fund, inaugurated in November 2014. Based in Beijing and domi-nated by Chinese investors, this nominally private operation, functioning like a private-equity venture fund, channels capital into promising projects along the New Silk Road.[69] And there is also the New Development Bank (NDB), formerly known as the BRICS Development Bank, headquartered in Shang-hai and led initially by an Indian president, which was launched in August 2015 with a capitalization of $50 billion.[70]

These Chinese initiatives reflect an underlying approach to international affairs that has deep roots in classical Chinese geopolitical thinking and histor-ical experience, as we have seen. Throughout the long period (third century BC to the nineteenth century AD) during which the traditional system of

international relations in East Asia prevailed, largely insulated from Western influence, the notions of *badao* ("hegemonic way") and *wangdao* (a more
consensual "kingly way") were common in Chinese political thought.[71] The
operation of these new, Chinese-initiated multilateral financial institutions
arguably represent a manifestation of the "kingly way" of influencing foreign
countries—relying on the unconstrained self-interest of recipients to encourage cooperation. The approach also manifestly serves the geo-economic
interest of contemporary China by maximizing the utility of its relative economic strength while minimizing the consequences of military weakness. It
is thus consistent with Chinese cultural norms, Chinese national interest, and
also the pluralist, nonregulatory approach to international order that we introduced in Chapter 1 as "distributive globalism."

A state following the "kingly way," according to Chinese thinking, does
not seek to impose its control over other countries but instead seeks to create conditions whereby foreign partners cooperating with it receive distinct
privileges and benefits. As a consequence, these countries themselves give
the beneficent donor state, in this case China, the opportunity to establish
control over them, or at least to receive the standing of "first among equals."
Establishing new institutions like the AIIB, the New Development Bank,
and the Silk Road Fund, while mobilizing them to dispense infrastructural
benefits of broad general utility, is a clear manifestation of the classical *wangdao*, providing distributive goods of general utility that also benefit centrally
located China as well.

"Distributive Globalism"

A related possibility, more fully developed in Beijing as actual policy than in
theory, is that global systemic transformation serving China's interests might
be achieved most effectively and painlessly not by conflict or even formal
creation of new institutions but through a softer, more incremental process of
subversion based on selective financial support. An aspiring hegemon could
simply bestow resources on strategically situated actors, as China has recently
done with Pakistan, for example, to encourage them to play more active
roles in support of the would-be hegemon. It could thereby create new geo-
economic realities conducive to the new hegemon's interests, without changing the embedded structures and rules of the established system. This essen-
tially distributive approach, oriented more toward consensus building than toward conflict, could be considered "distributive globalism," achieved through
the enhanced connectivity flowing from large-scale infrastructural outlays and

a related, incremental revision of global technical standards and operational rules in cooperation with a variety of partners outside the United States.

Distributive globalism, as applied to current world affairs, needs to be seen in geo-economic context. A geo-economic perspective, as we have stressed in previous chapters, helps greatly in understanding both the emerging order of world affairs in the early twenty-first century and also China's prospective role within that order. Land-based and hybrid land-sea transactions that have been underdeveloped for six hundred years and more are rapidly growing more economically and politically feasible, with the transformation being especially important across a Eurasian continent where overland connectivity has traditionally been poor. And a rapidly growing China lies at the economic heart of that reconnecting Eurasia.

As China grows and becomes more affluent, it is potentially also becoming a more and more attractive market and source of finance for the broader world. Conversely, the surrounding world is becoming an increasingly important source of resources, labor, and technology for a growing China. The problem has long been *connectivity*—China's infrastructure and communications links with the world, born in an earlier, more parochial age, have not been adequate to the present. That problem is addressed distributively—by providing infrastructure that solves the connectivity problem.

Many surrounding nations, especially in the developing world, experience an analogous challenge. Thus, connectivity is rapidly becoming a "win-win" proposition for both China and its neighbors—enhancing at once both regional prosperity and Chinese influence, provided the projects in question are economically and financially viable. Ensuring connectivity through distributive benefits like roads, railways, electric power grids, and telecommunications systems also could spread benefits across Eurasia, due to China's geo-economically central position.

Enhanced connectivity through ambitious infrastructure construction under the BRI can have strategic implications in many directions. Acquisition of ports like Piraeus in Greece or China's massive new dry ports in Khorgos and Minsk can enhance control of trade. Construction of railroads such as the Athens to Budapest high-speed rail line can have a parallel impact. Cooperation between Huawei and European counterparts can help set global standards in 5G telecommunications. Superhighways and power grids across Pakistan can check Indian efforts to expand its influence westward beyond the subcontinent.

China under Xi Jinping in 2013 began, through the BRI, to promote connectivity across the Eurasian continent. That could have been called "distributive regionalism." Increasingly, especially since early 2017, this approach has
morphed into full-scale "distributive globalism," with BRI projects spanning
the globe, including distant continents like South America.

China, to be sure, is continuing its efforts to promote connectivity across
Eurasia. Capitalizing on its continuing rapid growth, positive relations with
major global power centers in Europe, and failures of US global leadership
under Donald Trump, however, China is *expanding* its connectivity initiatives,
both to other continents and also to the global agenda-setting stage. In January 2017 at the World Economic Forum in Davos, and again in May 2017
at the inaugural Belt and Road Forum in Beijing, President Xi emphasized
the *global* scope of the BRI and its role in promoting global communication,
interdependence, and sustainable growth. Xi reiterated these themes at the
2018 Boao Forum for Asia. Premier Li Keqiang stressed similar themes in extensive meetings with European leaders in the immediate aftermath of Donald Trump's controversial visit to NATO headquarters and Trump's decision
to withdraw the US from the historic COP-21 global environmental agreement. China's distributive globalism, focused on providing connectivity infrastructure, is thus advancing into the vacuum created by Trump's abdication
of American global leadership, accelerating the coming of a Global Crossover
Point, under which a Beijing consensus gradually and quietly subverts the
already eroding legitimacy of the liberal world order, even as Chinese leadership ritually affirms many of its central tenets.

In Conclusion

The core institutions of the contemporary global political economy have
proven to be remarkably durable. The most basic ones—the IMF and the
World Bank—were born at the Bretton Woods conference of July 1944.
They have been supplemented by other bodies, such as the regional development banks. Yet the underlying structure has not changed. An American
continues to head the World Bank, and a European serves as managing director of the IMF, just as was true three quarters of a century ago.

Although the core institutions remain remarkably intact, with even their
leadership structure fundamentally unchanged, the political-economic context has shifted dramatically, as we have seen. Fueled by the recovery of the
former Axis powers, especially Germany and Japan, followed by the emergence of China and India, Europe and East Asia together comprise a much

larger portion of the global political economy than at the end of World War II, even if the ratios between them have shifted. Since the 1970s the oil producers of the Gulf have also come to play a more substantial role in the global political economy; since the early 1990s the nations of Eastern Europe have become more closely integrated into the international system as well.

Since the global financial crisis of 2008, a series of structural changes have begun to occur in the global political economy that generate strong pressures for a new paradigm of international relations. There has been a steady erosion of globalism, involving a deceleration of international trade and the failure of several global and large-scale regional trade negotiations. The advent of the Trump administration in the US, leading to American withdrawal from TPP and COP-21, as well as an escalation of trade conflict, has compounded the problem. Meanwhile, an increasingly interactive Eurasian playing field has emerged among nations with heretofore inadequate interconnections, necessitating a rapid expansion of transcontinental infrastructure and the birth of new institutions to facilitate it, including the AIIB, the New Development Bank, and the Silk Road Fund. China's new distributive globalism based on the BRI is working to create a new interdependence paradigm from the ground up, through infrastructural largesse and personal networks that do not directly contravene the Bretton Woods system. There are already normative policy objectives, such as sustainable development and green growth, being attached, and a few new institutions, such as the AIIB, being created to facilitate those objectives. The ongoing proliferation of intergovernmental and interagency MOUs will no doubt help clarify the currently vague formal structure.

It is already evident, however, that distributive globalism, potentially a halfway house to Chinese hegemony, will be less judgmental about and less intrusive into domestic political systems than liberal-internationalist alternatives. Beijing-led distributive globalism will be less legalistic and more reliant on distributive incentives to induce cooperation, as China warily moves halfway to hegemony under its subversive new supplement to the eroding liberal political-economic regime. In the distance, should the globalist framework continue to atrophy, looms the prospect of a more decentralized international structure of loose regional hegemonies, within which a nascent Eurasian Super Continent could quite plausibly loom large.

11

Prospects and Policy Implications

OVER THE PRECEDING TEN CHAPTERS we have explored the changing profile of an emerging Super Continent in the throes of reconnection. Eurasia has transformed itself from a static set of self-contained, autarkic states into a dynamically interactive group of countries, collectively exerting subtle but deepening influence over international relations as a whole. We have noted the importance of critical junctures, especially the Four Modernizations of China, the collapse of the Soviet Union, and the 2008 global financial crisis in provoking domestic transformation, relaxing the political constraints on interdependence, and then giving inhabitants of the continent deepening incentives for mutual interaction. Through this process Eurasia is returning to a centrality in global affairs to which its heartland position, in the view of so many geopolitical theorists, naturally entitles it. In the coming of the Eurasian continental Crossover Point and its global reverberations, Mackinder would see the inevitable unfolding of geopolitical logic in its fullness.

This chapter reviews the logic and detailed empirical evidence that have brought us to our provocative conclusion: a global transition to a new, multipolar era of rising Eurasian engagement in international affairs, and of enhanced continental collaboration, is now impending. Synergistic post-post Cold War transformations in China and Central Europe, as well as their interconnection, lie at the core of that process. The logic of integration, moving Eurasia increasingly beyond Brzezinski's paradigm of division, now more than two decades old, is a simple one: economic complementarities, plus the connectivity simulated by global shocks and nurtured by distributive globalism, render political divisions less and less central. The era of the Great Game is waning, and a more relevant political-economic paradigm is needed.

This chapter first outlines the eclectic methodological approach employed in creating that new paradigm: (1) understanding the geo-economic potential of geographic location, (2) conceptualizing geographically rooted national complementarities, and (3) showing how individual action, at historic critical junctures, relaxes political constraints on interdependence. Such relaxation in turn generates forces, including economic growth, energy demand, and logistical improvement, that propel such interdependence, thus generating systemic changes that give birth to a more integrated and interactive Eurasia, with a rising global profile. The analysis as a whole vindicates the deeply geo-economic approach, stressing the synergistic relation between geographic position and economic patterns, that is adopted throughout this book.

Key Findings in Review

Based on the foregoing assumptions about geo-economics and political-economic changes, we have argued that geographical location has intrinsic potential importance, although the significance of geography at any specific decision point ultimately depends on prevailing political, economic, and social structures. China is not Australia, which conveys both advantages and disadvantages to both. Today's China is also not the China of 1975 or even that of 2005; the important structural changes that unfold over time—conceived as critical junctures and Crossover Points—have fateful geo-economic implications.

The previous pages have contended that a fundamental transformation is occurring in world affairs, bringing to an end the unipolar American dominance that has persisted since the collapse of the Soviet Union in late 1991. This transformation is the result most fundamentally of synergistic subnational and transnational developments in China, Russia, and Central and Eastern Europe—with their origins in manufacturing, energy, finance, and logistics. Developments in these particular parts of the world are especially fateful due to their geographic *centrality*—changes there have powerful spill-over effects not present if change occurred in more geopolitically peripheral areas such as Australia or New Zealand. These historic changes in centrally located nations, themselves mutually synergistic, are bringing the countries of the continent closer in political-economic terms, while simultaneously increasing their overall self-sufficiency in relation to the broader world.

Contrary to the increasingly fashionable contentions of "fragile blossom" theorizing,[1] Eurasian growth is increasingly self-sustaining, with a declining reliance on the United States. This economic distancing opens corresponding prospects for a more decentralized system of global governance within which Washington's leverage declines, unless far-sighted countermeasures are taken. Recent isolationist steps by the Trump administration, including withdrawal from the multilateral Trans-Pacific Partnership and COP-21 agreements, as well as escalating economic conflicts with traditional allies, especially in Europe, further accelerate the demise of a US-centric world order that declining trade and financial reliance on America has already begun to provoke.

We have identified parallel and interrelated geo-economic transformations underway at three different levels: national, regional, and global. Together, these triple Crossover Points, or "transition periods to new forms of social activity of broader systemic relevance," have begun over the past four decades to radically and synergistically transform the global political economy, leading ultimately to the deepening challenges to American global credibility that the world witnesses today. These transformations have occurred discontinuously, we argue, through critical junctures like China's Four Modernizations (1978), the collapse of the Soviet Union (1991), the 2008 global financial crisis, and the Ukraine crisis (2013–2014). Collectively, these critical junctures, coupled with quieter, more technical revolutions in energy, finance, and logistics, have allowed Eurasia increasingly to exploit the implicit resource and demographic complementarities and geographic propinquities that endow this heartland continent with heretofore unexploited global strengths.

The national Crossover Point that first set broader transcontinental changes in motion was the shift within China from a coastal to a continental development approach. This shift occurred in three stages: (1) the Western Development regional policies of Jiang Zemin in the late 1990s; (2) the massive $586 billion stimulus package in 2008 of Hu Jintao, also oriented toward continental development; and (3) the Belt and Road Initiative (BRI; since 2013) of Xi Jinping. All were driven by embedded interests: party, military, heavy industry, local government, and real estate. Two-thirds of the distance from the Bohai Gulf to the Strait of Hormuz lies inside China, as does half the distance from Shanghai to the borders of the European Union; what geographically extensive and economically powerful China does for domestic reasons thus has broad continental and, indeed, global implications, due to its commanding geo-economic scale and continental centrality.

China's geo-economic expansion westward and southward is driven by its own parochial domestic growth dynamic more than explicit strategy, although influenced by opportunities created for China by parallel internal transformations in the EU and in Russia. Over the past two decades, propelled by economic growth, critical junctures, and implicit geo-economic logic, infrastructure has been built, red tape has been reduced, and production networks have evolved—both east from Germany and west from China's east coast. The collapse of communism in Eastern Europe during the 1990s and the ensuing structural changes in the center of Europe inspired eastward-oriented geoeconomic ties synergistic with the westward advance of China. The growing scale of consolidated Chinese and European markets, combined with a technical revolution in logistics, opened new prospects for intermodal road, rail, and maritime transport, not to mention e-commerce. Those innovations are profoundly reconfiguring commercial ties and supply chains across the continent.

Three decades ago, the Soviet Union would have stood solidly between Europe and China, easily frustrating any potential Sino-European entente. Historic geopolitical and technological changes have, however, radically transformed Russia's role, increasing transcontinental connectivity and allowing contemporary Eurasia to be born. The collapse of the Soviet Union, the explosive growth of China, the eastward expansion of democratic Europe, and changing transport logistics all combined to erode Moscow's control over transcontinental interchange and to transform Russia increasingly from a Euro-Asian hegemon into a transit country between the continent's dynamic poles to its east and its west.

National Crossover Points—particularly in China, Russia, and Central and Eastern Europe, including Germany—have thus been synergistic with the rise of a broader New Continentalism across Eurasia. Based on underlying resource and demographic complementarities, amplified by economic growth, these complementarities are being converted into real-world political-economic ties—a veritable Eurasian Crossover Point—through a relaxation of political constraints, impelled by critical junctures, such as the 1991 collapse of the USSR and the 2013–2014 Ukraine crisis. China's relations with Russia and Eastern Europe, in particular, have been strengthened by these continental transformations, even as backlash closer to the Atlantic also arises.

The portentous prospect of the Eurasian Crossover Point, from a broader global perspective, raises the specter of additional changes in worldwide governance. The Asian Infrastructure Investment Bank (AIIB), initially proposed by China, gained wider significance with the accession of Britain and other key European nations. So did the New Development Bank, by involving such major developing nations as Brazil, South Africa, and India, in addition to China. A third Crossover Point—that in global governance—is thus arguably impending, as a result of China's multiple connectivity initiatives, although its ultimate configuration remains unclear.

Such a global Crossover Point need not be imminent, and may well be nominally consistent with existing liberal institutions. Indeed, Chinese president Xi Jinping—at the 2017 Davos meetings, the 2017 Belt and Road Forum, and the 2018 Boao Forum for Asia—repeatedly stressed the global importance of free trade and multilateral institutions. The impending challenge from Eurasia, with China at the center, is far more subtle, flowing from the elemental distinction between regulatory and distributive policies made in Chapter 1. The classic Bretton Woods system is a "world of liberty under law," governed (at least in theory) by abstract, transparent norms.[2] The world now emerging will likely be a more relativistic one, subtly shaped by ad hoc, case-specific distributive decisions that both enhance connectivity and slowly transform underlying power relationships in revolutionary new directions.

In chronicling these three Crossover Points, with a focus on the critical Eurasian regional evolution, we have suggested three concrete implications for global affairs, apart from the structural shift outlined above. First, the balance between land and sea power is shifting—China is, through its BRI, gaining multifaceted leverage, with its land power and economic strength leveraging its maritime efforts to forge a Super Continent much as the United States did after construction of the transcontinental railway and the Panama Canal increased connectivity and mobility over a century ago. Changing logistics technology, plus massive infrastructure spending coupled with control of strategic seaports and dry ports, is giving China formidable influence over international channels of distribution.

The second broad implication of this research—and a critical one—is that we are by no means confronting the "end of the Asian century." To be sure, Asia may well face deepening demographic and financial challenges over the coming generation. At the same time, however, important political, economic, and technological constraints on transcontinental interdependence that have hampered flexible and intensive Eurasian interaction over the millennia are being relaxed. International political relationships are stable; trade restrictions are declining; and infrastructure—ranging from roads and railways to digital communications—is being rapidly upgraded. All of these developments are stimulating growth, offsetting negative developments on which pessimists traditionally dwell.

China's connectivity initiatives, epitomized in BRI, are playing a major role in making transcontinental transactions easier, stimulating growth. Meanwhile, the revolution in intermodal logistics is radically reducing the costs of trans-Eurasian manufacturing interdependence, just as e-commerce is magnifying the potential returns to such interaction. Continental Europe—and China, in particular—are growing rapidly, while developing unprecedented and synergistic value-chain relationships of global significance.

These transcontinental ties, in short, coupled with access to the resources of a weakened and more pliant Russia, are thus giving Asia unprecedented international leverage, and a new lease on political-economic life. China's distributive globalism, epitomized in BRI, is becoming a major transformative agent in international affairs. It fills a void created by recent American reluctance to play Washington's traditional role as multilateral leader, which is increasingly difficult to sustain in today's world. That role, after all, requires defending and enforcing abstract rules that inflict concentrated, clearly visible costs such as unemployment, while providing only diffuse, abstract rewards, such as the benefits of free trade. China's distributive globalism is thus reorienting global governance *away* from a liberal "liberty under law" paradigm toward a pragmatic approach that privileges sustainable growth and connectivity, while side-stepping human rights.

A third key feature of our emerging world is that traditional US alliance relationships, both in Europe and Asia, are cross-pressured and infinitely more fragile than at any time since the early post–World War II years. Rising interdependence across Eurasia, amply documented in these pages, creates a continentalist alternative to dependence on Washington, particularly when potential intra-Eurasian partners have attractive economic growth rates, natural resources, and rising technological sophistication. American parochialism and belligerence only compounds the danger, which is especially acute with European allies who have traditionally been accustomed to close and systematic consultation.

Future Prospects

Following from our review of past contentions presented in this book, which emphasize the rising cohesion of Eurasia and its rising profile in international affairs, we speculate regarding future prospects for Eurasia's role in the global system. Will it relate in stable fashion to the United States? Will it be inclined to participate constructively in the traditional globally inclusive institutions? Can it be considered a potentially constructive stakeholder in international affairs?

Due to its geo-economic scale and location, China has, as we observed in Chapter 1, the "wind at its back." That does not mean it will inevitably grow and become more influential, since structural factors are also at work.

Provided that its domestic politics and relations with other major powers are stable, however, there is that tendency, and connectivity initiatives to deepen China's international ties in a cooperative fashion will probably help. "Distributive globalism," through infrastructural initiatives like the BRI, is thus an astute grand strategy for Beijing to pursue in subtly promoting China's rise.

Another general conclusion is that a democratic evolution cannot be expected from the Eurasian continentalists, including China and Russia. Their soft authoritarian systems are mutually reinforcing and suppress the political emergence of middle-class interests that have been catalysts for "third-wave" democratic uprisings elsewhere in the world.[3] Many of the multilateral institutions that these continentalists support, including the Shanghai Cooperation Organization (SCO), are specifically directed to suppressing the upsurge of violence that has accompanied social mobilization across the continent over the past two decades. The SCO's Regional Anti-Terrorist Structure, based in Tashkent, is a case in point.[4]

The "world of liberty under law" idealized by Western liberals is not an inevitable development, we contend, across the bulk of Eurasia. It will likely persist in most of its European redoubts, but even there, in some of the newer democracies, it may be in danger.[5] More pervasive is likely to be the "Beijing consensus" that economic development should be strongly prioritized over civil liberty.[6]

Certainly "distributive globalism" promotes this outcome, since it magnifies the geo-economic advantages of China's geographic centrality in Eurasia by interconnecting the continent. Should Eurasian continentalism continue to deepen, as the analysis presented here suggests, and the autonomous role of the continent to rise, strongly influenced by China, the enduring post–World War II pattern of US global hegemony accompanied by a hub-and-spokes pattern of bilateral alliances centered on Washington, DC, could well be decisively compromised. In the short run, that would probably not have radical systemic consequences, as China would be loath to challenge the prevailing system directly or to impose a rule-based alternative of its own. More likely, as we have suggested, distributive globalism will grow more salient, in accordance with which China provides concrete, stabilizing benefits to key actors as the BRI itself proposes.

In Chapter I we presented four alternative paradigms of international order, based on a typology of leadership structure and rule orientation (Table 1.4). Of the four, three seem congenial to China, all of them based on human relationships rather than legal abstractions. One possibility, should China alone serve as hegemonic leader, could be a tributary system—a variant of China's historical relations with its neighbors, which involved formalistic benevolence on the part of China, but without transcendent systemic rules.[7] This approach, in its asymmetrical bilateralism, arguably bears structural similarity to the classical hub-and-spokes system that the US has employed to sustain its influence in East Asia over much of the post–World War II period, albeit with a contrasting approach to rules.[8] Closely related to the tributary system is the concept of *tianxia* or "all under heaven." The United Nations, sovereignty, globalization, and multilateral regionalism all potentially fit into a Chinese *tianxia* international order,[9] although applying classic concepts when China's known world was only its periphery to today's truly global society is a bit of a stretch.

A second possibility would be a "concert of powers" like that crafted by Metternich at the Congress of Vienna in 1814.[10] This paradigm has been proposed by prominent international relations scholars and practitioners, beginning with Henry Kissinger.[11] It combines the Western preference for a rules-based order with the multipolarity notions congenial to China. Chinese formulations of the basic concert concept assume various forms, including priority for the United Nations Security Council, BRICS, and the Six-Party Talks. All are formulations often supported explicitly by the Chinese government.

Some analysts propose a bilateral collaboration between China and the United States—a global, G-2 arrangement, which might be considered a variant of the concert of powers, in that it would not involve a unitary leadership structure. The late Zbigniew Brzezinski, national security adviser to President Jimmy Carter, who played a central role in promoting US recognition of the People's Republic of China (PRC) in 1979, himself endorsed an informal variant of this arrangement.[12] Brzezinski suggested that leaders of the two nations should "meet informally on a regular schedule for personal in-depth discussions not just about bilateral relations but about the world in general."[13] In addition, Brzezinski advocated deepened and widened cooperation between Washington and Beijing on matters ranging from global financial crises to climate change to Israeli-Palestinian peace talks.[14]

A more formalized version of Brzezinski's informal G-2 notion is the Chinese "new type of great-power relations" concept, proposed by Xi Jinping at the Sunnylands summit with US president Barack Obama in 2013.[15] The formula, as presented by Xi at Sunnylands, had three basic elements: (1) no conflict or confrontation, (2) mutual respect, and (3) mutually beneficial cooperation. The most important as well as controversial of the three is the second point—mutual respect, including for each other's core interests and major concerns. As Cheng Li argues, "By emphasizing the respect of 'core interests' as an element of the concept, China pushes its territorial claims to the forefront. . . . American adoption of the term would imply that the United States recognizes China's 'core interests' [in the East China Sea and the South China Sea]."[16]

A third alternative, and possibly the most congenial to China, is an eclectic one that can incorporate attractive elements of the other two options. That alternative is distributive globalism, involving plural, non–rule-based leadership. This avoids the legalistic, rule-based leadership that the US has pursued, and from which China has, in its view, suffered across the years. Distributive approaches also have elements of the tributary system, viewed as benevolent in China, without necessarily implying hierarchy. They are also compatible with pluralistic leadership approaches that are the heart of the concert of powers.

The one alternative presented in Table 1.4 that seems unlikely to be accepted in China over the long run is the post–World War II status quo—a rule and value-based order with a unitary leadership structure. That order has heretofore been dominated by the United States, and China sees no need, in the world of an emerging Eurasian Super Continent, to defer to such an external and culturally alien presence. Conversely, however, it shows no evident desire to assume the hegemonic role the US has recently played, or to dominate through regulatory norms, as the US has recently done.

Regardless of the global paradigm, the world in coming years will need to deal with a phenomenon it has not seen for over a century—the emergence of a Super Continent, coming into its own through the exhilarating act of physical connection. For America in the Age of Roosevelt at the beginning of the twentieth century, that was a matter of Manifest Destiny and emotional reconnection with the values of the nation's founders. For Eurasia in future years, a continent with much history, that awakening will likely be a subtler matter of rediscovery and reconnection with past glories. As a century ago, there will in any event be a new, emerging transcontinental force on the global horizon.

Policy Implications and Recommendations

The task for the rest of the world of dealing with a potential emerging Super Continent will not be an easy one. Building on the research presented in the foregoing pages, we consider here policy implications for the United States and likeminded nations, in four distinct areas: (1) relations with neighbors and formal allies; (2) key nonalliance bilateral relations; (3) issues of special importance, including energy, finance, and nuclear nonproliferation, as well as related institution building; and (4) specific responses to the challenge of BRI, including development of the vital relationship-building skills, including language and area-studies expertise, that are so vital to sustaining credible global ties. The transformation of Eurasia now underway is a historic development, and deserves a systematic response.

Relations with Neighbors and Allies

No doubt a key priority in our analysis must be revisiting the very logic of continentalism itself, to consider how we might benefit from the sort of solidarity with neighbors that we once valued, and that the Eurasians are fostering today. In what ways can a continent be greater than the sum of its parts? And what needs to be sacrificed to realize the benefits of that cohesion?

Domestic politics are making it difficult to appreciate North American continental economic relationships in the short run. Between 1994 and 2017, the US auto sector alone lost 350,000 jobs—fully one-third of its work force.[17] NAFTA was widely cited as responsible for that bitterness, especially by US politicians.

The United States, Canada, and Mexico, however, have potential synergies in energy, finance, technology, and labor-intensive manufacturing that make the whole much more competitive than any of the parts alone, if supply chains are allowed to be transcontinental. Despite the job losses and wage stagnation in a few noncompetitive sectors, such as US autos and steel, Canadian dairy products, or Mexican telecommunications, the impact on consumer prices and labor productivity has been highly positive, even in the US. Most estimates conclude that NAFTA has added several billion dollars of added growth to the US economy annually, amounting to close to 0.5 percent of GDP per year.[18] With more active job-retraining programs and offsetting domestic infrastructure spending, as on pipelines for exporting US shale gas, the positive impact could potentially be even higher. US President Donald Trump did come to terms with Mexico and Canada bilaterally in the fall of 2018, generating a US-Mexico-Canada (USMCA) agreement broadly similar to NAFTA, amidst lingering trilateral bitterness.[19]

Apart from rediscovering the virtues of a lost North American continental consciousness, Americans might also consider reviving the values of Atlantic

community. That should not prove insurmountable, despite recent recrimi-
nations, since cultural ties and personal familiarity are strong. Yet the payback
could be great—precisely to offset and dilute in the interest of a broader
globalism the incipient cohesion of Eurasia chronicled in these pages. It is a
tragedy that recent US policy has privileged trans-Atlantic confrontation over
solidarity.

One part of enhanced US engagement with Europe needs to be trade policy with a multilateralist dimension. Reviving the Transatlantic Trade and Investment Partnership (T-TIP) may be unrealistic in the short run, but the US
and the EU unquestionable share common interests in promoting "higher
standards" and "fairer rules." Another dimension of enhanced trans-Atlantic
relations could involve more dialogue on Asia policy, including supportive
background research.

Due to a history of longer and deeper involvement, European understanding of Central, Southern, and parts of Southeast Asia, in particular, is more
sophisticated in many ways than American. US support for dialogue could
potentially lead to more enlightened policies. Subtle US support for qualified
majority voting (QMV) within the EU could help the Europeans respond
more flexibly to a deepening Chinese challenge. Dialogues on global technology standards could serve a parallel purpose.

With Eurasia emerging, the US cannot forget about its longstanding
Northeast Asian allies, precariously hugging the Super Continent's rim. The
most exposed is South Korea, whose trade with China alone is now more significantly more than that with the US and Japan *combined*.[20] The most potent
economically and financially is Japan, with the third-largest economy and the
second-largest foreign-exchange reserves in the world.

With regard to both countries, especially Japan, the US must place greater
stress on the broad multilateral bodies that link these Northeast Asian out-
posts with the broader democratic world and market-capitalist economies,
countervailing the natural pull of the neighboring Super Continent. The
OECD and the G-7 are not fashionable of late, but do have a key role in the
international political-economic order. They need to be strengthened, and
rendered more relevant as agenda-setting bodies for more universal organizations like the G-20.

One key US priority must be encouraging better Japan-Korea relations,
which is often easier in multilateral contexts due to the difficult bilateral history between them. Including the two in US Southeast Asian initiatives could
be one way to do that, as could collaboration in cyber-security. Another pos-

sibility would be including this energetic duo in broader US-inspired or guaranteed consortia arrangements, especially in sectors like energy, since both are devoid of hydrocarbons.

Japan is a vital ally, of course, in its own right. Both the US and Japan want freedom and prosperity in the Indo-Pacific region, and Japan, with the largest ODA program in Asia of any democratic nation, together with important defensive capabilities like the world's largest minesweeping fleet, is in a position to powerfully support US security efforts. Its potential for technological cooperation, and for financing third-country projects through the Japan Bank for International Cooperation (JBIC), and other vehicles, should also be appreciated.

While working actively to deepen ties with both Japan and Korea, the US must accept the reality that they will not always agree—either with each other or the United States. The basic interests of Japan, in particular, are deeply aligned with the US, so Tokyo should be given benefit of the doubt in third-country diplomacy—with respect to AIIB involvement, for example. Japan, together with the Europeans, could be a powerful, pivotal force for transparency and market sensitivity in what otherwise would be a body more narrowly focused on Chinese geopolitical goals. Triangulation is a sophisticated form of diplomacy that natural allies like the US and Japan could practice more extensively, to mutual benefit.

In thinking about policies toward Eurasia as a whole, we must recall Brzezinski's observation, cited in Chapter 3. Eurasia united has formidable capacity to become a Super Continent. Yet precisely because it is so vast, it has a tendency toward division and fragmentation. The United States cannot avoid capitalizing on these fissiparous tendencies, but must recognize recent political-economic trends toward reintegration that are far stronger than Brzezinski supposed. It also must shun provocative and dangerous efforts to stimulate ethnic and other internal tensions.

Toward a Pluralist Super Continent

Before engaging in country-specific policy analysis, we should make a crucial policy-relevant geo-political observation. China's geographical centrality on the Eurasian continent almost by definition makes it a formidable land power, given its population, provided it is growing economically, politically stable, and connected logistically to its neighbors. The PRC's geopolitical endowments as a sea power, however, are much less clear. China does, however, have clear ambitions on the seas. Control over ports along the "string of pearls" across the Indian Ocean can foster its maritime interests, as can supporting powerful state-run shipping firms like COSCO. China has greater vulnerabilities on the seas than on land, however, which correspond to converse American political-military strengths.

If Eurasia as a whole is trending toward integration—evolving into a Super Continent, as suggested in these pages—this tendency implies a twofold US strategy in response: (1) engaging on the continent, where cost effective; and (2) exploiting comparative advantage around the maritime periphery. Both of these approaches naturally involve engaging Asian allies in the effort, as discussed above, especially as they are central to preserving Eurasian pluralism. Both of these approaches also require detailed area-studies expertise on Eurasia, supported by national policy, of a magnitude unknown since the days of the Sino-Soviet split in the late 1950s. Broad transnational trends across the continent, together with critical, understudied languages, need to be the educational and analytical focus.

On the continent itself, the policy emphasis needs to be on smaller yet pivotal countries with strong ethnic identities, some degree of internal pluralism, and powerful desires to preserve national independence. Mongolia, Uzbekistan, and Kazakhstan, as well as cosmopolitan Scandinavian nations such as Norway, Denmark, Sweden, and Finland appear to show special promise. A pluralistic continental Eurasia serves American interests, as it do the interests of these smaller nations as well.

Although American efforts to promote pluralism in post-post Cold War Eurasia should focus on dynamic, smaller states, they cannot totally neglect Russia. Precisely because it is a temporarily declining power, especially in world economic affairs, with a GDP now roughly on a par with South Korea, its injured pride and very real residual capabilities to both cooperate and obstruct should be treated with sensitivity. Cooperation on counterterrorism and nonproliferation are potential options. So is a compromise settlement in the Ukraine, or a frozen peace, that recognizes Russian strategic stakes in the Ukraine's neutrality, while also preserving Western leverage against future Russian pressures in the near abroad, and in the Middle East.

The Super Continent has growing cohesion, but it also remains heavily interdependent with the world. The bulk of its commerce still moves over the sea lanes, an area of American preeminence, as noted above. The US therefore has an interest in strengthening its own maritime capabilities and those of allies such as Japan, Korea, Singapore, and of course India, which all share a strategic interest in sea-lane security.

The US must not neglect the dual commercial and military dimensions of maritime security, especially given the inclination of China to enhance its comprehensive maritime capacities under the BRI. China has, after all, built COSCO through mergers and state support into one of the largest and most competitive shipping firms in the world, on both sea and land, with port ownership in such strategic locations as Piraeus, Gwadar, and Khorgos. And it has steadily expanded the capabilities of its navy, the PLA-N, as well, especially in the South China Sea. The US clearly needs to strengthen both the US Navy and the US commercial shipping fleet, even as it seeks expanded opportunities for security cooperation in areas like antipiracy and disaster relief—not only with India, Japan, and Australia, but with China as well. As the PRC becomes an ever larger energy importer over the sea lanes—a rising prospect for the coming two decades at least—the US should seek opportunities for maritime security cooperation with Beijing outside conflict zones like the South China Sea, that reduce China's sense of threat and incentives to accelerate its naval buildup still further. The US and China share deep common interests in global stability that must never be forgotten.

While not ignoring options for maritime security cooperation with Beijing, the US must reinforce its own strategic assets, especially in the Indian Ocean, which will become ever more important to US strategy as China's BRI itself gains greater momentum. The Trump administration's decision in March 2018 to rename the US Pacific Command as the Indo-Pacific Command was a positive symbolic step, although it involved no change in actual operating responsibilities. Diego Garcia, in the middle of the Indian Ocean and 2,000 miles south of the Persian Gulf, is especially important in that regard. Providing Diego with state-of-the-art defenses and facilities is one of the most cost-effective defense expenditures that the US could possibly make. Cooperation with Australia, Japan, and Singapore in defense intelligence is another high priority.

Our empirical analysis concludes, as suggested above, that the key nations of continental Eurasia—China, Russia, and the major Central Asian/Persian Gulf states—will remain stably soft authoritarian yet rising in global influence, particularly in relation to continental Europe. What does this mean for the United States? What does it mean for America's democratic allies, in both Europe and Asia? And what does it mean for the future of democracy and human rights as subjects of central policy importance in global affairs?

Given China's scale and centrality, its course will critically shape whether, and if so in what form, a Eurasian Super Continent ultimately emerges. China policy therefore inevitably lies at the heart of an American—and indeed a global—response. Such a policy needs to recognize China's rising global role in an affirmative way while also insisting on transparency about its initiatives (especially in the cyber realm), and supporting pluralism on the continent. US support for Japanese membership in AIIB, as well as selective US, Japanese, and South Korean involvement in some BRI projects, could be affirmative steps the US could take to dampen the confrontationist case toward China of US Indo-Pacific policies more generally.

The one large, stable democracy on the Eurasian land mass, outside Europe, is India. It is insulated from China's connectivity initiatives both by geo-political preference and also by the massive geo-economic barrier that the Himalayas create. And India is—critically—a maritime power, protruding deep into the Indian Ocean that bears its name. India shares a powerful strategic interest in sea lanes between the Strait of Malacca and the Persian Gulf with several neighboring maritime nations—Japan, Korea, the nations of the Association of Southeast Asian Nations (ASEAN), and Australia, virtually all of whom, like India, obtain the bulk of their energy from the Persian Gulf.

India's huge population of over 1.3 billion is currently growing much faster than that of China. Strong political leadership, a powerful military, and a deepening market orientation all strengthen India's prospective ability to project successfully on the international stage. India is clearly the only nation on the Eurasian continent capable of balancing the PRC in the long run, and such balance is clearly in America's strategic interest. India needs to be a priority topic in America's policy response to Eurasian continentalism, apart from the expansion of US Indo-Pacific capabilities noted above.

Enlisting India on behalf of American geopolitical interests will not be easy, as that South Asian giant has a long tradition of nonalignment and deep-seated suspicion of alliance relationships. Some of its interests also diverge from priorities that the US has conventionally considered key objectives of its own. India's tenuous natural overland route to Europe, for example, runs most easily through Iran and the former Soviet Union—that so-called International North-South Transport Corridor is estimated to be 40 percent shorter and 30 percent cheaper than from India to northern European ports by sea.[21] Promoting India as an alternative interlocutor to China thus involves considering deeper interaction with Iran and Russia as well.

Cultivating India needs to start with fostering multilateral, including trilateral, relationships such as the US-India-Japan triangle. Such multilateral arrangements could be a way of finessing delicate geo-economic issues such as transit and border-clearance procedures involving Iran. Case-by-case cooperative ventures building broader cooperation with India, such as the Malabar naval exercises, starting on a bilateral US-India basis and broadening to a multilateral format, should be another priority.[22] India's 2015 acceptance of Japan as a permanent member of the Malabar team was a positive sign.

The US also needs to stay engaged multilaterally with India and its smaller neighbors like Bangladesh, Myanmar, Sri Lanka, Nepal, and the Maldives, which are significant targets of China's BRI. It needs to pay more strategic attention to the Bay of Bengal. Like the South China Sea, that body of water is a key transit area for the commerce of America's Northeast Asian allies, which source more than three quarters of their oil consumption from the Persian Gulf, as noted previously. The US should fully utilize its observer status in the South Asian Regional Cooperation Council to help promote its interests in South Asia and the Indian Ocean, and consider closer ties with the Bay of Bengal Initiative for Multi-Sectoral Technical and Economic Cooperation, based in Bangladesh, at the head of the Bay of Bengal.

The US approach to India also naturally needs to have an active bilateral dimension. That approach could usefully include: (1) exchange of defense officials and bureaucrats, including expanded strategic dialogue between national defense universities; (2) joint US-India parliamentary committee studies to examine concerns common to the two democracies; (3) new defense manufacturing as well as research and development projects, including US-India coproduction and codevelopment,[23] in addition to intellectual, homeland security, and counterterrorism cooperation; and (4) expansion of defense contracts between private Indian and American firms, including potentially foreign subsidiaries of US defense firms in Europe and Japan.[24] The two countries could also pursue new initiatives to keep the Indian Ocean safe and secure, while likewise addressing cybersecurity threats in both bilateral and multilateral contexts.[25]

Functional Imperatives

Energy, as we have seen, is a key driver of Eurasian continentalism and a major geo-economic concern of India as well. The greatest long-term prospective energy consumers of Asia—China and India—are located immediately adjacent to the largest prospective suppliers—the Persian Gulf and Russia. This geographical propinquity could create a natural complementarity of interest between the large consumers and producers, despite its converse potential for deepening regional resource rivalries. Most of the pipeline infrastructure to consummate an intimate energy relationship is not yet in place. Building it would require massive capital investment and more stable transnational political-economic relations than have heretofore prevailed.

An autarkic, self-contained Eurasian energy economy is not in America's interest, as it would almost inevitably involve deep Asian reliance on Russia. Increasing political-economic interdependence across the continent of the sort predicted here, however, could nevertheless render such a self-contained Eurasian energy economy increasingly likely. To forestall or dilute such a development, it is important that the United States, together with allies possessing advanced energy-related technology, including Japan and South Korea, should intensify their energy cooperation with both India and China, especially in the energy efficiency and environmental protection sectors, despite the geopolitical differences with China outlined above. Since coal is so important in the energy economies of both China and India, its environmental perversities notwithstanding, coal remains the most cost-effective energy choice for many poor countries. The United States should modify its opposition to coal-fired power plants in such countries, and support the provision of clean coal technology, such as Integrated Gasification Combined Cycle (IGCC) technology developed in Japan.[26] China has already begun a pilot project in Tianjin to develop low-emission coal-fired power plants using this technology, and ultimately adding on carbon-capture capabilities.[27] Doing so would assure that emissions can be reduced to the fullest extent that is actually practicable.

The United States should also make certain that its nuclear policies toward continental Eurasia address not only nuclear proliferation issues, such as those considered in the recent negotiations with Iran, but also nuclear safety questions. Those inevitably will be important in India, China, and Southeast Asia, with their huge populations and sometimes inadequate transparency standards. Otherwise, the prospects for even more serious variants of the Fukushima tragedy are looming.

Finance, as we saw in Chapter 4, is a second critical driver of deepening Eurasian continentalism and of the related transformation in international affairs now leading us toward a global Crossover Point. New, Chinese-sponsored institutions like the AIIB, the Silk Road Fund, and the New Development Bank could potentially assume geopolitical importance—not only by further integrating the Eurasian political-economy through infrastructural spending. They could also enhance China's own soft power, as an altruistic benefactor to nations of the Middle East, the Soviet Union, and Europe as well. Distributive regionalism and globalism based on infrastructure spending can be highly seductive politically, due to the way that such spending diffuses actual costs, as we have noted. China has recently tempted nations like Sri Lanka into irresponsible borrowing, as in the case of Hambantota port construction. Encouraging American allies such as Japan to consider joining the AIIB, should they be offered voting rights commensurate with their economic scale, should be considered, as noted above, as a means of pressing the Chinese to adopt more transparent and even-handed governance. Another option could be offering recipient developing countries alternative financing to that provided under the BRI, as the Japan recently did at Matarbari, Bangladesh.

Needed trans-Eurasian infrastructure will not automatically emerge, even if financing is available. And even if the infrastructure does emerge, using it will not automatically be commercially viable. Clear, transparent border-clearance procedures are crucial. And credible adjudication procedures for disputes, in which global firms can expect to participate on a nondiscriminatory basis in accordance with the rule of international law, would be highly desirable.

Clearly, the new institutions China is building represent a significant challenge for American policy—not least because their activities potentially further the economic priorities of multiple nations, including several American allies, while also serving Chinese geopolitical interests. The appropriate response, however, is not to quietly deprecate these Chinese initiatives, as the Obama administration initially did, without providing a viable alternative. It needs a much more substantive dimension.

A Response to BRI

The US desperately needs, in particular, a response to the panoply of China-dominated development finance institutions established since 2014, including the Silk Road Fund. Such a response must capitalize on fundamental insights of other development-finance institutions, while avoiding weaknesses of the statist Chinese approach, such as moral hazard and inadequate risk-assessment mechanisms. "Distributive globalism," for all its defects, is a powerful if seductive tool for appealing to recipient nations, especially those with pressing infrastructural needs, that needs to be countered in kind.

In February 2018 there was a start.[28] Eight US Senators, together with colleagues in the House of Representatives, introduced legislation on a bipartisan basis to establish a United States International Development Finance Corporation (USIDFC). This body, relying primarily on investment guarantees rather than direct government funding, would be more market oriented and risk sensitive than its Chinese counterparts, but would more than double the US government's development-finance capability to over $60 billion under the so-called BUILD Act of 2018.[29] In October, 2018 this proposal was signed into law by President Donald Trump. It is an important start in the concrete American response to China's BRI.

Other elements of an American institutional response to BRI should leverage this much-needed development-finance expansion. Some options are necessarily or preferably taken unilaterally, including (a) exploration of new public-private partnership (PPP) options beyond the BUILD Act, for a composite, market-oriented response, that is sensitive to the important changes in distribution and logistics, now occurring worldwide; (b) dispatch of more technical specialists, conversant with the issues above, to US embassies abroad; (c) public diplomacy stressing the importance of transparency in development lending; and (d) a more active role for US embassies in mobilizing a coordinated, on-the-ground response of like-minded nations to BRI.

Other options, however, are easily and even preferably undertaken with allies, or in a G-7 context, with subsequent expansion to G-20. These could include: (a) Codification of international standards for high-quality infrastructure; (b) a coherent response to the digital dimensions of BRI, including intermodal logistics, 5G communications; and B2B e-commerce; (c) assistance to developing countries in developing analytical capabilities to objectively evaluate BRI projects; and (d) systematic research on emerging transnational supply chains, particularly across Eurasia, and their geo-economic implications. American response to the emerging Eurasian Super Continent needs to involve fundamental changes in US research capability and policy-making institutions back home.

The United States should also combine with affluent allies such as Japan to respond to the Chinese initiatives by offering selective cooperation projects of mutual interest, through established, credible institutions like the Asian Development Bank. The US and allies could also pursue independent infrastructural initiatives through their national development assistance programs, comprising a veritable Southern Silk Road, from east to west across Southeast and South Asia. Such efforts could serve joint allied geopolitical interests even more directly than multilateral programs, as China is already doing.

As we have seen throughout this book, a historic transformation is unfolding in Eurasia today—comparable only to the epic construction projects and impulses toward unity that made America a global power a century and more ago. As in the days of Abraham Lincoln and Theodore Roosevelt, a Super Continent is emerging, with global scope and ambition. This development requires a thoughtful response, not just from America, but from all the world.

In Conclusion

The geographic location of both China and Eurasia in the world is fateful but hardly determining, despite the contentions of classical continentalist geo-politicians such as Halford Mackinder. Political-economic structure, not to mention technological configurations, play a critical supplementary roles. For the bulk of the twentieth century, the nations of Eurasia were economically stagnant and politically disconnected—autarky was the order of the day, and domestic politics were often chaotic, as in Republican China (1912–1949).[30] That era of stagnation and chaos has largely ended, due to historic transformations in key countries at both the national level, and at the regional level as well. A new, dynamic, and interactive Eurasian continentalism has emerged, particularly since the global financial crisis of 2008, followed by the advent of the third Putin administration in Russia (2012) and the birth of the Xi Jinping government in China soon thereafter (2013).

Critical junctures of the recent past—the Ukraine crisis of 2013–2014 and the protracted European sovereign-debt financial crisis that erupted in late 2009 and came to a head in Greece during the summer of 2015—are enabling Eurasian continentalist trends, accelerated further by technological advance and a connectivity revolution, and deepening China's relationship with the European Union. Synergistic with Europe's new political-economic vulnerability in the age of Euro-crisis, China's new institutional innovations in development finance—the AIIB in particular—and the emergence of new transit routes across the continent from China to the EU are supporting emerging continentalist patterns, while giving them broader global geo-political importance. China's massive foreign-exchange reserves give further leverage. The distributive character of these resources enhances the political attractiveness of Chinese overtures. As the Trump administration shrinks from the nurturing of global public goods, China has confidently asserted a strategy of "distributive globalism," based on its BRI, that leverages its own geo-economic centrality in Eurasia to serve its own national geostrategic interests while also promoting connectivity and sustainable development. Significantly, this strategy does not directly challenge the Bretton Woods system, even as it weakens the West-centric "regulatory" foundations beneath it.

The US-China relationship is by no means necessarily a zero-sum game. China's distributive globalism, by promoting connectivity, is likely to promote more rapid international economic growth. It also, however, is provoking subtle yet undeniable continental and global geo-economic shifts that it is in the interest of the US and its democratic allies to counteract. To offset China's rising leverage on land, it is important for the US and its allies to strengthen both civilian and military maritime capabilities and coordination. The linchpins of a US balancing strategy are inevitably Japan, India, and Australia, with a geographic focus on the Indian Ocean.

The new developments in Eurasian continentalism are not simply a matter of balance of power diplomacy, however, that might be easily reversed by more attention and favors from Washington. They flow from deep political, economic, and technological transformations—critical junctures and Crossover Points—at the national and regional levels. Those developments also have novel institutional dimensions—ranging from the emergence of the AIIB to the real construction of Eurasian pipelines and actual Sino-Russian defense cooperation. These institutional changes give the new Eurasian continentalism, spearheaded by China, a long-term significance without parallel since the dispatch of Soviet advisors to the PRC in the 1950s, and necessitate a substantial US response in kind, ranging from alliance reinforcements to the BUILD Act. The new institutions on all sides, fledgling though they may be, are a quantum leap forward toward the dawning of a new, more multipolar and arguably transformational era in world affairs that could significantly reconfigure the role of the United States, China, and other major powers in global governance. The era of the Eurasian Super Continent has begun.

Notes

PREFACE

1. Linda Hall Library, "The Pacific Railway," *The Transcontinental Railroad*, https://railroad.lindahall.org/essays/brief-history.html

2. Paul Leicester Ford (ed.), *The Writings of Thomas Jefferson* (New York, 1892–99), IX, 351, quoted in Dan E. Clark, "Manifest Destiny and the Pacific," *Pacific Historical Review* 1, no. 1 (March 1932): 3, http://www.jstor.org/stable/3633743.

3. Benton asserted that "Upon the people of East Asia . . . the establishment of a civilized power on the opposite coast of America, could not fail to produce great and wonderful benefits. Science, liberal principles in government, and the true religion, might cast their lights across the intervening sea." See ibid., 4. Benton was elected as one of Missouri's first senators in 1821, and continued advocating westward expansion throughout his thirty-year service in the Senate.

4. Jon Debo Galloway, *The First Transcontinental Railroad: Central Pacific, Union Pacific* (New York: Simmons-Boardman, 1950), 32–33.

5. Ibid., 38.

6. Felix Rohatyn, *Bold Endeavors* (New York: Simon & Schuster, 2009), 51–54.

7. Ibid.

8. Heather Cox Richardson, *The Greatest Nation of the Earth: Republican Economic Policies during the Civil War* (Cambridge, MA: Harvard University Press, 1997), 170–208.

9. William Gilpin, *Mission of North American People: Geographical, Social, and Political* (Philadelphia: J. B. Lippincott & Co., 1873), 8.

10. Richardson, *The Greatest Nation*, 178–79, 194–95.

11. Philip F. Anschutz, William J. Convery, and Thomas J. Noel, *Out Where the West Begins: Profiles, Visions & Strategies of Early Western Business Leaders* (Denver: Cloud Camp Press, 2015), 141–52.

12. Ibid., 153–59.

13. Rohatyn, *Bold Endeavors*, 112–18.

14. Alfred Thayer Mahan, *The Influence of Sea Power upon History, 1660–1783* (Boston: Little, Brown, and Co., 1890).

15. Dension Kitchel, *The Truth About the Panama Canal* (New Rochelle, NY: Arlington House, 1978), 155–57.

16. The Treaty of Paris was signed in 1898 but became effective in 1899.

17. Rohatyn, *Bold Endeavors*, 118–20. The USS Oregon was called to fight on March 19, over a month before war began on April 21, 1898.

18. Ibid., 124–26.

19. Ibid., 128–30.

20. Alfred Thayer Mahan, "The Panama Canal and the Distribution of the Fleet," *North American Review* 200, no. 706 (September 1914): 416, http://www.jstor.org/stable/25108252.

21. Ibid.

22. Roger D. Lapham, "World-Wide Changes in Trade Due to Panama Canal," *Current History* (July 1929): 652. Figures are for fiscal years, although the canal opened in calendar 1914.

CHAPTER 1

1. A Near Eastern religion (Christianity) became central to European culture, for example; Genghis Khan's mother was also a Nestorian. The Zoroastrians of Persia influenced both the Hebrews of Israel and the Parsis of India. Middle Eastern spices enriched cuisine both in Europe and in China.

2. "Eurasia" here includes all of Europe and Asia. See Figure 1.1.

3. See Angus Maddison, *The World Economy: Historical Statistics* (Paris: OECD, 2003), Table 8b. Share of World GDP, 20 Countries and Regional Totals, 1–2001 AD. https://doi.org/10.1787/9789264104143-en.

4. Ibid.

5. On the social transformation, see Karl Polanyi, *The Great Transformation: The Political and Economic Origins of Our Time* (New York: Farrar & Rinehart, 1944) and Barrington Moore, *Social Origins of Dictatorship and Democracy: Lord and Peasant in the Making of the Modern World* (Boston: Beacon, 1966).

6. In 1950, the US shared 27 percent of global output, compared to Asia's 18 percent. See Maddison, *World Economy*, Table 8b.

7. The US population was 152.3 million, while that of Asia was 1.38 billion. See Maddison, *World Economy*, Table 8a: World Population, 20 Countries and Regional Totals, 1–2001 AD.

8. See "Record Number of Freight Trains Link China, Europe," *Xinhua*, November 18, 2017, http://www.xinhuanet.com/english/2017-11/18/c_136762654.htm.

9. See Benjamin Kentish, "First Direct Train Service from China to the UK Arrives in London," *Independent*, January 18, 2017, https://www.independent.co.uk/news/uk/home-news/first-direct-train-china-to-uk-arrives-east-london-yiwu-city-barking-channel-tunnel-a7533726.html; "First Freight Train Linking UK with China Arrives in Yiwu," *DW*, April 29, 2017, http://www.dw.com/en/first-freight-train-linking-uk-with-china-arrives-in-yiwu/a-38635908.

10. According to IHS Markit, Huawei shared 28 percent of the global mobile infrastructure market in 2017, followed by Ericsson (27 percent), Nokia (23 percent), and ZTE (13 percent). See Natalie Bannerman, "Ericsson, Nokia Lost Infrastructure Market

Share While Huawei Continues to Grow," *Capacity Media*, March 15, 2018, http://www
.capacitymedia.com/Article/3794074/News/Ericsson-Nokia-lose-infrastructure-market
-share-while-Huawei-continues-to-grow.

11. See Huawei, "Huawei Obtains the World's First CE-TEC for 5G Products," April
16, 2018, http://www.huawei.com/en/press-events/news/2018/4/World-First-CE-TEC
-5G-Products.

12. See Karen Freifeld and Eric Auchard, "U.S. Probing Huawei for Possible Iran
Sanctions Violations: Sources," *Reuters*, April 25, 2018, https://www.reuters.com/article/
us-usa-huawei-doj/u-s-probing-huawei-for-possible-iran-sanctions-violations-sources
-idUSKBN1HW1YG.

13. See Niall Ferguson et al., *The Shock of the Global: The 1970s in Perspective* (Cambridge, MA: Harvard University Press, 2010).

14. The overland shipping distance between Shanghai and Rotterdam, for example,
is 10,867 km, while the maritime distance between the two ports is 18,711 km. Also see
Map 1.1.

15. The actual figure is around 41 percent. See Table 1.4. On the importance of Eurasia in various geo-economic dimensions, see Zbigniew Brzezinski, *The Grand Chessboard:
American Primacy and Its Geostrategic Imperatives* (New York: Basic Books, 1997), 31.

16. In 2016, China produced 26 percent of the world's manufacturers, the EU 19 percent, and the US less than 18 percent. See World Bank, "Manufacturing, value added
(current US$)," *World Development Indicators*, accessed October 7, 2018.

17. Population growth, however, is sharply decelerating in China, as well as in Southeast Asia, while modestly decelerating in West Asia, making much of Asia's advantage
ephemeral.

18. A critical juncture is defined here as a historical decision point at which there are
alternative paths to the future. Descriptively, crisis, stimulus for change, and intense time
pressure are necessary and sufficient. See Kent E. Calder, *The New Continentalism: Energy
and Twenty-First Century Eurasian Geopolitics* (New Haven: Yale University Press, 2012), 53.

19. "Crossover Points" are transition periods to new forms of social activity of broad
social relevance.

20. On the determinants of system transition and the notion of a crossover transition
point, see A.F.K. Organski, *World Politics* (New York: Knopf, 1959); Klaus Knorr, *Power
and Wealth: The Political Economy of International Power* (New York: Basic Books, 1973);
Robert Gilpin, *War and Change in International Relations* (Cambridge: Cambridge University Press, 1981); Paul Kennedy, *The Rise and Fall of the Great Powers: Economic Change
and Military Conflict from 1500 to 2000* (New York: Random House, 1987); and Charles F.
Doran, "Explaining Ascendancy and Decline: The Power Cycle Perspective," *International
Journal* 60, no. 3 (Summer 2005): 685–701.

21. "Distributive globalism" is a variety of globally oriented activity involving distribution of material benefits by multiple state and/or multilateral actors on an ad hoc basis,
without an explicit regulatory framework.

22. According to the World Bank, China's nominal GDP was $6.1 trillion in 2010,
higher than Japan's $5.7 trillion. World Bank, "GDP (current US$)," *World Development
Indicators*, accessed March 13, 2017.

23. World Bank, "GDP, PPP (constant 2011 international $)," *World Development Indi-
cators*, accessed March 13, 2017.

24. The literal geographic center of Eurasia, of course, lies further to the north and
west, in Central Asia or Russia depending on the method of calculation used. As much

of the land north and west of China is arid, subject to extreme climatic change, or both, however, China lies at the heart of populated Eurasia, surrounded by the similarly populated and dynamic nations of Southeast Asia, the Indian subcontinent, and the Korean peninsula.

25. Deng Xiaoping's famous foreign policy slogan says, "Coolly observe, calmly deal with things, hold your position, hide your capacities, bide your time, accomplish things where possible." See "Less Biding and Hiding," *The Economist*, December 2, 2010, https://www.economist.com/node/17601475.

26. Since 2015 this has been known formally as the Belt and Road Initiative. See National Development and Reform Commission, Ministry of Foreign Affairs, and Ministry of Commerce of the People's Republic of China, "Full Text: Action Plan on the Belt and Road Initiative," *State Council of the People's Republic of China*, March 30, 2015, http://english.gov.cn/archive/publications/2015/03/30/content_281475080249035.htm.

27. This set of redistributive preferences began under President Jiang Zemin, although it has been greatly expanded and integrated into broader regional strategies much more systematically under President Xi. See Nancy Huang, Joie Ma, and Kyle Sullivan, "Economic Development Policies for Central and Western China," *China Business Review,* November 10, 2010, www.chinabusinessreview.com/economic-development-policies-for -central-and-western-china/; and "Rich Province, Poor Province," *The Economist*, October 1, 2016, https://www.economist.com/news/china/21707964-government-struggling -spread-wealth-more-evenly-rich-province-poor-province.

28. See, for example, John Markoff and Matthew Rosenberg, "China's Intelligent Weaponry Gets Smarter," *New York Times,* February 3, 2017, https://www.nytimes.com/ 2017/02/03/technology/artificial-intelligence-china-united-states.html. Also Ankit Panda, "China's First Domestically Manufactured Carrier Launches. What's Next for the PLAN?" *The Diplomat*, April 27, 2017, https://thediplomat.com/2017/04/chinas-first-domestically -manufactured-carrier-launches-whats-next-for-the-plan/. China's second aircraft carrier—the first to be produced domestically—was launched in late April 2017 and will be completed by 2020. It is worth noting that the People's Liberation Army is formally the army of the Chinese Communist Party (CCP), rather than the armed forces of China per se. It is thus inseparably linked to the perpetuation of CCP rule.

29. International Institute for Strategic Studies, *The Military Balance*, 2017 edition (London: Routledge, 2017), 251–60.

30. See Shen Dingli, Elizabeth Economy, Richard Haass, Joshua Kurzlantzik, Sheila A. Smith, and Simon Tay, "China's Maritime Disputes," *Council on Foreign Relations*, www.cfr .org/asia-and-pacific/chinas-maritime-disputes/p31345#!/?cid=otr-marketing_use-china _sea_InfoGuide.

31. "China-Europe freight trains steam ahead," Global Times, November 29, 2018, http://www.globaltimes.cn/content/1129613.shtml.

32. World Bank, "Population, Total," *World Development Indicators* (2017), accessed October 18, 2018.

33. For details, see Kent E. Calder, *The New Continentalism: Energy and Twenty-First- Century Eurasian Geopolitics* (New Haven, CT: Yale University Press, 2012), 223–27.

34. For a pessimistic view of these geopolitically tinged conflicts, see Bill Emmott, *Rivals: How the Power Struggle Between China, India and Japan Will Shape our Next Decade* (Orlando, FL: Harcourt, 2008).

35. See "SCO Member Countries Reap Tangible Benefits from China's Belt and Road Initiative, Play Bigger Role," *Xinhua*, May 9, 2018, http://www.xinhuanet.com/english/2018-05/09/c_137167093.htm.

36. See Theodore J. Lowi, "Review: American Business, Public Policy, Case Studies, and Political Theory," *World Politics* 16, no. 4 (July 1964): 677–693+695+697+699+701+703+705+707+711+713+715, http://www.jstor.org/stable/2009452.

37. Kent E. Calder, *Crisis and Compensation: Public Policy and Political Stability in Japan, 1949–1986* (Princeton, NJ: Princeton University Press, 1988), 162.

38. The author thanks Yun Han for helping to elucidate this distinction.

39. Kent E. Calder, *The Bay of Bengal: Political-Economic Transition and Strategic Implications* (Tokyo: Sasakawa Peace Foundation, 2018).

CHAPTER 2

1. The literal geographic locus of Eurasia, of course, is in the former Soviet Union—further north and west. The northern half of Eurasia, however, has limited geo-economic significance, as it is frigid, underpopulated, and lacking in developmental potential.

2. On Ibn Sina, and his use of the "syndrome" paradigm, see Lenn E. Goodman, *Islamic Humanism* (New York: Oxford University Press, 2003), 155.

3. According to UNESCO's "Silk Road: Dialogue, Diversity, and Development" project, Zhang Qian was sent to the West by Emperor Wu in 139 BC to build alliances with smaller states against the Xiongnu, and his first mission took thirteen years. Emperor Wu dispatched him on another mission in 119 BC, finally establishing the early routes between China and Central Asia. See United Nations Educational, Scientific and Cultural Organization, "About the Silk Road," *Silk Roads: Dialogue, Diversity & Development*, accessed June 24, 2018, https://en.unesco.org/silkroad/about-silk-road.

4. For a broad popular discussion of the varied Silk Roads across history, see Peter Frankopan, *The Silk Roads: A New History of the World* (New York: Alfred A. Knopf, 2016).

5. The Huns (ancestors of modern-day Hungarians) moved out of Western Asia into Europe from the first to the seventh centuries AD, while the Turks followed on their heels from the sixth through the eleventh centuries. See Christopher I. Beckwith, *Empires of the Silk Road: A History of Central Eurasia from the Bronze Age to the Present* (Princeton, NJ: Princeton University Press, 2009), especially 93–112.

6. Many Hungarian babies, for example, continue to manifest the "blue spot" racially characteristic of Asian peoples.

7. Xinru Liu, *The Silk Road in World History* (Oxford: Oxford University Press, 2010), 1.

8. Ibid.

9. There is substantial scholarly debate as to the origins of the Xiongnu. Some posit that Mongolians descend from the Xiongnu, but others have theorized that the Xiongnu are of mixed Asian and European ancestry. See Ryan W. Schmidt and Noriko Seguchi, "Craniofacial Variation of the Xiongnu Iron Age Nomads of Mongolia Reveal Their Possible Origins and Population History," *Quaternary International* 405, Part B (2016): 110–121; and Hyun Jin Kim, *The Huns* (Abingdon, UK: Routledge, 2016). Kim argues that

the Xiongnu are actually the Huns of the fourth to fifth centuries AD who invaded the Roman Empire.

10. Sima Qian's *History* and the official *History of the Han*, for example, preserve large portions of it. See Liu, *The Silk Road in World History*, 7.

11. Khanbaliq was the Mongol name for the Yuan Dynasty Chinese capital Dadu, later to be known as Beijing.

12. By AD 565, after overrunning the Avars, the Turks created their own empire of Turkestan, including modern-day Turkmenistan, Uzbekistan, Kyrgyzstan, Kazakhstan, Tajikistan, and Xinjiang. The Turks challenged the Persian monopoly over east–west trade by allying themselves with Byzantium in AD 568 in opening their own direct trading route. This political-economic alliance only lasted ten years, but permanently opened the northern Silk Road route, heading northwest from Samarkand to Astrakhan on the way to the Black Sea, or across the Caspian to Baku and then through the Caucasus rather than south through Persia. On the details, see Paul Wilson, *The Silk Roads: A Route and Planning Guide* (Hindhead, UK: Trailblazer, 2003), 41.

13. Jonathan Tucker, *The Silk Road: Central Asia, Afghanistan, and Iran: A Travel Companion* (London: I. B. Tauris, 2015), 54.

14. Paper reputedly diffused out from China, for example, in the pockets of Chinese prisoners of war, captured by Arabs at the Battle of Talas River. The story of paper transmission appears to be one of those illustrative historical anecdotes that today's historians enjoy pointing out to establish the difficulty of substantiation. What is clear is that the Muslim control of Central Asia—cemented by the Battle of the Talas River in 751—allowed for the transmission of papermaking techniques from Central Asia to the Middle East, and from there onward to other Muslim areas. See Jonathan Bloom, *Paper Before Print: The History and Impact of Paper in the Islamic World* (New Haven, CT: Yale University Press, 2001), 41–45.

15. Mongolian President Elbegdorj Tsakhia in November 2014 announced the Prairie Road Program, later renamed the Development Road Strategy, with the objective of improving trade and transport infrastructure between Mongolia and surrounding countries. This program involves building nearly 1,000 kilometers of expressway linking Russia and China across Mongolia, as well as gas/oil pipelines, railways, and power grids, with a total projected investment of US $50 billion. See Alicia J. Campi, "Mongolia's Place in China's 'One Belt, One Road'" *China Brief* 15, no. 16, accessed online August 18, 2015, https://jamestown.org/program/mongolias-place-in-chinas-one-belt-one-road/ and Meng Gencang, "Initiative a Win-Win Deal for China and Mongolia," *China Daily*, July 17, 2017, http://www.chinadaily.com.cn/opinion/2017-07/17/content_30133964.htm.

16. Kazakhstani president Nursultan Nazarbayev announced a $9 billion "Nurly Zhol (Bright Path)" program aiming at driving state and foreign investment into the country's critical infrastructure and priority sectors—agribusiness, transport and logistics, manufacturing, and so on. See Embassy of the Republic of Kazakhstan in the USA, "Nurly Zhol," accessed October 18, 2018, https://www.kazakhembus.com/content/nurly-zhol-0.

17. In addition to high-profile support for China's BRI, Iran is actively engaged in a number of transport corridors, most notably the International North-South Transport Corridor (INSTC or NSTC), Kyrgyzstan-Tajikistan-Afghanistan-Iran Corridor (KTAI), and Chabahar-Herat Corridor. Iran, together with India and Russia, founded the INSTC in 2000. The corridor links Mumbai with St. Petersburg and beyond through the Persian Gulf and Caspian Sea and has now fourteen country members and observers. See Martand

Jha, "India's Eurasia Policy Gets a Boost with Long-Awaited Trade Corridor," *The Diplomat*, December 9, 2017, https://thediplomat.com/2017/12/indias-eurasia-policy-gets-a -boost-with-long-awaited-trade-corridor/.

18. On the building of the Trans-Siberian Railway, see Benson Bobrick, *East of the Sun: The Epic Conquest and Tragic History of Siberia* (New York: Poseidon, 1992), 350–81.

19. This sum amounted to over 38 million pounds sterling or ¥358.36 million. Japan's annual military spending in 1894 was around ¥125 million. On the details, see Liwen Jiang, "The First Sino-Japanese War Indemnity Revisited," *Social Sciences in China* 36, no. 4 (2015): 113–37.

20. Today, European Russia has roughly less than one-quarter of the country's area, but more than 75 percent of its population. That ratio was even greater before the Russian Revolution of 1917, as heavily populated Ukraine, Belarus, the Baltics, and parts of contemporary Poland were still part of the Russian Empire.

21. See David McHugh, "Putin Set to Visit Dresden, Scene of His Work as KGB Spy, to Tend Relations with Germany," *International Herald Tribune*, October 9, 2006.

22. Dmitry Trenin, "Vladimir Putin's Fourth Vector," *Russia in Global Affairs*, June 30, 2013, http://eng.globalaffairs.ru/number/Vladimir-Putins-Fourth-Vector—16048.

23. See, for example, Morena Skalamera, "Putin's Asia Strategy for 2015," *National Bureau of Asian Research Commentary*, December 16, 2014, http://www.nbr.org/research/ activity.aspx?id=505.

24. Ibid.

25. For more details on Putin's Siberian infrastructure development plans, see "Russia Offers a Bridge across History to Connect Tokyo to the Trans-Siberian Railway," *Siberian Times*, September 7, 2017, https://siberiantimes.com/business/investment/news/russia -offers-a-bridge-across-history-to-connect-tokyo-to-the-trans-siberian-railway/.

26. See Michael Khodarkovsky, "So Much Land, Too Few Russians," *New York Times*, September 16, 2016, https://www.nytimes.com/2016/09/17/opinion/so-much-land-too -few-russians.html.

27. See Samuel Charap, John Drennan, and Pierre Noel, "Russia and China: A New Model of Great-Power Relations," *Survival* 59, no.1 (2017): 30, http://dx.doi.org/10 .1080/00396338.2017.1282670.

28. The principles of Korean reunification included three elements: (1) autonomous resolution by the two Koreas themselves, (2) use of peaceful means, and (3) priority to unity as one people. See "The July 4 South-North Joint Communique," *United Nations Peacemaker*, July 4, 1972, http://peacemaker.un.org/sites/peacemaker.un.org/files/KR%20KP_720704 _The%20July%204%20South-North%20Joint%20Communiqu%C3%A9.pdf.

29. Kim Taehwan, "Beyond Geopolitics: South Korea's Eurasia Initiative as a New Nordpolitik," *Asan Forum*, February 16, 2015, http://www.theasanforum.org/beyond -geopolitics-south-koreas-eurasia-initiative-as-a-new-nordpolitik/.

30. "Agreement on Reconciliation, Non-Aggression, and Exchanges and Cooperation Between South and North Korea (Basic Agreement)," February 19, 1992, Council on Foreign Relations, https://peacemaker.un.org/korea-reconciliation-nonaggression91.

31. See David Holley, "South Korea, China Forge Official Ties," *Los Angeles Times*, August 24, 1992, http://articles.latimes.com/1992-08-24/news/mn-5421_1_south-korea.

32. "Koryo" refers to the classic Korean dynasty (AD 918–1392), including the 1270–1356 period as a vassal of the Mongol Yuan Dynasty. "Koryo" is synonymous with "Korean." "Saram" simply means "person" in Korean. "Koryo" is also often spelled

"goryeo," which is more accurate in phonetic terms. The term typically refers to the Koreans deported to Central Asia by Stalin in the 1930s, and their descendants.

33. See Taehwan, "Beyond Geopolitics."

34. See "Kim Calls for 'Cyber Silk Road' between Asia, Europe," *Asian Economic News*, December 17, 2001, https://www.thefreelibrary.com/Kim+calls+for+%27cyber+silk +road%27+between+Asia%2C+Europe.-a083312904.

35. See Richard Weitz, "New South Korean Leader Affirms Strategic Partnership with Kazakhstan," *Eurasia Daily Monitor*, Jamestown Foundation, March 15, 2013, https://jamestown .org/program/new-south-korean-leader-affirms-strategic-partnership-with-kazakhstan/.

36. Tae-jun Kang, "South Korea's Quest to Be a Major Space Power," *The Diplomat*, March 27, 2015, http://thediplomat.com/2015/03/south-koreas-quest-to-be-a-major -space-power/.

37. He-suk Choi, "Park Seeks 'Eurasia Initiative' to Build Energy, Logistics Links," *Korea Herald*, October 18, 2013, http://www.koreaherald.com/view.php?ud=20131018000620.

38. "South Korea Eyes Express Train Project Linking Eurasia," *Yonhap*, January 13, 2015, http://english.yonhapnews.co.kr/news/2015/01/13/0200000000AEN20150113003 100315.html.

39. Jonathan E. Hillman, "South Korea's Emerging Vision," *CSIS Reconnecting Asia*, December 15, 2017, https://reconnectingasia.csis.org/analysis/entries/south-korea -emerging-vision/.

40. AP, "Moon Faces Toughest Challenge Yet in Third Summit with Kim," *CNBC*, September 15, 2018, https://www.cnbc.com/2018/09/15/korea-moon-faces-toughest -challenge-yet-in-third-summit-with-kim.html.

41. Kanehara Nobukatsu, "The Power of Japan and Its 'Grand Strategy,'" in *Japan's World Power: Assessment, Outlook, and Vision*, ed. Guibourg Delamotte (New York: Routledge, 2017), 19.

42. See Kent E. Calder, *The New Continentalism: Energy and Twenty-First-Century Eurasian Geopolitics* (New Haven, CT: Yale University Press, 2012), 24–25.

43. Kawanishi Seikan 川西正鑑, *Tōa Chiseigaku no Kōsō* 東亜地政学の構想 [The Concept of Oriental Geopolitics] (Tokyo: Jitsugyo no Nihon Sha, 1942).

44. Asano Risaburō 浅野利三郎, *Nichi-doku-so Tairiku Burokku Ron: So no Chiseigaku-teki Kōsatsu* 日独ソ大陸ブロック論：その地政学的考察 [Theory on the Japanese-German-Soviet Continental Bloc: A Geopolitical Perspective] (Tokyo: Tōkaidō, 1941).

45. Mark R. Peattie, *Ishiwara Kanji and Japan's Confrontation with the West* (Princeton, NJ: Princeton University Press, 1975).

46. On the Battle of Nomonhan and its implications, see Alvin D. Coox, *Nomonhan: Japan Against Russia, 1939* (Stanford, CA: Stanford University Press, 1985).

47. Christopher Len, "Understanding Japan's Central Asian Engagement," in *Japan's Silk Road Diplomacy: Paving the Road Ahead*, ed. Christopher Len, Uyama Tomohiko, and Hirose Tetsuya (Washington, DC: Central Asia-Caucasus Institute, 2008), 35.

48. Ibid.

49. Kawato Akio, "What Is Japan Up To in Central Asia?" in *Japan's Silk Road Diplomacy*, 18. For full text of the speech, see Prime Minister and His Cabinet, "Address by Prime Minister Ryutaro Hashimoto to the Japan Association of Corporate Executives," July 24, 1997, https://japan.kantei.go.jp/0731douyukai.html.

50. Kawato, "What Is Japan Up To in Central Asia?" 23; and Ministry of Foreign Affairs of Japan, "Central Asia Plus Japan Dialogue," updated May 1, 2017, https://www .mofa.go.jp/region/europe/dialogue/index.html.

51. Kawato, "What Is Japan Up To in Central Asia?" 27.

52. Ministry of Foreign Affairs of Japan, "Prime Minister Abe Visits Mongolia and the Five Central Asian Countries (October 22–28, 2015)," updated November 2, 2015, https://www.mofa.go.jp/region/page3e_000397.html.

53. Kawato, "What Is Japan Up To in Central Asia?" 28. For Aso, this Arc of Freedom and Prosperity extended geographically from the Baltics around the central and southern portions of Eurasia to Southeast Asia. For details, see Ministry of Foreign Affairs of Japan, "Speech by Mr. Taro Aso, Minister of Foreign Affairs, on the Occasion of the Japan Institute of International Affairs Seminar 'Arc of Freedom and Prosperity: Japan's Expanding Diplomatic Horizons,'" November 30, 2006, https://www.mofa.go.jp/announce/fm/aso/speech0611.html.

54. Jagannath Panda, "The Asia-Africa Growth Corridor: An Indian-Japan Arch in the Making?" *Focus Asia: Perspective & Analysis*, no. 21, August, 2017, http://isdp.eu/content/uploads/2017/08/2017-focus-asia-jagannath-panda.pdf.

55. Cemil Aydin, "From a 'Civilized' to an 'Islamic' Empire: Ottoman Grand Strategy during the Long Nineteenth Century, 1815–1923," Presentation at the American Historical Association Annual Convention, January 10, 2010.

56. James M. Dorsey, "Eurasianism Wins in Turkey Even If Ideologue Loses Election," *Real News Network*, June 23, 2018, https://therealnews.com/eurasianism-wins-in-turkey -even-if-ideologue-loses-election.

57. The most influential of which is Ahmet Davutoğlu, *Stratejik Derinlik, Türkiey'nin Uluslararası Konumu* [Strategic Depth: Turkey's International Position] (Istanbul: Kure Yayınları, 2001).

58. See Joshua W. Walker, "Ambitions of Grandeur: Understanding Turkey's Foreign Policy in a Changing World," in *China, the United States, and the Future of Central Asia: U.S.-China Relations, Volume I*, edited by David B. H. Denoon (New York: New York University Press, 2015), 298–99.

59. Ahmet Davutoğlu, *Civilizational Transformation and the Muslim World* (Kuala Lumpur: Mahir, 1994).

60. "Turkey," *Gazprom Export*, accessed December 1, 2018, http://www.gazpromex port.ru/en/partners/turkey/.

61. See Masanori Tobita, "China money flows into Turkey as crisis creates opening," *Nikkei Asian Review*, August 22, 2018, https://asia.nikkei.com/Politics/International -Relations/China-money-flows-into-Turkey-as-crisis-creates-opening; and Julia Famularo, "Erdogan Visits Xinjiang," *The Diplomat*, April 14, 2012, https://thediplomat.com/ 2012/04/erdogan-visits-xinjiang/.

62. For details on the Middle Corridor Initiative and other Turkish Silk Road policies, see Republic of Turkey Ministry of Foreign Affairs, "Turkey's Multilateral Transportation Policy," accessed June 24, 2018, http://www.mfa.gov.tr/turkey_s-multilateral -transportation-policy.en.mfa.

63. Among the major construction projects undertaken under the Middle Corridor Initiative are the Marmaray underwater subterranean rail passage connecting Asia and Europe under the Bosporus, the Eurasia Tunnel Project, and the Edirne-Kars High-Speed Railway across Anatolia, a natural continuation of the BTK railroad project into Georgia and Azerbaijan. See ibid.

64. Presidency of the Republic of Turkey, "A New Era Will Be Heralded in Our Region Based on Stability and Prosperity," May 14, 2017, accessed June 24, 2018, https:// www.tccb.gov.tr/en/news/542/75199/a-new-era-will-be-heralded-in-our-region-based -on-stability-and-prosperity.

65. In September 2013 President Xi introduced the "Silk Road Economic Belt" concept, in a major speech delivered at Nazarbayev University in Kazakhstan. The next month, in October 2013, he offered guidance on constructing a "Twenty-First-Century Maritime Silk Road," at the Indonesian parliament in Jakarta, where he also proposed establishing the Asian Infrastructure Investment Bank. See "Chronology of China's Belt and Road Initiative," *Xinhua*, March 28, 2015, http://news.xinhuanet.com/english/2015-03/28/c_134105435.htm.

66. The Silk Road Economic Belt concept was unveiled at Nazarbayev University in Almaty by President Xi Jinping in September 2013. The Maritime Silk Road was proposed before the Indonesian parliament in October 2013. The Chinese terminology for the two has never changed, although the original English express ("One Belt One Road"), a literal translation of the Chinese, was changed to "Belt and Road Initiative" in English during 2015.

67. On these synergistic relationships between the Belt and the Road, see, for example, Kent E. Calder, *Singapore: Smart City, Smart State* (Washington, DC: Brookings Institution, 2016); and Jacopo Maria Pepe, *Continental Drift: Germany and China's Inroads in the "German-Central Eastern European Manufacturing Core": Geopolitical Chances and Risks* (Washington, DC: Edwin O. Reischauer Center for East Asian Studies, 2017).

68. See, for example, Yiwei Wang, *The Belt and Road Initiative: What Will China Offer the World in Its Rise?* (Beijing: New World, 2016). Also, Chinese Academy of Social Sciences National Institute for Global Strategy, "International Seminar on the One-Belt and One-Road Initiative in the Global Context: Conference Papers," October 10–11, 2016, Beijing.

69. Shannon Tiezzi, "Who Is Actually Attending China's Belt and Road Forum?" *The Diplomat*, May 12, 2017, https://thediplomat.com/2017/05/who-is-actually-attending-chinas-belt-and-road-forum/.

70. Wang, *The Belt and Road Initiative*, 37.

71. Ibid., 191.

CHAPTER 3

1. Zbigniew Brzezinski, *The Grand Chessboard: American Primacy and Its Geostrategic Imperatives* (New York: Basic Books, 1997), 31.

2. For the classic study of Deng Xiaoping and his key role in making Chinese political-economic history, see Ezra F. Vogel, *Deng Xiaoping and the Transformation of China* (Cambridge, MA: Belknap Harvard, 2011).

3. On the early genesis of the Four Modernizations, see Immanuel Chung-yueh Hsu, *China without Mao: The Search for a New Order*, 2nd ed. (New York: Oxford University Press, 1990); and Vogel, *Deng Xiaoping*, 184–248.

4. Hsu, *China Without Mao*, 92–93.

5. Ibid., 94.

6. Hua thus, in Vogel's view, deserves more credit for China's opening than conventionally given, especially for instituting the SEZ concept. See Vogel, *Deng Xiaoping*, 185 and 190.

7. On the differences in the Hua and Deng approaches to Chinese economic development, see Edwin Moise, *Modern China: A History*, 2nd ed. (New York: Longman, 1994),194.

8. Kent E. Calder, *The New Continentalism: Energy and Twenty-First-Century Eurasian Geopolitics* (New Haven, CT: Yale University Press, 2012), 66.

9. Ibid.

10. For China's response to this, see John Garver, *China's Quest: The History of the Foreign Relations of the People's Republic of China* (New York: Oxford University Press, 2016), 416–19.

11. Calder, *The New Continentalism*, 67.

12. Ibid.

13. Ibid.

14. Shenzhen and Zhuhai were picked in August 1980, followed by Xiamen in October 1980 and Guangdong in October 1981. Hainan did not become an SEZ until April 1988.

15. Vogel, *Deng Xiaoping*, 403.

16. See Vogel, *Deng Xiaoping*, Chapter 14; and Barry Naughton, "China's Emergence and Prospects as a Trading Nation," *Brookings Papers on Economic Activity* 2 (1966): 273–344.

17. On the Soviet decline, see David Remnick, *Lenin's Tomb: The Last Days of the Soviet Empire* (New York: Random House, 1993).

18. Fatalities included 11,321 Red Army, 548 KGB, and 28 Ministry of Internal Affairs combat deaths. See G. F. Krivosheev, *Soviet Casualties and Combat Losses in the Twentieth Century* (London: Greenhill, 1997), 287.

19. Calder, *The New Continentalism*, 76.

20. Neil Robinson, "The Global Economy, Reform and Crisis in Russia," *Review of International Political Economy* 6, no. 4 (Winter 1999): 531–64.

21. Jacopo M. Pepe, *Continental Drift—Germany and China's Inroads in the "German-Central European Manufacturing Core": Geopolitical Chances and Risks* (Washington, DC: Reischauer Center for East Asian Studies, 2017), 12–13.

22. World Bank, "GDP Growth (Annual %)," *World Development Indicators* (2017), accessed October 18, 2018. The only one of the ten fastest growing members of the EU that joined before 2004 was Ireland.

23. See Grażyna Szymańska-Matusiewicz, "The Vietnamese Communities in Central and Eastern Europe as Part of the Global Vietnamese Diaspora," *Central and Eastern European Migration Review* 4, no. 1 (June 2015): 5.

24. See Rudolf Fürst, "Czechia's Relations with China: On a Long Road Toward a Real Strategic Partnership?" in *China's Relations with Central and Eastern Europe: From "Old Comrades" to New Partners*, ed. Weiqing Song (New York: Routledge, 2018), 199–200.

25. See China National Petroleum Corporation (CNPC), "Shanghai Xiying Zhongya Tianranqi Ruwang [Shanghai Welcomes First Natural Gas Delivery from Central]," www .china5e.com, June 27, 2012, https://www.china5e.com/news/news-229779-1.html.

26. See CNPC, "Flow of Natural Gas from Central Asia," *CNPC*, accessed June 26, 2018, http://www.cnpc.com.cn/en/FlowofnaturalgasfromCentralAsia/Flowofnaturalgas fromCentralAsia2.shtml.

27. Hasan H. Karrar, *The New Silk Road Diplomacy: China's Central Asian Foreign Policy Since the Cold War* (Vancouver: University of British Columbia Press, 2009), 57.

28. In 2016, Azerbaijan's trade with Turkey totaled $2.31 billion, higher than its $2.05 billion trade with Russia. See International Monetary Fund, *Direction of Trade Statistics*, accessed October 18, 2018.

29. Karrar, *The New Silk Road Diplomacy*, 60.

30. Ibid.

31. Calder, *The New Continentalism*, 78.

32. On the expanding export-processing activities in Urumqi Special Economic and Export Zone, see "Urumqi Economic and Technological Development Zone," *China Daily*, http://xinjiang.chinadaily.com.cn/urumqi_toutunhe/.

33. Erdoğan served as Turkish prime minister from March 2003 until August 2014, and then as president from August 2014. On domestic political linkages that animate Erdoğan's foreign policy, see Lisel Hintz, *Identity Politics Inside Out: National Identity Contestation and Foreign Policy in Turkey* (New York: Oxford University Press, 2018).

34. See Steven Erlanger, "Turkey-Iran Gas Deal: A Test of U.S. Law on Terror?" *New York Times*, August 13, 1996, accessed October 8, 2018, https://www.nytimes.com/1996/08/13/world/turkey-iran-gas-deal-a-test-of-us-law-on-terror.html.

35. See "Another Victory for Diversification as Turkmenistan Opens New Gas Pipeline to Iran," *IHS Markit*, January 6, 2010.

36. On the genesis of the Tengiz and Kashagan projects, see Steve Levine, *The Oil and the Glory: The Pursuit of Empire and Fortune on the Caspian Sea* (New York: Random House, 2007), 82–101, 327–44.

37. For more detail on the Indian changes and their implications, see Kent E. Calder, *The New Continentalism: Energy and Twenty-First Century Eurasian Geopolitics* (New Haven, CT: Yale University Press, 2012), 70–73.

38. Kent E. Calder, *The Bay of Bengal: Political-Economic Transition and Strategic Implications* (Tokyo: Sasakawa Peace Foundation, 2018), 72.

39. IMF, *Direction of Trade Statistics*, accessed October 18, 2018.

40. See Nirmala Joshi, ed., *Reconnecting India and Central Asia: Emerging Security and Economic Dimensions* (Washington, DC: Central Asia-Caucasus Institute, Paul H. Nitze School of Advanced International Studies, 2010).

41. ONGC in 2010 held a 20 percent interest in the Sakhalin I project, unaffected by Russian reduction of foreign shares in Sakhalin II. See "India Said Looking to Sakhalin I for LNG; Would Compete with China for Supply, Report Says," *Platts Oilgram News*, December 14, 2006. For the 2008 acquisition, see "India's ONGC Buys into Russian Oil Sector with Takeover of British Energy Company," *Nikkei Weekly*, February 2, 2009; "Energy: Indian Suitor Wins 1.4bn Bid Battle for Imperial Oil," *Guardian*, August 27, 2008.

42. John Ryan, "The Iran Nuclear Deal and Asia," *National Bureau of Asian Research*, January 2016, http://nbr.org/downloads/pdfs/psa/sa15_essay_iran_jan2016.pdf; and Hrishabh Sandilya, "India, Iran, and the West," *The Diplomat*, November 9, 2014, http://thediplomat.com/2014/11/india-iran-and-the-west/.

43. See Thomas L. Friedman and Michael Mandelbaum, *That Used to Be Us: How America Fell Behind in the World It Invented and How We Can Come Back* (New York: Farrar, Straus and Giroux, 2011).

44. The Medicare Prescription Drug, Improvement, and Modernization Act (MMA) was signed into law in 2003. See Henry J. Aaron, "Prescription Drug Bill: The Good, the Bad, and the Ugly," *The Brookings Institution*, January 15, 2004, https://www.brookings.edu/articles/prescription-drug-bill-the-good-the-bad-and-the-ugly.

45. Rob Atkinson and Paul Durden, "Housing Policy in the Thatcher Years," in *Public Policy under Thatcher*, ed. Stephen P. Savage and Lynton Robins (London: Macmillan, 1990), 117–30.

46. See James Rickards, "Repeal of Glass-Steagall Caused the Financial Crisis," *US News*, August 27, 2012, http://www.usnews.com/opinion/blogs/economic-intelligence/2012/08/27/repeal-of-glass-steagall-caused-the-financial-crisis.

47. See Eileen J. Canavan and Jason Bucelato, *Federal Elections 2004: Election Results for the U.S. President, the U.S. Senate and the U.S. House of Representatives* (Washington, DC: Federal Election Commission, 2005), 29, http://www.fec.gov/pubrec/fe2004/federalelections2004.pdf.

48. Shares fell by $3.03. The sharp drop in the stock's value came in light of Lehman's near $4 billion loss revealed on the previous day. See David Ellis, "Lehman Suffers Nearly $4 Billion Loss," *CNN Money*, September 10, 2008, http://money.cnn.com/2008/09/10/news/companies/lehman.

49. The KDB deal fell apart because KDB and Lehman could not agree on specific terms and market conditions. The deal could have potentially exposed KDB to fallout from the US housing crisis. And KDB reportedly wanted to pay only one-third of Lehman's asking price. See Tina Wang, "For Lehman, a Deal with KDB Appears Dead," *Forbes*, September 10, 2008, http://www.forbes.com/2008/09/10/lehman-korean-bank-markets-equity-cx_tw_0910markets3.html.

50. On the chronology of the Lehman crisis, see "Timeline: Key Events in Financial Crisis," *USA Today*, September 8, 2013, http://www.usatoday.com/story/money/business/2013/09/08/chronology-2008-financial-crisis-lehman/2779515/; and "The Fall of Lehman Brothers," *Market Watch*, http://projects.marketwatch.com/fall-of-lehman-brothers-timeline/#0.

51. On March 9, 2009, the S&P 500 reached a low below $667, and on October 3, 2018 recorded a high over of $2,939. See Yahoo! Finance, "S&P 500 (^GSPC)," https://finance.yahoo.com/quote/%5EGSPC?p=%5EGSPC.

52. "China Seeks Stimulation," *The Economist*, November 10, 2008, https://www.economist.com/asia/2008/11/10/china-seeks-stimulation.

53. See "Full Text of Geithner's Speech at Peking University," *Wall Street Journal*, June 1. 2009, https://blogs.wsj.com/chinarealtime/2009/06/01/full-text-of-geithners-speech-at-peking-university/; "Paulson Praises China's Cooperation in Easing Financial Crisis," *New York Times*, October 22, 2008, https://www.nytimes.com/2008/10/22/business/worldbusiness/22iht-22paulson.17155092.html; and Roger C. Altman, "Globalization in Retreat: Future Geopolitical Consequences of the Financial Crisis," *Foreign Affairs* (July/August 2009), accessed October 19, 2018, https://www.foreignaffairs.com/articles/2009-07-01/globalization-retreat.

54. For more details on the Ukraine crisis, see "Ukraine Crisis: Timeline," *BBC*, November 13, 2014, http://www.bbc.com/news/world-middle-east-26248275.

55. "EU Signs Pacts with Ukraine, Georgia and Moldova," *BBC*, June 27, 2014, http://www.bbc.com/news/world-europe-28052645.

56. For more details, see "Ukraine Crisis: Russia and Sanctions," *BBC*, December 19, 2014, http://www.bbc.com/news/world-europe-26672800.

57. See U.S. Department of the Treasury, "Treasury Sanctions Russian Officials, Members of the Russian Leadership's Inner Circle, and an Entity for Involvement in the Situation in Ukraine," March 20, 2014, https://www.treasury.gov/press-center/press-releases/Pages/jl23331.aspx. The Council of the European Union also imposed restrictive measures on twenty-one persons. See "Council Regulation (EU) No 269/2014," *Official Journal of the European Union*, March 17, 2014, http://eur-lex.europa.eu/legal-content/EN/TXT/?uri=uriserv:OJ.L_.2014.078.01.0006.01.ENG

58. See U.S. Department of the Treasury, Office of Foreign Assets Control, "Specially Designated Nationals List Update," April 28, 2014, https://www.treasury.gov/resource -center/sanctions/OFAC-Enforcement/Pages/20140428.aspx.

59. See "Council Implementing Decision 2014/238/CFSP," *Official Journal of the European Union*, April 28, 2014, http://eur-lex.europa.eu/legal-content/EN/TXT/?uri= uriserv:OJ.L_.2014.126.01.0055.01.ENG.

60. Raziye Akkoc and Roland Oliphant, "MH17 Airliner Destroyed by Buk Missile Fired from Eastern Ukraine, Dutch Report Confirms," *The Telegraph*, October 13, 2015, http://www.telegraph.co.uk/news/worldnews/europe/ukraine/11928778/MH17-hit-by -Buk-missile-Ukraine-plane-crash-Russia-live.html.

61. Leigh T. Hansson, Michael J. Lowell, Sian Fellows, David Myers, Alexandra E. Allan, Alexandra Gordon, Hena M Schommer, Laith Najjar, Michael A. Grant, Paula A. Salamoun, and Tom C. Evans, "Overview of the US and EU Sanctions on Russia," *Reed-Smith*, Client Alert 14-255, October 2014, https://www.reedsmith.com/files/Publication/ 9221cf81-e4f7-4907-ab2c-f7dc249eac58/Presentation/PublicationAttachment/441e0ec9 -dbd8-4c3a-b1fa-0bf7ed4d5872/alert_14-255.pdf.

62. "Ukraine Crisis: Russia and Sanctions," *BBC*.

63. On the 2018 extension of sanctions, see "Executive Order on the President's Continuation of the National Emergency with Respect to Ukraine," The White House, March 2, 2018, https://www.whitehouse.gov/presidential-actions/executive-order-presidents -continuation-national-emergency-respect-ukraine/.

64. See Yasmine Salam, "EU Extends Sanctions over Russia's Annexation of Crimea," *POLITICO*, June 18, 2018, https://www.politico.eu/article/crimea-russia-eu-extends -sanctions-over-annexation/; and Council of the EU, "Misappropriation of Ukrainian State Funds: EU Prolongs Asset Freezes against 13 Persons by One Year," Press Office – General Secretariat of the Council, March 6, 2018.

65. Lucy Hornby and Jamil Anderlini, "China and Russia Sign $400bn Gas Deal," *Financial Times*, May 21, 2014, https://www.ft.com/content/d9a8b800-e09a-11e3-9534 -00144feabdc0.

66. Interfax-Ukraine, "China's Xi Jinping Greets Ukraine on Independence Day," *KyivPost*, August, 24, 2016, https://www.kyivpost.com/article/content/ukraine-politics/ chinas-xi-jinping-greets-ukraine-on-independence-day-421532.html.

67. Benjamin Zhang, "China and Ukraine Are Going to Build the Largest Plane in the World," *Business Insider*, September 1, 2016, http://www.businessinsider.com/china -ukraine-build-antonov-an-225-2016-9.

68. Shannon Tiezzi, "China's Xi Brings 'Belt and Road' to Serbia, Poland," *The Diplomat*, June 24, 2016, http://thediplomat.com/2016/06/chinas-xi-brings-belt-and-road -to-serbia-poland/; and Ivana Sekularac, "Chinese President Visits Serbia, Trade Deals to Be Signed," *Reuters*, June 17, 2016, http://www.reuters.com/article/serbia-china -idUSL8N19921L.

CHAPTER 4

1. Apart from being director of the London School of Economics from 1903 to 1908, Mackinder was also founder of Oxford University's School of Geography. The published version of his historic remarks appeared as Halford Mackinder, "The Geographical Pivot

of History," *Geographical Journal* 23, no. 4 (April 1904): 435, http://www.jstor.org/stable/1775498.

2. On German and Russian pre–World War II geopolitical thinking, see Edward Hallett Carr, *German-Soviet Relations between the Two World Wars* (Baltimore, MD: Johns Hopkins University Press, 1951); as well as Lionel Kochan, *Russia and the Weimar Republic* (Cambridge: Bowes and Bowes, 1954). On the Japanese literature see, for example, Kawanishi Seikan 川西正鑑, *Tōa Chiseigaku no Kōsō* 東亜地政学の構想 [The Concept of Oriental Geopolitics] (Tokyo: Jitsugyo no Nihon Sha, 1942); and Asano Risaburō 浅野利三郎, *Nichi-doku-so Tairiku Burokku Ron: So no Chiseigaku-teki Kōsatsu* 日独ソ大陸ブロック論：その地政学的考察 [Theory on the Japanese-German-Soviet Continental Bloc: A Geopolitical Perspective] (Tokyo: Tōkaidō, 1941).

3. See Justin Vaisse, *Zbigniew Brzezinski: America's Grand Strategist*, trans. Catherine Porter (Cambridge, MA: Harvard University Press, 2018), 380–85.

4. Halford Mackinder, *Democratic Ideals and Reality: A Study in the Politics of Reconstruction* (Washington, DC: National Defense University Press, 1996), 74.

5. Christianity, for example, arose in the Near East and spread across Europe, also profoundly influencing parts of Southeast and Northeast Asia. Hellenistic thought arose in southern Europe and profoundly influenced Europe, the Near East, and South Asia. Middle Eastern spices shaped cuisine in India, Europe, and China, while paper, invented in China, had revolutionary social implications in Europe.

6. Nick Miller, "China Undermining US 'with Sticks and Carrots': Outgoing German Minister," *Sydney Morning Herald*, February 19, 2018, https://www.smh.com.au/world/europe/china-undermining-us-with-sticks-and-carrots-outgoing-german-minister-20180219-p4z0s6.html. Sigmar Gabriel served as German foreign minister from January 2017 until March 2018. Before that, he was minister of economic affairs and energy (December 2013–January 2017), and leader of the SPD from November 2009 until March 2017.

7. See, for example, Jacopo Maria Pepe, *Beyond Energy: Trade and Transport in a Reconnecting Asia* (Wiesbaden: Springer VS, 2018).

8. This includes 6.3 percent in Russia and 1.8 percent in Kazakhstan. See BP, "Oil: Proved Reserves," *Statistical Review of World Energy*, June 2018.

9. This includes 18.1 percent in Russia and 10.1 percent in Turkmenistan. See Table 4.2.

10. On the geo-economic implications of this transformation, see Meghan L. O'Sullivan, *Windfall: How the New Energy Abundance Upends Global Politics and Strengthens America's Power* (New York: Simon and Schuster, 2017).

11. The US in 2017 exported more oil to Asia (14.7 million tons) than to Europe (10.8 million tons), as well as more LNG to Asia (7.1 bcm) than to Europe (2.6 bcm). See BP, *Statistical Review of World Energy*, June 2018. According to the US Energy Information Agency, American LNG exports quadrupled in 2017, albeit from a small base. More than half went to three countries: Mexico (20 percent); South Korea (18 percent); and China (15 percent). China's imports declined in late 2018 due to trade frictions. The EIA predicts that by 2020 the US will become the world's third largest LNG exporter. See Victoria Zaretskaya, "U.S. liquefied natural gas exports quadrupled in 2017," *U.S. Energy Information Agency*, March 27, 2018, https://www.eia.gov/todayinenergy/detail.php?id=35512.

12. Such fluctuations are common in Iraq. In 2015 62.2 percent of Iraqi exports went to Asia; in 2016 this ratio fell to 47.4 percent, and in 2017 it rose back to 53.8%.

13. In 1991, 64.5 percent of Japan's oil imports came from the Persian Gulf, and the share rose to 79.6 percent in 2017. Similarly, Korea's oil imports from the Persian Gulf increased from 70.3 percent in 1991 to 75.2 percent in 2017. China's oil imports from the Persian Gulf went up from 30.3 percent in 1992 to 42.7 percent in 2017. See UN Comtrade, "Petroleum Oils and Oils Obtained from Bituminous Minerals; Crude," accessed October 9, 2018.

14. In 1991, 80.4 percent of India's oil imports came from the Persian Gulf, and the share dropped to 61.0 percent in 2016. See ibid.

15. Ibid.

16. Ibid. Imports from the Gulf has been rising since 2014, likely as a result of Russian sanctions.

17. This includes 2.36 mmbbl/d to China, 2.06 mmbbl/d to India, 2.32 mmbbl/d to Japan, 0.64 mmbbl/d to Singapore, and 3.56 mmbbl/d to other Asia Pacific states. See BP, "Oil: Inter-area Movements," *Statistical Review of World Energy*, June 2018.

18. Oil flows from the four Gulf states of Iraq, Kuwait, Saudi Arabia, and the UAE to Asia (550.2 million tonnes) shared 25.2 percent of global oil flows (2184.2 million tonnes) in 2017. See ibid.

19. Author's calculation based on OPEC, "OPEC Members' Crude Oil Exports by Destination," *Annual Statistical Bulletin*, 1999, 2004, 2008–2010, and 2016–2018.

20. International Energy Agency, "Executive Summary," *World Energy Outlook*, 2015 edition.

21. Ibid.

22. This includes 29.0 percent by Japan, 13.4 percent by China, and 13.0 percent by South Korea. See BP, "Gas: Trade Movements LNG," *Statistical Review of World Energy*, June 2018.

23. Ibid.

24. Daniel Yergin, *The Prize: The Epic Quest for Oil, Money & Power* (New York: Free Press, 2003), 779.

25. Ibid., 133.

26. Ibid., 515.

27. On Russia's natural gas endowments, see Per Hogselius, *Red Gas: Russia and the Origins of European Energy Dependence* (New York: Palgrave Macmillan, 2013).

28. The US R/P ratio for proved natural gas is 11.9 years and Canada's is 10.7 years, although both countries have substantial shale gas reserves.

29. Nord Stream II is at an advanced stage of preparation, although it has yet to gain approval from Sweden and Denmark. Although the pipelines do not pass through Poland's territorial waters, as a Baltic country Poland does have a say regarding the environmental impact of the pipeline's construction and has strongly opposed Nord Stream II. Gazprom still indicates that Nord Stream II will become operational by late 2019.

30. See BP, "Gas—Trade Movement Pipeline," *Statistical Review of World Energy*, June 2018.

31. Ibid. In 2017 virtually all of Russia's LNG exports went to Asia—9.9 bcm to Japan, 2.6 to South Korea, 2.3 to Taiwan, and 0.6 to the PRC.

32. Ibid.

33. "Power of Siberia," *Gazprom Export*, updated June 8, 2018, http://www.gazpromexport.ru/en/projects/3/.

34. At end 2017, Turkmenistan has 19.5 trillion cubic meters of proved natural gas reserves, Azerbaijan has 1.3 tcm, and Kazakhstan has 1.1 tcm. See BP, "Gas: Proved Reserves," *Statistical Review of World Energy*, June 2018.

35. At end 2017, Kazakhstan has 3,900 million tonnes of proved oil reserves, and Azerbaijan has 1,000 million tonnes. See BP, "Oil: Proved Reserves," *Statistical Review of World Energy*, June 2018.

36. See BP, "Coal: Proved Reserves," *Statistical Review of World Energy*, June 2018.

37. To be precise, the Chayandinskoye-Amur section of the Power of Siberia pipeline, which delivers natural gas from Irkutsk and Yakutia to Daqing, will be completed during 2018, and start pumping gas by the end of 2019.

38. See "Alexey Miller: Russia and China Signed the Biggest Contract in the Entire History of Gazprom," *Gazprom*, March 21, 2014, http://www.gazprom.com/press/news/2014/may/article191451.

39. Bryan Harris, Song Jung-a, and Peter Wells, "Plan for North-East Asian Electricity 'Super Grid' Boosted," *Financial Times*, November 2, 2017, https://www.ft.com/content/4b04ed8e-bf8b-11e7-b8a3-38a6e068f464.

40. Marc Levinson, *The Box: How the Shipping Container Made the World Smaller and the World Economy Bigger* (Princeton, NJ: Princeton University Press, 2008), chapters 6–8.

41. United States Postal Service Office of Inspector General, *The Global Logistics Revolution: A Pivotal Moment for the Postal Service*, June 3, 2013, Table 2, https://www.uspsoig.gov/document/global-logistics-revolution-pivotal-moment-postal-service.

42. See "The Global Logistics Business Is Going to Be Transformed by Digitisation," *The Economist*, April 26, 2018, https://www.economist.com/briefing/2018/04/26/the-global-logistics-business-is-going-to-be-transformed-by-digitisation. Alibaba predicts that cross-border e-commerce shipments worldwide could rise from $400 billion in 2016 to nearly $11 trillion by 2020.

43. World Bank, "Industry, Value-Added (Constant 2010 US$)," *World Development Indicators* (2016).

44. See Jost Wubbeke, Mirjam Meissner, Max J. Zenglein, Jaqueline Ives, and Bjorn Conrad, "Made in China 2015: The Making of a High-Tech Superpower and Consequences for Industrial Countries," Mercator Institute for China Studies, *MERICS Papers on China*, no. 2, December 2016.

45. Jakub Jakóbowski, Konrad Popławski, and Marcin Kaczmarski, *The Silk Railroad: The EU-China Rail Connections: Background, Actors, Interests* (Warsaw: Centre for Eastern Studies, 2018), 62.

46. See "China's High-Speed Trains Are Back on Track," *The Economist*, September 1, 2017, https://www.economist.com/graphic-detail/2017/09/01/chinas-high-speed-trains-are-back-on-track.

47. Lu Hui, "China's High-Speed Rail Tracks to Hit 38,000 km by 2025," *Xinhua*, January 2, 3018, http://www.xinhuanet.com/english/2018-01/02/c_136867206.htm.

48. Ibid.

49. This was about 56 percent of the total 3.04 billion passenger trips made on railways. See ibid. According to 2015 statistics, 50 percent of global HSR passengers were in China, and 22 percent in Japan. See US High Speed Rail Association, "High Speed Rail Around the World," accessed October 23, 2018, http://www.ushsr.com/hsr/hsrworldwide.html.

50. Ibid.

51. Rail freight, however, was growing at a faster pace (10.7 percent annually) than highway traffic (10.1 percent). See "China's Freight Growth Steady in 2017, *China Daily*, February 1, 2018, http://www.chinadaily.com.cn/a/201802/01/WS5a72a540a3106e7dcc13a316.html.

52. For details, see Kent E. Calder, *Singapore: Smart City, Smart State* (Washington, DC: Brookings Institution Press, 2016), 155–56.

53. Jacopo Maria Pepe, *Beyond Energy: Trade and Transport in a Reconnecting Asia* (Wiesbaden, Germany: Springer, 2018), 279. Data from Manin Askar's presentation at the Seventh 1520 Business Forum, June 2012.

54. Ibid.

55. Ibid.

56. Jakóbowski et al., *The Silk Railroad*, 69.

57. See Sina Tavsan, "'Iron Silk Road' Threatens to Sidetrack Russia," *Nikkei Asian Review*, October 31, 2017, https://asia.nikkei.com/Economy/Iron-silk-road-threatens-to-sidetrack-Russia.

58. Recent calculations suggest that the simplification of customs clearance due to the advent of the EAEU helps reduce trans-Eurasian travel duration by 4–6 days. In May 2018, China and member states of the EAEU signed agreements on customs clearance, trade facilitation, and e-commerce that should further enhance trade-related cooperation, beginning in early 2019. See Jakóbowski et al., *The Silk Railroad*, 33; and Jing Shuiyu and Zhong Nan, "China Signs Trade Deal with Eurasian Economic Union," *China Daily*, May 18, 2018, http://www.chinadaily.com.cn/a/201805/18/WS5afe4aaba3103f6866ee941b.html.

59. The so-called Visegrad Four are the Czech Republic, Slovakia, Poland, and Hungary. The Visegrad Group was formed in February 1991 at a meeting in Visegrad, Hungary, of leaders from Czechoslovakia, Poland, and Hungary. After the 1993 dissolution of Czechoslovakia into the Czech Republic and Slovakia, the Visegrad Triangle became the Visegrad Four.

60. On this development, see Jacopo M. Pepe, *Continental Drift—Germany and China's Inroads in the "German-Central European Manufacturing Core": Geopolitical Chances and Risks* (Washington, DC: Reischauer Center for East Asian Studies, 2017), 9–23.

61. Chem China, a Chinese firm, in 2016 acquired Krauss Maffei, a world leader in the production of industrial robots and engineering plastics. Another Chinese firm, Midea, in early 2017 also acquired the German robotics manufacturer KUKA, one of the world's leading suppliers of intelligent automation and a leader in digitalization of production processes that is one of the main suppliers of industrial robotics for Hungary's Mercedes plant. See Pepe, *Continental Drift*, 43–45.

62. China Railway Corporation was the third largest freight carrier in the world in 2018, even though freight service only made up 26 percent of the company's total revenue. COSCO ranks fourteenth globally, and Deutsche Bahn fifteenth. See "Top 50 Global Freight," *Transport Topics*, https://www.ttnews.com/top50/globalfreight/2018.

63. See The State Council Information Office of the People's Republic of China, "China's Arctic Policy," *The State Council of the People's Republic of China*, January 26, 2018, http://english.gov.cn/archive/white_paper/2018/01/26/content_281476026660336.htm.

64. In October 2013, for example, Hyundai Glovis, a Korean firm, completed a pilot voyage from Ust-Luga port in European Russia to Gwangyang, South Korea. See Kim Kwang-tae, "S. Korea Successfully Completes Pilot Service on Arctic Shipping Route,"

Yonhap, October 22, 2013, http://english.yonhapnews.co.kr/business/2013/10/22/17/
0501000000AEN20131022010900320F.html.

65. This 2017 estimate of $1.7 trillion/year in needed infrastructural investment was
more than double the $750 billion/year figure estimated in 2009. See Asian Development
Bank, *Meeting Asia's Infrastructure Needs: Highlights* (Mandaluyong City, Philippines: Asian
Development Bank, 2017); and Asian Development Bank, *Infrastructure for a Seamless Asia*
(Tokyo: Asian Development Bank Institute, 2009).

66. This project was approved in November 2007. For details, see Asian Development
Bank, "Regional: VIE: GMS Southern Coastal Corridor Project," https://www.adb.org/
projects/36353-013/main#project-overview.

67. This project was approved in May 2012. For details, see Asian Development Bank,
"Regional: Turkmenistan-Afghanistan-Pakistan-India Natural Gas Pipeline Project, Phase
3," https://www.adb.org/projects/44463-013/main#project-overview. The ADB were
also involved in the first two phases of the TAPI pipeline project, which are now closed.

68. For details, see Central Asia Regional Economic Cooperation, "CAREC Program,"
https://www.carecprogram.org/?page_id=31.

69. World Bank, "World Bank Lending—fiscal 2016," *World Bank*, http://pubdocs
.worldbank.org/en/634801473443116208/WBAR16-FY16-Lending-Presentation.pdf.

70. See European Bank for Reconstruction and Development, "South-West Corridor
Road Project," https://www.ebrd.com/work-with-us/projects/psd/southwest-corridor
-road-project.html.

71. See, for example, Kyle Ferrier, "How a Northeast Asian Development Bank
Could Succeed," *Korea Economic Institute of America*, http://keia.org/how-northeast
-asian-development-bank-could-succeed; as well as Lee-Jay Cho and S. Stanley Katz, "A
Northeast Asian Development Bank?" *NIRA Review* (Winter 2001): 41.

72. China Investment Corporation, the second largest sovereign wealth fund in the
world, possessed $941 billion in assets as of August 2018, and SAFE Investment Com-
pany (seventh largest) had $441 billion in assets. See Sovereign Wealth Fund Institute,
"Sovereign Wealth Fund Rankings," updated August 2018, https://www.swfinstitute.org/
sovereign-wealth-fund-rankings/.

73. See "Boao Forum for Asia Annual Conference 2009 Opens: Wen Jiabao Attends
the Conference and Delivers a Keynote Speech," *Ministry of Foreign Affairs of the People's
Republic of China*, April 18, 2009, http://www.fmprc.gov.cn/mfa_eng/wjdt_665385/zyjh
_665391/t558306.shtml.

74. "Full Text of Li Keqiang's Speech at Opening Ceremony of Boao Forum," *Ministry
of Foreign Affairs of the People's Republic of China*, April 11, 2014, http://www.fmprc.gov
.cn/mfa_eng/zxxx_662805/t1145980.shtml.

75. See Jamil Anderlini, "UK Move to Join China-led Bank a Surprise Even to Beijing," *Financial Times*, March 26, 2015, https://www.ft.com/content/d33fed8a-d3a1-11e4
-a9d3-00144feab7de; and Simon Mundy, "South Korea to Join China-Led Development
Bank," *Financial Times*, March 26, 2015, https://www.ft.com/content/7587ad1c-d429
-11e4-b041-00144feab7de.

76. "Full Text of Chinese President's Speech at Boao Forum for Asia," *Xinhua*, March
29, 2015, http://www.xinhuanet.com/english/2015-03/29/c_134106145.htm.

77. Martin A. Weiss, "Asian Infrastructure Investment Bank (AIIB)," *Congressional Research Service*, February 3, 2017, https://fas.org/sgp/crs/row/R44754.pdf.

78. Ibid.

79. Canada was the last of the G-7, apart from the US and Japan, to join. The AIIB approved Canada's application in March 2017. See Reuters Staff, "China-Led AIIB Approves 13 New Members, Canada Joins," *Reuters*, March 23, 2017, https://www.reuters.com/article/us-china-aiib/china-led-aiib-approves-13-new-members-canada-joins-idUSKBN16U0CG.

80. New Development Bank, "About Us: History," accessed March 31, 2017.

81. "China to Establish $40 Billion Silk Road Infrastructure Fund," *Reuters*, November 8, 2014, http://www.reuters.com/article/us-china-diplomacy-idUSKBN0IS0BQ20141108; and Wang Junlin, "Sharing 'One Belt One Road' Business Opportunities with the World," *Peoples' Daily Overseas Edition*, March 27, 2018. Sectors of special interest include energy development and electric power, construction machinery, petrochemicals, communications networks, marine engineering, shipbuilding, and financial cooperation. Concrete projects supported included the Yamal LNG facility in Russia's Arctic; a major hydroelectric project in Pakistan; and a stake in Pirelli Tires of Italy.

82. Wang Junling, "Tong Shijie Fenxiang 'Yidaiyilu" Shangji [Sharing 'Belt and Road Initiative' Business Opportunities with the World]," *People.cn*, March 27, 2018, http://world.people.com.cn/n1/2018/0327/c1002-29890532.html.

83. An Baijie, "Xi Vows Belt, Road Support," *China Daily*, May 15, 2017, http://www.chinadaily.com.cn/china/2017-05/15/content_29343505.htm.

84. Ibid.

85. The Marshall Plan provided total aid of $13 billion in 1947 dollars, equivalent to around $100 billion today. The AIIB alone has a capitalization of $100 billion, with $50 billion to be provided by China, and the PRC also contributes to the New Development Bank (formerly BRICS Development Bank), the Silk Road Fund, and other development institutions related to the BRI as well. See Melvyn P. Leffler, "The United States and the Strategic Dimensions of the Marshall Plan," *Diplomatic History* 12, no. 3 (July 1988): 277–306, doi: DOI: 10.1111/j.1467-7709.1988.tb00477.x; and Simon Shen, "How China's 'Belt and Road' Compares to the Marshall Plan, *The Diplomat*, February 6, 2016, http://thediplomat.com/2016/02/how-chinas-belt-and-road-compares-to-the-marshall-plan/.

86. The physical base of the previously virtual Central Asia Regional Economic Cooperation (CAREC) Institute was established at Urumqi in March 2018 to conduct research on BRI and related issues.

87. Statistics from Kaztransservice, *Kazlogistics*, 2014.

88. The sixteen European members are Albania, Bosnia and Herzegovina, Bulgaria, Croatia, Czech Republic, Estonia, Hungary, Latvia, Lithuania, Macedonia, Montenegro, Poland, Romania, Serbia, Slovakia, and Slovenia. See Cooperation between China and Central and Eastern European Countries official website, http://www.china-ceec.org/eng/.

CHAPTER 5

1. On the early genesis of the Four Modernizations, see Immanuel Chung-yueh Hsu, *China without Mao: The Search for a New Order*, 2nd ed. (New York: Oxford University Press, 1990), 92–126; and Ezra F. Vogel, *Deng Xiaoping and the Transformation of China* (Cambridge, MA: Harvard University Press, 2011), 184–248.

2. Along the way, China moved to seventh in 1997, sixth in 2000 (passing Italy), fifth in 2005 (passing France), third in 2007 (past Germany), and second in 2010 (eclipsing Japan). Only the US remains larger in nominal terms; in 2013 China passed even the US, accord-

ing to PPP criteria. See World Bank, "GDP (current US$)," *World Development Indicators*, accessed December 21, 2018.

3. Vogel, *Deng Xiaoping and the Transformation of China*, 406.

4. Between 2000 and 2008, for example, retained earnings did account for 71 percent of gross capital formation. See Nicholas R. Lardy, *Markets over Mao: The Rise of Private Business in China* (Washington, DC: Peterson Institute for International Economics, 2014), 95.

5. Ibid., 97–99.

6. Among the new Chinese government demands were mandatory licensing of foreign patents and revelation of corporate source and encryption codes. On the details, see John W. Garver, *China's Quest: The History of the Foreign Relations of the People's Republic of China* (New York: Oxford University Press, 2016), 699–701.

7. See Scott Kennedy, "Made in China 2025," *Center for Strategic & International Studies*, June 1, 2015, https://www.csis.org/analysis/made-china-2025.

8. For example, the MIIT will in cooperation with China Development Bank provide 300 billion yuan of loans and bonds to support "Made in China 2025" projects during 2016–2020. See Xinhua, "China to Invest Big in 'Made in China 2025' Strategy," *State Council of the People's Republic of China*, October 12, 2017, http://english.gov.cn/state_council/ministries/2017/10/12/content_281475904600274.htm.

9. See Ma Si, "Made in China 2025 Roadmap Updated," *China Daily*, January 27, 2018, http://www.chinadaily.com.cn/a/201801/27/WS5a6bb8b9a3106e7dcc137168.html.

10. See Mark J. Greeven and Wei Wei, *Business Ecosystems in China: Alibaba and Competing Baidu, Tencent, Xiaomi and LeEco* (New York: Routledge, 2018), 13–14.

11. World Bank, "GDP, PPP (Constant 2011 International $)," *World Development Indicators*, accessed October 23, 2018.

12. World Bank, "GDP Growth (Annual %)," *World Development Indicators*, accessed October 23, 2018.

13. Central Intelligence Agency, "Country Comparison: Public Debt," *The World Factbook*, accessed October 23, 2018.

14. See Zongyuan Liu, "Sovereign Leveraged Funds: Comparative Analysis of Using Foreign-Exchange Reserves as a Source of State-Led Finance and Investment in China and Japan." Unpublished doctoral dissertation, Johns Hopkins University, 2019.

15. See China Development Bank, *Annual Report 2017* (Beijing: China Development Bank), 6. At the end of 2017, the CDB maintained a balance of foreign currency loans of $261.7 billion. See ibid., 15. For a succinct summary of CDB activities, see Chris Wright, "Making Sense of Belt and Road—The Chinese Policy Bank: China Development Bank," *Euromoney*, September 26, 2017, https://www.euromoney.com/article/b14toydvx7zvmc/making-sense-of-belt-and-road-the-chinese-policy-bank-china-development-bank.

16. By the end of 2016, China had made over $292 billion in outstanding loans or equity investments under the BRI, with the China Development Bank as the largest single lender. See Gabriel Wildau and Nan Ma, "In Charts: China's Belt and Road Initiative," *Financial Times*, May 10, 2017, https://www.ft.com/content/18db2e80-3571-11e7-bce4-9023f8c0fd2e.

17. Ibid.

18. See CK Tan, "China to Step Up Financing for Belt and Road Projects," *Nikkei Asian Review*, March 7, 2018, https://asia.nikkei.com/Spotlight/China-people-s-congress-2018/China-to-step-up-financing-for-Belt-and-Road-projects.

19. Since the fund is denominated in RMB, it does not fall under the jurisdiction of US sanctions. See Max Seddon and Kathrin Hille, "China and Russia Strike $11bn Funding Deal," *Financial Times*, July 4, 2017, https://www.ft.com/content/323f8254-60d2 -11e7-8814-0ac7eb84e5f1.

20. See Martin Arnold, "Western Banks Race to Win China's Belt and Road Initiative Deals," *Financial Times*, February 26, 2018, https://www.ft.com/content/d9fbf8a6-197d -11e8-aaca-4574d7dabfb6.

21. On the 1994 tax reform and its fateful significance for the Chinese political economy, see Arthur Kroeber, *China's Economy: What Everyone Needs to Know* (New York: Oxford University Press, 2016), 115–18.

22. In 1978, China produced 31.8 million metric tons of crude steel, compared to 124.3 million tons by the US and 102.1 million tons by Japan. See International Iron and Steel Institute (now World Steel Association), "Crude Steel Production," *Steel Statistical Yearbook* (1986).

23. In 1996, China produced 101.2 million tons of crude steel, compared to 95.5 million tons by the US and 98.8 million tons by Japan. See World Steel Association, "Total Production of Crude Steel," *Steel Statistical Yearbook* (2006).

24. In 2015, China produced 803.8 million tons of crude steel, compared to 105.1 million tons by Japan and 78.8 million tons by the US. See World Steel Association, "Total Production of Crude Steel," *Steel Statistical Yearbook* (2016).

25. Ibid.

26. In 2006, China exported 51.7 million tons of steel products, compared to 34.6 million tons exported by Japan. See World Steel Association, "Exports of Semi-finished and Finished Steel Products," *Steel Statistical Yearbook* (2016).

27. World total steel products exports were 462.4 million tons in 2015. See ibid.

28. International Trade Administration, "Global Steel Trade Monitor," *U.S. Department of Commerce*, March 2017, http://www.trade.gov/steel/countries/pdfs/2016/annual/exports-china.pdf.

29. In one 2010 study, for example, Chinese scholars found that local governments in Jiangsu province provided land at 28 percent of market prices. See Lukas Brun, "Overcapacity in Steel: China's Role in a Global Problem," *Duke Center on Globalization, Governance, and Competitiveness*, September 2016, 27, https://aamweb.s3.amazonaws.com/uploads/resources/OvercapacityReport2016_R3.pdf.

30. Ibid., 23.

31. See Lukas Brun, "Overcapacity in Steel: China's Role in a Global Problem," *Duke Center on Globalization, Governance, and Competitiveness*, September 2016, 30.

32. The Bingtuan, it should be noted, was not organizationally part of the PLA. See Tai Ming Cheung, *China's Entrepreneurial Army* (New York: Oxford University Press, 2001); and Alexa Olesen, "China's Vast, Strange, and Powerful Farming Militia Turns 60," *Foreign Policy*, October 8, 2014, http://foreignpolicy.com/2014/10/08/chinas-vast-strange -and-powerful-farming-militia-turns-60/.

33. Chazen Global Insights, "Alibaba: A Dictatorship?" *Columbia Business School*, November 7, 2016, https://www8.gsb.columbia.edu/articles/chazen-global-insights/alibaba -dictatorship.

34. Bloomberg News, "Cosco Shipping Offers $6.3 Billion to Buy Orient Overseas," *Bloomberg*, July 9, 2017, https://www.bloomberg.com/news/articles/2017-07-09/cosco -agrees-to-buy-orient-overseas-in-6-billion-deal-wsj-says. Tung Chee-hwa, a prominent

family member, was the first governor of Hong Kong following the 1997 reversion to China.

35. In 2016 COSCO held an 11.6 percent global market share, exceeded only by APM-Maersk (16.4 percent) and Mediterranean Shipping Co. (14.7 percent). See Ben Bland, "Cosco Takeover of Orient Overseas Affirms China's Trade Ambitions," *Financial Times,* July 10, 2017, https://www.ft.com/content/11eca6ea-6545–11e7–8526–7b38d-caef614.

36. Reynolds Hutchins, "Cosco Beefs Up European Terminal Footprint Further," *Journal of Commerce,* June 12, 2017, https://www.joc.com/maritime-news/container-lines/cosco/cosco-beefs-european-terminal-footprint-further_20170612.html.

37. Ibid.

38. Bruce Barnard, "Cosco Pacific Buys Stake in Rotterdam Terminal," *Journal of Commerce,* May 12, 2016, https://www.joc.com/port-news/european-ports/port-rotterdam/cosco-pacific-buys-stake-rotterdam-terminal_20160512.html.

39. Staley Carvalho and Maha el Dahan, "China's Cosco to Invest $400 Million in New Abu Dhabi Container Terminal," *Reuters,* September 28, 2016, https://www.reuters.com/article/us-cosco-shipping-emirates-idUSKCN11Y1N1.

40. Sheridan Prasso, "A Chinese Company Reshaping the World Leaves a Troubled Trail," *Bloomberg Businessweek,* September 18, 2018, https://www.bloomberg.com/news/features/2018-09-19/a-chinese-company-reshaping-the-world-leaves-a-troubled-trail.

41. See Engineering News-Record, "ENR's 2017 Top 250 International Contractors," August 2017, https://www.enr.com/toplists/2017-Top-250-International-Contractors-1.

42. Shi Yinglun, "All Aboard: China's High-Speed Rail 10 Years On," *Xinhua,* August 1, 2018, http://www.xinhuanet.com/english/2018-08/01/c_137361580.htm.

43. See "High Speed Rail around the World," *US High Speed Rail Association,* accessed October 19, 2018, http://www.ushsr.com/hsr/hsrworldwide.html.

44. CRRC supplies over 90 percent of the Chinese market, and also makes metro cars for the Massachusetts Bay Transit Association (MBTA) in Springfield, Massachusetts. See Bruce Wilds, "Mergers Hit Rail Equipment Sector—What Is the Lesson?" *Seeking Alpha,* September 28, 2017, https://seekingalpha.com/article/4110463-mergers-hit-rail-equipment-sector-lesson; and Keith Barrow, "CNR Selected to Supply New Trains for Boston," *International Railway Journal,* October 22, 2014, https://www.railjournal.com/regions/north-america/cnr-selected-to-supply-new-trains-for-boston/.

45. See "Top 5 Best-Selling Smartphone Brands in the World," *Business Tech,* February 23, 2018, https://businesstech.co.za/news/mobile/227509/top-5-best-selling-smartphone-brands-in-the-world/.

46. Huawei, "Huawei Investment & Holding Co., Ltd. 2017 Annual Report," http://www.huawei.com/en/press-events/annual-report/2017.

47. See Jan Drahokoupil, Angieszka McCaleb, Peter Pawlicki, and Agnes Szunomar, "Huawei in Europe: Strategic Integration of Local Capabilities in a Global Production Network," in *Chinese Investment in Europe: Corporate Strategies and Labour Relations,* ed. Jan Drahokoupil (Brussels: European Trade Union institute, 2017), 211–29.

48. Daniel Morial, "Huawei Is Now More Popular than Apple in Central and Eastern Europe," *Gadget Match,* August 16, 2017, https://www.gadgetmatch.com/huawei-more-popular-than-apple-central-and-eastern-europe/.

49. Huawei Europe, "A High-Powered Innovator in Poland," *Huawei,* September 27, 2017, https://huawei.eu/blog/high-powered-innovator-poland-0.

50. Huawei, "Huawei in Europe," accessed May 7, 2018, http://www.huawei.com/ch -en/about-huawei/ch/huawei-europe.

51. "Record Year for International Patent Applications in 2016; Strong Demand Also for Trademark and Industrial Design Protection," *World Intellectual Property Organization*, March 15, 2017, http://www.wipo.int/pressroom/en/articles/2017/article_0002.html.

52. Raymond Zhong, "China's Huawei Is at Center of Fight Over 5G's Future," *New York Times*, March 7, 2018, https://www.nytimes.com/2018/03/07/technology/china -huawei-5g-standards.html.

53. Ibid.

54. On the history of Alibaba, see Duncan Clark, *Alibaba: The House that Jack Ma Built* (New York: Harper Collins, 2016).

55. See ibid., 109–30.

56. Mark J. Greeven and Wei Wei, *Business Ecosystems in China: Alibaba and Competing Baidu, Tencent, Xiaomi and LeEco* (New York: Routledge 2018), 22.

57. Alibaba Group, "Alibaba Group Announces March Quarter 2018 Results and Full Fiscal Year 2018 Results," May 4, 2018, https://www.alibabagroup.com/en/news/press _pdf/p180504.pdf.

58. See Reuters Staff, "Alibaba's Ma Meets Trump, Promises to Bring One Million Jobs to U.S." *Reuters*, January 9, 2017, https://www.reuters.com/article/us-usa-trump-alibaba -idUSKBN14T1ZA.

59. On Ma's speech at Davos, see Alanna Petroff, "Jack Ma: 'Don't Use Trade as a Weapon,'" *CNN Money*, January 24, 2018, http://money.cnn.com/2018/01/24/news/jack -ma-trade-davos-2018-wef/index.html.

60. See Rachel Brown, "Beijing's Silk Road Goes Digital," *Council on Foreign Relations*, https://www.cfr.org/blog/beijings-silk-road-goes-digital; and "Alibaba to Set Up NW China HQ to Boost Belt and Road Initiative," *GBTimes*, August 21, 2017, https://gbtimes .com/alibaba-set-nw-china-hq-boost-belt-and-road-initiative.

61. The five coastal provinces are Shandong, Jiangsu, Zhejiang, Fujian, and Guangdong. The three municipalities are Beijing, Tianjin, and Shanghai. See National Bureau of Statistics of China, "Total Value of Imports and Exports by Operating Units," "Value Added by Industry," and "Gross Regional Product," *National Data*, accessed October 9, 2018.

62. David Barboza, "China Unveils $586 Billion Stimulus Plan," *New York Times*, November 10, 2008, http://www.nytimes.com/2008/11/10/world/asia/10iht-10china .17673270.html.

63. The Marshall Plan involved $13 billion expenditures in 1947 dollars—the equivalent of around $100 billion today. Funding for the BRI at the end of 2016 was around $292 billion. See Simon Shen, "How China's 'Belt and Road' Compares to the Marshall Plan," *The Diplomat*, February 6, 2016, http://thediplomat.com/2016/02/how-chinas-belt -and-road-compares-to-the-marshall-plan/; and Gabriel Wildau and Nan Ma, "In Charts: China's Belt and Road Initiative," *Financial Times*, May 10, 2017, https://www.ft.com/ content/18db2e80-3571-11e7-bce4-9023f8cofd2e

64. The Silk Road Fund at the end of 2016 provided $4 billion, followed by the New Development Bank ($2 billion), and the Asian Infrastructure Investment Bank ($2 billion). See Wildau and Ma, "In Charts: China's Belt and Road Initiative."

65. Reuters Staff, "China-Led AIIB Approves 13 New Members, Canada Joins," *Reuters*, March 23, 2017, https://www.reuters.com/article/us-china-aiib/china-led-aiib -approves-13-new-members-canada-joins-idUSKBN16U0CG. Hungary and Belgium were also included in this expansion.

66. Shannon Tiezzi, "Who Is Actually Attending China's Belt and Road Forum?" *The Diplomat*, May 12, 2017, http://thediplomat.com/2017/05/who-is-actually-attending -chinas-belt-and-road-forum/.

67. See "List of Deliverables of Belt and Road Forum," *Xinhua*, May 15, 2017, http:// news.xinhuanet.com/english/2017-05/15/c_136286376.htm.

68. In 2017 South Korea's total trade with China recorded $238.2 billion, compared to $199.4 billion trade with the US and Japan combined. See International Monetary Fund, *Direction of Trade Statistics* (2017).

69. U.S. Energy Information Administration, "China Surpassed the United States as the World's Largest Crude Oil Importer in 2017," *Today in Energy*, February 5, 2018, https://www.eia.gov/todayinenergy/detail.php?id=34812.

70. According to the OECD/IEA *World Energy Outlook* 2016, China's oil demand and net oil imports will rise to 15.1 million bbl/day and 12 million bbl/day by 2040. At that point, China would prospectively be importing 80 percent of its oil needs.

71. See Tom DiChristopher, "US Will Be a Net Energy Exporter by 2022, Four Years Sooner than Expected, Energy Department Says," *CNBC*, February 7, 2018, https:// www.cnbc.com/2018/02/07/united-states-will-be-a-net-energy-exporter.html ; and Timothy Cama, "Perry: US to become net energy export within 18 months," *The Hill*, July 31, 2018, https://thehill.com/policy/energy-environment/399670-perry-us-to-become -net-energy-exporter-in-18-months.

72. Susan L. Shirk, *How China Opened Its Door: The Political Success of the PRC's Foreign Trade and Investment Reforms* (Washington, DC: Brookings Institution, 1994).

73. Ibid.

74. G. John Ikenberry and Anne-Marie Slaughter, *Forging a World of Liberty under Law: U.S. National Security in the 21st Century* (Princeton, NJ: Princeton University Press, 2006).

75. See National Development and Reform Commission, "CHINA RAILWAY Express Construction and Development Plan for 2016–2020," released on October 17, 2016.

76. See BP, "Carbon Dioxide Emissions (Million Tons)," *Statistical Review of World Energy*, June 2017.

77. See Chris Rhodes, "Manufacturing: International Comparisons," Briefing Paper No. 05809, *House of Commons Library*, August 18, 2016; Verband der Automobilindustrie, "Annual Report 2015," 20–21; Phillip Kissonergis, "Smartphone Ownership, Usage And Penetration By Country," *The Hub*, October 13, 2015, http://thehub.smsglobal.com/ smartphone-ownership-usage-and-penetration; Daimler, "Annual Report 2015," and Yum Food Inc., "Yum! Brands 2015 Annual Report."

78. E. F. Denison and W. K. Chung, "Economic Growth and Its Sources," in *The Japanese Economy: Vol. 2 Postwar Growth*, ed. Peter Drysdale and Luke Gower (New York: Routledge, 1998–1999), 30; and "Top 20 Semiconductor Companies 2016," *AnySilicon*, May 23, 2016, http://anysilicon.com/top-20-semiconductor-companies-2016/. South Korea is the world's second largest semiconductor producer, after the US. Samsung is the second largest corporate semiconductor producer, and SK Hynix (also South Korean) is sixth.

CHAPTER 6

1. Kent G. Deng, "Why Shipping 'Declined' in China from the Middle Ages to the Nineteenth Century," in *Shipping and Economic Growth 1350–1850*, ed. Richard W. Unger (Leiden: Brill, 2011), 219.

2. Zheng He's seventh voyage left China in the winter of 1431. He reputedly died in Calicut in the spring of 1433, and the fleet returned to China that summer. See Jung-pang Lo, "Zheng He," *Encyclopædia Britannica*, https://www.britannica.com/biography/Zheng -He.

3. See Craig A. Lockard, "Chinese Migration and Settlement in Southeast Asia Before 1850: Making Fields from the Sea," *History Compass* 11, no. 9 (September 2013): 765–81, doi: 10.1111/hic3.12079.

4. Ibid., 770.

5. "Bangkok Population 2017," *World Population Review*, October 26, 2016, http://worldpopulationreview.com/world-cities/bangkok-population/.

6. See Maria Fernanda Pargana Ilheu, "Cultural Characteristics and Effective Business in China," in *The China Information Technology Handbook*, ed. Patricia Ordonez de Pablos and Miltiadis D, Lytras (New York: Springer, 2009), 206.

7. See Suzanne Nam, "Thailand's 40 Richest," *Forbes*, September 1, 2010, https://www .forbes.com/2010/09/01/thailands-richest-dhanin-wealth-thailands-rich-10_lander.html.

8. Yenni Kwok, "The Memory of Savage Anticommunist Killings Still Haunts Indonesia, 50 Years On," *Time*, September 29, 2015, http://time.com/4055185/indonesia -anticommunist-massacre-holocaust-killings-1965/.

9. On Singapore's approach to relations with China, and its historical background, see Kent E. Calder, *Singapore: Smart City, Smart State* (Washington, DC: Brookings Institution Press, 2016), 13–14.

10. On these issues, see ibid., 151–56.

11. Official figures are conflicting, but reliable estimates indicate at least seven thousand Chinese military deaths and at least ten thousand Vietnamese civilian fatalities, plus Vietnamese military casualties. See Xiaoming Zhang, "China's 1979 War with Vietnam: A Reassessment," *China Quarterly*, no. 184 (December 2005): 851–74, http://www.jstor .org/stable/20192542.

12. China imported $500 billion from East Asia, $245 billion from the EU, and $235 billion from ASEAN in 2017, according to International Monetary Fund, *Direction of Trade Statistics*. If the European Union is not counted as a region, Southeast Asia could be second.

13. Author's calculation based on ibid.

14. Fully 17 percent of the integrated circuits China imported in 2016, together with 12 percent of its computer imports, originated in Malaysia. See "Where Does China Import Computers From? (2016)" and "Where Does China Import Integrated Circuits From? (2016)" in A.J.G. Simoes and C. A. Hidalgo. *The Economic Complexity Observatory: An Analytical Tool for Understanding the Dynamics of Economic Development*. Workshops at the Twenty-Fifth AAAI Conference on Artificial Intelligence. (2011), accessed online October 9, 2018, https://www.aaai.org/ocs/index.php/WS/AAAIW11/paper/view/3948.

15. Author's calculation based on American Enterprise Institute/Heritage Foundation, *China Global Investment Tracker*, updated January 2018.

16. Robert D. Kaplan, *Asia's Cauldron: The South China Sea and the End of a Stable Pacific* (New York: Random House, 2014), 41.

17. The US Energy Information Administration (EIA) estimates that there are some 11 billion barrels of oil and 190 trillion cubic feet of natural gas proved and probable reserves in the South China Sea. China's CNOOC estimated in late 2012 that the area holds some 125 billion barrels of oil and 500 trillion cubic feet of natural gas in undiscovered

reserves. See Energy Information Administration (EIA), "South China Sea," *U.S. Department of Energy*, February 7, 2013, https://www.eia.gov/beta/international/regions-topics.cfm?RegionTopicID=SCS.

18. On the South China Sea as "China's Caribbean," see Kaplan, *Asia's Cauldron*, 32–50.

19. Southeast Asian nations began asserting these views with particular intensity following Hillary Clinton's remarks at the 2010 ASEAN Regional Forum in Hanoi.

20. "The South China Sea Arbitration (The Republic of Philippines v. The People's Republic of China)," *Permanent Court of Arbitration*, https://pca-cpa.org/en/cases/7/.

21. Katie Hunt, "Showdown in the South China Sea: How Did We Get Here?" *CNN*, August 2, 2016, http://www.cnn.com/2015/10/28/asia/china-south-china-sea-disputes-explainer/.

22. Jane Perlez, "Tribunal Rejects Beijing's Claims in South China Sea," *New York Times*, July 12, 2016, https://www.nytimes.com/2016/07/13/world/asia/south-china-sea-hague-ruling-philippines.html.

23. Andreo Calonzo and Cecilia Yap, "China Visit Helps Duterte Reap Funding Deals Worth $24 Billion," *Bloomberg*, October 21, 2016, https://www.bloomberg.com/news/articles/2016-10-21/china-visit-helps-duterte-reap-funding-deals-worth-24-billion.

24. Associated Press, "Philippines to 'Set Aside' South China Sea Tribunal Ruling to Avoid Imposing on Beijing," *The Guardian*, December 17, 2016, https://www.theguardian.com/world/2016/dec/17/philippines-to-set-aside-south-china-sea-tribunal-ruling-to-avoid-imposing-on-beijing.

25. Ben Blanchard and Manny Mogato, "China Welcomes ASEAN Summit Declaration on South China Sea," *Reuters*, May 2, 2017, http://www.reuters.com/article/us-asean-summit-china-idUSKBN17Y0SL.

26. U.S. Energy Information Administration, "China Surpassed the United States as the World's Largest Crude Oil Importer in 2017," *Today in Energy*, February 5, 2018, https://www.eia.gov/todayinenergy/detail.php?id=34812.

27. The IEA projects that China's oil demand will reach 15.1 million bbl/day in 2040. With imports projected at 12 million bbl/day, China would be importing 79.5 percent of its oil demand by that time. See International Energy Agency, *World Energy Outlook 2016* (Paris: IEA, 2016), 115 and 143, http://dx.doi.org/10.1787/weo-2016-en.

28. "What Does Indonesia Export to China? (2016)" in *Observatory of Economic Complexity*, accessed online October 9, 2018, https://atlas.media.mit.edu/en/. Interestingly, coal (lignite and coal briquettes) accounted for over half of the mineral products exported to China in 2016.

29. "What Does Philippines Export to China? (2016)," "What Does Malaysia Export to China? (2016)," "What Does Singapore Export to China? (2016)," "What Does Vietnam Export to China? (2016)," and "What Does Thailand Export to China? (2016)," in *Observatory of Economic Complexity*, accessed online October 9, 2018, https://atlas.media.mit.edu/en/.

30. As previously indicated, China sources 17 percent of its integrated circuits, and 12 percent of its finished computers—mostly low-end versions—from Malaysia. In 2016 it also imported substantial volumes of both integrated circuits and finished computers from Singapore, Thailand, the Philippines, and Vietnam as well. On this significant intraregional electronics trade involving China, see "Where Does China Import Computers From? (2016)" and "Where Does China Import Integrated Circuits From? (2016)" in *Observatory of Economic Complexity*, accessed online October 9, 2018, https://atlas.media.mit.edu/en/.

31. Author's calculation based on data provided by American Enterprise Institute/Heritage Foundation, *China Global Investment Tracker*, updated January 2018.

32. Ibid.

33. Billy Wong, "Guangxi: Enhancing ASEAN Supply Chain Connectivity," *Hong Kong Trade Development Council*, May 25, 2017, http://economists-pick-research.hktdc .com/business-news/article/Research-Articles/Guangxi-Enhancing-ASEAN-Supply -Chain-Connectivity/rp/en/1/1X000000/1X0AA5PW.htm.

34. The Beihai Industrial Zone, for example, employed thirty thousand workers in 2017, mainly from Vietnam, up 50 percent from the previous year. See ibid.

35. Ibid.

36. See AFP-Jiji, "Under New Leader Mahathir, China's Infrastructure Projects in Malaysia Are Under Threat," *Japan Times*, June 17, 2018, https://www.japantimes.co .jp/news/2018/06/17/asia-pacific/new-leader-mahathir-chinas-infrastructure-projects -malaysia-threat/#.WzE7O6dKiUk.

37. On the Singapore-Kunming Rail Link, see Shang-su Wu, "Singapore-Kunming Rail Link: A 'Belt and Road' Case Study," *The Diplomat*, June 17, 2016, http:// thediplomat.com/2016/06/singapore-kunming-rail-link-a-belt-and-road-case-study/.

38. Peter Janssen, "China Train Project Runs Roughshod over Laos," *Asia Times*, August 18, 2018, http://www.atimes.com/article/china-train-project-runs-roughshod-over -laos/.

39. Xinhua, "Construction of Thai-Chinese High-Speed Rail to Start Fully: Thai Official," *New China*, June 3, 2018, http://www.xinhuanet.com/english/2018-06/03/c _137226904.htm.

40. The link was originally scheduled to be completed in March 2018. Delays were caused by concerns from the Thai side. See Chris Horton, "Capital of Laos Seeks Stronger Ties to China," *New York Times*, September 25, 2018, https://www.nytimes.com/2018/ 09/25/business/vientiane-laos-china-investment.html.

41. Charissa Yong, "Malaysia, Singapore Ink Agreement to Defer High-Speed Rail Project for 2 Years; KL to Pay S$15m for Suspending Work," *Strait Times*, September 5, 2018, https://www.straitstimes.com/singapore/malaysia-singapore-ink-agreement-to -defer-high-speed-rail-project-for-two-years.

42. Matt Steinglass, "Vietnam Assembly Derails High-Speed Rail Link," *Financial Times*, June 21, 2010, https://www.ft.com/content/65255d72-7d6f-11df-a0f5 -00144feabdc0.

43. Doan Loan and Dat Nguyen, "Feasibility Report Ready for Vietnam's $58 Billion High-Speed Railroad," *VNExpress*, "August 29, 2018, https://e.vnexpress.net/news/ business/companies/feasibility-report-ready-for-vietnam-s-58-billion-high-speed-railroad -3800113.html.

44. AP, "Cambodia's Missing Railway Link to Thailand Rebuilt after 45 years," *South China Morning Post*, April 4, 2018, https://www.scmp.com/news/asia/southeast-asia/ article/2140314/cambodias-missing-railway-link-thailand-rebuilt-after-45.

45. See David Briginshaw, "CRRC to Supply Indonesia High-Speed Trains," *International Railway Journal*, April 13, 2017, http://www.railjournal.com/index.php/high-speed/ crrc-to-supply-indonesian-high-speed-trains.html; and Amy Qin, "China Exports High-Speed Rail Technology to Turkey," *New York Times*, July 28, 2014, https://sinosphere .blogs.nytimes.com/2014/07/28/china-exports-high-speed-rail-technology-to-turkey/.

46. Wu, "Singapore-Kunming Rail Link."

47. China has, for example, established a regional management center, manufacturing factory, and other facilities in Malaysia. See Wu, "Singapore-Kunming Rail Link."

48. In mid-2015 there were rumors that Chinese and Thai companies had agreed to a joint study of the Kra Isthmus as a canal site, but both governments denied the existence of such an agreement. See Gaku Shimada, "Kra Isthmus Shortcut Would Mean Big Shifts in Southeast Asia," *Nikkei Asian Review,* June 25, 2015, http://asia.nikkei.com/magazine/20150625-IS-ASIA-READY/Politics-Economy/Kra-Isthmus-shortcut-would-mean-big-shifts-in-Southeast-Asia.

49. On Kunming's felicitous location and the implications for its continental relationships, see Kent E. Calder, "A Tale of Two Cities: Kunming, Urumqi, and the New Continentalism," *Boao Review,* January 10, 2014.

50. See Xinhua, "Ever Expanding Chinese Rail Network Boosts German 'China City,'" *China Daily,* November 28, 2017, http://www.chinadaily.com.cn/business/2017-11/28/content_35092415.htm.

51. An, "Road-Rail Freight Route Delivers Cargo from SE Asia to Europe," *Xinhua,* September 29, 2017, http://www.xinhuanet.com/english/2017-09/29/c_136646445.htm.

52. Xiang Bo, "Regular Sea-Rail Route Links Chongqing, Singapore," *Xinhua,* September 25, 2017, http://www.xinhuanet.com/english/2017-09/25/c_136637079.htm.

53. Chong Koh Ping, "Singapore and Chongqing Aim to Cut Freight Time between the Two Cities to as Little as 5 Days," *Strait Times,* April 13. 2018, https://www.straitstimes.com/asia/east-asia/singapore-and-chongqing-aim-to-cut-freight-time-between-the-two-cities-to-as-little.

54. See Du Juan, "Myanmar-China Gas Pipeline Completed," Official Website of Guizhou, China, October 21, 2013, http://www.chinadaily.com.cn/m/guizhou/2013-10/21/content_17056468.htm.

55. See "China Opens Delayed Myanmar Oil Pipeline to Get Mideast Crude Faster," *Bloomberg,* April 11, 2017, https://www.bloomberg.com/news/articles/2017-04-11/china-opens-delayed-myanmar-oil-link-to-get-mideast-crude-faster.

56. Kunming has been a "national economic and technological development zone" since February, 2000. See National Economic and Technological Development Zones, "Kunming Economic and Technological Development Zone," accessed May 30, 2017, http://www.china.org.cn/english/SPORT-c/75845.htm.

57. See Atul Aneja, "China, India Fast-Track BCIM Economic Corridor Project," *The Hindu,* updated April 9, 2016, http://www.thehindu.com/news/national/china-india-fasttrack-bcim-economic-corridor-project/article7355496.ece.

58. Nineteen of the twenty richest individuals in Southeast Asia are also reportedly of Chinese descent. See Dorothea Slevogt, "Southeast Asia: The True Extent of Chinese Influence," *Schlegel und Partner,* May 11, 2015, https://www.schlegelundpartner.com/cn/news/suedost-asien-china/u/1126/.

59. On that visit, see Ezra F. Vogel, *Deng Xiaoping and the Transformation of China* (Cambridge, MA: Harvard University Press, 2011), 287–91.

60. Graham Allison and Robert D. Blackwill, *Lee Kuan Yew: The Grand Master's Insights on China, the United States, and the World* (Cambridge, MA: MIT Press, 2013).

61. From 2000 to 2016, the EU accounted for 22 percent of all FDI flows to ASEAN, leading all other foreign investors, with Japan second. European investment, however, has been quite volatile, and represented less than 2 percent of the EU's global outflows for that period. For Japan, investment in ASEAN has been more important, accounting for 13

percent of Japan's entire FDI outflows. See ASEAN Secretariat, *ASEAN Investment Report 2017: Foreign Direct Investment and Economic Zones in ASEAN* (Jakarta: ASEAN Secretariat, October 2017), Table 1.2.

62. Following Chinese prime minister Li Keqiang's Tokyo visit in May 2018, and Japanese prime minister Abe Shinzō's Beijing visit in October 2018, China and Japan have begun to pursue joint infrastructure projects in Southeast Asia. One of the first is a $45 billion high-speed rail project in Thailand, connecting the country's three main airports. See Gaku Shimada, "Japan and China take first step toward joint infrastructure abroad," *Nikkei Asia Review,* September 4, 2018, https://asia.nikkei.com/Politics/International-Relations/Japan-and-China-take-first-step-toward-joint-infrastructure-abroad.

63. For details, see Calder, *Singapore,* 151–56.

CHAPTER 7

1. The Sino-Russian border is currently 2,265 miles long, while that between the US and Mexico is 1,951 miles long. See "10 Longest Land Borders in the World," *10 Most Today,* November 22, 2015, http://10mosttoday.com/10-longest-land-borders-in-the-world/.

2. In 1991 the former Soviet Union and China began the process of delineating their borders, but a set of final deals was not concluded until 2004. The border dispute was formally concluded in 2008, when Russian foreign minister Sergei Lavrov signed an agreement to hand back two border islands to China. See "Timeline: Russia-China Relations," *Reuters,* May 19, 2008, http://www.reuters.com/article/us-russia-medvedev-foreign-timeline-idUSL1912530020080519; and Xiaokun Li, "China, Russia Sign Border Agreement," *China Daily,* July 22, 2008, http://www.chinadaily.com.cn/china/2008-07/22/content_6865847.htm.

3. The entire Russian Far East has a population of 6.3 million, compared to 38.3 million living across the Amur River in Heilongjiang. See Alexander Gabuev and Maria Repnikova, "Why Forecasts of a Chinese Takeover of the Russian Far East Are Dramatic Myth," *Carnegie Moscow Center,* July 14, 2017, http://carnegie.ru/2017/07/14/why-forecasts-of-chinese-takeover-of-russian-far-east-are-just-dramatic-myth-pub-71550.

4. O. Edmund Clubb, *China and Russia: The "Great Game"* (New York: Columbia University Press, 1971), 13.

5. On the details of seventeenth-century Sino-Russian interaction, see Benson Bobrick, *East of the Sun: The Epic Conquest and Tragic History of Siberia* (New York: Poseidon Press, 1992), 79–95.

6. On aggressive Russian steps to create new political-economic realities on the Amur in the mid-nineteenth century, see ibid., 255–62.

7. Ibid., 262.

8. Peter Hopkirk, *Setting the East Ablaze: Lenin's Dream of an Empire in Asia* (New York: Kodansha International, 1995).

9. Deborah A. Kaple, "Soviet Advisors in China in the 1950s," in *Brothers in Arms: The Rise and Fall of the Sino-Soviet Alliance, 1945–1963,* ed. Odd Arne Westad (Washington, DC: Woodrow Wilson Center Press, 1998), 117–20.

10. Kathryn Weathersby, "Stalin, Mao, and the End of the Korean War," in *Brothers in Arms: The Rise and Fall of the Sino-Soviet Alliance, 1945–1963,* ed. Odd Arne Westad (Washington, D.C.: Woodrow Wilson Center Press, 1998).

11. The Sino-Soviet border conflict began on March 2, 1969. On the details, see "Sino-Soviet Border Clashes," *Global Security*, http://www.globalsecurity.org/military/world/war/prc-soviet.htm.

12. See Richard M. Nixon, *Six Crises* (New York: Pyramid Books, 1962).

13. James Mann, *About Face: A History of America's Curious Relationship with China, from Nixon to Clinton* (New York: Alfred Knopf, 1999), 95.

14. These border talks, concluding successfully with a 1997 treaty on military frontier force reduction, were paralleled by bilateral border discussions by both the Chinese and the Russians with Kazakhstan, Kyrgyzstan, and Tajikistan, all of which ultimately proved successful. See Kent E. Calder, *The New Continentalism: Energy and Twenty-First Century Eurasian Geopolitics* (New Haven, CT: Yale University Press, 2012), 203; Elizabeth Wisnick, *Mending Fences: The Evolution of Moscow's China Policy from Brezhnev to Yeltsin* (Vancouver: University of Washington Press: 2015), 98–117 ; and "Timeline: Russia-China Relations," *Reuters*, May 19, 2008, http://www.reuters.com/article/us-russia-medvedev-foreign-timeline-idUSL1912530020080519.

15. Yukos accumulated $28 billion in tax claims, interest, and penalties in 2004; Khodorkovsky and Lebedev were sentenced in 2005; and Rosneft acquired any remaining Yukos assets at bankruptcy auctions in 2007. The timeline of events can be found at: Courtney Weaver, "Timeline: The Rise and Fall of Yukos," *Financial Times*, July 28, 2014, https://www.ft.com/content/f371c836-1645-11e4-93ec-00144feabdc0.

16. See International Monetary Fund, *Direction of Trade Statistics*.

17. Alexander Gabuev, "Friends with Benefits? Russian-Chinese Relations After the Ukraine Crisis," *Carnegie Endowment for International Peace*, June 29, 2016, http://carnegie.ru/2016/06/29/friends-with-benefits-russian-chinese-relations-after-ukraine-crisis-pub-63953.

18. U.S. Energy Information Agency, "China Surpassed the United States as the World's Largest Crude Oil Importer in 2017," *Today in Energy*, February 5, 2018, https://www.eia.gov/todayinenergy/detail.php?id=34812.

19. Beijing is ranked second with 22 million people, and Tianjin is sixth with 15 million. See "Largest Cities in China 2016," *Country Digest*, http://countrydigest.org/largest-cities-china/.

20. The Daqing and Shengli oilfields, located in Heilongjiang and Shandong provinces respectively, were discovered in 1959 and 1961 respectively. On Daqing, see: Daqing Oilfield, "History of Daqing Oilfield," http://dqyt.cnpc.com.cn/dqen/HoDO/dqen_common.shtml; and on Shengli, see: Sinopec Group, "About Sinopec," http://www.sinopecgroup.com/group/en/companyprofile/.

21. The distance from Fateh Oil Terminal (UAE) to Mawei Port (China) is 6232 nautical miles. See http://ports.com/sea-route/fateh-oil-terminal,united-arab-emirates/mawei-port,china/.

22. On the Power of Siberia project, see "Power of Siberia," *Gazprom*, http://www.gazprom.com/about/production/projects/pipelines/built/ykv/.

23. See Samuel Charap, John Drennan, and Pierre Noel, "Russia and China: A New Model of Great-Power Relations," *Survival* 59, no. 1 (2017): 30, http://dx.doi.org/10.1080/00396338.2017.1282670.

24. Ibid.

25. In 2010 four ships circumnavigated the Arctic Ocean between Northeast Asia and Europe. This number increased to 34 in 2011, 46 in 2012, and 71 in 2013. See Jonathan Masters, "The Thawing Arctic: Risks and Opportunities," *Council on Foreign Relations*, December 16, 2013, http://www.cfr.org/arctic/thawing-arctic-risks-opportunities/p32082.

26. The shipping distance between Shanghai and Hamburg via the Suez Canal is about 20,000 kilometers, whereas the Arctic route is only 14,000 kilometers. See Marco Evers, "Northeast Passage: Russia Moves to Boost Arctic Shipping," *Spiegel Online*, August 22, 2013, http://www.spiegel.de/international/world/russia-moves-to-promote-northeast -passage-through-arctic-ocean-a-917824.html.

27. "China's New Shipping Frontier," *Wall Street Journal*, July 9, 2014.

28. See Masters, "The Thawing Arctic."

29. Ibid.

30. Trude Pettersen, "Chinese Icebreaker Concludes Arctic Voyage," *Barents Observer*, September 27, 2012, http://wayback.archive-it.org/10184/20180413031500/http:// barentsobserver.com/en/arctic/chinese-icebreaker-concludes-arctic-voyage-27-09.

31. Stephanie Pezard and Timothy Smith, "Friends If We Must: Russia and China in the Arctic," *War on the Rocks*, May 6, 2016, http://warontherocks.com/2016/05/friends-if-we-must-russia-and-chinas -relations-in-the-arctic/.

32. Ibid.

33. The Silk Road Fund came in to fill a funding gap created when Exxon Mobil and other Western majors were forced to leave the Yamal project due to Western sanctions. See "China, Russia Jointly Launch Yamal LNG Project in the Arctic," *People.cn*, December 11, 2017, http://en.people.cn/n3/2017/1211/c90000-9302698.html.

34. Donald Gasper, "China and Russia Want to Develop Arctic Energy Resources Together, and US Disapproval May Not Deter Them," *South China Morning Post*, September 12, 2018, https://www.scmp.com/comment/insight-opinion/asia/article/2163719/china -and-russia-want-develop-arctic-energy-resources.

35. See "Offshore Oil Feels Pain of Spare Parts Come Short," *Barents Observer*, September 2015, http://wayback.archive-it.org/10184/20180412073929/http://barentsobserver .com/en/energy/2015/09/offshore-oil-feels-pain-spare-parts-come-short-18-09.

36. Associated Press, "A Timeline of US Troop Levels in Afghanistan Since 2001," *Military Times*, July 6, 2016, http://www.militarytimes.com/story/military/2016/07/06/ timeline-us-troop-levels-afghanistan-since-2001/86755782/.

37. Manas Air Force Base was returned to Kyrgyzstan in June 2014. On the details, see Olga Dzyubenko, "The US Military Just Closed Its 'Gateway to Afghanistan," *Business Insider*, June 4, 2014, http://www.businessinsider.com/olgha-dzyubenko-the-us-has-handed -back-manas-airbase-2014-6.

38. On the US military presence in Central Asia, see Kent E. Calder, *Embattled Garrisons: Comparative Base Politics and American Globalism* (Princeton, NJ: Princeton University Press, 2007), 54–55 and 201–2; as well as Alexander Cooley, *Base Politics: Democratic Change and the US Military Overseas* (Ithaca, NY: Cornell University Press, 2008).

39. Thomas Lum and Ben Dolven, "Mongolia," *Congressional Research Service*, July 10, 2018, https://fas.org/sgp/crs/row/IF10926.pdf

40. Xinjiang borders on Mongolia, Russia, Kazakhstan, Kyrgyzstan, Tajikistan, Afghanistan, Pakistan, and India.

41. World Bank, *Russian Economic Report*, no. 35 (April 2016): 55.

42. World Bank, "GDP (Current US$)" and "Exports of Goods and Services (BoP, Current US$)," *World Development Indicators*.

43. Kathrin Hille, "Russia's Economy: Challenges Facing Vladimir Putin." *Financial Times*, February 28, 2018, https://www.ft.com/content/3aac3faa-1bb6-11e8-aaca-4574d7dabfb6.

44. See Figure 7.1.

45. Alibaba will hold 48 percent of equity in the new venture, with Mega Fon, the next largest partner, holding 24 percent. See Max Seddon, "Alibaba to Set Up Online Retail Service in Russia," *Financial Times,* September 12, 2018, https://www.ft.com/content/453b58ac-b5a8-11e8-bbc3-ccd7de085ffe.

46. See Ezra F. Vogel, *Deng Xiaoping and the Transformation of China* (Cambridge, MA: Harvard University Press, 2011) 714. Vogel suggested that Deng's phrasing applied only to "hiding capabilities." It appeared first in the context of Sino-Russian relations, and not in 1979.

47. See Don Oberdorfer, *The Turn: From the Cold War to a New Era: The United States and the Soviet Union, 1983–1990* (New York: Poseidon, 1991).

48. Putin's third term as president began in 2012. His second term as president was during 2004–2008.

49. On rising Russian disillusionment toward prospects for an integrated Europe, see Fyodor Lukyanov, "May You Live in Interesting Times," *Russia in Global Affairs,* no 2: (April–June, 2015): 5–8; and Sergei Karaganov, "Eurasian Way Out of the European Crisis," *Russia in Global Affairs,* no. 2 (April–June, 2015): 8–21.

50. See Eastern Economic Forum, "Outcomes of the EEF 2018," https://forumvostok.ru/en/outcomes-of-the-eef-2018/.

51. Russia has reportedly been interested in returning to Cam Ranh Bay, although its opposition to "internationalization" of the South China Sea might make it difficult for Moscow to cooperate with Vietnam. See Yevgen Sautin, "This Vietnamese Base Will Decide the South China Sea's Fate," *National Interest,* May 8, 2016, http://nationalinterest.org/feature/vietnamese-base-will-decide-the-south-china-seas-fate-16093?page=2.

52. Xi visited Turkmenistan, Kazakhstan, Uzbekistan, and Kyrgyzstan. He also met with leaders from Mongolia and Iran, while attending the G-20 and SCO Summits. These events all occurred from March 2013 through September 2014. See ibid.

53. For an outline of the "new continentalism," and the political-economic forces driving it, published fifteen months before Xi's announcement of "One Belt, One Road," see Calder, *The New Continentalism.*

54. National Development and Reform Commission (NDRC) of the People's Republic of China, "Vision and Actions on Jointly Building Silk Road Economic Belt and 21st-Century Maritime Silk Road," *NDRC,* March 28, 2015, http://en.ndrc.gov.cn/newsrelease/201503/t20150330_669367.html.

55. See "Alexey Miller: Russia and China Signed the Biggest Contract in the Entire History of Gazprom," *Gazprom,* March 21, 2014, http://www.gazprom.com/press/news/2014/may/article191451.

56. "Gazprom and CNPC Sign Technical Agreement on Gas Supplies via Eastern Route," *Gazprom,* October 13, 2014, http://www.gazprom.com/press/news/2014/october/article203444/.

57. The EAEU was founded on October 10, 2000, and focuses on four policy areas: (1) transportation; (2) energy, especially improving electricity and water supply; (3) workforce migration (protecting migrant rights); and (4) agrarian-sector reform, especially reducing costs and creating market institutions in the countryside.

58. Shannon Tiezzi, "At Russia's Military Parade, Putin and Xi Cement Ties," *The Diplomat,* May 9, 2015. http://thediplomat.com/2015/05/at-russias-military-parade-putin-and-xi-cement-ties/.

59. Paul Sonnet, "China to Design New Russian High-Speed Railway," *Wall Street Journal,* June 19, 2015, https://www.wsj.com/articles/china-to-design-new-russian-high-speed-railway-1434729400.

60. Wade Shepard, "Investors from East and West Eager to Get a Piece of Russian High-Speed Rail Action," *Forbes*, November 16, 2016, https://www.forbes.com/sites/wadeshepard/2016/11/16/investors-from-east-and-west-eager-to-get-a-piece-of-russian-high-speed-rail-action/#e9a3fd749d25.

61. Channel NewsAsia, "Putin Arrives in Beijing for China's V-Day Parade," September 3, 2015, https://web.archive.org/web/20151107205030/http://www.channelnewsasia.com/news/asiapacific/putin-arrives-in-beijing/2096496.html.

62. See Agencies, "'Friends Forever': Xi Talks Up China's Ties with Russia During Putin Trade Trip," *The Guardian*, June 25, 2016, https://www.theguardian.com/world/2016/jun/26/friends-forever-xi-talks-up-chinas-ties-with-russia-during-putin-trade-trip; and AFP, "Ice Cream Gift from Vladimir Putin to Xi Jinping Warms Ties between Russia, China at G20 Summit," *The Straits Times*, September 4, 2016, http://www.straitstimes.com/asia/east-asia/ice-cream-gift-from-putin-to-xi-warms-ties-between-russia-china-at-g20-summit.

63. Israel and Ukraine (before President Viktor Yanukovych was deposed) provided most of the remainder. Ukraine, for example, provided China with its first aircraft carrier, in a 1998 $20–$30 million deal. The carrier was second hand, as production had ceased in Ukraine following the collapse of the Soviet Union. The aircraft carrier was officially supposed to be used for civilian use, but was remodeled to be used by the PLA Navy. See the SIPRI Arms Transfer Database.

64. For a thorough description of Sino-Russian relations in the wake of the Ukraine crisis, see Alexander Gabuev, "A Soft Alliance: Russia-China Relations after the Ukraine Crisis," *European Council on Foreign Relations*, February 10, 2015, http://www.ecfr.eu/publications/summary/a_soft_alliance_russia_china_relations_after_the_ukraine_crisis331; and Gabuev, "Friends with Benefits?"

65. Ethan Meick, "China-Russia Military-to-Military Relations: Moving Toward a Higher Level of Cooperation," *U.S.-China Economic and Security Review Commission Staff Research Report*, March 20, 2017, 14, https://www.uscc.gov/sites/default/files/Research/China-Russia%20Mil-Mil%20Relations%20Moving%20Toward%20Higher%20Level%20of%20Cooperation.pdf.

66. Office of the Secretary of Defense, *Military and Security Developments Involving the People's Republic of China 2015: Annual Report to Congress* (Washington, DC: US Government Printing Office, April 2015), 60. The Defense Department asserts that "resistance (to Russian technology transfer) is waning as Russia looks to China to relieve the effects of Western sanctions."

67. Meick, "China-Russia Military-to-Military Relations," 14.

68. Ibid., 21.

69. See Franz-Stefan Gady, "Russia Completes Delivery of 1st S-400 Missile Defense Regiment to China," *The Diplomat*, May 10, 2018, https://thediplomat.com/2018/05/russia-completes-delivery-of-1st-s-400-missile-defense-regiment-to-china/.

70. The two nations signed a contract in November 2015 that called for twenty-four fighters, at a price of $2 billion, suggesting further Russia's weakened leverage in relation to China. See ibid., 15.

71. Russian Su-35 turbo-fan engine technology, for example, could enable the Chinese J-20 to supercruise, thus putting its performance on a par with the F-22. See ibid.

72. Franz-Stefan Gady, "Russia Confirms Delivery of 10 Su-35 Fighter Jets to China by Year's End," *The Diplomat*, August 29, 2018, https://thediplomat.com/2018/08/russia-confirms-delivery-of-10-su-35-fighter-jets-to-china-by-years-end/; and "Emei: Eluosi yi wancheng xiang zhongfang jiaofu su-35 zhandouji gongzuo 俄媒：俄罗斯已完成向中

方交付苏-35战斗机工作 [Russian media: Russia has completed delivery of Su-35 fighters to China]," www.huanqiu.com, November 27, 2018, http://world.huanqiu.com/article/2018-11/13653522.html.

73. See Wendell Minnick, "Russia-China Su-25 Deal Raises Reverse Engineering Issue," *Defense News*, November 20, 2015, http://www.defensenews.com/story/defense/air-space/strike/2015/11/20/russia-china-su-35-deal-raises-reverse-engineering-issue/76102226/.

74. China was, for example, reportedly able to develop the Chengdu J-20 stealth jet fighter using technology extracted from parts of an American F-117 Nighthawk that was shot down over Serbia in 1999. See Mail Foreign Service, "China Used Downed U.S. Fighter to Develop First Stealth Jet," *Daily Mail*, April 19, 2011, http://www.dailymail.co.uk/news/article-1349906/Chengdu-J-20-China-used-downed-US-fighter-develop-stealth-jet.html.

75. SIPRI Arms Transfer Database.

76. In 2007 the US sold advanced Patriot missile defense systems to Taiwan, immediately after which China refused port access for several US naval vessels. Taiwan's defense budget, however, actually decreased by 25 percent during 2001–2006, in spite of vows by then president Chen Shui-bian (DPP) to increase military spending during his tenure. See Esther Pan and Youkyung Lee, "China-Taiwan Relations," *Washington Post*, January 15, 2008, http://www.washingtonpost.com/wp-dyn/content/article/2008/01/15/AR2008011501347.html.

77. SIPRI Arms Transfer Database.

78. Ibid.

79. India signed a deal with Russia to update its 194 Su-30s for $8 billion. India eventually wants to upgrade all of its fighters, in addition to procuring Russia's fifth generation fighter aircraft. During the 1980–2015 period, Russia still sold more Su fighters to China (347 vs. 290). China, however, has a contract for the advanced Su-35 fighters, which India does not. Further, Russia has sold twelve Kilo submarines to China (1994–2005), and six to Vietnam. See Vivek Raghuvanshi, "India to Upgrade Sukhoi Fleet with Russia's Help," *Defense News*, July 27, 2016, http://www.defensenews.com/story/defense/international/asia-pacific/2016/07/27/india-sukhoi-russia-upgrade-su-30mki-fgfa/87609150/; and Greg Torode, "Vietnam Building Deterrent Against China in Disputed Seas with Marines," *Reuters*, September 7, 2014, http://www.reuters.com/article/us-vietnam-submarines-china-insight-idUSKBN0H20SF20140907.

80. See Meick, "China-Russia Military-to-Military Relations," March, 2017; Andrew Higgins, "China and Russia Hold First Joint Naval Drill in the Baltic Sea," *New York Times*, July 25, 2017, https://www.nytimes.com/2017/07/25/world/europe/china-russia-baltic-navy-exercises.html; and "Russia, China to Hold Joint Naval Drills in Yellow Sea," *TASS*, April 26, 2018, http://tass.com/defense/1001880.

81. Martin Andrew, "Power Politics: China, Russia, and Peace Mission 2005," *China Brief* 5, no. 20, September 27, 2005, https://jamestown.org/program/power-politics-china-russia-and-peace-mission-2005/.

82. Meick, "China-Russia Military-to-Military Relations," Appendix 1. In addition to the 28 bilateral or SCO exercises, China and Russia also had a quadrilateral exercise with Kazakhstan and Tajikistan in 2009 and a trilateral military exercise with Mongolia in 2018.

83. Ibid., 19 and 27.

84. Christopher Harress, "Russia and China Begin Mediterranean Military Exercises with Black Sea Port Visit," *IB Times*, May 5, 2015, http://www.ibtimes.com/russia-china-begin-mediterranean-military-exercises-black-sea-port-visit-1916868.

85. Russia and China began their exercises in the South China Sea on September 12, 2016. These exercises focused on "island seizing," a particularly controversial topic at the time, since they followed the ruling at the Permanent Court of Arbitration in The Hague, declaring China's South China Sea claims null and void. See Sam LaGrone, "China, Russia Kick Off Joint South China Sea Naval Exercise: Includes 'Island Seizing' Drill," *USNI News*, September 12, 2016, https://news.usni.org/2016/09/12/china-russia-start-joint -south-china-sea-naval-exercise-includes-island-seizing-drill.

86. See Dmitry Gorenburg, "5 Things to Know about Russia's Vostok-2018 Military Exercises," *Washington Post*, September 13, 2018, https://www.washingtonpost .com/news/monkey-cage/wp/2018/09/13/5-things-to-know-about-russias-vostok-2018 -military-exercises/?noredirect=on&utm_term=.94931757ee47.

87. Chen Aizhu and Meng Meng, "Russia Beats Saudi Arabia as China's Top Crude Oil Supplier in 2016," *Reuters*, January 23, 2017, http://www.reuters.com/article/us -china-economy-trade-crude-idUSKBN1570VJ; and Daniel Workman, "Top 15 Crude Oil Suppliers to China," *World's Top Exports*, April 1, 2018, http://www.worldstopexports .com/top-15-crude-oil-suppliers-to-china/.

88. The Su-37 is only in the experimental stage, and development has reportedly ceased. See: "Sukoi Su-37 Flanker-E," *Military Today*, http://www.military-today.com/ aircraft/su_37.htm.

CHAPTER 8

1. World Bank, "GDP (Current US$)," *World Development Indicators* (2017), accessed June 26, 2018.

2. J. Thorley, "The Development of Trade between the Roman Empire and the East under Augustus," *Greece and Rome* 16, no. 2 (October 1969): 209–23, http://www.jstor .org/stable/642851.

3. Marco Polo and Ronald Latham, *The Travels of Marco Polo* (London: Penguin, 1958).

4. On Ricci's views of China, see Jonathan D. Spence, *The Memory Palace of Matteo Ricci* (New York: Viking Penguin, 1984).

5. Jonathan D. Spence, *The Search for Modern China* (New York: Norton, 1990), 132.

6. Ibid., 132–33.

7. See Derk Bodde, "Chinese Ideas in the West," *Columbia University*, http://projects .mcah.columbia.edu/nanxuntu/html/state/ideas.pdf.

8. In France, the earliest civil service system was established in 1791, shortly after outbreak of the French Revolution. For more details on China's influence upon the European civil service, see Ssu-yu Teng, "Chinese Influence on the Western Examination System," *Harvard Journal of Asiatic Studies* 7, no. 4 (September 1943): 267–312, http://www.jstor .org/stable/2717830.

9. Spence, *Search for Modern China*, 133.

10. Ibid., 134.

11. Michael Yahuda, "The Sino-European Encounter: Historical Influences on Contemporary Relations," in *China-Europe Relations: Perceptions, Policies and Prospects*, ed. David Shambaugh, Eberhard Sandschneider, and Zhou Hong (New York: Routledge, 2008), 13–32.

12. Spence, *Search for Modern China*, 134.

13. EU investment in China, as measured in stock, expanded from $37.87 billion in 2003 to $79.93 billion in 2012, and to $154.43 billion in 2017. Meanwhile, Chinese investment in the EU grew exponentially, from $422 million in 2003 to $31.55 billion in 2012,

and to $153.96 in 2017. For FDI statistics for 2003–2012, see United Nations Conference on Trade and Development, *Bilateral FDI Statistics,* 2014 edition; for FDI statistics thereafter, see Thilo Hanemann and Mikko Huotari, "EU-China FDI: Working Towards Reciprocity in Investment Relations," *Mercator Institute for China Studies,* April 17, 2018, https://www.merics.org/en/papers-on-china/reciprocity.

14. Jamil Anderlini, "UK Move to Join China-Led Bank a Surprise Even to Beijing," *Financial Times,* March 26, 2015, https://www.ft.com/content/d33fed8a-d3a1-11e4-a9d3-00144feab7de.

15. Embassy of the People's Republic of China in the United Kingdom of the Great Britain and Northern Ireland, "Backgrounder: Sino-British Relations," October 10, 2003, http://www.chinese-embassy.org.uk/eng/wjzc/zygx/t27071.htm.

16. See "Table 4 Diplomatic Relations, 1949–87" in *China: A Country Study,* 4th ed., ed. Robert L. Worden, Andrea Matles Savada, and Ronald E. Dolan (Washington, DC: Library of Congress, 1988), 630–31.

17. André Malraux, *Man's Fate (La Condition Humaine),* trans. Haakon M. Chevalier (New York: Random House, 1968).

18. See European Union External Action, "EU-China Dialogue Architecture," updated November 2015.

19. Anthony Williams, "China Becomes EBRD Member as Suma Chakrabarti Visits Beijing," European Bank for Reconstruction and Development, January 15, 2016, http://www.ebrd.com/news/2016/china-becomes-ebrd-member-as-suma-chakrabarti-visits-beijing.html.

20. The Six include the original signatories to the Treaty of Rome in 1957: France, the Federal Republic of Germany, the Netherlands, Belgium, Luxembourg, and Italy.

21. The additional three Cold War entrants were Britain, Ireland, and Denmark, who all joined in 1973.

22. Greece joined the European Union in 1981, followed by Spain and Portugal in 1986.

23. The Czech Republic, Hungary, Poland, Slovakia, Slovenia, Estonia, Latvia, and Lithuania entered the EU in 2004. Bulgaria and Romania entered in 2007, and Croatia joined in 2013.

24. Serbia and Bulgaria, in particular, have historically maintained more positive relations with Russia, but they have been the exception in Eastern Europe rather than the rule.

25. The eleven original members were Austria, Belgium, Finland, France, Germany, Ireland, Italy, Luxembourg, the Netherlands, Portugal, and Spain. Later entrants included Greece (2001), Slovenia (2007), Cyprus and Malta (2008), Slovakia (2009), Estonia (2011), Latvia (2014), and Lithuania (2015). See Cynthia Kroet, "A Timeline of the Eurozone's Growth," *Politico,* January 30, 2015, http://www.politico.eu/article/a-timeline-of-the-eurozones-growth/.

26. In 2017, for example, Greece prevented the European Union from formally criticizing China's human-rights record at a United Nations Forum; Greece and Hungary similarly prevented the EU from supporting a court ruling against China's expansive territorial claims in the South China Sea. See "China's designs on Europe," *The Economist,* October 4, 2018, https://www.economist.com/leaders/2018/10/04/china-has-designs-on-europe-here-is-how-europe-should-respond.

27. Thilo Hanemann and Mikko Huotari, "EU-China FDI: Working Towards Reciprocity in Investment Relations," *MERICS Papers on China,* no. 3 (May 2018), Figure 4, accessed online October 19, 2018, https://www.merics.org/en/papers-on-china/reciprocity.

28. "Gaining wisdom, marching forward," *The Economist*, October 4, 2018, https://www.economist.com/briefing/2018/10/04/chinese-investment-and-influence-in-europe-is-growing.

29. See International Monetary Fund, *Direction of Trade Statistics*.

30. Chinese investment in Greece, Spain, and Italy, for example, was rising during 2009–2015, even as overall inbound FDI to those countries was falling. In Portugal, overall FDI during this period was rising, together with Chinese inbound FDI also. On a sectoral basis, Chinese FDI into the Mediterranean region was concentrated in port infrastructure, energy, telecommunications, and finance.

31. "Ukraine Crisis: Timeline," *BBC*, November 13, 2014, http://www.bbc.com/news/world-middle-east-26248275.

32. "Speech by Mikhail Gorbachev to the Council of Europe in Strasbourg, 'Europe as a Common Home,' July 6, 1989," Wilson Center Digital Archive, http://digitalarchive.wilsoncenter.org/document/134162.pdf?v=d7297bf2c85bb3e59f62a01a47a90fca.

33. On the evolution of the GCEMC and its broader global implications, see Jacopo Maria Pepe, *Continental Drift: Germany and China's Inroad in the German Central European Manufacturing Core— Geopolitical Changes and Risks* (Washington, DC: Reischauer Center for East Asian Studies, 2017).

34. See World Bank, "Industrial Production, Constant US$, Sea. Adj.," *Global Economic Monitor*, https://data.world/worldbank/global-economic-monitor, accessed online June 5, 2017.

35. On the implications of "Made in China 2025" for the GCEMC, see Jost Wubbeke, Mirjam Meissner, Max J. Zenglein, Jaqueline Ives, and Bjorn Conrad, "Made in China 2025: The Making of a High-Tech Superpower and Consequences for Industrial Countries," Mercator Institute for China Studies, December 2016, https://www.merics.org/sites/default/files/2017-09/MPOC_No.2_MadeinChina2025.pdf.

36. Henk Bekker, "2017 (Full Year) China and Worldwide German Car Sales," *Car Sales Statistics*, January 16, 2018, https://www.best-selling-cars.com/china/2017-full-year-china-worldwide-german-luxury-car-sales/.

37. Jakub Jakóbowski, Konrad Popławski, and Marcin Kaczmarski, *The Silk Railroad: The EU-China Rail Connections: Background, Actors, Interests* (Warsaw: Centre for Eastern Studies, 2018), 95.

38. See Pepe, *Continental Drift*, 28.

39. IMF, *Direction of Trade Statistics*, http://data.imf.org/?sk=9D6028D4-F14A-464C-A2F2-59B2CD424B85.

40. Rene Wagner and Michael Nienaber, "China Steams Past U.S., France to be Germany's Biggest Trading Partner," *Reuters*, February 24, 2017, https://www.reuters.com/article/us-germany-economy-trade-idUSKBN1622SO.

41. Author's calculation based on AEI/Heritage Foundation, *China Global Investment Tracker*, http://www.aei.org/china-global-investment-tracker/, updated January 2018.

42. See Bloomberg News, "China's Geely Buys $9 Billion Daimler Stake," *Bloomberg*, Februar 24, 2018, https://www.bloomberg.com/news/articles/2018-02-23/china-s-geely-is-said-to-be-buying-9-billion-stake-in-daimler.

43. BMW is sourcing raw materials for the cells itself, to pass on to CATL, under long-term contracts. On this arrangement, see Irene Preisinger and Victoria Bryan, "China's CATL to build its first European battery factory in Germany," *Reuters*, July 9, 2018, https://www.reuters.com/article/us-bmw-catl-batteries/chinas-catl-to-build-its-first-european-ev-battery-factory-in-germany-idUSKBN1JZ11Y.

44. CNOOC bought 100 percent of Awilco Offshore of Norway for $2.5 billion in 2008. Geely Auto bought 100 percent of Sweden's Volvo for $2.7 billion in 2010. Fosun bought 80 percent of Caixa Seguros, Portugal's largest insurer, in 2014 for $1.4 billion. It also bought 100 percent of Club Med in 2015 for $1.1 billion. See ibid.

45. Nineteen percent of Chinese investment in Europe during 2005–2017 went to energy, followed by 17 percent in transport, 9 percent in real estate, and 6 percent in logistics. See ibid.

46. In a January 8, 1973, agreement between the US and Greek navies, the Greek government granted homeporting facilities to serve around nine thousand US military personnel and dependents assigned to escort ships, and ultimately a carrier. US defense secretary James Schlesinger postponed the second stage of homeporting involving the carrier deployment while accelerating a parallel project in Japan. The carrier homeporting initiative in Greece was never revived, although a US Navy carrier has remained deployed in Japan to this day. See Stephen G. Xydis, "Coups and Countercoups in Greece, 1967–1973 (with postscript)," *Political Science Quarterly* 89, no. 3 (Autumn 1974): 507–38, http://www.jstor.org/stable/2148452; and U.S. Department of State, *Foreign Relations of the United States Vol. XXX, Greece, Cyprus, Turkey, 1973–1976* (Washington, DC: United States Government Printing Office, 2007).

47. COSCO now has a 67 percent stake in Piraeus, as a result of a deal signed in July 2016. COSCO initially acquired a 51 percent stake, for €280.5 million, and will take over the remaining 16 percent for €88 million in 2021, on the condition that it spends €350 million on expanding and modernizing the port. The overall value of the deal is close to €1.5 billion, including the mandatory investments and concession payments. See "Greece, China Cosco Finally Seal Piraeus Port Sale," *Journal of Commerce*, July 5, 2016, http://www.joc.com/port-news/european-ports/port-piraeus/greece-cosco-china-finally-seal-piraeus-port-sale_20160705.html.

48. Newsroom, "Piraeus' Port Ranks 7th in Europe," *The Greek Observer*, May 31, 2018, http://thegreekobserver.com/greece/article/43983/piraeus-port-ranks-7th-in-europe/.

49. Altay Atli, "China in the Balkans: Serbia Wants Business but Its Future Lies in Europe," *Asia Times*, June 28, 2016, http://www.atimes.com/article/serbia-wants-to-do-business-with-china-but-its-future-lies-in-europe/; and Altay Atli, "China in the Balkans: Macedonia, Albania Seek Beijing's Funds for Projects," *Asia Times*, July 11, 2016, http://www.atimes.com/article/china-in-the-balkans-macedonia-albania-seek-beijings-help-in-building-infrastructure/.

50. Jakóbowski, Popławski, and Kaczmarski, *The Silk Railroad*, 68–73.

51. Philippe Le Corre, "Europe's Mixed Views on China's One Belt, One Road Initiative," *Order from Chaos* (blog), May 23, 2017, https://www.brookings.edu/blog/order-from-chaos/2017/05/23/europes-mixed-views-on-chinas-one-belt-one-road-initiative/.

52. Jost Wubbeke, Mirjam Meissner, Max. K. Zenglein, Jaqueline Ives, and Bjorn Conrad, "Made in China 2025: The Making of High-Tech Superpower and Consequences for Industrial Countries," *Mercator Institute for China Studies Papers on China No. 2* (December 2016).

53. Bloomberg News, "Merkel Tells China It Risks European Backlash over Investments," *Bloomberg*, May 24, 2018, https://www.bloomberg.com/news/articles/2018-05-24/merkel-china-s-li-pledge-to-defend-global-order-tested-by-trump.

54. Oleg Livitin, Jakov Milatovic, and Peter Sanfey, "China and South-Eastern Europe: Infrastructure, Trade, and Investment Links," European Bank for Reconstruction and Development EBRD Paper (July 2016), 4–5, cited in Pepe, *Continental Drift*, 34.

55. See Zhu Sheng, "Ever Expanding Chinese Rail Network Boosts German 'China City,'" *Xinhua*, November 11, 2017, http://www.xinhuanet.com/english/2017-11/27/c _136783113.htm.

56. See Tim Maughan, "Yiwu: The Chinese City Where Christmas Is Made and Sold," *BBC*, December 18, 2014, http://www.bbc.com/future/story/20141218-the -hidden-home-of-christmas.

57. See Harriet Alexander, "World's Longest Train Journey Ends in Madrid," *The Telegraph*, December 10, 2014, http://www.telegraph.co.uk/news/worldnews/europe/spain/ 11284911/Worlds-longest-train-journey-ends-in-Madrid.html.

58. See Greg Knowler, "Huge Subsidies Keep China-Europe Rail Network on Track," *Journal of Commerce*, May 23, 2018, https://www.joc.com/rail-intermodal/huge-subsidies -keep-china-europe-rail-network-track_20180523.html.

59. Chu Daye, "Blueprint for Continental Cargo Train to Open Markets in Eurasia," *Global Times*, October 18, 2016, http://www.globaltimes.cn/content/1012168.shtml; and Li Guo, "2017 China Railway Express Report: 3,271 Trips Covering 35 Cities and a Future Turn Towards 'High Quality,'" *21st Century Economic Herald*, January 8, 2018.

60. See "First China to UK Rail Freight Service Arrives in London," *Railway Gazette*, January 18, 2017, http://www.railwaygazette.com/news/single-view/view/first-china-to -uk-rail-freight-service-arrives-in-london.html; and "First Freight Train Linking UK with China Arrives in Yiwu," *Deutsche Welle*, April 29, 2017, http://www.dw.com/en/first -freight-train-linking-uk-with-china-arrives-in-yiwu/a-38635908.

61. Navoi, a joint venture between KAL and Uzbekistan Airways, handles even perishables, animals, and dangerous goods. For more details on the terminal, see Uzbekistan Airways, "Cargo Terminal," *Navoi International Airport*, http://www.navoi-airport.com/ en/content/cargo_service/cargo_terminal/.

62. Nicholas Winning, "U.K., China Give Clearance for More Passenger, Cargo Flights," *Wall Street Journal*, October 11, 2016, https://www.wsj.com/articles/u-k-china -give-clearance-for-more-passenger-cargo-flights-1476208837.

63. In 2000 China accounted for 5.7 percent of global industrial production. By 2016 that ratio had risen to 24.8 percent. World Bank, "Industrial Production, Constant US$, Sea. Adj.," *Global Economic Monitor*, https://data.world/worldbank/global-economic- monitor, accessed online June 5, 2017.

64. Sailing time from China's east coast ports to Hamburg is around 30 days, so rail freight offers time savings of 14 to 18 days. See John Kemp, "China Develops Continent-Spanning Railroad to Europe," *Reuters*, April 8, 2016, https://www.reuters.com/article/ us-china-railway-kemp/china-develops-continent-spanning-railroad-to-europe-kemp -idUSKCN0X41U7.

65. See Andrew Higgins, "China's Ambitious New 'Port': Landlocked Kazakhstan," *New York Times*, January 1, 2018, https://www.nytimes.com/2018/01/01/world/asia/china -kazakhstan-silk-road.html.

66. Eurasian Economic Commission, "Eurasian Economic Integration: Facts and Figures," 1H 2016, http://www.eurasiancommission.org/en/Documents/Forms/AllItems .aspx.

67. In October, 2018, for example, BMW announced plans to assume 75 percent majority control of its automobile manufacturing joint venture in Shenyang, northeastern China, currently employing over 16,000 people. See Trevor Moss, "BMW to Take Control of China Joint Venture in $4 Billion Deal," *Wall Street Journal*, October 12, 2018,

https://www.wsj.com/articles/bmw-to-take-control-of-china-joint-venture-in-4-1-billion-deal-1539233722.

68. See "China-Europe Rail Has Air Cargo in the Crosshairs," *Journal of Commerce*, July 28, 2015, http://www.joc.com/rail-intermodal/international-rail/china-europe-rail-has-air-cargo-crosshairs_20150728.html.

69. See "S. Korea, Norway to Bolster Cooperation in Ships, Arctic Region Use," *Yonhap News Agency*, April 15, 2016, http://english.yonhapnews.co.kr/business/2016/04/15/0503000000AEN20160415005400315.html.

70. See "Northern Sea Route Handles Record 9.7 Mn Tons," *World Maritime News*, January 23, 2018, https://worldmaritimenews.com/archives/241571/northern-sea-route-handles-record-9-7-mn-tons/.

CHAPTER 9

1. Joyce Yanyun Man, "China's Property Tax Reform: Progress and Challenges," *Lincoln Institute of Land Policy*, April 2012, http://www.lincolninst.edu/publications/articles/chinas-property-tax-reform.

2. This debt is unsettling, but down from 41 percent of GDP in 2015. See Gabriel Wildau, "China Local Governments Revive Off-Budget Stimuls," *Financial Times*, September 21, 2016, https://www.ft.com/content/b303f280-7f14-11e6-8e50-8ec15fb462f4. Local governments also reportedly use various tactics to accumulate hidden liabilities, however. See Sidney Leng, "Chinese Local Governments' US$2.4 Billion of Concealed Debt Is Uncovered by Audit Office," *South China Morning Post*, April 21, 2018, http://www.scmp.com/news/china/economy/article/2142692/chinese-local-governments-us24-billion-concealed-debts-revealed.

3. Brian Spegele, Peter Wonacott, and Nicholas Bariyo, "China's Workers Are Targeted as Its Overseas Reach Grows," *Wall Street Journal*, February 1, 2012, https://www.wsj.com/articles/SB10001424052970204652904577194171294491572.

4. In 2017 Asia and Europe together were home to over 5.2 billion people, or 69.1 percent of the global total, of which 4.16 billion were living in Asia. See World Bank, "Population, Total," *World Development Indicators*, accessed October 10, 2018, https://data.worldbank.org/products/wdi.

5. The youth unemployment problem appears to be more serious in Eastern and Southern Europe than in Southeast Asia, with youth unemployment in 2017 reaching almost 47 percent in Northern Macedonia, 43 percent in Greece, 39 percent in Spain, 37 percent in Italy, and 33 percent in Serbia. See World Bank, "Unemployment, Youth Total (% of Total Labor Force Ages 15–24) (Modeled ILO Estimate)," *World Development Indicators*, https://data.worldbank.org/products/wdi, accessed June 27, 2018.

6. World Bank, "Unemployment, Total (% of Total Labor Force) (Modeled ILO Estimate)" and "Unemployment, Youth Total (% of Total Labor Force Ages 15–24) (Modeled ILO Estimate)," *World Development Indicators*, https://data.worldbank.org/products/wdi, accessed June 27, 2018.

7. Ibid.

8. World Bank, "Unemployment, Youth Total (% of Total Labor Force Ages 15–24) (Modeled ILO Estimate)," *World Development Indicators*, https://data.worldbank.org/products/wdi, accessed June 27, 2018.

9. Indonesia's median age, for example, is only 30.2, while India's is 27.9 and that of the Philippines is 23.5. See Central Intelligence Agency, "Median Age," *World Factbook*,

2017 estimates, https://www.cia.gov/library/publications/the-world-factbook/fields/2177.html.

10. Russia's population increased by 1.6 million during 2008–2016, but remains much lower than in 1992. See World Bank, "Population, Total," "Life Expectancy at Birth, Female (Years)," and "Life Expectancy at Birth, Male (Years)," *World Development Indicators*, https://data.worldbank.org/products/wdi, accessed June 28, 2018. On Russia's post–Cold War demographic crisis more generally, see Nicholas Eberstadt, "The Dying Bear: Russia's Demographic Disaster," *Foreign Affairs*, November/December 2011, accessed online on April 17, 2017, https://www.foreignaffairs.com/articles/russia-fsu/2011-11-01/dying-bear.

11. As of September 2018, there were 69,785 centenarians in Japan, according to the Ministry of Internal Affairs and Communications. 88 percent of this number were women. See Justin McCurry, "Japanese Centenarian Population Edges toward 70,000," *The Guardian*, September 14, 2018, https://www.theguardian.com/world/2018/sep/14/japanese-centenarian-population-edges-towards-70000.

12. See World Bank, "Population, Total," *World Development Indicators*, https://data.worldbank.org/products/wdi, accessed June 28, 2018.

13. World Bank, "Population Ages 65 and Above (Percent of Total)," *World Development Indicators* (2017), https://data.worldbank.org/products/wdi.

14. See World Bank, "Fertility Rate, Total (Births per Woman)," *World Development Indicators* (2016), https://data.worldbank.org/products/wdi.

15. The one-child policy, peppered with numerous exceptions, has now been fully abandoned and replaced by a two-child policy.

16. United States Census Bureau, "Demographic Overview—Custom Region—China," *International Data Base*, https://www.census.gov/data-tools/demo/idb/region.php?N=%20Results%20&T=13&A=separate&RT=0&Y=2018&R=-1&C=CH, accessed April 17, 2017; Wan He, Daniel Goodkind, and Paul Kowal, "An Aging World: 2015: International Population Reports," U.S. Census Bureau, March 2016, Table B-3, https://www.census.gov/content/dam/Census/library/publications/2016/demo/p95-16-1.pdf.

17. Rob Preston, "Why Demographic Trends Spell Trouble for China and Russia—and Prosperity for US," *Forbes*, November 3, 2015, https://www.forbes.com/sites/oracle/2015/11/03/why-demographic-trends-spell-trouble-for-china-and-russia-and-prosperity-for-us/#5b05ae60cfcc; and Andrea den Boer and Valerie M. Hudson, "The Security Risks of China's Abnormal Demographics," *Washington Post*, April 30, 2014, https://www.washingtonpost.com/news/monkey-cage/wp/2014/04/30/the-security-risks-of-chinas-abnormal-demographics/?utm_term=.a06213f0477c.

18. China had 755.8 million people living on less than $1.90 a day (2011 PPP) in 1990. By 2013, that number has fallen to 25.2 million. See World Bank, "Number of People Living on Less Than $1.90 a day (2011 PPP)," *Poverty & Equity Data*, accessed on May 2, 2017, http://povertydata.worldbank.org/poverty/country/CHN.

19. In 1990, for example, the average income of Americans was more than 75 times that of Chinese. By 2017, however, that multiple had narrowed to less than 7 times. See World Bank, "GDP Per Capita (Current US$)," *World Development Indicators*, accessed October 10, 2018, https://data.worldbank.org/products/wdi.

20. Sonali Jain-Chandra, "Chart of the Week: Inequality in China," *IMFBlog*, September 20, 2018, https://blogs.imf.org/2018/09/20/chart-of-the-week-inequality-in-china/.

21. Gini coefficients of income inequality have risen in all regions of the world except Latin America, sub-Saharan Africa, and the Middle East/North Africa, although

Notes to Chapter 9

they were already high in those areas. The coefficient has risen most sharply in China. See ibid.

22. Thomas Piketty, *Capital in the Twenty-First Century*, trans. Arthur Goldhammer (Cambridge, MA: Belknap Press of Harvard University Press, 2014).

23. Fareed Zakaria, "Populism on the March: Why the West Is in Trouble," *Foreign Affairs*, November/December 2016 issue, accessed online May 2, 2017, https://www.foreignaffairs.com/articles/united-states/2016-10-17/populism-march.

24. Ibid.

25. According to the United Nations, an international migrant is "a person who is living in a country other than his or her country of birth." See United Nations Department of Economic and Social Affairs, *International Migration Report 2017: Highlights* (New York: United Nations, 2017).

26. Joseph S. Nye Jr., "The Future of American Power: Dominance and Decline in Perspective," *Foreign Affairs* 89, no. 6 (November/December 2010): 2–12.

27. Amitav Acharya, *The End of American World Order* (Malden, MA: Polity, 2014), 1–12.

28. Ethnic conflict has, for example, already complicated and delayed the China-Pakistan Economic Corridor, the China-Myanmar Economic Corridor, and the Bangladesh-China-India-Myanmar (BCIM) Economic Corridor projects proposed under BRI. See Usman Shahid, "Balochistan: The Troubled Heart of the CPEC," *The Diplomat*, August 23, 2016, https://thediplomat.com/2016/08/balochistan-the-troubled-heart-of-the-cpec/; and Xing Yun, "Secure Borderlands Needed Before Launch of BCIM Corridor Project," *Myanmar Business Today*, February 18, 2014, https://www.mmbiztoday.com/articles/secure-borderlands-needed-launch-bcim-corridor-project.

29. "'780 Languages Spoken in India, 250 Died Out in Last 50 Years,'" *Hindustan Times*, July 17, 2013, http://www.hindustantimes.com/books/780-languages-spoken-in-india-250-died-out-in-last-50-years/story-Y3by800YbXRA77xP2AEWKN.html.

30. See First Post, "India Has 79.8% Hindus, 14.2% Muslims, Says 2011 Census Data on Religion," *First Post India*, August 26, 2015, http://www.firstpost.com/india/india-has-79-8-percent-hindus-14-2-percent-msulims-2011-census-data-on-religion-2407708.html.

31. See Vali Nasr, *The Shia Revival: How Conflicts within Islam Will Shape the Future* (New York: W. W. Norton, 2006), 185–210, 234–36; and "Mapping the Global Muslim Population," Pew Research Center, http://www.pewforum.org/2009/10/07/mapping-the-global-muslim-population.

32. "Sunnis and Shia: Islam's Ancient Schism," *BBC*, January 4, 2016, https://www.bbc.com/news/world-middle-east-16047709.

33. Ibid.

34. On the Iranian Revolution and its broader implications for political-economic development across Eurasia, also see Kent E. Calder, *The New Continentalism: Energy and Twenty-First Century Eurasian Geopolitics* (New Haven, CT: Yale University Press, 2012), 80–89.

35. The SDF did indeed retake Raqqa, but other groups, including the Iraqi Army, the Iranian Revolutionary Guards, and even at times the Syrian Army also fought IS.

36. See Igor Rotar, "Hizb ut-Tahrir in Central Asia Publication," *Terrorism Monitor* 4, no. 2 (2005), http://www.jamestown.org/single/?tx_ttnews%5Btt_news%5D=419#.V9mSqEOrJpg.

37. These groups include Lashkar-e-Taiba (Pakistan based, with some cells in India), Hizb-ul-Mujahideen (mostly in isolated pockets in the mountains), Harkat-ul-Mujahideen (local seminaries in Pakistan), and the Jammu and Kashmir Liberation Front (nationalist secular group largely destroyed by 1990, with many of its factions now renouncing militancy).

38. Charles Haviland, "The Darker Side of Buddhism," *BBC*, May 30, 2015, http://www.bbc.com/news/magazine-32929855.

39. Ibid.

40. On the history of the Rohingya conflict, see Kent E. Calder, *The Bay of Bengal and Its Strategic Transformation* (Tokyo: Sasakawa Peace Foundation, 2018), 46–47.

41. Kiyya Baloch, "Chinese Operations in Balochistan Again Targeted by Militants," *The Diplomat*, March 27, 2015, http://thediplomat.com/2015/03/chinese-operations-in-balochistan-again-targeted-by-militants/.

42. Uyghur Human Rights Project, "Spatial Results of the 2010 Census in Xinjiang," March 7, 2016, http://uhrp.org/featured-articles/spatial-results-2010-census-xinjiang.

43. The third nation, Tajikistan, considers itself Persian rather than Turkic.

44. Austin Ramzy, "A Year After Xinjiang Riots, Ethnic Tensions Remain," *Time*, July 5, 2010, http://content.time.com/time/world/article/0,8599,2001311,00.html.

45. "Timeline: Xinjiang Unrest," *BBC*, July 20, 2009, http://news.bbc.co.uk/2/hi/asia-pacific/8138866.stm.

46. Although attacks beyond Xinjiang thereafter subsided, under the pressure of intensified counterterrorist measures, incidents closer to the Uyghur ancestral homeland continued. For example: April 2014: Bombing and knife attack at Urumqi Railway Station immediately following a visit to Xinjiang by Xi Jinping; May 2014: 43 killed in a suicide attack at an Urumqi street market; October 2014: 22 killed in a knife and bombing attack at a farmer's market; September 2015: Over 50 workers killed at a coal mine.

47. Michael Schwirtz, "Ethnic Rioting Ravages Kyrgyzstan," *New York Times*, June 13, 2010, http://www.nytimes.com/2010/06/14/world/asia/14kyrgyz.html. While Uzbeks only make up 15 percent of Kyrgyzstan's population overall, they are the majority in the Kyrgyz portion of the Fergana Valley.

48. The Kyrgyz government appears to believe that the act was ordered by the Nusra Front, a militant terrorist group active in Syria with some Uyghur members. The actual attack was coordinated by a Kyrgyz expatriate living in Turkey. See Ivan Nechepurenko, "Suicide Bomber Attacks Chinese Embassy in Kyrgyzstan," *New York Times*, August 30, 2016, https://www.nytimes.com/2016/08/31/world/asia/bishkek-china-embassy-kyrgyzstan.html.

49. Kurt M. Campbell, Robert J. Einhorn, and Mitchell B. Reiss, *The Nuclear Tipping Point: Why States Reconsider Their Nuclear Choices* (Washington, DC: Brookings Institution Press, 2004).

50. See, for example, William J. Broad and David E. Sanger, "North Korea's Missile Success Is Linked to Ukrainian Plant, Investigators Say," *New York Times*, August 14, 2017, https://www.nytimes.com/2017/08/14/world/asia/north-korea-missiles-ukraine-factory.html.

51. Moon Jae-in and Kim Jong-un met at the DMZ in April 2018 and May 2018, as well as in Pyongyang in September 2018.

52. Ten tons of this plutonium is reportedly held domestically within Japan, and another thirty-seven tons held overseas, mainly at French and British reprocessing facilities.

See Robin Harding, "Japan Plutonium Stockpile Fuels US Unease," *Financial Times*, June 25, 2018, https://www.ft.com/content/9d245eca-7781-11e8-bc55-50dafi1b720d.

53. See World Food Programme, "Where We Work: Tajikistan," http://www1.wfp .org/countries/tajikistan, accessed online May 2, 2017.

54. David Trilling, "Water Wars in Central Asia," *Foreign Affairs*, August 24, 2016, https://www.foreignaffairs.com/gallerys/2016-08-24/water-wars-central-asia.

55. See IEA, *World Energy Outlook Special Report: Energy and Climate Change* (Paris: OECD Publishing, 2015), 51–52. It should be noted, however, that the IEA focuses on forecasting consumption and production, with import-export balances only a secondary analytical issue.

56. IEA, *World Energy Outlook 2016* (Paris: OECD Publishing, 2016), 143. China's oil imports reached 8.4 million bbl/day in 2017.

57. IEA, *World Energy Outlook 2015: Executive Summary* (Paris: OECD Publishing, 2015), 2.

58. IEA, *World Energy Outlook 2016*, 143.

59. In 2017, 60.3 percent of primary energy consumed in China was coal generated, compared to 53.8 percent in India. See BP, "Primary Energy: Consumption by Fuel," *Statistical Review of World Energy*, June 2018.

60. BP, "Carbon Dioxide Emissions," *Statistical Review of World Energy*, June 2018.

61. See World Health Organization (WHO), *WHO Global Urban Ambient Air Pollution Database (update 2018)*, http://www.who.int/airpollution/data/cities/en/. Twelve Chinese cities, however, ranked between 21 and 40 on the most-polluted list. On the list, India's Kanpur ranked first place, Patna the fifth, and Delhi the sixth in 2018.

62. Deaths attributed to PM 2.5 pollution in India increased by 14 percent during 2010–2015, to almost exactly China's level, although the Indian population is somewhat smaller than that of China. See Health Effects Institute and Institute for Health Metrics and Evaluation, *State of Global Air 2017*, https://www.stateofglobalair.org/data, accessed May 1, 2017.

63. According to a recent study by the Center for Global Development, 23 of the 69 countries identified as potential BRI borrowers were found to already be at a "quite high" level of debt distress. All of those listed here are identified as having problems servicing debt. See John Hurley, Scott Morris, and Gailyn Portelance, "Examining the Debt Implications of the Belt and Road Initiative from a Policy Perspective," *CGD Policy Paper 121*, March 2018, 16–19, https://www.cgdev.org/publication/examining-debt-implications -belt-and-road-initiative-a-policy-perspective.

64. For a pessimistic view of these great power relationships, see Bill Emmott, *Rivals: How the Power Struggle between China, India, and Japan Will Shape Our Next Decade* (Orlando, FL: Harcourt, 2008).

65. See, for example, Gaku Shimada, "Japan and China Take First Step toward Joint Infrastructure Abroad," *Nikkei Asia Review*, September 4, 2018, https://asia.nikkei .com/Politics/International-Relations/Japan-and-China-take-first-step-toward-joint -infrastructure-abroad.

66. Trade, now over $70 billion, also has great long-term potential, as does foreign investment. Chinese president Xi Jinping has promised that China will invest $20 billion in India. China has also wanted to incorporate India into BRI, but India has yet to endorse the program. See IMF, *Direction of Trade Statistics*, 2015, http://data.imf.org/ ?sk=9D6028D4-F14A-464C-A2F2-59B2CD424B85; and Sana Hashmi, "Building the

Basis for India-China Cooperation," *East Asia Forum*, November 25, 2015, http://www
.eastasiaforum.org/2015/11/25/building-the-basis-for-india-china-cooperation/. For
bilateral trade and investment figures, see Ram Kumar Jha and Saurabh Kumar, "The
Case for Stronger India-China Economic Relations," *The Diplomat*, May 21, 2015, http://
thediplomat.com/2015/05/the-case-for-stronger-india-china-economic-relations/.

67. Over 60 percent of all international migrants live in either Asia (80 million) or Europe (78 million). North America hosts the third largest number, with the United States
(50 million) hosting the largest number for any one country. Although slightly more migrants live in Asia than Europe, the concentration is much higher in Europe since Asia's
population is so much larger. See UN Department of Economic and Social Affairs, *International Migration Report 2017: Highlights*, https://www.un.org/development/desa/
publications/international-migration-report-2017.html,

68. Turkey in 2016 hosted 3.1 million refugees and asylum seekers, followed by Jordan
(2.9 million), the State of Palestine (2.2 million), Lebanon (1.6 million), and Pakistan (1.4
million). See ibid.

69. See Julia Gillard, "Why the Syrian Refugee Crisis Is Just the Tip of the Iceberg,"
World Economic Forum, March 18, 2016, https://www.weforum.org/agenda/2016/03/why
-the-syrian-refugee-crisis-is-just-the-tip-of-the-iceberg.

70. Cas Mudde, "Europe's Populist Surge: A Long Time in the Making," *Foreign Affairs*, November/December 2016, https://www.foreignaffairs.com/articles/europe/2016
-10-17/europe-s-populist-surge, accessed online May 2, 2017.

71. See Steven Erlanger, "In Eastern Europe, Populism Lives, Widening a Split in the
E.U.," *New York Times*, November 28, 2017, https://www.nytimes.com/2017/11/28/
world/europe/populism-eastern-europe.html.

72. See John B. Judis, *The Populist Explosion: How the Great Recession Transformed American and European Politics* (New York: Columbia Global Reports, 2016), 89–153.

73. See John Burn-Murdoch, Billy Enrenberg-Shannon, Aleksandra Wisniewska,
and Aendrew Rininskand, "French Election Results: Macron's Victory in Charts," *Financial Times*, May 8, 2017, https://www.ft.com/content/62d782d6-31a7-11e7-9555
-23ef563ecf9a.

74. Jean-Marie Le Pen won only 17.7 percent of the vote, compared to Jacques Chi-
rac's 82.2 percent, in the second round of the 2002 French presidential election. See
Tracy McNicoll, "French Election History: Jean-Marie Le Pen's 'Thunderclap' Shocker
15 Years On," *France 24*, April 21, 2017, http://www.france24.com/en/20170420-france
-presidential-history-looking-back-jean-marie-le-pen-thunderclap-election-shocker.

75. See Kate Connolly, "German Election: Merkel Wins Fourth Term but Far-Right
AfD Surges to Third," *The Guardian*, September 24, 2017, https://www.theguardian.com/
world/2017/sep/24/angela-merkel-fourth-term-far-right-afd-third-german-election. The
National Democratic Party entered seven West German state parliaments during 1966–68.

76. In July 2016, COSCO acquired a 51 percent stake in Piraeus port for €280.5 million, with a commitment to take over the remaining 16 percent for €88 million after five
years, on the condition that it spend €350 million on expanding and modernizing the port.
The overall value of the deal is around €1.5 billion, including mandatory investments and
concession payments. See "Greece, China Cosco Finally Seal Piraeus Port Sale," *Journal
of Commerce*, July 5, 2016, http://www.joc.com/port-news/european-ports/port-piraeus/
greece-cosco-china-finally-seal-piraeus-port-sale_20160705.html.

77. US Department of Labor, Bureau of Labor Statistics, "Union Members Summary,"
Economic News Release, January 19, 2018, https://www.bls.gov/news.release/union2.nr0.htm.

78. Heather Long, "U.S. Inequality Keeps Getting Uglier," *CNN Money*, December 22, 2016, http://money.cnn.com/2016/12/22/news/economy/us-inequality-worse/.

79. Zakaria, "Populism on the March."

80. Author's calculation based on World Bank, "GDP, PPP (Constant 2011 International $)," *World Development Indicators*, 2015, https://data.worldbank.org/products/wdi.

81. Congressional Budget Office, "Historical Budget Data," April 2018, https://www.cbo.gov/about/products/budget-economic-data#2.

82. Zakaria, "Populism on the March."

83. During 2018 Trump's tariff threats became reality. In March 2018 he signed tariffs on imported steel (25%) and aluminum (10%) from all nations except Mexico and Canada. In June the US announced tariffs on $50 billion in Chinese imports, with China responding in kind. And in September the US announced 10 percent tariffs on $200 billion of additional Chinese exports, to rise to 25 percent from the end of 2018. See Bloomberg News, "The Trade War Is On: How We Got Here and What's Next," *Bloomberg*, September 18, 2018, https://www.bloomberg.com/news/articles/2018-10-09/asia-stocks-point-to-mixed-start-treasuries-rise-markets-wrap. In late November, this latest increase was postponed.

84. Acharya, *The End of American World Order*, 4.

CHAPTER 10

1. Negotiations on GATT were held in Geneva at the same time as the ITO negotiations. GATT was signed in October 1947, and took effect on January 1, 1948. It lasted until the establishment of the WTO on January 1, 1995. See Chad P. Bown, *Self-Enforcing Trade: Developing Countries and WTO Dispute Settlement* (Washington, DC: Brookings Institution Press, 2009), 10–21.

2. The WTO was proposed in 1944 and formally established in 1995.

3. See Yale Law School, "Security Treaty Between the United States and Japan, September 1, 1951"; "Security Treaty Between the United States, Australia, and the New Zealand (ANZUS), September 1, 1951"; "Mutual Defense Treaty Between the United States and the Republic of the Philippines, August 30, 1951"; and "Mutual Defense Treaty Between the United States and the Republic of Korea, October 1, 1953"; *The Avalon Project: Documents in Law, History and Diplomacy*, http://avalon.law.yale.edu/default.asp.

4. Nationalist China and the US signed a Mutual Defense Treaty on December 2, 1954. There was no specific treaty committing the US to the defense of South Vietnam, but the US normalized relations with Vietnam in 1950, after its independence within the French Union, and continued close relations until the fall of Saigon in April 1975.

5. See Yale Law School, "Southeast Asia Collective Defense Treaty (Manila Pact); September 8, 1954," *The Avalon Project: Documents in Law, History and Diplomacy*, http://avalon.law.yale.edu/default.asp; and US Department of State, Bureau of East Asian and Pacific Affairs, "US Relations with Thailand: Fact Sheet," *US Department of State*, January 24, 2017, http://www.state.gov/r/pa/ei/bgn/2814.htm.

6. Ministry of Foreign Affairs of the People's Republic of China, "Conclusion of the 'Sino-Soviet Treaty of Friendship, Alliance and Mutual Assistance,'" http://www.fmprc.gov.cn/mfa_eng/ziliao_665539/3602_665543/3604_665547/t18011.shtml.

7. United Nations Treaty Series Online, "No. 6045. Treaty of Friendship, Co-operation and Mutual Assistance Between the Union of Soviet Socialist Republics and the Democratic People's Republic of Korea; Signed at Moscow, on 6 July 1961," https://

treaties.un.org/doc/Publication/UNTS/Volume%20420/volume-420-I-6045-English .pdf; and Kevin Klose, "Soviets and Vietnamese Sign Treaty, Warn Chinese," *Washington Post*, November 4, 1978, https://www.washingtonpost.com/archive/politics/1978/11/ 04/soviets-and-vietnamese-sign-treaty-warn-chinese/e7be2390-fc73-441d-b91c-2a196d 6476b7/?utm_term=.9518b58aa08c.

8. See North Atlantic Treaty Organization, "What Is NATO," http://www.nato.int/ nato-welcome/.

9. U.S. Department of State, "The Baghdad Pact (1955) and the Central Treaty Organization (CENTO)," https://2001-2009.state.gov/r/pa/ho/time/lw/98683.htm.

10. The multilateral treaty establishing SEATO was signed at Manila on September 8, 1954. On February 19, 1955, SEATO was formally established in Bangkok, where its headquarters were located. It was abolished, as noted above, on June 30, 1977, following the US withdrawal from Vietnam.

11. SEATO held its final exercise on February 20, 1976, and formally dissolved on June 30, 1977. Encyclopædia Britannica, "Southeast Asia Treaty Organization (SEATO)," July 20, 1998, https://www.britannica.com/topic/Southeast-Asia-Treaty-Organization.

12. Robert Gilpin, *War and Change in World Politics* (Cambridge: Cambridge University Press, 1981).

13. Gerhard Peters and John T. Woolley, "George Bush: Remarks Following Discussions with Prime Minister Toshiki Kaifu of Japan in Palm Springs, California," *The American Presidency Project*, March 3, 1990, http://www.presidency.ucsb.edu/ws/?pid=18214.

14. Gerhard Peters and John T. Woolley, "George Bush: The President's News Conference with President Boris Yeltsin of Russia in Moscow," *The American Presidency Project*, January 3, 1993, http://www.presidency.ucsb.edu/ws/index.php?pid=20409.

15. See, for example, Robert O. Keohane and Joseph S. Nye, *Power and Interdependence: World Politics in Transition* (Boston: Little, Brown, 1977); Robert O. Keohane, *After Hegemony: Cooperation and Discord in the World Political Economy* (Princeton, NJ: Princeton University Press, 1984); Raymond Vernon, *Sovereignty at Bay: The Multinational Spread of U.S. Enterprises* (New York: Basic Books, 1971); Raymond Vernon, *Storm over the Multinationals: The Real Issues* (Cambridge, MA: Harvard University Press, 1977); and Daniel Yergin and Joseph Stanislaw, *The Commanding Heights: The Battle between Government and the Marketplace That Is Remaking the Modern World* (New York: Simon & Schuster, 1998).

16. On those battles for hegemonic supremacy, see Robert Gilpin, *War and Change in International Relations* (Cambridge: Cambridge University Press, 1981).

17. World Trade Organization, "What Is the WTO?" https://www.wto.org/english/ thewto_e/whatis_e/whatis_e.htm.

18. Chad P. Bown and Douglas A. Irwin, "The GATT's Starting Point: Tariff Levels circa 1947" (NBER Working Paper No. 21782, National Bureau of Economic Research, December 2015), doi: 10.3386/w21782.

19. Barry Eichengreen, "Globalization's Last Gasp," *Project Syndicate*, November 17, 2016, https://www.project-syndicate.org/commentary/growth-before-globalization-by -barry-eichengreen-2016-11?barrier=accessreg.

20. For USTR Michael Froman's view at Nairobi that the Doha Round should be terminated, see Michael Froman, "We Are at the End of the Line on the Doha Round of Trade Talks," *Financial Times*, December 13, 2015, https://www.ft.com/content/4ccf5356 -9eaa-11e5-8ce1-f6219b685d74.

21. Peter Baker, "Trump Abandons Trans-Pacific Partnership, Obama's Signature Trade Deal," *New York Times*, January 23, 2017, https://www.nytimes.com/2017/01/23/us/politics/tpp-trump-trade-nafta.html?_r=0.

22. World Economic Forum, "Enabling Trade: Valuing Growth Opportunities," 2013, http://www3.weforum.org/docs/WEF_SCT_EnablingTrade_Report_2013.pdf.

23. World Economic Forum, "Digital Transformation of Industries: Digital Enterprise," January 2016, http://reports.weforum.org/digital-transformation-of-industries/wp-content/blogs.dir/94/mp/files/pages/files/digital-enterprise-narrative-final-january-2016.pdf.

24. PC laptop exports from Chongqing alone amounted in 2016 to 45 million units, for a total export value of $15.9 billion. "16–09 Main Export Commodities in Volume and Value," *Chongqing Statistical Yearbook*, 2017.

25. Within Europe, transport deregulation occurred in various countries internally between 1986 and 1990. It continued to expand cross-nationally within the EU in 1995, particularly with respect to border controls (as within the Schengen border-free area) and in access to international intraunion markets. See B. T. Bayliss and A. I. Millington, "Deregulation and Logistics Systems in a Single European Market," *Journal of Transportation Economics and Policy* 29, no. 3 (September 1995): 305–16; and Francesco Saverio Montesano and Maaike Okano-Heijmans, "Economic Diplomacy in EU-China Relations: Why Europe Needs Its Own 'OBOR,'" *Netherlands Institute of International Relations (Clingendael)*, June 2016, https://www.clingendael.nl/sites/default/files/Policy%20Brief%20Economic%20Diplomacy%20in%20EU%E2%80%93China%20relations%20-%20June%202016.pdf.

26. The ADB's 2017 estimates of infrastructure needs are more than triple those that the ADB itself estimated in 2009, and include $14.7 trillion over the 2016–2030 period for electric power, $8.4 trillion for transportation, $2.3 trillion for telecommunications, and $800 billion for water and sanitation. See Asian Development Bank, *Meeting Asia's Infrastructure Needs: Highlights* (Manila, Philippines: Asian Development Bank, 2017).

27. For conceptual details, see Jordan Wirfs-Brock, "Lost in Transmission: How Much Electricity Disappears between a Power Plant and Your Plug?" *IE Inside Energy*, November 6, 2015, http://insideenergy.org/2015/11/06/lost-in-transmission-how-much-electricity-disappears-between-a-power-plant-and-your-plug/.

28. On this revolutionary development, see Marc Levinson, *The Box: How the Shipping Container Made the World Smaller and the World Economy Bigger* (Princeton, NJ: Princeton University Press, 2008), especially chapter 9.

29. Michel Beuthe, "Intermodal Freight Transport in Europe," in *Globalized Freight Transport: Intermodality, E-Commerce, Logistics and Sustainability*, ed. Thomas R. Leinbach and Cristina Capineri (Northampton, MA: Edward Elgar, 2007), 78.

30. Michael Dunford and Weidong Liu, eds., *The Geographic Transformation of China* (Hoboken, NJ: Routledge, 2014), 269.

31. On transcontinental supply chains, see, for example, Christopher Minasians, "Where Are Apple Products Made? How Much Does the iPhone Cost to Make? A Comprehensive Breakdown of Apple's Product Supply Chain," *Macworld*, November 24, 2016, http://www.macworld.co.uk/feature/apple/where-are-apple-products-made-how-much-does-iphone-cost-make-india-3633832/.

32. On COSCO's trans-Eurasian supply-chain management, see Frans-Paul van der Putten, Mikko Huotari, John Seaman, Alice Ekman, and Miguel Otero-Iglesias, "The

Role of OBOR in Europe-China Relations," in *Europe and China's New Silk Roads: A Report by the European Think-Tank Network on China (ETNC)*, ed. Frans-Paul van der Putten et al. (Wassenaar, Netherlands: Netherland Institute of International Relations (Clingendael), 2016), 5, https://www.clingendael.nl/sites/default/files/Europe_and_Chinas_New_Silk_Roads_0.pdf.

33. Gilpin, *War and Change in World Politics*.

34. Charles P. Kindleberger, *The World in Depression, 1929–1939* (Berkeley: University of California Press, 1973), 291–308.

35. Aaron L. Friedberg, "Ripe for Rivalry: Prospects for Peace in a Multi-polar Asia," *International Security* 18, no. 3 (1993): 5–33; Aaron L. Friedberg, "Will Europe's Past Be Asia's Future?" *Survival* 42, no. 3 (Autumn 2000): 147–59; and Kent E. Calder, *Pacific Defense: Arms, Energy, and America's Future in Asia* (New York: William Morrow, 1996).

36. In September 2017, 20.7 percent of Chinese exports went to the United States—a share that had fallen to 17.6 percent by March 2018. See International Monetary Fund, *Direction of Trade Statistics*, http://data.imf.org/?sk=9D6028D4-F14A-464C-A2F2-59B2CD424B85, accessed June 29, 2018.

37. On this transition, see Barry Eichengreen, "The Dollar and Its Discontents," *Japan Times*, October 19, 2018, https://www.japantimes.co.jp/opinion/2018/10/19/commentary/world-commentary/the-dollar-and-its-discontents/#.W83ZaBNKjeQ.

38. Unemployment spiked in 1921 and again in 1931–1932, before dropping abruptly around 1941 as World War II intensified. For more on the UK's interwar unemployment situation, see James Denman and Paul McDonald, "Unemployment Statistics from 1881 to the Present," *Labor Market Trends*, January 1996.

39. In the 1920s, the UK's difficult domestic economic situation (falling demand, rising unemployment) made the pound less competitive vis-à-vis the dollar as a reserve currency. The British government nevertheless insisted on keeping to the gold standard, thus further weakening the strength of the pound. See Tajvan Pettinger, "The UK Economy in the 1920s," *Economics Help*, October 16, 2012; and Barry Eichengreen, *Globalizing Capital: A History of the International Monetary System* (Princeton, NJ: Princeton University Press, 1998), 78–83.

40. For more details on the Indonesian *Konfrontasi*, see "Konfrontasi (Confrontation)," *Global Security*, November 7, 2011, http://www.globalsecurity.org/military/world/war/konfrontasi.htm.

41. Jeffrey Pickering, *Britain's Withdrawal from East of Suez: The Politics of Retrenchment* (New York: Palgrave, 1998), 150–76.

42. See International Monetary Fund, *Currency Composition of Official Foreign Exchange Reserves*, http://data.imf.org/?sk=E6A5F467-C14B-4AA8-9F6D-5A09EC4E62A4, accessed June 30, 2018.

43. See Michael Selby-Green, "'Europe Should Not Allow the US to Act Over Our Head': Germany Is Challenging the US's Financial Monopoly as the Iran Row Deepens," *Business Insider*, August 22, 2018, https://www.businessinsider.com/germany-wants-european-rival-to-us-backed-swift-payment-system-2018-8; and Mehreen Khan and Jim Brunsden, "Juncker vows to turn euro into reserve currency to rival US dollar," *Financial Times*, September 12, 2018, https://www.ft.com/content/7358f396-b66d-11e8-bbc3-ccd7de085ffe.

44. Society for Worldwide Interbank Financial Telecommunication (SWIFT), "RMB Tracker November 2011," November 25, 2011; "RMB Tracker January 2014," Janu-

ary 23, 2014; "RMB Tracker January 2015," January 28, 2015, https://www.swift.com/our-solutions/compliance-and-shared-services/business-intelligence/renminbi/rmb-tracker.

45. The October 2016 weights for the five basket currencies were US dollar (41.73 percent); euro (30.93 percent); Chinese RMB (10.92 percent); Japanese yen (8.33 percent); and British pound sterling (8.09 percent). See International Monetary Fund, "IMF Adds Chinese Renminbi to Special Drawing Rights Basket," *IMF News*, September 30, 2016, http://www.imf.org/en/News/Articles/2016/09/29/AM16-NA093016IMF-Adds-Chinese-Renminbi-to-Special-Drawing-Rights-Basket.

46. See SWIFT, "RMB Internationalisation: Where We Are and What We Can Expect in 2018," January 2018, 7, https://www.swift.com/resource/rmb-tracker-january-2018-special-report.

47. Ibid.

48. See International Monetary Fund, *Currency Composition of Official Foreign Exchange Reserves*.

49. SWIFT, "RMB usage by country for commercial payments ending in China and Hong Kong," RMB Tracker January 2018 (Special Report), January 31, 2018.

50. Ibid.

51. Ibid.; and SWIFT, RMB Tracker May 2015, May 27, 2015.

52. Gabriel Wildau, "Renminbi Drops to Sixth in International Payment Ranking," *Financial Times*, July 21, 2016, https://www.ft.com/content/bbcaef78-4efd-11e6-8172-e39ecd3b86fc.

53. SWIFT is an acronym for Society for Worldwide Interbank Financial Telecommunications.

54. G. John Ikenberry, *After Victory: Institutions, Strategic Restraint, and the Rebuilding of Order After Major Wars* (Princeton, NJ: Princeton University Press, 2011), 244.

55. Kindleberger, *The World in Depression*.

56. Henry Kissinger, *A World Restored: Metternich, Castlereagh, and the Problems of Peace, 1812–22* (Boston: Houghton Mifflin, 1973); and Henry Kissinger, *World Order* (New York: Penguin Press, 2014).

57. Kissinger, *World Order*, 367–71.

58. Ibid., 225.

59. The only serious case of an adversary nearby, following American independence, was Britain during the War of 1812. Britain did continue to rule Canada formally until 1867, and France had a powerful presence in Mexico under Emperor Maximillian during the 1860s, but neither of those latter contingencies led to armed conflict.

60. Kissinger, *World Order*, 226.

61. Yan Xuetong, *Ancient Chinese Thought, Modern Chinese Power* (Princeton, NJ: Princeton University Press, 2011), 5–6.

62. Ren Xiao, "Traditional Chinese Theory and Practice of Foreign Relations: A Reassessment," in *China and International Relations: The Chinese View and the Contribution of Wang Gungwu*, ed. Zheng Yongnian (New York: Routledge, 2010), 115.

63. Zheng Yongnian, "Organizing China's Inter-state Relations: From 'Tianxia' (All-Under-the-Heaven) to the Modern International Order," in *China and International Relations: The Chinese View and the Contribution of Wang Gungwu*, ed. Zheng Yongnian (New York: Routledge, 2010), 304.

64. Paul Evans, "Historians and Chinese World Order: Fairbank, Wang, and the Matter of 'Intermediate Relevance,'" in *China and International Relations: The Chinese View and the Contribution of Wang Gungwu*, ed. Zheng Yongnian (New York: Routledge, 2010), 46.

65. Kissinger, *World Order*, 5.

66. Theodore J. Lowi, "American Business, Public Policy, Case Studies, and Political Theory," *World Politics* 16, no. 4 (July 1964): 677–693+695+697+699+701+ 703+705+707+711+713+715, http://www.jstor.org/stable/2009452.

67. According to the AIIB's articles of agreement, China contributed $29.78 billion (initial subscription) of the AIIB's $100 billion authorized capital, and is the bank's largest shareholder. As of December 18, 2018, China held 26.6% votes in the AIIB. See Asian Infrastructure Investment Bank, "Articles of Agreement," https://www.aiib.org/en/about -aiib/basic-documents/_download/articles-of-agreement/basic_document_english-bank _articles_of_agreement.pdf; and "Members and Prospective Members of the Bank," updated December 18, 2018, https://www.aiib.org/en/about-aiib/governance/members-of -bank/index.html.

68. See ADB, *Meeting Asia's Infrastructure Needs*.

69. See Lauren Dodillet, "$40 Billion Silk Road Fund Kicks Off China's 'Belt and Road' Initiatives," *China Business Review*, March 10, 2015, https://www.chinabusinessreview .com/40-billion-silk-road-fund-kicks-off-chinas-belt-and-road-initiatives/. Substantial sovereign wealth fund assets were also involved.

70. The NDB has a rotating presidential structure, with Kundapur Vaman Kamath of India serving as the first president. He has argued that the NDB could be seen as an alternative to the IMF and the World Bank. See "Brics Countries Launch New Development Bank in Shanghai," *BBC News*, July 21, 2015, http://www.bbc.com/news/33605230.

71. Yaroslav Zaitsev, "The 'Hegemonic Way' and the 'Kingly Way': How Russia and China Define Their National Interests," *Russia in Global Affairs*, June 19, 2015, http://eng .globalaffairs.ru/number/The-Hegemonic-Way-and-the-Kingly-Way-17540.

CHAPTER II

1. See, for example, Michael R. Auslin, *The End of the Asian Century: War, Stagnation, and the Risks to the World's Most Dynamic Region* (New Haven, CT: Yale University Press, 2017); and Zbigniew Brzezinski, *The Fragile Blossom: Crisis and Change in Japan* (New York: Harper and Row, 1972).

2. See G. John Ikenberry and Anne-Marie Slaughter, *Forging a World of Liberty under Law: U.S. National Security in the 21st Century* (Princeton, NJ: Princeton University Press, 2006).

3. On the "third wave," see Samuel P. Huntington, *The Third Wave: Democratization in the Late Twentieth Century* (Norman: University of Oklahoma Press, 1991).

4. On this center and SCO counterterrorist activities more generally, see Zhao Xiaodong, *The Shanghai Cooperation Organization and Counter-Terrorism Cooperation* (Singapore: Institute for Security and Development Policy, 2012).

5. See, for example, Dalibor Rohac, "Hungary and Poland Aren't Democratic. They're Authoritarian," *Foreign Policy*, February 5, 2018.

6. Stefan A. Halper, *The Beijing Consensus: Legitimizing Authoritarianism in Our Time* (New York: Basic Books, 2010).

7. On the tributary system concept, see David Kang, *East Asia Before the West: Five Centuries of Trade and Tribute* (New York: Columbia University Press, 2010).

8. See Ren Xiao, "Traditional Chinese Theory and Practice of Foreign Relations: A Reassessment," in *China and International Relations: The Chinese View and the Contribution of Wang Gungwu*, ed. Zheng Yongnian (New York: Routledge, 2010), 102–16.

9. Zheng Yongnian, "Organizing China's Inter-state Relations: From '*Tianxia*' (All-Under-Heaven) to the Modern International Order," in *China and International Relations: The Chinese View and the Contribution of Wang Gungwu*, ed. Zheng Yongnian (New York: Routledge, 2010), 293–321.

10. Henry Kissinger, *A World Restored: Metternich, Castlereagh, and the Problems of Peace, 1812–22* (Boston: Houghton Mifflin, 1973).

11. He Baogang of Nanyang Technological University in Singapore, for example, proposes a concert of powers between China and the US, also involving ASEAN, that could allow small and middle powers to work with both the US and China. See He Baogang, "Sponsored Post: The Rise of China, a Concert of Asian Powers and Hybrid Asian Regionalism," *The Diplomat*, June 26, 2015, http://thediplomat.com/2015/06/sponsored-post-the-rise-of-china-a-concert-of-asian-powers-and-hybrid-asian-regionalism/.

12. See Zbigniew Brzezinski, "The Group of Two Could Change the World," *Financial Times*, January 13, 2009.

13. Ibid.

14. Ibid.

15. Pam Price, "Sunnylands Summit with US and China President Ends on Positive Note," *Forbes*, June 10, 2013, http://www.forbes.com/sites/pamprice/2013/06/10/sunnylands-summit-with-u-s-and-china-presidents-ends-on-positive-note/#23bdb7a33687.

16. Cheng Li and Lucy Xu, "Chinese Enthusiasm and American Cynicism: The 'New Type of Great Power Relations,'" Brookings, December 4, 2014, https://www.brookings.edu/opinions/chinese-enthusiasm-and-american-cynicism-over-the-new-type-of-great-power-relations/.

17. See James McBride and Mohammed Aly Sergie, "NAFTA's Economic Impact," Council on Foreign Relations, October 4, 2017, https://www.cfr.org/backgrounder/naftas-economic-impact.

18. Ibid. Also, Joe Terino, "Is Your Supply Chain Ready for a NAFTA Overhaul?" *Harvard Business Review*, June 30, 2017, https://hbr.org/2017/06/is-your-supply-chain-ready-for-a-nafta-overhaul.

19. The new agreement did address several of NAFTA's flaws, including: (a) country of origin rules; (b) lack of labor provisions; (c) US access to the Canadian dairy market; (d) intellectual property and digital trade; and (e) Sunset clause (sixteen years in this case). For details, see Jen Kirby, "USMCA, Trump's new NAFTA deal, explained in 500 words," *Vox*, October 3, 2018, https://www.vox.com/2018/10/3/17930092/usmca-nafta-trump-trade-deal-explained.

20. In 2017 Korea's trade with China was $238.2 billion, compared to $199.4 billion for Japan and the United States combined. See International Monetary Fund, *Direction of Trade Statistics*, accessed October 23, 2018.

21. Bipul Chatterjee and Surendar Singh, "An Opportunity for India in Central Asia," *The Diplomat*, May 4, 2015, http://thediplomat.com/2015/05/an-opportunity-for-india-in-central-asia/.

22. Prashanth Parameswaran, "US, Japan, and India Kick Off 2016 Malabar Exercise," *The Diplomat*, June 12, 2016, http://thediplomat.com/2016/06/us-japan-and-india-kick -off-malabar-2016/.

23. The Defense Technology and Trade Initiative (DTTI), inaugurated in 2012, begins this process. In 2015 the US and India agreed to implement government-to-government DTTI projects to develop mobile hybrid electric power sources and next-generation protective ensembles for chemical and biological protection. Cooperative work is also being done on aircraft engine and aircraft carrier development. See US Department of Defense, "Fact Sheet: US-India Defense Relationship," *US Department of Defense Archives*, http:// archive.defense.gov/pubs/US-IND-Fact-Sheet.pdf.

24. Stephen P. Cohen and Michael E. O'Hanlon, "Enhancing India-US Defense and Security Cooperation," *Brookings Institution*, January 20, 2015, https://www.brookings .edu/opinions/enhancing-india-u-s-defense-and-security-cooperation/.

25. Dean Cheng and Lisa Curtis, "The China Challenge: A Strategic Vision for US-India Relations," *The Heritage Foundation*, July 18, 2011, http://www.heritage.org/asia/ report/the-china-challenge-strategic-vision-us-india-relations.

26. IGCC is a process through which coal is turned into synthetic gas (syngas) by means of a high-pressure gasifier. IGCC has many environmental advantages, including reduced SO_2, NO, and PM emissions levels, compared to pulverized coal. The greatest challenges are cost, availability, and complexity. See U.S. Department of Energy, National Energy Technology Laboratory, "Commercial Power Production based on Gasification," https://www.netl.doe.gov/research/coal/energy-systems/gasification/gasifipedia/igcc.

27. The China Huaneng Group's "Green Gen" project in Tianjin, begun in 2009 and extending to after 2020, gasifies 2,000 tons/day of pulverized coal and will entail constructing carbon-capture facilities. See Global CCS Institute, "Huaneng Green Gen IGCC Project (Phase 3)," https://www.globalccsinstitute.com/projects/huaneng -greengen-igcc-project-phase-3.

28. Daniel F. Runde and Romina Bandura, "The BUILD Act Has Passed: What's Next?" *Center for Strategic & International Studies*, October 12, 2018, https://www.csis.org/ analysis/build-act-has-passed-whats-next.

29. BUILD stands for "Better Utilization of Investments Leading to Development."

30. The Qing Dynasty fell in 1911, but the Republic of China was not established until 1912.

Bibliography

Aggarwal, Vinod K., and Charles E. Morrison, eds. *Asia-Pacific Crossroads: Regime Creation and the Future of APEC*. New York: St. Martin's Press, 1998.

Acharya, Amitav. *The End of American World Order*. Malden, MA: Polity, 2014.

Allison, Graham T., and Phillip Zelikow. *Essence of Decision: Explaining the Cuban Missile Crisis*. 2nd ed. New York: Longman, 1999.

Asano, Risaburō 浅野利三郎. *Nichi-doku-so Tairiku Burokku Ron: So no Chiseigaku-teki Kōsatsu* 日独ソ大陸ブロック論 ： その地政学的考察 [Theory on the Japanese-German-Soviet Continental Bloc: A Geopolitical Perspective]. Tokyo: Tōkaidō, 1941.

Asian Development Bank. *Meeting Asia's Infrastructure Needs: Highlights*. Mandaluyong City, Philippines: Asian Development Bank, 2017.

Auslin, Michael R. *The End of the Asian Century: War, Stagnation, and the Risks to the World's Most Dynamic Region*. New Haven, CT: Yale University Press, 2017.

Beckwith, Christopher I. *Empires of the Silk Road: A History of Central Eurasia from the Bronze Age to the Present*. Princeton, NJ: Princeton University Press, 2009.

Binder, Leonard. *Crises and Sequences in Political Development*. Princeton, NJ: Princeton University Press, 1971.

Blackwill, Robert D., and Jennifer W. Harris. *War by Other Means: Geoeconomics and Statecraft*. Cambridge, MA: Harvard University Press, 2016.

Bobrick, Benson. *East of the Sun: The Epic Conquest and Tragic History of Siberia*. New York: Poseidon, 1992.

Boulnois, Luce. *Silk Road: Monks, Warriors & Merchants on the Silk Road*. Hong Kong: Odyssey, 2004.

Brzezinski, Zbigniew. *The Fragile Blossom: Crisis and Change in Japan*. New York: Harper and Row, 1972.

Brzezinski, Zbigniew. *The Grand Chessboard: American Primacy and Its Geostrategic Imperatives*. New York: Basic Books, 1997.

Calder, Kent E. *The Bay of Bengal: Political-Economic Transition and Strategic Implications*. Tokyo: Sasakawa Peace Foundation, July 2018.

Calder, Kent E. *Crisis and Compensation: Public Policy and Political Crisis in Japan.* Princeton, NJ: Princeton University Press, 1988.

Calder, Kent E. *The New Continentalism: Energy and Twenty-First Century Eurasian Geopolitics.* New Haven, CT: Yale University Press, 2012.

Calder, Kent E. *Pacific Defense: Arms, Energy, and America's Future in Asia.* New York: William Morrow, 1996.

Calder, Kent E. *Singapore: Smart City, Smart State.* Washington, DC: Brookings Institution, 2016.

Calder, Kent E., and Min Ye. *The Making of Northeast Asia.* Stanford, CA: Stanford University Press, 2010.

Campbell, Kurt M., Robert J. Einhorn, and Mitchell B. Reiss. *The Nuclear Tipping Point: Why States Reconsider Their Nuclear Choices.* Washington, DC: Brookings Institution, 2004.

Carr, Edward Hallett. *German-Soviet Relations between the Two World Wars.* Baltimore, MD: Johns Hopkins University Press, 1951.

Clubb, O. Edmund. *China and Russia: The "Great Game."* New York: Columbia University Press, 1971.

Cooley, Alexander. *Base Politics: Democratic Change and the US Military Overseas.* Ithaca, NY: Cornell University Press, 2008.

Cumings, Bruce. *Korea's Place in the Sun: A Modern History.* New York: W. W. Norton, 2005.

Davutoğlu, Ahmet. *Civilizational Transformation and the Muslim World.* Kuala Lumpur: Mahir, 1994.

Davutoğlu, Ahmet. *Stratejik Derinlik, Turkiye'nin Uluslararasi Konumu* [Strategic depth: Turkey's international position]. Istanbul: Küre Yayınları, 2001.

De Blij, Harm. *Why Geography Matters More than Ever.* Oxford: Oxford University Press, 2012.

Dennon, David B. H., ed. *China, the United States, and the Future of Central Asia: U.S.-China Relations,* Volume I. New York: New York University Press, 2015.

Deudney, Daniel. "Geopolitics as Theory: Historical Security Materialism." *European Journal of International Relations* 6, no. 1 (2000): 77–107.

Doran, Charles F. "Explaining Ascendancy and Decline: The Power Cycle Perspective." *International Journal* 60, no. 3 (Summer 2005): 685–701.

Dugin, Aleksandr. *Foundations of Geopolitics.* Moscow: Arktogeya, 1997.

Dunford, Michael, and Weidong Liu, ed. *The Geographic Transformation of China.* Hoboken, NJ: Routledge, 2014.

Drysdale, Peter, and Luke Gower, eds. *The Japanese Economy: Vol. 2 Postwar Growth.* New York: Routledge, 1998–1999.

Eichengreen, Barry. *Globalizing Capital: A History of the International Monetary System.* Princeton, NJ: Princeton University Press, 1998.

Emmott, Bill. *Rivals: How Power Struggle between China, India, and Japan Will Shape our Next Decade.* New York: Harcourt, 2008.

Encarnation, Dennis. *Dislodging Multinationals: India's Strategy in Comparative Perspective.* Ithaca, NY: Cornell University Press, 1989.

Esposito, John L., ed. *The Iranian Revolution: Its Global Impact.* Miami: Florida International University Press, 1990.

Ferguson, Niall, ed. *The Shock of the Global: The 1970s in Perspective.* Cambridge, MA: Belknap Press of Harvard University Press, 2010.

Friedberg, Aaron L. "Ripe for Rivalry: Prospects for Peace in a Multi-polar Asia," *International Security* 18, no. 3 (1993): 5–33.

Frankopan, Peter. *The Silk Roads: A New History of the World*. New York: Alfred A. Knopf, 2016.

Friedberg, Aaron L. "Will Europe's Past Be Asia's Future?" *Survival* 42, no. 3 (Autumn 2000): 147–59.

Friedman, Thomas L., and Michael Mandelbaum. *That Used to Be Us: How America Fell Behind in the World It Invented and How We Can Come Back*. New York: Farrar, Straus, and Giroux, 2011.

Garver, John W. *China's Quest: The History of the Foreign Relations of the People's Republic of China*. New York: Oxford University Press, 2016.

Gilpin, Robert. *War and Change in World Politics*. Cambridge: Cambridge University Press, 1981.

Goldman, Marshall I. *Petrostate: Putin, Power, and the New Russia*. Oxford: Oxford University Press, 2008.

Gourevitch, Peter, "Second Image Reversed: The International Sources of Domestic Politics." *International Organization* 32, no. 4 (Autumn 1978): 881–912.

Greeven, Mark J., and Wei Wei. *Business Ecosystems in China: Alibaba and Competing Baidu, Tencent, Xiaomi and LeEco*. New York: Routledge, 2018.

Grygiel, Jakub. *Great Powers and Geopolitical Change*. Baltimore, MD: Johns Hopkins University Press, 2006.

Halper, Stefan, *The Beijing Consensus: Legitimizing Authoritarianism in Our Time*. New York: Basic Books, 2010.

Herodotus. *The History*, translated by David Grene. Chicago: University of Chicago Press, 1987.

Hiro, Dilip. *Inside Central Asia*. New York: Peter Mayer, 2009.

Hopkirk, Peter. *Setting the East Ablaze: Lenin's Dream of an Empire in Asia*. New York: Kodansha, 1984.

Hsu, Immanuel Chung-yueh. *China without Mao: The Search for a New Order*, 2nd ed. New York: Oxford University Press, 1990.

Huntington, Samuel P. *Political Order in Changing Societies*. New Haven, CT: Yale University Press, 1968.

Huntington, Samuel P. *The Third Wave: Democratization in the Late Twentieth Century*. Norman: University of Oklahoma Press, 1991.

Ikenberry, G. John, and Anne-Marie Slaughter. *Forging a World of Liberty under Law: U.S. National Security in the 21st Century*. Princeton, NJ: Princeton University Press, 2006.

Johnston, Alastair Iain. *Cultural Realism: Strategic Culture and Grand Strategy in Chinese History*. Princeton, NJ: Princeton University Press, 1995.

Joshi, Nirmala, ed. *Reconnecting India and Central Asia: Emerging Security and Economic Dimensions*. Washington, DC: Central Asia-Caucasus Institute, Paul H. Nitze School of Advanced International Studies, 2010.

Kang, David. *East Asia before the West: Five Centuries of Trade and Tribute*. New York: Columbia University Press, 2010.

Kaplan, Robert D. *Asia's Cauldron: The South China Sea and the End of a Stable Pacific*. New York: Random House, 2014.

Karaganov, Sergei. "Eurasian Way Out of the European Crisis." *Russia in Global Affairs*, 2 (April–June, 2015): 8–21.

Katzenstein, Peter J., ed. *The Culture of National Security: Norms and Identity in World Politics*. New York: Columbia University Press, 1996.

Katznelson, Ira, and Helen Milner, eds. *Political Science: State of the Discipline*. New York: W. W. Norton, 2002.

Kawanishi, Seikan 川西正鑑. *Tōa Chiseigaku no Kōsō* 東亜地政学の構想 [The Concept of Oriental Geopolitics]. Tokyo: Jitsugyo no Nihon Sha, 1942.

Kennan, George F. *Memoires: 1925–1050*. Boston: Little, Brown, 1962.

Kennedy, Paul. *The Rise and Fall of the Great Powers: Economic Change and Military Conflict from 1500 to 2000*. New York: Random House, 1987.

Keohane, Robert O. *After Hegemony: Cooperation and Discord in the World Political Economy*. Princeton, NJ: Princeton University Press, 1984.

Keohane, Robert O., and Joseph S. Nye. *Power and Interdependence: World Politics in Transition*. Boston: Little, Brown, 1977.

Khanna, Parag. *Connectography: Mapping the Future of Global Civilization*. New York: Random House, 2016.

Kindleberger, Charles P. *The World in Depression, 1929–1939*. Berkeley: University of California Press, 1973.

Kissinger, Henry. *A World Restored: Metternich, Castlereagh, and the Problems of Peace, 1812–22*. Boston: Houghton Mifflin, 1973.

Kissinger, Henry. *On China*. New York: Penguin, 2011.

Kissinger, Henry. *World Order*. New York: Penguin, 2014.

Knorr, Klaus. *Power and Wealth: The Political Economy of International Power*. New York: Basic Books, 1973.

Krasner, Stephen. "Approaches to the State: Alternative Conceptions and Historical Dynamics." *Comparative Politics* 16, no. 2 (1984): 223–46.

Krasner, Stephen ed. *International Regimes*. Ithaca, NY: Cornell University Press, 1983.

Laruelle, Marlene. *Russian Euroasianism: An Ideology of Empire*. Baltimore, MD: Johns Hopkins University Press, 2008.

Leinbach, Thomas R., and Cristina Capineri, eds. *Globalized Freight Transport: Intermodality, E-Commerce, Logistics and Sustainability*. Northampton, MA: Edward Elgar, 2007.

Levinson, Marc. *The Box: How the Shipping Container Made the World Smaller and the World Economy Bigger*. Princeton, NJ: Princeton University Press, 2008.

Liu, Xinru. *The Silk Road in World History*. Oxford: Oxford University Press, 2010.

Lowi, Theodore J. "American Business, Public Policy, Case Studies, and Political Theory." *World Politics* 16, no. 4 (July 1964): 677–693+695+697+699+701+703+705+707+711+713+715, http://www.jstor.org/stable/2009452.

Mackinder, Halford John. "The Geographical Pivot of History." *Geographical Journal* 23, no. 4 (1904): 421–37.

Mahan, Alfred Thayer. *The Influence of Sea Power on History, 1660–1783*. Boston: Little, Brown, 1890.

Mahan, Alfred Thayer. *The Problem of Asia and Its Effect on International Policies*. Boston: Little, Brown, 1900.

Mann, James. *About Face: A History of America's Curious Relationship with China, from Nixon to Clinton*. New York: Alfred Knopf, 1999.

Marshall, Tim. *Prisoners of Geography: Ten Maps that Explain Everything about the World*. New York: Scribner, 2015.

Mattli, Walter. *The Logic of Regional Integration: Europe and Beyond*. Cambridge: Cambridge University Press, 1999.

Nasr, Vali. *The Shia Revival: How Conflict within Islam Will Shape the Future.* New York: W. W. Norton, 2006.

National Development and Reform Commission. "China Railway Express Construction and Development Plan for 2016–2020," released on October 17, 2016.

Oberdorfer, Don. *The Turn: From the Cold War to a New Era: The United States and the Soviet Union, 1983–1990.* New York: Poseidon, 1991.

Omrani, Bijan. *Asia Overland: Tales of Travel on the Trans-Siberian and Silk Road.* Hong Kong: Odyssey Books, 2010.

Organski, A.F.K. *World Politics.* New York: Knopf, 1959.

Ó'Tuathail, Gearóid. *Critical Geopolitics: The Politics of Writing Global Space.* Minneapolis: University of Minnesota Press, 1996.

Palmer, Michael A. *Guardians of the Gulf: A History of America's Expanding Role in the Persian Gulf, 1833–1992.* New York: Simon & Schuster, 1992.

Pepe, Jacopo Maria. *Beyond Energy: Trade and Transport in a Reconnecting Eurasia.* Berlin: Springer VS, 2018.

Pepe, Jacopo Maria. *Continental Drift: Germany and China's Inroads in the "German-Central Eastern European Manufacturing Core": Geopolitical Chances and Risks.* Washington, DC: Edwin O. Reischauer Center for East Asian Studies, 2017.

Polanyi, Karl. *The Great Transformation: The Political and Economic Origins of Our Time.* New York: Farrar & Reinhart, 1944.

Polo, Marco, and Ronald Latham. *The Travels of Marco Polo.* London: Penguin, 1958.

Putnam, Robert D. "Diplomacy and Domestic Politics: The Logic of Two-Level Games." *International Organization* 42 (Summer 1988): 427–60.

Rosecrance, Richard. *The Rise of the Virtual State: Wealth and Power in the Coming Century.* New York: Basic Books, 1999.

Shambaugh, David, Eberhard Sandschneider, and Zhou Hong, eds. *China-Europe Relations: Perceptions, Policies and Prospects.* New York: Routledge, 2008.

Shirk, Susan L. *How China Opened Its Door: The Political Success of the PRC's Foreign Trade and Investment Reforms.* Washington, DC: Brookings Institution, 1994.

Spence, Jonathan. *The Memory Palace of Matteo Ricci.* New York: Viking Penguin, 1984.

Spence, Jonathon. *The Search for Modern China.* New York: Norton, 1990.

Spykman, Nicholas. *The Geography of the Peace,* edited by Helen R. Nicholl. New York: Harcourt, Brace, 1944.

Vogel, Ezra F. *Deng Xiaoping and the Transformation of China.* Cambridge, MA: Harvard University Press, 2011.

Wang, Yiwei. *The Belt and Road Initiative: What Will China Offer the World in Its Rise?* Beijing: New World, 2016.

Wisnick, Elizabeth. *Mending Fences: The Evolution of Moscow's China Policy from Brezhnev to Yeltsin.* Seattle: University of Washington Press, 2015.

Yan, Xuetong, Daniel Bell, Zhe Sun, and Edmund Ryden. *Ancient Chinese Thought, Modern Chinese Power.* Princeton, NJ: Princeton University Press, 2011.

Yergin, Daniel. *The Prize: The Epic Quest for Oil, Money, and Power.* New York: Simon & Schuster, 1991.

Yergin, Daniel, and Joseph Stanislaw. *The Commanding Heights: The Battle between Government and the Marketplace That Is Remaking the Modern World.* New York: Simon & Schuster, 1998.

Zhang, Weiwei. *The China Wave: Rise of a Civilizational State.* Hackensack, NJ: World Century, 2012.

Zheng, Yongnian, ed. *China and International Relations: The Chinese View and the Contribution of Wang Gungwu.* New York: Routledge, 2010.

Zhirinovskii, Vladimir. *Geopolitika I russkii vopros* [Geopolitics and the Russian question]. Moscow: Galeriia, 1998.

Ziuganov, Gennady A. Ziuganov, *Geografiia pobedy: osnovy rossiiskoigeopolitiki* [The geography of victory: Foundations of Russian geopolitics]. Moscow: G. Ziuganov, 1997.

Index

Page numbers followed by *f*, *m*, or *t* indicate material in figures, maps, or tables.

CPSIA information can be obtained
at www.ICGtesting.com
Printed in the USA
LVHW041308110619
620848LV00004B/320